£27.50nn

DISABILITY DISCRIMINATION
LAW AND PRACTICE

DISABILITY DISCRIMINATION
LAW AND PRACTICE

Brian J Doyle LLB, LLM, PhD, *Barrister*
Professor of Law
The University of Liverpool

JORDANS
1996

Published by
Jordan Publishing Limited
21 St Thomas Street
Bristol BS1 6JS

British Library Cataloguing-in-Publication Data
A catalogue record for this book is available from the British Library.

ISBN 0 85308 403 3

Typeset by Mendip Communications Limited, Frome, Somerset
Printed by Biddles Ltd, Guildford and King's Lynn

For Jackie and Herbert McDonald

PREFACE

Disability Discrimination Law and Practice is in effect the second edition of *Disability Discrimination: The New Law* which was published in early 1996, shortly after the Disability Discrimination Act 1995 had received Royal Assent. At that time, the substantive provisions of this new, important and challenging Act had not yet been brought into force. Moreover, in to order to flesh out the bare bones of the statute, we awaited statutory guidance, regulations and codes of practice. In a remarkably short space of time – in fact, less than one year after the Act reached the statute book – a whole raft of secondary legislation and supporting extra-statutory sources has been published. Already some parts of the Act have been brought into force and the central thrust of the new legislation (the rights affecting employment and the provision of goods, facilities and services) will be largely (although not entirely) effective from 2 December 1996.

Accordingly, not only is a new edition – to coincide with the implementation of these measures – timely and warranted, but it is also appropriate to retitle the book. The law is no longer strictly *new* and the commentary has been expanded to take account of the practical implications of the secondary sources. The promulgation of statutory guidance, regulations and codes of practice, to some extent at least, has clarified many of the difficult issues of interpretation and application which were highlighted in *Disability Discrimination: The New Law*. This has prompted me to revise and to rewrite some of my initial analysis. In turn, these novel points of reference may have produced new twists and problems of their own, and so I have seen fit to add to the interpretation of the new law which I first offered. Where possible, I have appended to this edition many of the secondary sources.

Undoubtedly, much is yet to come. We can expect further regulations from 1997 onwards (indeed, there may also be some which have been published towards the end of 1996 but which were too late to be included in this edition) and a further timetable to be announced setting out the schedule for implementing those parts of the Act which are not yet in force. By mid-1997, we should also see the earliest first instance decisions, particularly those of industrial tribunals under the employment provisions of Part II of the Act. But it will be at least one year after that before the appellate courts get an opportunity to provide authoritative and binding guidance on some of the difficult questions that this legislation will pose. At that time, it may be appropriate to consider a further edition.

As with the first edition, I have incurred a number of debts, not least to Jackie and Herbert McDonald, Gillian Howard, Jenny White, Maria Dand (again) and my wife, Antoinette, in addition to those I acknowledged in the preface to the first edition. I am also grateful to Martin West, Mollie Dickenson and

Brendan Farrell at Jordans for their continued support. The first edition was well received and I thank those reviewers and readers who provided constructive criticism (some of which I have accepted and incorporated in this edition). Writing a new edition of a book admidst a flurry of commencement orders is like trying to hit a moving target. Nevertheless, I have attempted to state the law as I understand it to be on 1 October 1996, with an indication of which parts of the law are in force and those which will be before the end of 1996.

Brian Doyle
Liverpool
October 1996

CONTENTS

TABLE OF CASES

References in the right-hand column are to paragraph numbers.

TABLE OF STATUTES

References in the right-hand column are to paragraph numbers.
References in italics are to page numbers of appendices.

TABLE OF STATUTORY INSTRUMENTS

References in the right-hand column are to paragraph numbers.

TABLE OF EUROPEAN AND UN LEGISLATION

References in the right-hand column are to paragraph numbers.

TABLE OF CODES AND GUIDANCE

Chapter 1

INTRODUCTION

1.1 BACKGROUND

1.1.1 Moving the Third Reading of the Disability Discrimination Bill in the House of Commons on 28 March 1995, the then Minister for Social Security and Disabled People, Mr William Hague claimed:

> 'It is a landmark Bill. It is the only comprehensive Bill for disabled people ever introduced by a British Government. It will mark the United Kingdom out as one of the world leaders and the leader in Europe in the move towards comprehensive anti-discrimination legislation for disabled people. It is a profound measure with significant implications for every part of the economy.[1]

In responding to the debate which followed, Mr Hague further asserted:

> 'It sets this country on a clear, workable and unambiguous course to ending discrimination against disabled people. It will make a genuine difference to the opportunities and lives of millions of our fellow citizens...'[2]

---

1   HC Deb, vol 257, col 904. See the similar comments made by the lead Minister in the House of Lords: HL Deb, vol 566, col 1070 (Lord Mackay of Ardbrecknish).
2   HC Deb, vol 257, col 928.

1.1.2 Despite this positive tone, the Government had been a belated convert to the case for disability discrimination legislation in the UK. The evidence that disabled people faced discrimination and barriers to equal participation and opportunity in education, employment, health and social services, housing, transport, the built environment, leisure and social activities, and civic rights has been long established by volumes of research.[1] Yet the Government was reluctant or unwilling to recognise that the disadvantage and experience of many disabled people could be explained by discrimination and negative attitudes.[2]

If disability discrimination was recognised as a phenomenon, then inevitably the argument would be raised that anti-discrimination legislation would be too complex to draft and uncertain in its application.[3] As recently as 1993, for example, the Prime Minister felt it necessary to state that his Government had 'no plans to introduce generalized anti-discrimination legislation because we foresee problems in both approach and implementation'.[4] The preferred approach was to eliminate unjustified discrimination by education and persuasion, supported by specific legislation to target particular problems.

---

1   The most cogent and comprehensive account of this research is to be found in Colin Barnes, *Disabled People in Britain and Discrimination: A Case for Anti-Discrimination Legislation* (1991, London: Hurst & Company/British Council of Organizations of Disabled People).

2   Although see the limited concessions in Department of Employment, *Employment and Training for People with Disabilities: Consultative Document* (1990, London: Department of Employment) at p 16.
3   Department of Employment, *Employment and Training for People with Disabilities: Consultative Document* (1990, London: Department of Employment) at paras 5.14–5.15.
4   HC Deb, vol 217, col 485 (Mr J. Major) 22 January 1993.

1.1.3 Beyond Parliament, however, disabled people themselves were arguing for anti-discrimination legislation. The disability rights movement was especially inspired by the comprehensive and universal civil rights agenda set for disabled people in the United States by that country's Americans with Disabilities Act 1990 which built upon the earlier limited provisions of the Rehabilitation Act 1973.[1] In 1992, the Australian federal government passed its Disability Discrimination Act 1992 (adding to comparable laws at State level) and, the following year, New Zealand's Human Rights Act 1993 explicitly addressed the civil rights of disabled citizens. Canada has also long experimented in its human rights codes in attempting to legislate for the mischief of disability discrimination. These comparative examples demonstrated that anti-discrimination legislation could be framed and might be made to work with the necessary political will.[2]

---

1   See Caroline Gooding, *Disabling Laws, Enabling Acts: Disability Rights in Britain and America* (1994, London: Pluto Press).
2   See Gerard Quinn, Maeve McDonagh and Cliona Kimber, *Disability Discrimination Law in the United States, Australia and Canada* (1993, Dublin: Oak Tree Press/National Rehabilitation Board); Brian Doyle, *Disability, Discrimination and Equal Opportunities: A Comparative Study of the Employment Rights of Disabled Persons* (1995, London: Mansell Publishing).

1.1.4 International legal standards had also provided some comfort for advocates of disability rights. The International Labour Organisation (ILO) had established minimum labour standards for persons with physical and mental disabilities.[1] The United Nations (UN) Declaration on the Rights of Disabled Persons also provided a touchstone for equal rights and anti-discrimination principles.[2] It pre-dated the UN's Decade of Disabled Persons which ended in 1992 and which witnessed many of the legislative developments in other industrial democracies already alluded to. Perhaps the most tangible evidence of the fruits of the UN Decade are the UN Standard Rules on the Equalization of Opportunities for Persons with Disabilities.[3] The Standard Rules set the framework and establish the principles for nation States to adopt domestic anti-discrimination and equal opportunities legislation.

---

1   See ILO Convention no 159 and Recommendation no 168 (1983). Note also ILO Convention no 99 (1955).
2   General Assembly Resolution 3447 (XXX) 9 December 1975.
3   General Assembly Resolution 48/96 (20 December 1993). See Theresia Degener and Yolan Koster-Dreese (eds), *Human Rights and Disabled Persons: Essays and Human Rights Instruments* (1995, Dordrecht: Martinus Nijhoff Publishers).

1.1.5 The law of the European Union (EU) and European Communities (EC) also provides some little assistance to the disability rights movement. The EC adopted a soft law measure in the form of the 1986 Recommendation on the Employment of Disabled People,[1] while Article 26 of the EC Charter of Fundamental Social Rights of Workers expressed the right of disabled people to expect Member States to take steps to improve their social and professional integration.[2] However, there has always been doubt about the legal competence of the EU/EC to legislate for the social rights of disabled Europeans, although a legal basis for such legislation can be found in the Treaty provisions.[3] Nevertheless, the 1994 White Paper on Social Policy has heralded a clear intention by the EC Commission to introduce anti-discrimination legislation (perhaps in the form of a Directive) addressing the question of disability, and the 1996 Inter-Governmental Conference will provide the opportunity to revise the EU/EC treaties to achieve that end.[4]

---

1 Council Recommendation 86/376/EEC (24 July 1986) OJ L225/43 (12 August 1986).
2 Adopted by 11 of the then 12 Member States (excluding the UK) at Strasbourg on 9 December 1989. See also Article 2 of the Social Chapter Agreement annexed to the EC Protocol on Social Policy (February 1992).
3 See Lisa Waddington, *Disability, Employment and the European Community* (1995, Ontwerp: MAKLU).
4 EC Commission, *European Social Policy: A Way Forward for the Union* (COM (94) 333 final) (1994, Luxembourg: EC Commission).

1.1.6 None the less, it has not been European, international or comparative pressure which has brought about a sea change in the Government's attitude towards disability discrimination legislation. Rather, it has been domestic political forces that have been at work. Backbench Members of Parliament first introduced a private members' bill modelled after the Americans with Disabilities Act in the 1991–92 parliamentary session. This was the Civil Rights (Disabled Persons) Bill. Similar bills were introduced in subsequent sessions but, without frontbench support, failed to make progress, despite cross-party approval. When, in 1993–94, another Civil Rights (Disabled Persons) Bill completed the Committee stage in the House of Commons for the first time, disability rights activists were optimistic that the Bill would reach the statute book. However, the Bill was defeated at Report stage by procedural means in May 1994 and the role of the then Minister for Disabled People (Sir Nicholas Scott) in the affair was called into question.[1]

---

1 HC Deb, vol 242, cols 960–1017 and HC Deb, vol 243, cols 1077–1102.

1.1.7 Sir Nicholas Scott lost his portfolio in a government reshuffle during the summer of 1994, but not before he had published in July 1994 a Green

Paper which set out proposals for limited law reform to prevent discrimination against disabled people in the labour market and in access to goods and services.[1] His successor as Minister for Disabled People, Mr William Hague, followed the Green Paper in January 1995 with a White Paper committing the Government to legislate to end discrimination against disabled people in employment, access to goods and services, transport and education.[2] At the same time, the Minister published the Disability Discrimination Bill as the vehicle for implementing many (but not all) of the proposals contained in the White Paper. It is perhaps noteworthy that neither the Bill nor the Government statements of policy which prefaced it make any mention of an intention to legislate in conformity with European or international developments. This is purely a domestic initiative.

---

1 *A Consultation on Government Measures to Tackle Discrimination Against Disabled People* (1994, London: Department of Social Security).
2 *Ending Discrimination Against Disabled People* Cm 2729 (1995, London: HMSO).

1.2 LEGISLATIVE PROGRESS OF THE ACT

1.2.1 The Disability Discrimination Bill received its First Reading in the House of Commons on 12 January 1995 and was ordered to be printed as HC Bill 32. Although the Bill was presented by the Secretary of State for Social Security (Mr Peter Lilley), it was steered through the House of Commons by the then Minister for Social Security and Disabled People (Mr William Hague). Mr Hague was aided by Mr James Paice, the Parliamentary Under-Secretary of State for Employment. Mr Alistair Burt subsequently succeeded Mr Hague as Minister for Disabled People and handled the final stages of the Bill's progress towards Royal Assent when it returned from the House of Lords in October 1995.

1.2.2 The Bill received its Second Reading on 24 January 1995 and was committed to a Standing Committee.[1] On that same day, the House of Commons also approved a money resolution, for the purposes of the Act, to authorise the payment out of public funds of any sums required for paying persons appointed under the Act, for paying expenses incurred by the National Disability Council and for any other expenditure to be incurred directly or indirectly as a result of the Act.[2]

During a total of 13 sittings between 31 January 1995 and 28 February 1995, the Bill was given line-by-line scrutiny in Standing Committee E and was subject to a small number of Government amendments.[3] The Bill, as amended in Committee (HC Bill 59), was reported to the House of Commons and considered on Report on 27 and 28 March 1995.[4] The Bill received its Third Reading on 28 March 1995 and was sent to the House of Lords.[5]

1 HC Deb, vol 253, cols 147–239.
2 HC Deb, vol 253, cols 238–239. A further money resolution was approved by the House of Commons on 31 October 1995 (HC Deb, vol 265, col 108). See also s 69 of the Act.
3 HC Deb Standing Committee E (Disability Discrimination Bill).
4 HC Deb, vol 257, cols 697–799 and cols 840–904.
5 HC Deb, vol 257, cols 904–928.

1.2.3 The Bill was brought from the House of Commons and given its First Reading in the House of Lords on 29 March 1995. It was ordered to be printed as HL Bill 54. Lord Mackay of Ardbrecknish (Minister of State, Department of Social Security) piloted the Bill through the upper chamber, aided by Lord Inglewood (Parliamentary Under-Secretary of State, Department of National Heritage), Lord Lucas and, subsequently, by Lord Henley (Minister of State, Department for Education and Employment).

1.2.4 The Second Reading debate in the House of Lords took place on 22 May 1995.[1] The Bill was committed to a Committee of the Whole House and considered in detail in Committee over three days on 13 June 1995, 15 June 1995 and 27 June 1995.[2] The Government introduced a number of extensive and substantive amendments and additions to the Bill in Committee (and again on Report). The Bill was reported with amendments as HL Bill 120 and was considered by the House of Lords on Report on 18 and 20 July 1995.[3] The Bill as amended on Report (HL Bill 135) did not have time for a Third Reading debate before the upper chamber rose for the summer recess on 21 July 1995. Instead, it received its Third Reading on 24 October 1995 and was returned to the House of Commons.[4]

1 HL Deb, vol 564, cols 800–815 and 830–892.
2 HL Deb, vol 564, cols 1640–1718, 1723–1784, 1895–1954 and 1975–2054; HL Deb, vol 565, cols 608–680 and 686–744.
3 HL Deb, vol 566, cols 114–141, 168–186, 205–280 and 386–476.
4 HL Deb, vol 566, cols 969–1080.

1.2.5 The House of Lords' amendments to the Bill were considered by the House of Commons on 31 October 1995 (HC Bill 182).[1] The House of Commons disagreed with one of the substantive amendments to the Bill (made in the House of Lords against the wishes of the Government) and, rather unusually, made some additional amendments to the Bill itself (including introducing what is now s 33 of the Act). Accordingly, the Bill returned to the House of Lords on 6 November 1995 (as HL Bill 146) for consideration of the House of Commons' amendments and its reasons for rejecting one of the amendments made in the House of Lords.[2] The upper chamber accepted the lower chamber's will and the Bill received Royal Assent as the Disability Discrimination Act 1995 (Chapter 50 of 1995) on 8 November 1995.

1.2.6   Following Royal Assent, preparation for the various regulations and extra-statutory instruments began. Consultation on the statutory guidance on the meaning of disability and on regulations to further refine the definition of disability under Part I of the Act took place between December 1995 and March 1996. During the same period, the Government also consulted on regulations and a code of practice in respect of the employment provisions of Part II of the Act. In the first quarter of 1996, consultation on the further education measures contained in Part IV was undertaken. At the same time, the National Disability Council and the Northern Ireland Disability Council were established in February 1996. Finally, consultation on the first rights of access to goods, facilities and services in Part III of the statute was pursued between March and May 1996. Further consultations under Part III are proposed for the future.

1.3   SHORT TITLE, COMMENCEMENT AND EXTENT

1.3.1   The long title of the Act seeks:

> 'to make it unlawful to discriminate against disabled persons in connection with employment, the provision of goods, facilities and services or the disposal or management of premises; to make provision about the employment of disabled persons; and to establish a National Disability Council.'

In fact, the Act also makes provision in respect of education and public transport. Section 70(1) establishes the conventional right to refer to the Act by its short title, namely the Disability Discrimination Act 1995.

Commencement provisions

1.3.2   Section 70 of the Act makes general provision as to the statute's short title, commencement and extent. That section came partly into force on Royal Assent (s 70(2)). Section 70(3), which also had immediate effect, states that the remaining provisions of the 1995 Act are to come into force on such day or days as the Secretary of State may appoint by order.[1] Different days of commencement may be appointed for different purposes. Section 70(8) allows consultations required under the Act to be conducted by the Secretary of State (or the appropriate Northern Ireland department) before the coming into force of any relevant provision.

1   In Northern Ireland, the power to make commencement orders lies with the Department of Health and Social Services (Sch 8, para 48(1)).

1.3.3 The first provisions of the Act to be brought into force were those dealing with the establishment and functions of the National Disability Council.[1] These provisions came into effect on 1 January 1996.[2] The provisions relating to the meaning of 'disability' and 'disabled person,[3] were given effect from 17 May 1996.[4] The second commencement order also applied to a host of other miscellaneous provisions from 17 May 1996.[5]

The Disability Discrimination Act 1995 (Commencement No 3 and Saving and Transitional Provisions) Order 1996 gave effect from 6 June 1996 to various provisions of the Act which authorise the making of regulations or provide essential statutory definitions.[6] This Order also brought into force the measures relating to codes of practice issued by the Secretary of State and to help for persons suffering discrimination.[7] On 31 July 1996, sections relating to the functions of the Teacher Training Agency, and to the further education and higher education of disabled persons, were given effect.[8] This means that not all aspects of Part IV are yet in force at the time of writing.

---

1   DDA 1995, ss 50–52 and Sch 5.
2   Article 2 of the Disability Discrimination Act 1995 (Commencement No 1) Order 1995, SI 1995/3330.
3   DDA 1995, Part I (ss 1–3) and Schs 1–2.
4   Articles 2, 3(a)–(c) and 3(m)–(n) of the Disability Discrimination Act 1995 (Commencement No 2) Order 1996, SI 1996/1336. Schedule 1, para 7 (persons deemed to be disabled) was not brought into force on this date. This was also the date upon which the definitions of 'sub-lease' and 'sub-tenancy' in s 16(3) and (5) and Sch 4, para 4 were brought into force: ibid, arts 3(d) and (o).
5   Ibid, art 3(e) (s 28 on provision of advice and assistance), art 3(f) (s 59 on statutory authority and national security), art 3(g) (s 62(1)–(2) and (7) on restriction of publicity in industrial tribunals), art 3(h) (s 63(1)–(2), (4)–(6) on restriction of publicity in the Employment Appeal Tribunal), art 3(l) (s 67 on regulations and orders), art 3(j) (s 68(1) on interpretation), art 3(k) (s 69 on financial provisions), and art 3(l) (s 70(7) on House of Commons disqualification).
6   SI 1996/1474, art 2(1) and Sch, Part I. The relevant provisions are detailed in the text and are to be found in ss 5(6)–(7), 6(8)–(10), 8(6)–(7), 12(3) and (6), 14(6), 16(5) (to the extent not already in force – see note 4 above), 17(3), 18(3)–(4), 19(5)(c), 20(6)–(8), 24(5), and Sch 4 (Part I, para 3).
7   Ibid, art 2(1) and Sch, Part I. See DDA 1995, ss 53–54 and 56.
8   Ibid, art 2(2) and Sch, Part II. See DDA 1995, ss 29(3), 30(1)–(6) and 31.

1.3.4 Many of the remaining substantive provisions of the Act are given effect from 2 December 1996. That is the date in particular on which the remaining provisions of Part II of the Act on employment discrimination are brought into force.[1] Exceptionally, the duty placed upon trade organisations[2] to make reasonable adjustments is not yet effective.[3] The provisions of Part III on discrimination in relation to goods, facilities and services, and in relation to the disposal and management of premises, are also brought partly into force on 2 December 1996.[4] The exceptions relate to the duty to make reasonable adjustments. During the consultation process, the Government indicated that service providers might be required to adjust policies, practices and procedures from 1998, provide auxiliary aids and services from 2000, and remove physical barriers (or provide a service by reasonable alternative means) from 2005.

---

1 Disability Discrimination Act 1995 (Commencement No 3 and Saving and Transitional Provisions) Order 1996, art 2(3) and Sch, Part III subject to the saving and transitional provisions set out in art 3.
2 By DDA 1995, ss 14(2), 14(4)–(5) and 15.
3 Curiously, that part of s 16(3) which provides the definition of 'lease' for the purposes of s 16 has not been brought into force. This would seem to be an oversight.
4 SI 1996/1474, art 2(3) and Sch, Part III. See DDA 1995, ss 19(1)(b), 20(2), 20(5), 20(9), 21, 27 and Sch 4, Part II which are not yet in force.

1.3.5 To summarise, most of the provisions of the Act have been brought into force on or before 2 December 1996. Apart from the exceptions already detailed, the following provisions are also not yet in effect:

- s 29(1)–(2) (on education of disabled persons in schools);
- s 30(7)–(9) (on functions of local education authorities in respect of further education);
- Part V generally (ss 32–49) (on public transport);
- s 62(3)–(6) (restriction of publicity: industrial tribunals);
- s 63(3) (applying s 62(3)–(6) to the Employment Appeal Tribunal);
- s 70(5) and Sch 7 (so far as they apply to the prospective repeal of s 22(4) of the Disabled Persons (Employment) Act 1944; s 16 of the Chronically Sick and Disabled Persons Act 1970 and consequential amendments of the Employment Protection (Consolidation) Act 1978;[1] the Local Government and Housing Act 1989; and the Education Act 1993).

A firm timetable for the bringing into force of these remaining Parts and provisions is not yet clear. Certain saving and transitional provisions are also made to deal with the repeal of certain provisions of the Disabled Persons (Employment) Act 1944.[2] These provisions are explained in the text below.

---

1 Now the Employment Rights Act 1996.
2 Disability Discrimination Act 1995 (Commencement No 3 and Saving and Transitional Provisions) Order 1996, art 3.

Application to Northern Ireland

1.3.6 The Act is expressed in language which appears to suggest that its substantive provisions only apply to England and Wales and to Scotland. However, by virtue of s 70(6) the provisions of the 1995 Act are extended to Northern Ireland also. The application of the Act in Northern Ireland has effect to the extent of (and subject to the textual modifications set out in) Sch 8 to the legislation. Where appropriate, these are indicated in the text below. Separate commencement orders have been made for Northern Ireland.[1]

1   Disability Discrimination Act 1995 (Commencement No 1) Order (Northern Ireland) 1996, SR 1996/1; Disability Discrimination Act 1995 (Commencement No 2) Order (Northern Ireland) 1996, SR 1996/219.

Amendment of the Act

1.3.7   The Disability Discrimination Act 1995 has already been the subject of contextual amendment necessitated by the consolidating measures contained in the Employment Rights Act 1996 (ERA 1996) and the Industrial Tribunals Act 1996 (ITA 1996) with effect from 22 August 1996.[1] These amendments are accounted for in the text of the statute appended below and will be referred to at appropriate points in the text.

The ITA 1996, Sch 1, para 12 makes consequential amendments to ss 8(7) and 9(2)(a) of the 1995 Act (interest on industrial tribunal compensation awards and compromises or settlements). Schedule 2, Part II to the ITA 1996 makes transitional provision for ss 62–63 of the 1995 Act (restriction of publicity in the industrial tribunal and Employment Appeal Tribunal). This is because those provisions are effectively repealed by Sch 3 to the ITA 1996 and replaced in identical terms by ss 12 and 32 of the ITA 1996. The ITA 1996, Sch 3 also repeals and replaces Sch 3, para 1 (complaints to industrial tribunals) and Sch 6, para 2 (appeals to the Employment Appeal Tribunal) (see ITA 1996, ss 18 and 21).

Consequential amendments to ss 50(9)(a) (affecting the advisory functions of the National Disability Council) and 65(2) (application to Parliament) of the 1995 Act are wrought by Sch 1 to the ERA 1996. Transitional provision is made in para 18 of Sch 2 to the ERA 1996 in respect of para 3 of Sch 6 to the 1995 statute (continuous service and reinstatement or re-engagement of dismissed employees), which in turn is repealed by Sch 3 to the ERA 1996 and relocated in s 219 of the ERA 1996.

1   See the like effect in Northern Ireland of the Employment Rights (Northern Ireland) Order 1996, SI 1996/1919 and the Industrial Tribunals (Northern Ireland) Order 1996, SI 1996/1921.

1.4   OVERVIEW OF THE ACT

1.4.1   Part I of the Act (ss 1–3) and Schs 1–2 to the Act address the problem of defining the meaning of 'disability' and 'disabled person'. These are key provisions of the new legislation and are considered in detail in Chapter 2.

1.4.2   Part II of the Act deals with the issue of discrimination in the employment field. Section 4 outlaws discrimination (in a way defined in s 5) against disabled persons by employers in respect of employment opportunities generally. Employers are placed under a duty to make reasonable adjustments where this will assist disabled persons to compete for such opportunities (s 6).[1] An exemption from Part II obligations is granted to small businesses by s 7. The provisions on employment discrimination are extended to contract workers by s 12, while ss 8–11 and Schs 3–4 deal with a number of matters relating to enforcement, remedies and procedures. The general anti-discrimination measures in the employment field are discussed in Chapter 3, while the question of enforcement and remedies is tackled in Chapter 10. Section 61 and Schs 6–7 amend and repeal certain existing employment laws and the effect of these parts of the Act is set out in Chapter 3.

---

1   Note also the provisions of s 16 dealing with alterations to premises occupied under a lease.

1.4.3   Part II of the Act also deals with discrimination against disabled persons by trade organisations. Section 13 lays down the general principles, while s 14 defines discrimination in this context. Section 15 places trade organisations under a duty to make adjustments for disabled applicants and members.[1] These provisions are discussed in Chapter 4, while ss 8–11 and Schs 3–4 deal with a number of matters relating to enforcement, remedies and procedures and are discussed in Chapter 10.

---

1   Note also the provisions of s 16 dealing with alterations to premises occupied under a lease.

1.4.4   Discrimination in non-employment areas is approached in Part III of the statute. The measures outlawing discrimination in relation to goods, facilities and services are detailed in ss 19–21 and these are analysed in Chapter 5. Discrimination in relation to the disposal and management of premises is addressed by ss 22–24, the discussion of which will be found in Chapter 6. Enforcement, procedure and remedies for transgressions of Part III are considered in Chapter 10.

1.4.5   Education and transport have been expressly excluded from the anti-discrimination formula contained in Part III of the 1995 Act. Instead, the statute's preferred approach in respect of education is to place educational institutions and funding bodies under specific duties to provide information about educational opportunities available to disabled pupils and students (ss 29–31). Chapter 7 looks at this alternative approach. With regard to public transport, the Act resembles enabling legislation, empowering the relevant minister to lay regulations in the future that will define new standards of accessibility for disabled people to taxis, public service vehicles and trains (ss 32–49). This framework for future change is outlined in Chapter 8.

1.4.6   The Act contains its own institutional framework for enforcement and review of the new principles contained within it. In particular, s 50 and Sch 5 establish the National Disability Council, while ss 51–54 provide powers to issue codes of practice to underpin the statutory provisions. Section 60 allows the Secretary of State to appoint advisers on disabled employment matters, while ss 64–66 address the application of the Act to the Crown, Parliament itself and government appointments. Section 67 sets out the procedure for making and laying regulations and orders under the Act. The institutional framework is considered in Chapter 9.

1.4.7   Finally, Chapter 10 deals with enforcement, procedure and remedies. As well as the relevant provisions briefly referred to above, Chapter 10 examines the effect of s 55 (on victimisation), s 56 (statutory questionnaires) and ss 57–59 (dealing with liability questions generally). Sections 62–63 provide for a measure of restricted reporting of disability discrimination cases in the employment field and these sections are also explained in Chapter 10.

1.4.8   For completeness, it should be mentioned that the Act contains a comprehensive interpretation section (s 68) and this is referred to at frequent intervals throughout the chapters that follow.

Chapter 2

DISABILITY AND DISABLED PERSON

2.1 INTRODUCTION

2.1.1 The twin concepts of 'disability' and 'disabled person' are central to the operation of the new Act. These are the terms that determine who has rights and expectations under the new legislation. Only someone who can satisfy the definition of disabled person within the meaning of the 1995 Act can enjoy the protection of its framework.

2.1.2 Part I of the Act (ss 1–3) and Schs 1 and 2 to the Act furnish definitions of 'disability' and 'disabled person' for the purposes of the statute. These provisions were given effect from 17 May 1996.[1] They are supplemented by regulations[2] and by the statutory guidance issued by the Secretary of State under s 3 (referred to hereafter as 'Guidance').[3] The Guidance does not impose any legal obligations in itself and is not designed to be an authoritative statement of law. Nevertheless, an industrial tribunal or court is required to take account of the Guidance, where relevant, when determining certain questions arising from the statutory definition of disability.[4]

Section 1(2) defines 'disabled person' as meaning 'a person who has a disability'. A person is then treated by s 1(1) as having a disability if he or she has a physical or mental impairment which has a substantial and long-term adverse effect on his or her ability to carry out normal day-to-day activities.[5]

---

1 Disability Discrimination Act 1995 (Commencement No 2) Order 1996, SI 1996/1336. See **1.3.3**.
2 Disability Discrimination (Meaning of Disability) Regulations 1996, SI 1996/1455 which came into force on 30 July 1996 and made under the authority of Sch 1, paras 1(2), 2(4), 3(2)–(3), 4(2)(a) and 5(a). See also Disability Discrimination (Meaning of Disability) Regulations (Northern Ireland) 1996, SR 1996/421.
3 *Guidance on matters to be taken into account in determining questions relating to the definition of disability* (1996, London: HMSO). The Guidance came into force on 31 July 1996 by virtue of the Disability Discrimination (Guidance and Code of Practice) (Appointed Day) Order 1996, SI 1996/1996, para 2. In Northern Ireland, the power to issue s 3 guidance is vested in the Department of Economic Development (Sch 8, para 2(1)) and a separate edition of the Guidance has been issued there.
4 See s 3(3). As to the legal status of the Guidance, see **9.3**.
5 Note that the definition is also extended to include persons who had such a disability in the past (s 2 and Sch 2). See **2.11**.

2.1.3 The concept of disability and the identification of who is a disabled person have previously been the concern of social welfare law generally.[1] Illustrative definitions are supplied by various statutory sources.[2] In social security law too, the qualification for disability-related benefits calls for the definition of the qualifying class.[3]

---

1 See, for example, *Halsbury's Laws of England* (4th edn) vol 33, paras 902 and 927–928.
2 See, for example, National Assistance Act 1948, ss 29(1) and 64(1); Mental Health Act 1959, s 8(2); Chronically Sick and Disabled Persons Act 1970, s 2; Health and Social Services Adjudications Act 1983, Sch 4; Mental Health Act 1983, s 1(2); Disabled Persons (Services, Consultation and Representation) Act 1986, ss 5, 9 and 16.
3 See *Halsbury's Laws of England* (4th edn) vol 33, paras 504 et seq and the Social Security Contributions and Benefits Act 1992.

2.1.4 Moreover, under the Disabled Persons (Employment) Act 1944, s 1(1) the status of registered disabled person has been determined by reference to:

> 'a person who, on account of injury, disease, or congenital deformity, is substantially handicapped in obtaining or keeping employment, or in undertaking work on his own account, of a kind which apart from that injury, disease or deformity would be suited to his age, experience and qualifications.'[1]

While these definitions are generally helpful in understanding the nature of the problem of identifying the protected class, considerable care must be exercised in any attempt to translate existing classifications of disabilities and disabled persons into the new legislative framework of the Disability Discrimination Act 1995.

---

1 See also Disabled Persons (Employment) Act (Northern Ireland) 1945. These provisions are repealed with effect from 1 December 1996. See **3.11.3**.

2.1.5 In order to enjoy the protection of the new rights afforded by the 1995 Act, applicants or complainants must bring themselves fairly and squarely within the definitional provisions of Part I of and Schs 1–2 to the Act and the Guidance issued under s 3. However, with that necessary caveat, it is likely that many (but not all) individuals who satisfy the definition of disability or disabled person under pre-existing legislation will be able do so under the 1995 Act. Indeed, in one particular case – that of a person registered as disabled under the 1944 Act at specified times – there is a deeming provision by which the existing status of an individual as a legally recognised disabled person is preserved for the purposes of disability discrimination law (Sch 1, para 7). This is explained further below.[1]

---

1 See **2.8**.

2.2 MEANING OF 'DISABILITY' AND 'DISABLED PERSON'

2.2.1 Section 1(2) defines a 'disabled person' for the purposes of the Act as a person who has a 'disability'. A person has a 'disability' in this context if he or she has a physical or mental impairment which has a substantial and long-term adverse effect on his or her ability to carry out normal day-to-day activities (s 1(1)). This is made expressly subject to the provisions of Sch 1 to the Act which supplement the definitions supplied by s 1.

2.2.2 It is clear, therefore, that attention must be given to three separate aspects of the definition of the protected class:

- What is a physical or mental impairment?
- What is meant by a person's ability to carry out normal day-to-day activities?
- In what circumstances does an impairment have a substantial and long-term adverse effect upon the ability to carry out normal day-to-day activities?

Each of these elements of the definition of disability is considered in turn below.

2.2.3 In approaching s 1 of the Act, it might be useful to take account of what the legislature hoped to achieve in defining the protected class in this way. In Committee, the Minister stated that the Government intended to create a commonsense definition, which fitted the generally accepted perception of what is a disability and who is a disabled person, and which provided certainty and avoided vagueness.[1] The ministerial view is that the definition, and the legislation which it underpins, would not be credible if it embraced individuals who were not fairly or generally recognised as disabled. The Government believes that the definition will cover the vast majority of the 6.5 million disabled persons in Britain identified by the 1988 Office of Population Census and Surveys report.[2]

---

1   HC Deb Standing Committee E, col 73 (Mr W. Hague, Minister for Social Security and Disabled People).
2   Martin, Meltzer and Elliott, *The Prevalence of Disability Among Adults: OPCS Surveys of Disability in Great Britain Report 1* (1988, London: HMSO).

2.3   PHYSICAL OR MENTAL IMPAIRMENT

2.3.1 The term 'impairment' is vital to an understanding of the concept of disability. Yet it is not defined in the legislation. A literal interpretation of the word would suggest a condition of weakness, injury or damage, but the term has a more precise meaning in medical circles. The World Health Organization's 1980 classification of impairment, disability and handicap defines impairment as 'any loss or abnormality of psychological, physiological, or anatomical structure or function'.[1] The tenor of the parliamentary debates on the Disability Discrimination Act suggests that the intention was to base the new legal framework upon a medical model of disability. In that regard, the WHO definition may be a helpful one (although not necessarily one that would be embraced by disabled people themselves).

The Guidance anticipates that in many cases there will be no dispute over whether or not a person has an impairment. It makes clear that the question of how an impairment was caused is not a relevant consideration. However, the Guidance does not go any further in explaining the term 'impairment'.[2]

---

1 World Health Organization, *International Classification of Impairments, Disabilities and Handicaps: A Manual of Classification Relating to the Consequences of Disease* (1980, Geneva: WHO).
2 Guidance, Part I, paras 10 et seq.

Physical impairment

2.3.2   The term 'physical impairment' is also not defined or further explained in the substantive provisions in the main body of the Act. Instead, it is necessary to refer to Sch 1 to the statute, which in turn is singularly unhelpful. Schedule 1, para 1(2)(a) states that regulations may be made for the purposes of the new legislation so as to provide that 'conditions of a prescribed description' are 'to be treated as amounting to impairments'. Equally, such regulations may provide that specified conditions of a prescribed description shall be treated as not amounting to impairments. The meaning of 'condition' for this purpose is not defined, but the regulations may, in due course, furnish a definition for this purpose too (Sch 1, para 1(3)).

Regulations which have now been made under these powers provide that addiction to (including dependency upon) alcohol, nicotine or any other substance is to be treated as not amounting to an impairment for the purposes of the DDA 1995.[1] That would not prevent liver disease which resulted from alcohol dependency or abuse from counting as an impairment, even though alcoholism itself would not be so treated.[2] This exclusion also does not prevent an addiction which was originally the result of administration of medically prescribed drugs or other medical treatment from amounting to an impairment, all other things being equal.[3] So, for example, an addiction to pain-killers, to sedatives or to a mood-altering drug may amount to an impairment, provided that the drug in question was *medically prescribed* and not simply bought over-the-counter without prescription or otherwise acquired. The regulations also treat seasonal allergic rhinitis (a form of severe hay fever) as not amounting to an impairment.[4] In this case, however, account might be taken of the condition so far as it aggravates the effect of another condition which does amount to an impairment (for example, a breathing impairment).[5]

---

1 Disability Discrimination (Meaning of Disability) Regulations 1996, regs 2 and 3(1).
2 Guidance, Part I, para 11.
3 Disability Discrimination (Meaning of Disability) Regulations 1996, reg 3(2).
4 Ibid, reg 4(2).
5 Ibid, reg 4(3).

2.3.3 The Minister for Disabled People has explained that the purpose behind the power to make exclusive and inclusive regulations is to provide flexibility to deal with future medical developments and to resolve problems of interpretation that arise through future case-law.[1] The Minister also indicated that this power may be exercised in 'cases where there is medical doubt or controversy about whether a particular manifestation should be rightly described as a "condition"'.[2] Note also that the Act treats a severe disfigurement as a relevant impairment in defined circumstances.[3]

---

1 HC Deb Standing Committee E, col 105 (Mr W. Hague).
2 HC Deb Standing Committee E, col 109 (Mr W. Hague).
3 See Sch 1, para 3 and the more detailed discussion of this provision at **2.6**.

2.3.4 Despite the absence of a definition of 'physical impairments', it is suggested that many commonly accepted conditions – such as orthopaedic impairments, cerebral palsy, epilepsy, muscular dystrophy, multiple sclerosis, cancer, heart disease, diabetes and tuberculosis – will qualify as impairments, all other things being equal.

Mental impairment

2.3.5 The term 'mental impairment' is equally not defined or explained in the substantive provisions of the Act. Again, it is necessary to refer to Sch 1 to the statute, which is also not particularly helpful. The Guidance is scarcely more helpful, indicating that the term refers to 'a wide range of impairments relating to mental functioning, including what are often known as learning disabilities (formerly known as "mental handicap")'.[1] Clearly, it is intended that learning, psychiatric and psychological impairments are to be included, but the Minister for Disabled People made it clear in debate that regulation-making powers would be used to exclude certain antisocial disorders and addictions.[2]

---

1 Guidance, Part I, para 13.
2 HC Deb Standing Committee E, cols 72 and 105 (Mr W. Hague).

2.3.6 As already noted, addiction to alcohol, nicotine or any other substance has been excluded (whether this amounts to a mental or a physical impairment).[1] Regulations made under Sch 1, para 1(2)–(3) go further. They provide that, for the purposes of the DDA 1995, the conditions of a tendency to set fires, to steal or to physical or sexual abuse of other persons, together with the conditions of exhibitionism and voyeurism, are to be treated as not amounting to impairments.[2]

1 See **2.3.2**.
2 Disability Discrimination (Meaning of Disability) Regulations 1996, reg 4(1). See HC Deb
   Standing Committee E, col 109 (Mr W. Hague). These exclusions do not go as far as the author
   originally predicted in the first edition of this book. See Doyle, *Disability Discrimination: The New
   Law* (Jordans, 1996) para 2.3.6.

2.3.7   Schedule 1 also makes it explicit that a mental impairment includes 'an impairment resulting from or consisting of a mental illness' – but only if 'the illness is a *clinically well-recognised illness*' (para 1(1), my emphasis). What amounts to a clinically well-recognised illness will be a question of fact for the decision of a tribunal or court.[1] This will clearly call for expert medical evidence in tribunal or court proceedings where there is any doubt about whether or not an apparent mental illness is well-recognised by medical opinion. In difficult cases, tribunals may be called upon to choose between opposing medical expert evidence. Clearly, merely *some* degree of recognition in *some* quarters of medical opinion will not be sufficient. General medical recognition of the condition as a mental illness will be called for and there is room for lengthy medical and legal dispute about whether a plaintiff is clinically mentally impaired.

1 The Guidance (Part I, para 14) refers to mental illnesses recognised by a respected body of
   medical opinion, including those specifically mentioned in publications such as the World
   Health Organisation's *International Classification of Diseases*.

2.3.8   It is also noteworthy here that the Government rejected an attempt during the passage of the legislation to import into the Disability Discrimination Act the broader and more embracing definition of mental illness or 'disorder' contained in the Mental Health Act 1983, s 1(2). This refers to 'mental illness, arrested or incomplete development of the mind, psychopathic disorder and any other disorder or disability of mind'. The Opposition was concerned that a person detained or 'sectioned' under the 1983 Act on grounds of mental disorder could nevertheless be excluded from the 1995 Act because the illness or disorder might not be clinically recognised.

The Government subsequently amended the Bill to make it clear that the definition of 'mental impairment' used in the 1995 Act is not the same as that used in the Mental Health Act 1983 or the Mental Health (Scotland) Act 1984 (see s 68(1)). The fact that an impairment would be a mental impairment for the purposes of the 1983 or 1984 Acts, does not prevent it from being a mental impairment for the purposes of the 1995 Act, but it is not to be treated as automatically so.

2.3.9   Some assistance might be gleaned from ministerial statements in this context.[1] It seems to be intended that mental impairments (including learning disabilities) that are not mental illnesses are nevertheless covered by s 1 and Sch 1, and that persons with recognised mental illnesses are to be treated as disabled persons for the purposes of the 1995 Act. This will include individuals experiencing schizophrenia, manic depression, severe and extended depressive psychoses and a range of other conditions recognised by clinical psychiatrists and psychologists.

1   HC Deb Standing Committee E, cols 103–105 (Mr W. Hague).

2.3.10   However, the Act is not intended to cover 'moods or mild eccentricities' nor 'obscure conditions unrecognised by reputable clinicians' (what the Minister also referred to as 'mild or tendentious' conditions). Nevertheless, the Government's view is that 'arrested or incomplete development of the mind, psychopathic disorder and any other disorder or disability of mind' does fall within the 1995 definition of mental impairment, provided they are conditions which have attracted clinical recognition and subject to the conditions excluded by regulation already noted at **2.3.6**.

Sensory impairment

2.3.11   Much discussion of the definition of an impairment ensued during the Committee stage of the Act when passing through the legislative process in the lower chamber. Concern was expressed that such a bald and spare definition of impairment would serve to exclude large numbers of otherwise disabled persons deserving of the statute's protection against disability-informed discrimination. The power to define what impairments were within the scope of the Act by secondary legislation which might exclude prescribed conditions from the law's compass was especially a source of debate.

2.3.12   Particular attention was focused upon the question of whether individuals with sensory impairments would be embraced within the definition of physical or mental impairment. Sensory impairments might include deafness, other hearing impairments or loss, blindness, partial sightedness and dual sensory impairments (such as combined loss of speech and hearing). The Government made it clear that it was not intended that persons with sensory impairments should be excluded from the legislation.[1]

1   HC Deb Standing Committee E, col 71 (Mr W. Hague).

2.3.13   The Minister's view was that the term 'sensory' did not add legal or medical meaning to the definition of impairment and that sensory disorders are either physical or mental impairments:

> 'The terms physical and mental are intended to be seen in their widest sense and should comprehensively cover all forms of impairment. All the advice that I have received suggests that a third category, in addition to physical and mental

impairment, might imply that those categories are not all-embracing ... Sensory conditions would generally be covered as physical conditions or, exceptionally, in cases such as hysterical deafness, as mental conditions.'[1]

That is as clear an expression of legislative intention as one could hope to receive and, should there be any doubt whether or not an individual who has a sensory impairment is entitled *ceteris paribus* to bring proceedings under the Act, reference should be made to the legislative history of the measure. In any event, the Guidance makes it clear that the concept of a physical or mental impairment includes sensory impairments, such as those affecting sight or hearing.[2]

---

1 HC Deb Standing Committee E, col 71 (Mr W. Hague).
2 Guidance, Part I, para 12.

2.3.14 Nevertheless, there remains some ground for doubt and argument about what impairments are of a physical or mental nature, and undoubtedly there will be difficult cases where the point will be taken in litigation. For example, the condition of chronic fatigue syndrome is one which is not universally recognised in medicine, but where it is, there is doubt about whether its origins are physical, viral or psychological. Similarly, there is disagreement about whether epilepsy is a physical disability (because of its physical manifestations) or a mental disability (because of its origins as a disturbance in the brain). It cannot be imagined that the new legislation will not afford protection against discrimination to persons with epilepsy, despite this dichotomy, whereas doubt will almost certainly be cast upon whether individuals with chronic fatigue syndrome are within the protected class.[1]

---

1 Other difficult areas for the definition of disability might include pre-menstrual tension (PMT) and conditions of obesity.

Effect of control by medical treatment

2.3.15 It should be noted that the Act continues to treat as an impairment one which satisfies the substantive definition of impairment but which is currently controlled or corrected by medical treatment, medication, prosthesis, auxiliary devices or other aids (Sch 1, para 6). This is discussed in more detail below (at **2.7**).

2.4 ABILITY TO CARRY OUT NORMAL DAY-TO-DAY ACTIVITIES

2.4.1 A person is a disabled person only if possessing an impairment that has an adverse effect, of the degree required, upon that person's 'ability to carry out normal day-to-day activities' (s 1(1)). The phrase 'normal day-to-day activities' is defined in Sch 1, para 4(1). This provides that an impairment is to be treated as affecting the ability of the person concerned to carry out normal day-to-day activities *only* if it affects one of the following:

- mobility;
- manual dexterity;
- physical coordination;
- continence;
- ability to lift, carry or otherwise move everyday objects;
- speech, hearing or eyesight;
- memory or ability to concentrate, learn or understand;
- perception of the risk of physical danger.

It is clear that it is the effect upon the complainant (and not persons generally) that matters. The Guidance explains what is meant by the scope of each of the eight listed activities.[1] It is not proposed to reproduce this here.

---

1 Guidance, Part II, paras C14–C21.

2.4.2 Regulations may be adopted to prescribe the circumstances in which an impairment that does not affect one of the above eight categories of day-to-day activities is nevertheless to be treated as affecting the ability of the person concerned to carry out normal day-to-day activities (Sch 1, para 4(2)(a)). Similarly, regulations may also provide that an impairment which does affect one of the above eight categories of day-to-day activities is nevertheless to be treated as not affecting the ability of the person concerned to carry out normal day-to-day activities (Sch 1, para 4(2)(b)). Otherwise the list is exhaustive. No regulations have been made under this provision at the time of writing.[1]

---

1 However, note the Disability Discrimination (Meaning of Disability) Regulations 1996, reg 6. This provides that, where a child under six years of age has an impairment which does not have an effect on the child's ability to carry out one of the normal day-to-day activities listed in Sch 1, para 4(1), the impairment is nevertheless to be taken to have a substantial and long-term adverse effect on the child's ability to carry out normal day-to-day activities if it would normally have such an effect on the ability of a person aged six years or over.

2.4.3 The reference to the effect which an impairment has upon the ability to carry out normal day-to-day activities is designed to achieve the result of excluding from the Act's remit mild or trivial conditions. Equally, by measuring the effect which an impairment or condition has upon 'normal day-to-day activities' the legislation excludes complaints from persons who might seek to show that, because of some physical or mental limitation, they are effectively excluded from participating in some specialised activity or pursuit which the majority of people would be incapable of enjoying in any event.[1] It also has the obvious effect of limiting the protected class of disabled persons.

---

1   It is not intended that activities which are normal only for a particular person or group of people should be included. Account must be taken of how far the activity is normal for most people and carried out by most people on a daily or frequent and fairly regular basis. See Guidance, Part II, para C2.

2.4.4   The 'ability to carry out normal day-to-day activities' formula will thus exclude individuals with temporary and non-chronic conditions, such as sprains, influenza, etc.[1] The effect is even more far-reaching, however, as the following examples will demonstrate.

A person with colour blindness will be disqualified from being a commercial airline pilot, but cannot usually be said to experience adverse effects on his or her ability to carry out normal day-to-day activities. A person who is left-handed will be disabled in using industrial machinery designed for right-handed use, but left-handedness is not usually recognised as a disability. An individual with a poor educational record because of comparatively low or average intelligence will be effectively disqualified from aspiring to the position of heart surgeon, but the majority of the population could be said to be 'disabled' to that extent. It is not thought that colour blindness, left-handedness or indifferent educational attainment are within the scope of the Act and the 'ability to carry out normal day-to-day activities' rubric emphasises that exclusion.[2]

---

1   This will be underlined by the 'substantial and long-term adverse effect' formula discussed at **2.5**.
2   See further: Guidance, Part II, para C3.

2.4.5   Furthermore, although the Act covers clinically well-recognised mental illnesses, it might be difficult for persons with such illnesses to be able to show that they have an adverse effect on normal day-to-day activities, as those activities are defined in the Act. In the employment sphere, many mental illnesses might have an adverse effect upon a person's full working capacity, but work is not one of the listed normal day-to-day activities.[1]

---

1   See Guidance, Part II, para C3.

2.5   SUBSTANTIAL AND LONG-TERM ADVERSE EFFECT

2.5.1   To satisfy the definition of a disability, the putative disabled person must demonstrate that he or she has a physical or mental impairment 'which has a substantial and long-term adverse effect' on the ability to carry out normal day-to-day activities (s 1(1)).

2.5.2   The Guidance issued by the Secretary of State (and by the Department of Economic Development in Northern Ireland) under s 3 (and Sch 8, para 2(1)) specifically refers to the matters which a court or tribunal ought to take into account when determining whether an impairment has a substantial adverse effect on a person's ability to carry out normal day-to-day activities or whether such an impairment has a long-term adverse effect (s 3(1)). A court or tribunal addressing these questions, for any purpose of the legislation, is obliged to take account of the Guidance where it appears to be relevant (s 3(3) and (12)).[1]

---

1   See **9.3**.

2.5.3   The power to issue Guidance under s 3 is at large, but s 3(2) makes it clear that such Guidance may give examples in four particular circumstances:

- effects which it would be reasonable to regard as substantial adverse effects in relation to particular activities;
- effects which it would not be reasonable to regard as substantial adverse effects in relation to particular activities;
- substantial adverse effects which it would be reasonable to regard as long term;
- substantial adverse effects which it would not be reasonable to regard as long term.

The Guidance gives detailed examples of what would or would not be reasonable to regard as substantial adverse effects in relation to each of the eight normal day-to-day activities.[1] It is not proposed to duplicate these examples here. Further interpretative assistance is to be found in Sch 1 to the Act.[2]

---

1   See Guidance, Part II, paras C5–C21.
2   Note also the provisions in respect of impairments controlled by medical treatment or special aids. See Sch 1, para 6 and the further discussion below at **2.7**.

2.5.4   As already noted, the Guidance was issued under s 3 during the course of 1996. In general terms, the Guidance is of some assistance in addressing the questions that might arise in respect of the definition of disability under the DDA 1995. However, it is important to note that the Guidance is not intended to weaken the definition of disability or to exclude particular impairments.[1] That is properly the function of any regulations made under the Act. Nevertheless, the Guidance does help the present discussion by illustrating and exemplifying how the statutory definition works in practice.

1   See the assurance given at HC Deb Standing Committee E, col 124 (Mr W. Hague).

Substantial adverse effects

2.5.5   Whether an impairment has a substantial adverse effect upon a person is not explained in the Act.[1] Nevertheless, it is the Government's stated intention that quite minor impairments should not provide a cause of action and that the use of the word 'substantial' is designed to ensure that trivial conditions are not brought within the scope of the legislation.[2] For example, persons with a minor vision impairment (such as 20/40 vision) might find it difficult to show that their impairment has a substantial adverse effect of the kind required by the statute.

The Guidance confirms that a substantial effect is one that is more than minor or trivial and indicates that the requirement that an adverse effect be substantial is designed to reflect the general understanding of disability as being a limitation going beyond the normal differences in ability between people.[3] In the final analysis, however, what is and what is not a 'substantial' adverse effect will be a matter for judicial interpretation of the statutory language, albeit assisted by the provisions of the Guidance and any appropriate regulations. Schedule 1, para 5 provides that regulations may be made to provide for an effect of a prescribed kind on the ability of a person to carry out normal day-to-day activities to be treated as being (or, alternatively, as not being) a substantial adverse effect. No general regulations have been made under this power.[4]

1   The word 'substantial' is also used, for example, in the employment provisions of ss 5 and 6. It will be interesting to see whether it is interpreted in different ways in different contexts. See the discussion of this question in Chapter 3 *passim.*

2   HC Deb Standing Committee E, col 114 (Mr W. Hague); HC Deb vol 566, col 174 (Mr A. Burt).

3   Guidance, Part II, para A1.

4   Although see the Disability Discrimination (Meaning of Disability) Regulations 1996, reg 5 (on tattoos and body piercing, discussed at **2.6.4**) and reg 6 (on babies and young children under six years of age, discussed at **2.4.2**).

2.5.6   The Guidance states that, in judging whether the adverse effects of an impairment upon a normal day-to-day activity are substantial, account should be taken of the time taken to carry out the activity and the way in which the activity is carried out.[1] If the impairment adversely affects the speed or manner in which that person can perform a particular activity in comparison with other persons, that is a relevant consideration. Environmental considerations will also be important (for example, the effect which temperature or stress has upon the impairment).[2] It will also be appropriate to take account of the cumulative effects of an impairment.[3] For example, someone with mild cerebral palsy may experience only minor effects upon any of a number of the listed activities in Sch 1, para 4(1), but the aggregate effect may be quite disabling and should be treated as so under the Act.[4] The cumulative effect of two or more impairments might also produce the substantial adverse effect on normal day-to-day activities called for by the statute even if, in isolation, each impairment could not be said to have such an effect.[5]

Account should also be taken of how far a person might reasonably be expected to modify their behaviour so as to prevent or reduce the adverse effects of an impairment on normal day-to-day activities.[6] For example, a person with a condition which manifests itself as an allergic reaction to certain substances might reasonably be expected to take steps to avoid those substances. To that extent, that person could not be said to experience a substantial adverse effect upon his or her normal day-to-day activities and would no longer satisfy the definition of disability. However, such avoidance or coping strategies must be subject to a test of reasonableness and might produce second order disabling effects in themselves. In any event, it must be recognised that such strategies might break down at times of stress and that must be weighed in the balance.[7]

---

1 Guidance, Part II, paras A2–A3.
2 Ibid, para A10.
3 Ibid, para A4.
4 Ibid, para A5 and see the examples provided there.
5 Ibid, para A6.
6 Ibid, para A7–A9.
7 Ibid, para A8. Note also para A9 discussed at **2.7.2**.

2.5.7 The Act also provides that if an impairment is one which has had a substantial adverse effect on a person's ability to carry out normal day-to-day activities, but subsequently ceased to have that effect, it will be treated as continuing to have such a substantial adverse effect (that is, during any intervening period of remission or good health) 'if that effect is likely to recur' (Sch 1, para 2(2)). However, the likelihood of an effect recurring shall be disregarded in circumstances which may be prescribed in future regulations (Sch 1, para 2(3)). No such regulations have been made at the time of writing.

2.5.8 This is an essential provision which recognises that there are many impairments whose effects upon day-to-day activities fluctuate. In the case of epilepsy or multiple sclerosis, for example, the underlying condition is constant, but the adverse effects of the condition are variable, with periods of impairment or disability alternating with periods of good health and normal activity. The Government has stated that such conditions are within the Act and that its regulation-making powers will not be used to exclude persons with such conditions.[1] Nevertheless, some conditions whose effects are recurring and can be substantial for a brief time are likely to be excluded by regulation.[2]

---

1 HC Deb Standing Committee E, col 113 (Mr W. Hague).
2 See the treatment of seasonal allergic rhinitis at **2.3.2**.

2.5.9 In respect of an impairment or condition with recurring effects, the Guidance states that an effect is likely to recur if 'it is more likely than not that the effect will recur'.[1] If the effects are likely to recur beyond 12 months after the first occurrence, then they are to be treated as long-term.[2] However, in judging the likelihood of recurrence, account should be taken of all the circumstances, including any reasonable expectation that the person concerned should take steps to prevent the recurrence.[3]

---

1   Guidance, Part II, para B3. It is likely an event will happen if it is more probable than not that it will happen: ibid, para B7.
2   Ibid, para B4.
3   Ibid, para B5 applying much the same behavioural expectations as were discussed at **2.5.6** (and see Guidance, Part II, paras A7–A9).

2.5.10 Two further provisions might be usefully introduced at this point and then returned to in more detail below. First, an impairment which consists of a severe disfigurement is to be treated as having a substantial adverse effect on the ability of the person concerned to carry out normal day-to-day activities (Sch 1, para 3). This is discussed further at **2.6**. Secondly, an impairment which is controlled or corrected by medical treatment or special aids is to be treated as continuing to have a substantial adverse effect on a person's ability to carry out normal day-to-day activities if it would have that effect were it not controlled or corrected (Sch 1, para 6). This provision is discussed at **2.7**.

Long-term effects

2.5.11 The Act is more expansive in its explication of what amounts to long-term effects of an impairment. Schedule 1 provides that the effect of an impairment is 'long-term' if it has lasted for at least 12 months (para 2(1)(a)) or the period for which it lasts is likely to be at least 12 months (para 2(1)(b)) or it is likely to last for the rest of the life of the person affected (para 2(1)(c)). Regulations may prescribe circumstances in which an effect which would not otherwise be long term is to be treated as a long-term effect or an effect which would otherwise be long term is not to be treated as a long-term effect (Sch 1, para 2(4)). No such regulations have been made at the time of writing.[1]

---

1   But note the discussion of children under six years of age at **2.4.2**.

2.5.12 The intention of the Act is to exclude from the protection of the anti-discrimination principle those persons whose impairment or disability is merely short term or temporary. To take an example that was cited in Committee,[1] suppose that an employee suffered a sudden onset of deafness and was dismissed within six months of medical diagnosis. Would the employee have redress under the law, all other things being equal? Even though at the time of dismissal the impairment had not lasted at least 12 months, nevertheless the employee should be able to show that the period for which the hearing impairment is likely to last is at least 12 months, and so the employee would be enabled to seek a remedy. However, a person refused access to a restaurant because he has a broken leg in plaster, or because she exhibits obvious signs of German measles, would not have redress because the impairments or conditions in question do not have, or are not likely to have, long-term effects.[2]

In Committee, the question was also raised as to how the Act would treat a person diagnosed as having a terminal illness with a prognosis that he or she would not live for more than a few months and less than 12 months.[3] Could such a person be lawfully refused, for example, provision of goods or services in a shop or restaurant? The ministerial view was that such a case would generally be covered by a commonsense interpretation of the law and that it was intended that terminal illnesses should be within the definition. On the face of it, such an individual satisfies neither of the first and second alternative conditions of the definition of 'long-term effects' contained in Sch 1, para 2(1), but would easily be caught by Sch 1, para 2(1)(c) in that the impairment can reasonably be expected to last for the rest of the life of the person affected.

---

1 HC Deb Standing Committee E, col 70 (Mr D. Hanson).
2 See further, HC Deb Standing Committee E, cols 77–78 (Mr W. Hague).
3 HC Deb Standing Committee E, col 78 (Mr N. Gerrard).

2.5.13 The Guidance states that, in judging whether the adverse effects of an impairment are long term, it is not necessary for the effect to be the same throughout the period in question. The effect may be variable or progressive. Provided the impairment continues to have (or is likely to have) an adverse effect on ability to carry out normal day-to-day activities throughout the period, there is a long-term effect.[1] The Guidance also states:

> 'In assessing the likelihood of an effect lasting for any period, account should be taken of the total period for which the effect exists. This includes any time before the point when the discriminatory behaviour occurred as well as time afterwards. Account should also be taken of both the typical length of such an effect on an individual, and any relevant factors specific to this individual (for example, general state of health, age).'[2]

Note, however, that provision is also made for recurring effects.[3] If the adverse effects are likely to recur beyond 12 months after the first occurrence, they are to be treated as long term.[4] It is likely that an event will happen if it is more probable than not that it will happen.[5]

---

1 Guidance, Part II, paras B1–B2.
2 Ibid, para B8.
3 See Sch 1, para 2(2) and the discussion at **2.5.7–2.5.9**.

4   Guidance, Part II, para B5.
5   Ibid, para B7.

2.5.14   As discussed below (at **2.11**), references in Parts II and III of the Act to a disabled person are also to be read as references to a person who has had a disability (s 2(2) and Sch 2, para 2). Some modification of the meaning of 'long-term effect' is necessary in order to accommodate the inclusion of past disabilities. Schedule 2, para 5 substitutes a modified version of Sch 1, para 2(1)—(3) when dealing with the question of whether a person with a past disability has experienced a long-term adverse effect on ability to carry out normal day-to-day activities.

For this purpose only, the effect of an impairment is a long-term effect if it has lasted for at least 12 months (modified Sch 1, para 2(1)). Where an impairment ceases to have a substantial adverse effect on a person's ability to carry out normal day-to-day activities, it is to be treated as continuing to have that effect if that effect recurs (modified Sch 1, para 2(2)).[1] For the purposes of the modified para 2(2), the recurrence of an effect shall be disregarded in circumstances that may be prescribed by future regulations (modified Sch 1, para 2(3)).

---

1   See Guidance, Part II, para B9.

2.6   SEVERE DISFIGUREMENT

2.6.1   Schedule 1, para 3(1) provides that an impairment which consists of a severe disfigurement is to be treated as having a substantial adverse effect on the ability of the person concerned to carry out normal day-to-day activities. Regulations may provide that in prescribed circumstances a severe disfigurement is not to be treated as having that effect, even if that is the effect (Sch 1, para 3(2)). These regulations may also make particular provision with respect to 'deliberately acquired disfigurements' (Sch 1, para 3(3)).

2.6.2   The inclusion of severe disfigurements within the definition of disability for the purposes of the Act is important. Persons with facial port wine stains, other birth marks, severe burns or scalds, and other disfiguring signs face discrimination based upon aesthetic appearance.[1] Such an impairment is rarely disabling in itself. Rather, the disability experienced by disfigured individuals is as a result of society's reaction to perceived imperfection. This is a rare example of the new legislation acknowledging a social model of disability rather than a purely medical one.

---

1   The Guidance also refers to scars, limb or postural deformation or diseases of the skin (Part II, para A17).

2.6.3   The potential exclusion by regulations of severe disfigurements which are 'deliberately acquired disfigurements' (Sch 1, para 3(3)) was always likely to give rise to contention. The obvious example of a deliberately acquired disfigurement would be a facial or bodily tattoo or tattoos. Society's reaction to tattoos – especially extensive tattooing – is frequently negative and, while the tattooed individual himself or herself might not regard the tattoo as a disfigurement, that will often not be a perception shared with or by others. However, in debate, the Minister made it apparent that the Government intended to use its regulatory powers to exclude tattoos and body-piercing from the scope of disfigurements otherwise within the Act.

Accordingly, the regulations stipulate that a severe disfigurement is not to be treated as having a substantial adverse effect on the ability of the person concerned to carry out normal day-to-day activities if it consists of a tattoo (which has not been removed) or body-piercing for decorative or other *non-medical purposes* (including any object attached through the piercing for such purposes).[1] *Quaere* whether a severe disfigurement resulting from an attempt to remove a tattoo would also be excluded? It is suggested that it would not be so excluded.

---

1   Disability Discrimination (Meaning of Disability) Regulations 1996, reg 5.

2.6.4   Note that the Act does not automatically exclude deliberately acquired severe disfigurements. This can only be done by regulation. For the moment, the regulations do not make any further exclusions and it does not appear that any more are being contemplated. Facial or bodily scarring caused by self-mutilation or self-administered injury – perhaps as a reaction to emotional stress, depression or as part of a suicide attempt – can be severely disfiguring and yet will also be deliberately acquired. In Committee, the specific example was given of a person who, as a child, had engaged in solvent abuse and suffered major burns in consequence. The Minister indicated that such a person would not be ruled out of inclusion under the Act, even though he or she might be said to have had some responsibility for the disfigurement.[1] The position in respect of self-mutilation or self-administered scars remains unclear, but their omission from the regulations seems to indicate that they will count as a severe disfigurement, *ceteris paribus,* and thus deemed to be a disability under the Act.[2]

---

1   HC Deb Standing Committee E, cols 110–111 (Mr W. Hague).
2   Note that the Guidance (Part II, para A17) assumes that the assessment of the severity of a disfigurement (whether deliberately acquired or not) will be a matter of degree and that account may be taken of where on the body the feature in question is to be found. The implication is that a facial disfigurement is more likely to pass the test of severity than one hidden by a person's clothing.

2.7   EFFECT OF MEDICAL TREATMENT

2.7.1   A problem which has been addressed in other jurisdictions which have disability discrimination laws is whether or not a person whose disability is controlled, corrected or adjusted by medical treatment, or by the use of medication, auxiliary devices or other aids, remains a person with an impairment for the purpose of protection against disability-related discrimination. In a strict sense, such a person might no longer be said to have an impairment which has an adverse effect on normal day-to-day activities. Yet, at the same time, the underlying condition or impairment remains and the person is disabled to the extent that the method of control or correction will involve residual or second order effects and inconveniences. Equally, such a person might experience continuing adverse treatment at the hands of others who might continue to regard the individual as disabled. That might be the case illustratively where an individual walks with the aid of a prosthesis or is mobile with the assistance of a motorised wheelchair.

2.7.2   As already briefly referred to above,[1] the Act provides that an impairment which would be likely to have a substantial adverse effect on the ability of the person concerned to carry out normal day-to-day activities, but for the fact that measures are being taken to treat or correct it, is nevertheless to be treated as continuing to be an impairment amounting to a disability (Sch 1, para 6(1)). The legislation gives examples of measures treating or correcting an impairment as including 'medical treatment and the use of a prosthesis or other aid' (Sch 1, para 6(2)).

---

1   At **2.3.15**.

2.7.3   Provided that the impairment would have had a substantial adverse effect on a person's ability to carry out normal day-to-day activities *but for* the fact that it has been treated or controlled or corrected in the manner described, then it is also to be treated as continuing to have such a substantial adverse effect even although no such effect is actually experienced because of such treatment or control or correction. An example of such an impairment might include insulin-controlled diabetes or medication-regulated epilepsy. A further illustration would be hearing loss improved by a hearing aid.

The Guidance states that this provision applies even if the measures in question result in the effects being completely under control or not at all apparent.[1] The question of whether or not a person has an impairment which has a substantial adverse effect upon the ability to carry out normal day-to-day activities is to be answered by reference to what would be the effect of the impairment or condition but for the treatment, aid or medication.[2] Note also that the Guidance proposes that if a disabled person is advised by a medical practitioner to behave in a certain way in order to reduce the impact of a disability, that might count as treatment to be disregarded under this provision.[3]

1 Guidance, Part II, para A12.
2 Ibid, para A13.
3 Ibid, para A9, and thus that behaviour should not be taken into account at all under paras A7–A8 (see **2.5.6**).

2.7.4 However, this provision does not extend to the impairment of a person's sight, to the extent that the impairment is, in the particular person's case, 'correctable by spectacles or contact lenses' or in such other ways as may be prescribed by regulations (Sch 1, para 6(3)(a)). Individuals with spectacles or contact lenses which compensate for an impairment to their sight do not usually regard themselves as disabled and are not to be treated as such for the purposes of the Act.

The use of the word 'correctable' seems to suggest also that an individual who has a sight impairment, but does not use spectacles or contact lenses that might otherwise correct the sight loss, would not qualify as a 'disabled person'. In other words, this provision of the Act only embraces involuntary disabilities. A person who chooses to take basic, non-surgical remedial action to correct a vision impairment cannot claim protection of the Act. Schedule 1, para 6(3)(a) does not suggest that a sight impairment correctable by surgical techniques is excluded from the coverage of the legislation, although the wording of the paragraph is wide enough to allow future regulations to make such provision.

However, it may be that the better interpretation of Sch 1, para 6(3)(a) is provided by the Guidance. This states that the only effects on ability to carry out normal day-to-day activities to be considered are *those which remain* when spectacles or contact lenses are used (or would remain if they were used).[1] There would seem to be some room for confusion here which will call for judicial resolution.

1 Guidance, Part II, para A14.

2.7.5 Regulations may also provide that this exception is to be extended to other impairments in such circumstances as may be prescribed by the regulations (Sch 1, para 6(3)(b)). No regulations of either kind have yet been laid before Parliament. It is not the Government's present intention to use the regulation-making powers in Sch 1, para 6(3)(b) at the commencement of the legislation and the powers are apparently purely precautionary.[1]

An example where the powers might be used in the future, however, is in respect of hearing aids. It is clear that a hearing-aid user will be presently covered by the Act, but future technological advances might produce aids that fully correct hearing loss in the way that spectacles or contact lenses correct loss of vision. In that light, it might be appropriate to exclude hearing-aid users from the law's protection in future.

1 HC Deb Standing Committee E, col 121 (Mr W. Hague).

2.8   PERSONS DEEMED TO BE DISABLED

2.8.1   It was observed previously that the existing classification of a person as disabled under other legislation would be of some assistance, but not conclusively so, in determining whether that individual satisfied the definition of a disabled person under the 1995 Act.[1] In other jurisdictions, the fact that persons had been recognised as disabled for other purposes (for example, for the purposes of social security, industrial injury compensation or social welfare law) would be at least persuasive that their status as a disabled person should be accepted for the purposes of a disability discrimination enactment.

---

1   See **2.1.5**.

2.8.2   That is not explicitly the case under the 1995 Act and one must be cautious of relying upon any implicit assumption that a court or tribunal would regard a pre-existing certification of a person as disabled under parallel legal provisions as conclusive or persuasive that they should be so treated under the Disability Discrimination Act 1995. However, there is one exceptional case provided for in Sch 1, para 7 in respect of so-called 'Green Card' holders under the 1944 and 1945 Acts.[1]

---

1   For the modification of these provisions in the Northern Ireland context see Sch 1, para 49.

Green Card holders

2.8.3   Schedule 1 to the 1995 Act deals with a person who was a 'registered disabled person' under s 6 of the Disabled Persons (Employment) Act 1944 (or its Northern Ireland equivalent) both on 12 January 1995 and 2 December 1996, the date on which para 7 in Sch 1 to the 1995 Act came into force (Sch 1, para 7(1)). Such a person who can meet those conditions is 'deemed to have a disability' and is thus treated as a disabled person for the purpose of the application of any provision of the Disability Discrimination Act 1995 in relation to 'the initial period' (Sch 1, para 7(2)(a)).

The significance of the two cut-off dates is that 12 January 1995 was the date upon which the draft statute was published as a Bill. Clearly, only those persons who were registered at that time and who maintained their registration until this provision came into force should be allowed to take advantage of a deeming and transitional provision. The repeal of the relevant provisions of the 1944 Act (by virtue of s 61(7), s 70(5) and Sch 7) was contemporaneous with the bringing into force of Part II of the 1995 Act (the employment provisions) on 2 December 1996.

2.8.4   A 'disabled person' within the meaning of s 1 of the Disabled Persons (Employment) Act 1944 (now repealed) was defined as someone who is substantially handicapped in obtaining or keeping employment because of injury, disease or congenital deformity. Being handicapped in undertaking work on his or her own account by reason of these causes also qualified an individual as a disabled person under the 1944 Act. The employment or work in question must be of a kind which, apart from the injury, disease or deformity, would be suited to that person's age, experience and qualifications.

2.8.5 The primary importance of this definition of disabled person was for the purpose of registering under the 1944 Act as a 'person registered as handicapped by disablement'. Only such registered disabled persons could qualify for *certain* employment assistance and services offered by government departments. Employers' obligations under the statutory quota scheme and in respect of designated employment were measured by reference to registered disabled persons alone. The Government maintained a register of disabled persons under s 6 of the 1944 Act. An individual who satisfied the definition of disabled person could apply at a Job Centre to be entered in the register, provided that the disablement was likely to last for at least 12 months. The applicant must also have attained the school leaving age, desire to engage in remunerative work, have a reasonable prospect of obtaining and keeping such work, and be ordinarily resident in Great Britain or Northern Ireland (unless a serviceman or merchant seaman).

2.8.6 A registered disabled person was issued with a certificate of registration, known as a 'Green Card', production of which an employer or prospective employer subject to the 1944 Act could demand. The significance of the certificate of registration is that it will now be treated as conclusive evidence, in relation to the person with respect to whom it was issued, in respect of the matters certified. Unless the contrary is shown, its validity is entitled to be taken at face value (Disability Discrimination Act 1995, Sch 1, para 7(3)–(4) and (7)). In other words, a Green Card holder will be deemed to be a disabled person for the purposes of the 1995 Act provided the certificate of registration satisfies the cut-off dates specified above. Such a person will not need to satisfy the various ingredients of 'disabled person' set out in s 1 of and Sch 1 to the new Act.

2.8.7 However, this deemed status only lasts for the so-called 'initial period' (Sch 1, para 7(2)(a)). This means the period of three years from 2 December 1996 (Sch 1, para 7(7)). Thereafter, such a person will need to meet the statutory definition of 'disabled person' contained in all its detail in the 1995 Act and the accompanying Guidance and regulations. In practice, that might not be an insurmountable task for a person who qualified under the 1944 Act and whose conditions and circumstances remain unchanged or comparable.

In any event, Sch 1, para 7(2)(b) regards such a person as being a person who had a disability, and thus to have been a disabled person, during the initial period. This means that they should be able to rely upon the extension of the Act to include persons who have had a disability in the past (s 2 and Sch 2) as discussed below.[1]

---

1   See **2.11**.

Other cases

2.8.8   Schedule 1 also anticipates the possibility that prescribed descriptions of persons might also be deemed to have disabilities and, therefore, be deemed to be disabled persons for the purposes of the new legislation. Such prescription will be made by regulations under Sch 1, para 7(5). The regulations might also provide that a person deemed to be a disabled person by virtue of a relevant registration under the 1944 Act, or by virtue of a deeming provision made under Sch 1, para 7(5) (in the 1995 Act), shall be treated as no longer deemed to be a disabled person (Sch 1, para 7(6)). No such regulations of the kinds described have been made to date.

2.9   PROGRESSIVE CONDITIONS

2.9.1   Schedule 1, para 8 deals with the situation where (a) a person has a 'progressive condition' and, (b) as a result of that condition, he or she has an impairment which has (or had) an effect on his or her ability to carry out normal day-to-day activities, but that effect is not (or was not) a *substantial* adverse effect. Such a person is nevertheless to be treated as having an impairment which has such a substantial adverse effect if the condition is likely to result in that person having such an impairment in the future (Sch 1, para 8(1)).

2.9.2   The Act illustrates the kind of 'progressive condition' which is contemplated here by reference to conditions 'such as cancer, multiple sclerosis, muscular dystrophy or infection by the human immunodeficiency virus' (Sch 1, para 8(1)(a)) but it is clear that this list is not intended to be exhaustive. Regulations may provide (for the purposes of this provision only) that conditions of a prescribed description are to be treated as being or not being progressive conditions (Sch 1, para 8(2)). No such regulations have yet been enacted.

2.9.3   It is apparent from the parliamentary debates that the legislature did not intend that the new legislation should protect individuals from discrimination where they possess asymptomatic conditions (for example, a person diagnosed as HIV positive but without manifest symptoms of the virus or a related illness).[1] That belief does not appear to be fully supported by the language of the statute. The Government's view must be based, if at all, upon Sch 1, para 4, in that it might be said that a symptomless illness or condition is not an impairment which has yet affected one of the designated normal day-to-day activities.[2]

1   HL Deb, vol 566, col 1061 (Lord Mackay of Ardbrecknish).
2   That is the assumption made by the Guidance, Part II, para A15.

2.9.4   It is submitted that a person known to have been diagnosed as HIV positive or as having multiple sclerosis or cystic fibrosis, but who is presently without patent symptoms of illness, ought to be protected from discrimination by virtue of the combined effect of s 1 and Sch 1, para 8 (that is, that a disability can include a progressive condition whose adverse effect is not yet substantial or long term but is likely to be so). However, that was not the legislative intention, as a Minister explained:

> 'We recognise that there is a need to protect people where the effect of the condition is not yet substantial but is expected to be so in the future. That is why the [Act] specifically includes people with progressive conditions as soon as there are any effects on their ability to carry out normal day-to-day activities. However, we do not believe that it would be right to include people with conditions which may remain latent, possibly for a considerable number of years ... The Disability Discrimination [Act] is designed to protect people who have, or ... have had, an actual disability. It is not a general anti-discrimination [Act] nor a general health discrimination [Act]. If we extend it to cover people who may develop a disability at some unspecified time in the future we will undermine the effectiveness of the [Act] by creating uncertainty about who is covered.'[1]

This point is now clarified by the Guidance which makes it clear that medical diagnosis is not enough by itself.[2]

1   HL Deb, vol 564, col 1682 (Lord Mackay of Ardbrecknish).
2   See the Guidance, Part II, para A15.

2.10   PERCEIVED DISABILITIES AND FUTURE DISABILITIES

2.10.1   Despite the inclusive tone of the statute's treatment of progressive conditions, the wording of the Act makes it plain that it is to be the *future* effects of a *presently existing* progressive condition only which the law intends to embrace. A person whose medical status or condition merely indicates that it is likely that he or she might suffer from a progressive condition *in the future* is not to be treated as having an impairment with substantial adverse effects on ability to carry out normal day-to-day activities. Thus the 'progressive conditions' provision does not include within the protection of the 1995 Act individuals who merely have a genetic or other predisposition to (or risk of) a progressive condition in the future.

A number of unsuccessful attempts were made during the legislative process to include within the category of 'disabled person' individuals who had undergone a medical test which indicated that they had a predictive propensity to develop an impairment at a later date (such as Usher syndrome, Huntingdon's chorea, Alzheimer's disease or multiple sclerosis). The Government consistently and successfully resisted such attempted amendments.[1]

---

1   On the problem of discrimination based upon genetic screening see: House of Commons Science and Technology Committee, *Human Genetics: The Science and Its Consequences* (HC Paper 41, July 1995, London: HMSO).

2.10.2   During the passage of the Act, attempts were also made to introduce into the definition of 'disabled person' provisions which would have had the effect of protecting from discrimination individuals who had a mistaken or erroneous reputation as a person who has or had an impairment or might do so in the future. These attempts were influenced by similar provisions in the United States.[1] The intention of the movers of these ultimately unsuccessful amendments was to ensure that a person with a degenerative condition which has not yet had an effect on ability to carry out normal day-to-day activities (such as multiple sclerosis in its early stages) or with a dormant or symptomless condition (such as asymptomatic Human Immunodeficiency Virus) would be automatically protected under the provisions of the Act. Concern was expressed that if an individual could not satisfy the definition of a disability in the present, they might nevertheless face discrimination today on the basis of being treated or perceived as disabled or because of a judgement as to their future disposition to illness.

---

1   See also the creative provisions in respect of supposed religious belief or political opinion in the Fair Employment (Northern Ireland) Act 1989, s 57(2).

2.10.3   For example, a person who had taken a medical test to detect the presence of HIV or a genetic disorder might be discriminated against without an avenue of redress. Even though at the time of discrimination he or she might be quite well or symptomless, such a person might nevertheless be treated by an employer or other party as if he or she were disabled or impaired in some way. To include such persons within the definition of 'disabled person' for the purposes of the Act would have been to recognise that disability involves a social construction as well as a medical diagnosis.

A further illustration would involve a person injured in an industrial or road traffic accident which resulted in fractures to his or her limbs. Ironically, the fractures themselves would not amount to an impairment because it is unlikely that they would cause long-term adverse effects on the activities of the individual. However, an employer might in the future refuse to employ such an individual on the basis of a perception or assumption – unsupported by any existing medical evidence – that he or she constitutes a safety risk because of the prior accident record or because of an ill-founded concern that the individual is left with a residual and inherent musculo-skeletal weakness. Such an employer has treated or regarded the individual in question as 'disabled'.

2.10.4 These amendments were rejected by the Government and do not form part of the substance of the Act. It remains to be seen whether persons who are treated as disabled, or who are perceived or reputed to have a disability, or who are predicted as likely to experience future disability, will be brought within the legislation's fold by creative judicial interpretation. Given the unambiguous wording of s 1 and Sch 1, and given the Government's express rejection of the amendments,[1] there would appear to be little scope for judicial expansionism. It is, in any event, the Government's view that the Act will indirectly benefit such persons because of the expected general improvement in attitudes to disabilities which it is hoped the new legislation will produce.

---

1   HC Deb Standing Committee E, cols 83–85 (Mr W. Hague); HL Deb, vol 564, cols 1648–1653 (Lord Mackay of Ardbrecknish).

2.11 PAST DISABILITIES

2.11.1   Following concessions made during the Second Reading of the Act in the House of Lords, amendments were moved by the Government in Committee so that Parts II and III of the Act (discrimination in relation to employment, contract work, trade organisations, goods, facilities, services and premises) now apply *pari passu* in relation to a person 'who has had a disability' as if that person was a person who has that disability at the present or relevant time (s 2(1)).

This is achieved by making appropriate modifications to the substantive provisions of the Act (s 2(2)) and such modifications are set out in Sch 2. In particular, references in Parts II and III of the Act to a disabled person are also to be read as references to a person who has had a disability (Sch 2, para 2). Any regulations or orders made under the powers bestowed by the Act may include provision with respect to persons who have had a disability (s 2(3)).

2.11.2   The Government's change of heart was explained by Lord Mackay of Ardbrecknish in the following terms:

'[A]fter very careful consideration we accepted that the [Act] should confer protection against discrimination for people who have had a disability. This decision was not made lightly. We have rightly been concerned that the protection conferred by the [Act] should be sharply focused on those people who are commonly accepted as being disabled ... It has become clear that people who have had a disability, although they may be no longer disabled as such, share with people who are currently disabled, a need for protection against discrimination in relation to their disability ... It is clearly a very important part of the whole process of recovery that someone who has been disabled is able not only to participate fully in employment and social activities but to feel confident in doing so . . . In addition, we have been persuaded that it is not always possible to tell when a person has fully recovered from a disability and when the condition is no longer likely to recur.'[1]

1   HL Deb, vol 564, col 1655.

2.11.3   In a case of alleged discrimination against a person who complains of an act based upon that person's past disability, it does not matter that the relevant provisions of the Act were not in force when that person was actually experiencing the disability in question. The question whether a person had a disability at a particular time shall be determined as if the relevant provisions of the Act in force at the time of the discriminatory act had been in force at the relevant time (ie at the time the person had the disability in issue) (s 2(4)). Furthermore, the past disability in question might have been experienced at a time before the passing of the new legislation (s 2(5)). These provisions will ensure consistency of treatment between persons who are presently disabled and those individuals who have recovered from the same condition.[1]

1   HL Deb, vol 564, col 1656 (Lord Mackay of Ardbrecknish).

2.11.4   The modification of the definition of 'long-term adverse effect' when dealing with a past disability is set out in Sch 2, para 5. This has been dealt with above.[1]

1   At **2.5.14**.

2.11.5   The inclusion of past disabilities within the Act's protection is an important concession and provides a potential remedy for those persons who are discriminated against because of their history or record of disability. For example, a person with a history of depression or mental or emotional illness might be unreasonably excluded from employment opportunity but would otherwise have no cause of action unless the depression or mental or emotional illness was a clinically recognised condition from which the individual suffered at the time the employment opportunity was denied. Section 2 and Sch 2 now make provision for such a case, all other things being equal.

However, it is important to note that, where a person seeks to rely upon the status of being 'a person who has had a disability', it will still be necessary for that person to show that, at the relevant time in the past, he or she had a physical or mental impairment which had a substantial and long-term adverse effect on his or her ability to carry out normal day-to-day activities within the meaning of s 1 and Sch 1.

Chapter 3

EMPLOYMENT AND CONTRACT WORK

3.1 INTRODUCTION

3.1.1 Part II of the Disability Discrimination Act 1995 addresses the problem of discrimination against persons with disabilities in the field of employment. It is modelled after the similar provisions in the Sex Discrimination Act 1975 (SDA) and the Race Relations Act 1976 (RRA). Case-law under that legislation will be instructive. However, there are important differences between the 1995 Act and the earlier statutes.

3.1.2 Part II of the Act, so far as it affects employment and contract work, came into force on 2 December 1996.[1] It is subject to regulations amplifying (and sometimes narrowing) the provisions on employment discrimination.[2] A new code of practice (referred to hereafter as 'Employment Code of Practice') has been issued by the Secretary of State under s 53(1)(a). It provides guidance and assistance to employers in respect of their new obligations under Part II.[3] It does not impose legal obligations of itself and is not intended to be an authoritative statement of law. However, it is admissible in proceedings before an industrial tribunal or court, and these bodies must take into account any provision of the Employment Code of Practice which appears to be relevant to the determination of a question in those proceedings.[4]

---

1 Disability Discrimination Act 1965 (Commencement No 3 and Saving and Transitional Provisions) Order 1996, SI 1996/1474, art 2(3) and Sch, Part III subject to the saving and transitional provisions set out in art 3. See **1.3.4**.

2 Disability Discrimination (Employment) Regulations 1996, SI 1996/1456 which came into force on 2 December 1996 and which were made under powers conferred by ss 5(6)–(7), 6(8) and (10), and 12(3), and Sch 4, para 3. See also Disability Discrimination (Employment) Regulations (Northern Ireland) 1996, SR 1996/419.

3 *Code of Practice for the elimination of discrimination in the field of employment against disabled persons or persons who have had a disability* (1996, London: HMSO). The Employment Code of Practice came into force on 2 December 1996 by virtue of the Disability Discrimination (Guidance and Code of Practice) (Appointed Day) Order 1996, SI 1996/1996, para 3. A separate (but essentially identical) Employment Code of Practice covers Northern Ireland and reflects the different institutional context of the province. Both codes came into force on 2 December 1996.

4 Employment Code of Practice, para 1.3 and DDA 1995, s 53(4)–(6). See generally, **9.2**.

3.1.3 By virtue of ss 61 and 70, and Schs 6 and 7, the Act repeals the statutory disabled workers' quota scheme and the reserved occupations under the Disabled Persons (Employment) Acts 1944 and 1958 and makes consequential amendments to other statutory provisions affecting disabled employment rights or opportunities with effect from 2 December 1996.

3.2 GENERAL PROHIBITION ON DISCRIMINATION IN EMPLOYMENT

3.2.1   Section 4 of the Act makes it unlawful, in relation to employment at establishments in Great Britain and in Northern Ireland,[1] for an employer to discriminate against disabled persons.[2] As the section explains, this covers both discrimination against disabled applicants in the recruitment and selection process, as well as discrimination against disabled employees while in an employer's employment.[3] The ministerial view is that:

> 'The [Act] prohibits an employer from discrimination against a disabled person in recruitment of new employees or against disabled employees. It uses broad and comprehensive general wording – as in race discrimination legislation – to cover all aspects of the recruitment process and the employment relationship. There is no need to deal with specific circumstances and forms of discrimination.'[4]

---

1   As originally drafted, the Bill upon which the Act was based only applied to discrimination in employment with establishments within Great Britain. This was amended to include employment in Northern Ireland. See s 4(6) as modified by s 70(6) and Sch 8, para 3.
2   As defined and discussed in Chapter 2. Note that the employment provisions of the Act apply in relation to a person who has had a disability as they apply in relation to a person who has that disability (s 2(1)).
3   This section is virtually identical to the similar provisions in SDA 1975, s 6 and RRA 1976, s 4.
4   HC Deb Standing Committee E, col 142 (Mr J. Paice, Parliamentary Under-Secretary of State for Employment).

3.2.2   The liability of an employer may be vicarious liability for the actions of employees in the course of employment (in accordance with s 58). The employer's liability may be shared with another person who knowingly aids in the commission of an unlawful act of discrimination (s 57). These concepts are discussed in more detail in Chapter 10.

Employment

3.2.3   The term 'employment' has the same extended definition as used in other discrimination statutes. The Act embraces discrimination in employment under a contract of service or a contract of apprenticeship, but it also includes employment under a contract personally to do any work (s 68(1)).[1] This extended definition of employment is subject to any provision prescribed by regulations. No such prescription has been made to date.

---

1   An almost identical definition of 'employment' (with the omission of the word 'any' before the word 'work') applies in Northern Ireland by virtue of s 70(6) and Sch 8, para 47 modifying s 68(1).

3.2.4   While Part II of the Act generally will cover employment by a partnership (all other things being equal), it does not extend to the business relationship of partners within a partnership.[1] Disabled persons have no right of action under the Act if they believe that they have been discriminated against by reason of their disability when seeking to enter a partnership as a would-be partner or while in a partnership in the capacity of partner. This may be simply a small anomaly, but it does seem rather strange that, for instance, a firm of solicitors may not generally discriminate against a disabled lawyer seeking articles or employment as an assistant solicitor, but can do so with impunity if that disabled lawyer, after some years of employment in the firm, were later to seek an equity partnership in the firm (*quaere* the position of a salaried partner?).

---

1 HC Deb Standing Committee E, cols 455–457 (Mr J. Paice). This is in contrast with SDA 1975, s 11 and RRA 1976, s 10.

Employment at an establishment in Great Britain

3.2.5 The phrase 'employment at an establishment in Great Britain' (and, by extension, Northern Ireland) as used in s 4(6) is to be construed in accordance with s 68(2)–(5).[1] It is provided that, where an employee does his or her work wholly or mainly outside Great Britain (or Northern Ireland), that employment is not to be treated as being work at an establishment in Great Britain (or Northern Ireland) even if he or she does some of that work at an establishment within Great Britain (or Northern Ireland) (s 68(2)). The determination of the question of where work is done is settled by the simple rules in s 68(5). Work is treated as done at the establishment *from* which it is done or *with* which it has the closest connection.

Employment on board a ship, aircraft or hovercraft is to be regarded as not being employment at an establishment in Great Britain (or Northern Ireland), unless regulations prescribe otherwise in respect of particular cases (s 68(3)). Furthermore, regulations may provide that employment of a prescribed kind, or in prescribed circumstances, is to be regarded as not being employment at an establishment in Great Britain (or Northern Ireland) (s 68(4)). No regulations under either subsection have been made to date.

---

1 See s 68(1) (as modified for Northern Ireland by Sch 8, para 47).

Exclusion of small businesses

3.2.6 The employment provisions of the Act will not apply in relation to certain small businesses. This exclusion is set at present to benefit employers with fewer than 20 employees (s 7(1)).[1] This threshold reflects the pre-existing

requirement for the operation of the statutory quota scheme under the 1944
Act and the Government's concern to protect the small business sector from
prescriptive regulation.[2] The question of whether an employer has fewer than
20 employees is to be answered by examining how many employees are
employed by that employer on the day the alleged discrimination took place
rather than the date upon which the statute came into force or the date of any
litigation or judicial proceedings.[3]

1   Note the expanded definition of 'employment' (and by inference 'employee') in s 68(1).
    Part-time and temporary employees will count towards the measurement of the threshold.
2   See, for example, HC Deb, vol 257, cols 727–728 (Mr J. Paice). The Minister calculated that,
    despite the small employer exemption, the Act will cover 83 per cent of employees (HC Deb, vol
    257 col 732).
3   HC Deb Standing Committee E, col 227 (Mr J. Paice).

3.2.7   Problems of interpretation might arise, nevertheless, in cases where
there is a series of discriminatory acts rather than one single incident of
discrimination. In the Government's view, no liability can arise for any actions
in a series of actions which occur while the employer has fewer than 20
employees, even if at other times the employer's workforce exceeds that
threshold.[1] This scenario might be particularly relevant to small employers who
rely upon a fluctuating workforce of seasonal, temporary or casual employees.
Nevertheless, a discriminatory act committed while the employer employed
fewer than 20 employees might have continuing effects and, if the employer
subsequently began to employ 20 or more employees, liability might arise from
a failure to correct the continuing effects of a previous discriminatory act for
which no liability had otherwise arisen because of s 7(1).

1   HC Deb Standing Committee E, col 249 (Mr J. Paice).

3.2.8   The statute also does not define how the number of employees is to be
determined in cases of associated employers or corporate groups. The
implication appears to be that, unless a tribunal or court is prepared to lift the
corporate veil, the separate legal entity within which the employee is employed
is to be the unit of calculation. For the purpose of determining the small
employer threshold, there seems to be no scope for adding together separate
workforces employed by the same employer through parent, holding and
subsidiary companies or via associated firms. The Employment Code of
Practice makes it clear that independent franchise holders are exempt if they
employ fewer than 20 people even if the franchise network has 20 or more
employees.[1]

1   Employment Code of Practice, para 2.6.

3.2.9   The exclusion of small businesses will be subject to future review under s 7(4).[1] The threshold figure of 20 employees may be adjusted in future by ministerial order under s 7(2),[2] but only after such a review, and any such order must be brought into force not later than one year after the commencement of the review (s 7(8)). The Government indicated that it would consult interested parties before such an adjustment could be made.[3] Statutory provision is now made for such consultations (s 7(7)).[4]

It was apparently not intended to use the power to raise the threshold above the original figure so as to exclude even more small employers. This point has been clarified by an amendment during the course of the legislative process. The s 7(2) power may not be used to substitute a different number *greater* than 20. In other words, if the small business exemption is to be changed in the future, it will be amended only to reduce the number of small employers excused liability under the Act rather than to increase the exempted class.

---

1   In Northern Ireland, responsibility for any review will lie with the Department of Economic Development (Sch 8, para 4).
2   See further **9.4.19**.
3   HC Deb Standing Committee E, col 251 (Mr J. Paice).
4   Discussed at **3.2.10**.

3.2.10   The Act commits the Secretary of State to review the small employer exemption threshold, if he or she has not already done so, at the latest immediately following the fourth anniversary of s 7 coming into force (s 7(5) as read with s 7(3)). Such a review must be completed within nine months (s 7(6)). Whether the Secretary of State undertakes a review of the small employer threshold before or following the fourth anniversary of s 7 coming into force, in conducting the review he or she shall consult such organisations (as he or she considers appropriate) representing the interests of employers and of disabled persons in employment or seeking employment (s 7(7)).

3.2.11   There is no obligation upon the Secretary of State to amend the small employer threshold following a review. Instead, the Act requires the Secretary of State, should he or she decide not to make an amending order, to lay before Parliament a report summarising the results of the review and giving reasons for the decision not to make an order (s 7(9)).[1] This must be done not later than one year after the commencement of a review. The report must include a summary of the views expressed to the Secretary of State in the statutory consultations (s 7(10)).

---

1   In Northern Ireland, the Department of Economic Development must lay such a report before the Northern Ireland Assembly (Sch 8, para 4(3)). In practice, because the Assembly is presently dissolved, power has reverted to Westminster.

Other exemptions

3.2.12 In addition, although the Act will apply to employment by the Crown, government departments, statutory bodies and statutory office-holders (s 64 (1)), the employment provisions of the Act will not apply to employment as:

- a statutory office-holder (such as a police officer);
- a member of the Ministry of Defence Police, British Transport Police, Royal Parks Constabulary or the United Kingdom Atomic Energy Authority Constabulary;
- a prison officer (except custody officers);
- a fire fighting member of a fire brigade;
- a member of the naval, military or air forces of the Crown;

by virtue of s 64(5)–(8). These exemptions and the wider question of the application of the Act to the Crown and to Parliament is considered in more detail in Chapter 9.

3.2.13 Exceptional treatment under Part II of the Act is also given to charities under s 10(1). By virtue of s 10(3) the term 'charity' as used in s 10 has the same meaning as in the Charities Act 1993.[1] Nothing in Part II of the Act (the employment provisions) affects any charitable instrument which provides for conferring benefits on one or more categories of person determined by reference to any physical or mental capacity (s 10(1)(a)). A charitable instrument is an enactment or other instrument (whenever taking effect) so far as it relates to charitable purposes (s 10(3)).[2]

Moreover, nothing in the employment provisions of the 1995 Act makes unlawful any act done by a registered or non-registered charity[3] in pursuance of any of its charitable purposes, so far as those purposes are connected with persons determined by reference to any physical or mental capacity (s 10(1)(b)).

---

1 In Northern Ireland, see the Charities Act (Northern Ireland) 1964 (by virtue of Sch 8, para 7(3)).
2 In England and Wales (and Northern Ireland), charitable purposes are purposes which are exclusively charitable according to the law of England and Wales (and Northern Ireland) (s 10(4) and Sch 7, para 7(4)). In Scotland only, charitable purposes are to be construed as if contained in the Income Tax Acts (s 10(5)).
3 By virtue of s 10(3), in Scotland only, a recognised body for the purposes of Part I of the Law Reform (Miscellaneous Provisions) (Scotland) Act 1990.

3.2.14 Special provision is also made for persons providing supported employment under the Disabled Persons (Employment) Act 1944 or the Disabled Persons (Employment) Act (Northern Ireland) 1945. Section 10(2)(a) of the 1995 Act provides that nothing in Part II of the Act (the employment provisions) prevents a person who provides supported employment from treating members of a particular group of disabled persons (or persons who have had a disability in the past) more favourably than other persons in providing supported employment. In this context, 'supported employment' means facilities provided or paid for under s 15 of the 1944 or 1945 Acts (s 10(3) and Sch 8, para 7).

Furthermore, nothing in Part II of the Act prevents the Secretary of State (or, in Northern Ireland, the Department of Economic Development) from agreeing to arrangements for the provision of supported employment which will (or may) have the effect of treating members of a particular group of disabled persons (or persons who have had a disability in the past) more favourably than other persons (s 10(2)(b) and Sch 8, para 7(2)).

3.2.15 The effect of s 10(2) is not to exclude persons employed under supported employment arrangements from the prohibition on disability-related discrimination per se. Rather, the intention is to allow employers providing supported employment to distinguish between different groups of disabled persons when extending supported employment opportunities. Providing supported employment opportunities for some disabled persons while excluding other persons with a disability would otherwise amount to less favourable treatment for a reason which related to those other persons' disability contrary to ss 4–5 of the Act.

For example, s 10(2) will allow an employer creating a supported employment environment for workers with sight impairments to do so without the need to provide similar facilities for other disabled workers. However, the supported employment in question must be within the framework provided by the 1944–45 legislation. Moreover, s 10(2) does not excuse acts of disability-related employment discrimination elsewhere in the employer's workplace.

3.3 DISCRIMINATION IN EMPLOYMENT

3.3.1 Part II of the Act is concerned with outlawing disability discrimination in employment. Disability discrimination does not take place in a vacuum. A complainant will need to show that the alleged act of disability discrimination falls within one of the prohibited acts of employment discrimination set out in s 4 of the Act. Section 4 makes it unlawful for an employer to discriminate against a disabled person (as defined in s 1) in specified circumstances.[1]

---

1   In the case of an act of victimisation which, by virtue of s 55, constitutes discrimination for the purposes of Part II, the categories of unlawful action or omission in s 4 also apply to discrimination against a person who is not disabled (s 4(5)).

3.3.2 First, it is unlawful for an employer to discriminate against a disabled person in the arrangements which the employer makes for the purpose of determining to whom the employer should offer employment (s 4(1)(a)). As intended, the concept of 'arrangements' as used in s 4(1)(a) has a wide meaning, and will cover job advertisements,[1] and the selection process (including job specifications, qualifications, the location and timing of interviews, the use of assessment techniques, the interview itself, and selection criteria).[2] For example, the inclusion of unnecessary or marginal requirements in a job specification, or blanket exclusions which do not take account of individual circumstances, can be discriminatory.[3] So too, if a disabled person is rejected for a job because he or she lacks a qualification specified by the employer, the rejection might be discriminatory if the lack of the particular qualification is related to that person's disability (for example, because of the effect of dyslexia). The employer would need to justify the stipulation of that qualification (for example, by reference to relevance and significance) or demonstrate that no reasonable adjustment in favour of the disabled applicant (for example, reallocating some duties to another employee or devising an alternative test of competence) could have been made.[4]

---

1   Note also the particular provisions of s 11 discussed below at **3.4.10** et seq.
2   Employment Code of Practice, para 5.2. On the use of aptitude tests and other forms of assessment techniques in the recruitment process, see ibid, para 5.21. On the selection and interview process generally, see ibid, paras 5.12–5.26.
3   Ibid, paras 5.2–5.4 and note the examples provided there.
4   Ibid, para 5.22.

3.3.3   Secondly, s 4(1)(b) provides that it is unlawful for an employer to discriminate against a disabled person in the terms on which the employer offers that person employment. The Employment Code of Practice reinforces this point.[1]

---

1   Employment Code of Practice, para 5.27.

3.3.4   Thirdly, it is equally unlawful for an employer to discriminate against a disabled person by refusing to offer that person employment (s 4(1)(c)). Discrimination by these means includes a deliberate failure or omission to offer employment to a disabled person, so that there does not have to be an express refusal to offer employment in order for potential discrimination to have occurred.

3.3.5   Fourthly, in respect of a disabled person in an employer's employment, it is unlawful for an employer to discriminate against a disabled employee in the terms of employment which the employer affords to such an employee (s 4(2)(a)). As the Employment Code of Practice notes, terms and conditions of service should not discriminate against disabled persons. That does not mean that an employer can never offer a disabled person a less favourable contract but, subject to any duty to make reasonable adjustments, the employer must be prepared to justify the differential.[1] The Employment Code of Practice also reminds employers that they must not discriminate in their induction procedures. If necessary, a newly recruited disabled employee may need an individually tailored induction programme.[2]

---

1 Employment Code of Practice, paras 5.27–5.28 (and note the examples provided there).
2 Ibid, paras 6.2–6.3

3.3.6 Fifthly, disability-based discrimination in employment opportunities is caught by s 4(2)(b). This subsection makes it unlawful for an employer to discriminate against a disabled employee in certain employment opportunities afforded to that person by the employer. The opportunities in question are exhaustively defined as promotion, transfer, training or the receipt of any other benefit.[1] Benefits include facilities and services (s 4(4)) and, subject to what is said below, plainly include entitlements to fringe benefits of employment (such as private health insurance provided to employees by the employer through an insurance company) and to occupational pensions.[2]

In addition, s 4(2)(c) ensures that it is unlawful for an employer to discriminate against a disabled person whom the employer employs where the employer refuses to afford the disabled employee any such opportunities as are mentioned in s 4(2)(b). A refusal in this context includes a deliberate omission to afford such opportunities to a disabled employee.

---

1 The Employment Code of Practice states (para 6.7) that 'benefits' might include canteens, meal vouchers, social clubs and other recreational activities, dedicated car parking spaces, discounts on products, bonuses, share options, hairdressing, clothes allowances, financial services, healthcare, medical assistance/insurance, transport to work, company car, education assistance, workplace nurseries, and rights to special leave. Note the examples provided there. In respect of promotion, transfer and training, see ibid, paras 6.4–6.6.
2 HL Deb, vol 566, col 169 (Lord Mackay of Ardbrecknish). On occupational pensions and insurance benefits, see **3.7** and **3.8**.

3.3.7 The separate wording of s 4(2)(b) and (c) is noteworthy. This ensures that discrimination in the form of a refusal to consider access to possible employment opportunities, facilities and benefits is prohibited as well as discrimination in access to existing employment opportunities, facilities and benefits. This circumvents the restrictive interpretation of the different, but parallel, provision in the SDA 1975. In *Clymo v London Borough of Wandsworth* [1989] IRLR 241, the Employment Appeal Tribunal regarded an employer's refusal to consider a job share proposal as not amounting to indirect sex discrimination because that statute had to be construed as only applying to opportunities or facilities which were already in existence. Such a construction cannot be placed upon the Disability Discrimination Act 1995 and would be simply inconsistent with an employer's quite separate duty under s 6 to make reasonable adjustments to employment arrangements so as to accommodate disabled persons.

3.3.8   Finally, it is unlawful for an employer to discriminate against a disabled employee by dismissing him or her,[1] or by subjecting that person to any other detriment (s 4(2)(d)). The term 'any other detriment' is broadly based and will provide a catch-all for any other forms of employment discrimination against disabled persons if not already caught by the specific categories previously set out. In particular, it is likely that harassment of a disabled person because of his or her disability (or for a reason related to his or her disability) will fall within s 4(2)(d).[2]

---

1   See Employment Code of Practice, paras 6.19–6.21
2   This is confirmed by the Employment Code of Practice (paras 6.22–6.23).

Exceptions

3.3.9   The s 4(2) prohibition on discrimination against disabled persons while in employment does not generally apply to discrimination in relation to benefits of any description if the employer is concerned with the provision of benefits of that description to the public (s 4(3)). For example, the employer might be a bank providing loans to the public and loans to its employees (perhaps at favourable rates of interest). Similarly, that prohibition does not apply if the employer is concerned with the provision of benefits of that description to a section of the public which includes the disabled employee in question (for example, a local authority providing welfare-related benefits to disabled persons in the community, including its own disabled employees). A benefit for this purpose includes facilities and services (s 4(4)) and it is immaterial whether or not the benefit is provided for payment.

3.3.10   However, these exceptions to s 4(2) do not apply in three cases set out in s 4(3).[1] First, discrimination is prohibited if the employer is concerned with the public provision of the relevant benefits, but that provision differs in a material respect from the provision of the benefits by the employer to the employer's employees (s 4(3)(a)). Secondly, discrimination is prohibited if the employer is concerned with the public provision of the relevant benefits, but the provision of the benefits to the employee in question is regulated by the employee's contract of employment (s 4(3)(b)). The application of these two cases might be seen at work in the illustrations given immediately above.[2] Thirdly, discrimination is prohibited if the employer is concerned with the public provision of the relevant benefits, but those benefits relate to training (s 4(3)(c)).

---

1   See Employment Code of Practice, para 6.8.
2   See **3.3.9**.

3.3.11 The s 4(3) exceptions are designed to prevent unnecessary overlap with the provisions in Part III of the Act outlawing discrimination in the provision of goods, facilities and services.[1] The intention is that if an employer offers goods, facilities or services to its employees in the same way as it offers them to members of the public, but disabled employees receive discriminatory treatment in that provision, then their right of action falls under Part III of the Act, if at all. Nevertheless, Part II of the Act will continue to apply to such discriminatory treatment if the provision of goods, facilities and services to the employer's employees is not identical to such provision to the public, or is an incident of the employment contract, or relates to training.[2]

---

1   There are similar exceptions in the SDA 1975, s 6(7).
2   See the special treatment of occupational pensions and other insurance-related benefits under ss 17–18 as discussed at **3.7** and **3.8**.

Pre-employment health screening

3.3.12 The Act does not expressly address the question of pre-employment medical examinations and screening. Many employers utilise health-related questions in application forms or medical examinations as a precondition of employment. By screening employment applicants for disability or medical conditions, many employers effectively exclude a proportion of applicants from further competition in the selection process. An applicant with a disability might be prematurely excluded from further consideration and may lose the opportunity to demonstrate ability and merit.

3.3.13 An attempt was made during the legislative process to prohibit pre-employment medical examinations or screening, but the amendments were rejected. The Government's view was that 'in general, employers should be free to use whatever recruitment procedures best meet their needs and to conduct medical examinations of employees where that seems appropriate'.[1] It was unwilling to forbid medical examinations or to limit inquiries about disability. Indeed, employers might find it necessary to question disabled applicants about a disability where such questions are designed to assist the disabled person in competing for employment opportunities.[2]

---

1   HC Deb Standing Committee E, col 151 (Mr J. Paice). Note also the protections provided in the Access to Medical Reports Act 1988.
2   See further, HL Deb, vol 564, cols 1935–1936 (Lord Inglewood).

3.3.14 Nevertheless, that does not mean that health screens and examinations might not fall foul of s 4 of the Act. Medical examinations, inquiries, questions or screening would undoubtedly constitute 'arrangements' made for the purpose of determining who should be offered employment within s 4(1)(a). If the effect of such arrangements was to amount to less favourable treatment of a disabled person for a reason related to disability, the employer would have to show that that treatment was justifiable. Even if all applicants and employees were medically examined, the effect might be to discriminate indirectly against disabled persons if the employer uses the evidence gleaned from the examination without further individualised inquiry as to the ability to do the job (including reasonable adjustments).

3.3.15   The Employment Code of Practice provides some useful guidance in this area. It indicates that employers may stipulate essential health requirements for a job, provided that they are capable of justification and if it would not be reasonable to waive them in an individual case.[1] Equally, stating that certain personal, medical or health-related characteristics are desirable or preferred may be discriminatory, unless justifiable.[2] A related issue is whether an employer should ask about disability at all? While the Act does not prevent such a question, the Employment Code of Practice recommends that the question should only be asked if disability is, or may be, relevant to the ability to do the job.[3] It might be appropriate – in order to counteract the negative impression left by such a question – to include a positive statement welcoming applications from disabled persons.[4] In any event, asking about the effects of a disability might be necessary as part of the process of considering what reasonable adjustments might be made under s 6 of the Act.[5]

While an employer can insist upon a disabled person having a pre-employment medical examination, the Employment Code of Practice warns employers that it may be discriminatory without justification to single out a disabled person (and not other applicants or employees) for a health check.[6] Employers are reminded that having a disability does not adversely affect a person's general health and, while medical evidence about a disability might justify an employment decision (for example, a dismissal or refusal of promotion), it cannot do so if the disability has little or no effect upon the person's ability to do the job.[7]

1   Employment Code of Practice, para 5.5.
2   Ibid, para 5.6.
3   Ibid, para 5.20.
4   Ibid, para 5.10.
5   Ibid, paras 5.11 and 5.20.
6   Ibid, para 5.23 and see the examples given there.
7   Ibid, para 5.24.

3.4   MEANING OF DISCRIMINATION

3.4.1   For the purposes of Part II of the Act, the meaning of discrimination is set out in s 5.[1] An employer discriminates against a disabled person if: (a) for a reason which relates to the disabled person's disability, the employer treats that person less favourably than the employer treats or would treat others to whom that reason does not or would not apply; and (b) the employer cannot show that the treatment in question is justified (s 5(1)). This definition of discrimination is closely (but not exactly) related to the definition of *direct* discrimination in the sex and race discrimination statutes,[2] but with the addition of a justification defence which is normally an adjunct of *indirect* discrimination.

---

1 By virtue of s 55, victimisation of a person in specified circumstances also amounts to discrimination.

2 The formula of 'a reason which relates to the disabled person's disability' has much in common with the provisions in the Employment Rights Act 1996, s 99 dealing with dismissal on grounds of pregnancy or childbirth.

3.4.2 Section 5 does not set out a test or formula for indirect discrimination. However, in the Government's view, s 4(1) and (2):

> 'already firmly cover – and are intended to cover – the use of standards, criteria, administrative methods, work practices or procedures that adversely affect a disabled person. That applies whether determining who should be employed or dismissed or establishing terms on the basis of which people are employed and their access to opportunities is structured.'[1]

Furthermore, the Minister has stated that:

> 'The broad term "arrangements" has been deliberately used in both [ss 4(1)(a) and 6(1)(a)] to cover anything done by or for an employer as part of his recruitment process or in making available opportunities in employment.'[2]

This would, in principle, address work practices and procedures which have an indirectly adverse effect upon the employment opportunities of disabled persons. The Government clearly intended that indirect discrimination would be prohibited and that this should be underlined by the duty to make reasonable adjustments under s 6.[3]

---

1 HC Deb Standing Committee E, col 142 (Mr J. Paice).

2 HC Deb Standing Committee E, col 142 (Mr J. Paice).

3 HC Deb Standing Committee E, col 143 (Mr J. Paice).

Less favourable treatment

3.4.3 The key concept which underpins the meaning of unlawful discrimination is the idea of less favourable treatment. An employer only discriminates against a disabled person if the employer treats the disabled individual 'less favourably than' the employer 'treats or would treat others' to whom the reason which relates to the disabled person's disability does not or would not apply (s 5(1)(a)).[1]

This concept of less favourable treatment calls for a comparative approach. The question is how has the disabled person been treated in comparison with other persons to whom the reason relating to the disabled person's disability does not apply. If the treatment of the comparator is more favourable than the treatment of the complainant, one of the necessary (but not sufficient) criteria for establishing unlawful direct discrimination is in place. Three points should be noted about this definition of discrimination.

---

1   See the example provided in the Employment Code of Practice at para 4.2.

3.4.4   First, it seems to admit the possibility that a disabled complainant could seek to show that he or she has been treated less favourably than a hypothetical (rather than an actual) comparator. The double use of the word 'would' in s 5(1)(a) supports that reasoning. If this interpretation is correct, this is especially important where a disabled person has been refused or denied employment opportunities in a context which is not an immediately competitive one. For example, a disabled employee denied promotion would not need to show that a colleague was actually promoted instead. It might be sufficient to show that a similarly situated employee without disability would have been promoted in those circumstances.[1]

---

1   This reasoning appears to be supported by the Employment Code of Practice at para 4.3.

3.4.5   Secondly, the actual or hypothetical comparison is between the disabled complainant and a comparator to whom the reason relating to the disabled complainant's disability does not or would not apply. It is important to note that the Act does not call for a simplistic comparison between a disabled person and a person who is not disabled or who does not have the disability in question (although that is how the Bill was originally drafted). The Government has considered that 'it is important to define the test correctly to avoid confusion and unnecessary litigation' and to ensure that the test in s 5(1)(a) 'correctly reflects the need to show that the treatment was for a reason relating to the disability and not necessarily the mere fact of disability'.[1]

---

1   HL Deb, vol 566, col 1200 (Lord Henley).

3.4.6   The Minister gave the example of two employees who cannot type: one because he or she is disabled with arthritis and the other, who is not disabled, because he or she has never been taught to type. If the disabled person with arthritis is refused employment as a typist that is not discriminatory treatment provided the non-disabled person who has never been taught to type is also refused employment in such a position. In a strict sense, the disabled person has been refused employment because of a reason related to disability (the inability to type being due to arthritis), but he or she has not been treated less favourably in comparison with the other person if the employer has rejected all candidates who cannot type. If the employer offers the position to someone who is able to type, then on the face of it that may be less favourable treatment of the person with arthritis for a reason related to his or her disability, but, subject to the duty to make adjustments, the employer will probably be able to explain the treatment if typing skills are a requirement of the position applied for.

3.4.7 Thirdly, the phrasing of the definition of discrimination will allow a disabled person to seek to show that he or she has been treated less favourably than another disabled person has been or would be. Section 5 does not necessarily call for an analysis of discriminatory behaviour which distinguished between disabled and non-disabled individuals.

For example, two equally well-qualified applicants might be in competition for an employment vacancy. One has a physical disability and the other a mental disability. If, without interviewing both candidates and considering their respective merits, the employer automatically rejects the applicant with a mental disability, that action could form the basis of a complaint of disability-informed discrimination brought by the rejected applicant. Again, the employer might be able to justify the differential treatment, but the individual with a mental disability was entitled to be given due consideration.[1]

---

1   See Employment Code of Practice, para 4.3.

3.4.8 Where an employer has failed to comply with any duty under s 6 of the Act to make reasonable adjustments in relation to a disabled person,[1] the employer is deemed to have discriminated against the disabled person, unless the employer can show that the failure to comply with that duty is justified (s 5(2)). Where the conditions in s 5(2) are satisfied, there is *prima facie* discrimination. This extended definition of discrimination is re-examined in greater depth in the discussion of the duty to make reasonable adjustments.[2]

---

1   The reference to a s 6 duty in s 5 rather obviously means any duty imposed by or under s 6 (s 68(1)).
2   At **3.6**.

Reason related to disability

3.4.9 In order for unlawful discrimination to be established, any less favourable treatment of a disabled person by an employer must be 'for a reason which relates to the disabled person's disability' (s 5(1)(a)). The employer's intention, purpose or motive for so acting is not relevant. However, there must be a nexus or causal connection between the discriminatory treatment and the complainant's disability.

For example, a disabled person who is refused or denied an employment opportunity because he or she does not have the necessary vocational qualifications, or is not the best person for the job on merit, has not been discriminated against contrary to the Act.[1] That person has been treated less favourably than the person who was awarded the employment opportunity, at least in the sense that his or her employment aspirations have been disappointed. Nevertheless, the reason for the apparently less favourable treatment is not that person's disability, but rather a reason which is unrelated to disability, namely merit or qualification.

---

1   As the Employment Code of Practice puts it (para 2.2): 'The Act does not prohibit an employer from appointing the best person for the job. Nor does it prevent employers from treating disabled people more favourably than those without a disability'. See also ibid, para 5.26.

Employment advertisements

3.4.10   Unlike sex and race discrimination legislation, the 1995 Act does not make separate provision for the outlawing or prohibition of discriminatory employment advertisements.[1] However, s 11 enables industrial tribunals to make assumptions about an employer's reason for refusing employment to a disabled person where the employer has published an advertisement suggesting that it will discriminate against disabled persons. There are a number of conditions which must be satisfied before the tribunal can make such assumptions.

---

1   For the Government's reasoning on this point, see HL Deb, vol 565, col 676 (Lord Inglewood).

3.4.11   First, and most obviously, the disabled person must have presented a complaint to an industrial tribunal under s 8 and that complaint must be against the employer in question (s 11(1)(c)). Secondly, the disabled person must have applied for employment with the employer (s 11(1)(a)) and the employer has refused to offer, or has deliberately not offered, the disabled person that employment (s 11(1)(b)). Thirdly, the employer must have advertised the employment for which the disabled person has applied (whether before or after the disabled person applied for it) (s 11(1)(d)). An advertisement for this purpose includes every form of advertisement or notice, whether to the public or not (s 11(3)).[1]

Fourthly, and most crucially, the advertisement must have indicated (or might reasonably be understood to have indicated) that any application for the advertised employment would, or might, be determined to any extent by reference to the successful applicant not having any disability or any category of disability which includes the disabled person's disability (s 11(1)(e)(i)). Alternatively, the advertisement must have indicated (or might reasonably be understood to have indicated) that any application for the advertised employment would, or might, be determined to any extent by reference to the employer's reluctance to take any action of a kind mentioned in the employer's s 6 duty to make reasonable adjustments (s 11(1)(e)(ii)).

---

1   An advertisement would include the internal publication of a vacancy only within an office or company: Employment Code of Practice, para 5.8. See generally, ibid, para 5.7 and the example provided there. Note also that advertising a job might call for a reasonable adjustment (for example, providing information about the post in alternative media or formats): ibid, para 5.9.

3.4.12   If all the conditions detailed in s 11(1) are satisfied, then the industrial tribunal hearing the disabled person's complaint under s 8 shall assume, unless the contrary is shown, that the employer's reason for refusing employment to the disabled person was related to the complainant's disability (s 11(2)). In other words, where the employer has published a discriminatory advertisement, there is a rebuttable presumption that any subsequent less favourable treatment of the disabled person was for a reason related to the complainant's disability. The requirement in s 5(1)(a) that the less favourable treatment of a disabled person must be for a reason 'which relates to the disabled person's disability' will be presumed to have been satisfied. Note, however, that this presumption only operates where the complaint is brought under s 4(1)(c) and is that the employer has refused to offer, or has deliberately not offered, the disabled person the employment so advertised.

3.4.13   Section 11 is a difficult and convoluted provision. The definition of 'advertisement' in s 11(3) is broad enough to embrace job particulars or details sent to would-be applicants as well as job advertisements placed in newspapers or other media. The Government's intention is to prevent employers using job advertisements as a means of discouraging disabled employment applicants, although s 11 does not apply to exempted small businesses under s 7.[1] At the same time, however, it is not intended that this provision should prevent employers from specifying reasonable or justifiable health or other ability requirements, even if these might cause difficulties of compliance for persons with disabilities.[2]

---

1   HL Deb, vol 565, col 678 (Lord Inglewood).
2   HC Deb Standing Committee E, cols 282–284 (Mr J. Paice).

Discrimination by association

3.4.14   The Act does not explicitly address the problem of discrimination against non-disabled persons because of their association with (or relationship to) a disabled person. In debate, the relevant Minister stated that it was the Government's intention 'that the concept of reasonable adjustment could include the need to make arrangements to take into account the particular difficulties that carers face because of their caring responsibilities'.[1] However, he later recanted and explained that the 'needs of carers might be taken into account as a reasonable adjustment for a disabled person. If the needs were such that a disabled person had to fit in with the position of a carer, the carer's needs could be taken in as part of the reasonable adjustment'.[2]

---

1   HC Deb Standing Committee E, col 168 (Mr J. Paice).
2   HC Deb Standing Committee E, col 172 (Mr J. Paice). To this effect, see Employment Code of Practice, para 4.20.

3.5   DEFENCE OF JUSTIFICATION

3.5.1   An employer discriminates against a disabled person if there is less favourable treatment of a disabled person for a reason related to the disabled person's disability (s 5(1)(a)) and the employer cannot show that the less favourable treatment is justified (s 5(1)(b)). The burden of proof will be upon the employer who relies upon a justification defence. For the purposes of s 5(1),[1] such less favourable treatment is justified 'if, but *only if*, the reason for it is *both* material to the circumstances of the *particular* case *and* substantial' (s 5(3) with emphasis added). What is novel about this justification defence is that, in contrast to the existing discrimination jurisdictions, this justification defence is available in both cases of direct and indirect disability discrimination.

---

1   There is a justification defence in s 5(2) also (introduced at **3.4.8**) and this defence is explained in s 5(4). See further the discussion at **3.6**.

3.5.2   The first thing to note about the justification defence is that it goes beyond merely showing that a disabled person was treated less favourably than others for a reason unconnected with or unrelated to his or her disability. An employer will always be able to defend a discrimination complaint by proving that the alleged discriminatory act was not for a reason which relates to the disabled complainant's disability. That is implicit in the wording of s 5(1)(a). The justification defence in s 5(3) clearly only applies where an employer *has* treated a disabled person less favourably for a disability-related reason. In other words, the Act envisages that there will be cases where, despite the merit principle, an employer could take lawful account of a person's disability.

For example, the disabled person might be otherwise well qualified for the position, but the evidence might support a real fear that there is a clear and unacceptable health and safety risk to the disabled worker or others, or that the disability will prevent the employee from attending work regularly and predictably. However, such conclusions must be based upon hard evidence and not merely assumptions or stereotypes.

3.5.3 Moreover, s 5(3) contemplates that the justification defence is a particular, rather than general, defence. The use of the phrase 'if, but only if' in s 5(3) clearly limits the scope for justifying less favourable treatment of a disabled person for a reason related to disability. An employer might have no difficulty in subjectively justifying to itself or to other employers the discriminatory treatment of disabled persons, but that is not enough to satisfy the legislative test of justification. The Act does not admit a general defence of justification. Furthermore, where the employer is under a s 6 duty to make reasonable adjustments, the justification defence must take account of that duty. This is considered further below.[1]

---

1   See **3.6.19–3.6.21**.

3.5.4   The statutory defence of justification in s 5(3) requires the employer to show that the reason for the less favourable treatment of a disabled person, for a reason related to that person's disability, is both 'material' to the circumstances of the particular case and 'substantial'. This final version of the defence reduces the complexity inherent in earlier drafts of the Bill that eventually became the 1995 Act. The Government believes that it has provided 'a simpler and clearer test for reasons which would justify less favourable treatment'.[1] The defence of justification must take account of the circumstances of the particular case, including 'the type of job, the type of disability and its effects, the nature of the position being taken and many other factors'.[2]

---

1   HL Deb, vol 566, col 118 (Lord Henley).
2   HL Deb, vol 566, col 119 (Lord Henley). See also Employment Code of Practice, para 4.6.

3.5.5   The interpretation given to the terms 'material' and 'substantial' will be crucial to an understanding of the justification defence. The word 'material' has been used in other discrimination law contexts.[1] It conveys a sense that the reason for the discriminatory treatment must be important, essential or relevant in the circumstances of the case. The word 'substantial' is used in s 1 of the 1995 Act to measure the adverse effect that a person's disability has upon normal day-to-day activities.[2] In that context, a disabled person will wish to argue that the word denotes something more than minor or trivial, whereas in the context of the employer's justification defence, a complainant might understandably contend that the word carries a weightier implication. It would seem that the combination of the words 'material' and 'substantial' in s 5(3) and (4) produces a relatively high threshold for the operation of the justification defence. However, the Employment Code of Practice states that the justification defence in s 5(3) 'means that the reason has to relate to the individual circumstances in question and *not just be trivial or minor*'.[3] That suggests, not without some logic, that the term 'substantial' should be interpreted consistently wherever it appears in the Act and simply denotes something that is more than minor or trivial. The authoritative resolution of this question must await judicial attention.

---

1   Equal Pay Act 1970, s 1(3) as amended.
2   See **2.5.5** et seq. See also its use in s 6(1) of the 1995 Act where it qualifies the disadvantage that
    must be faced by a disabled person before the employer's duty to make reasonable adjustments
    is triggered (**3.6.8**).
3   Employment Code of Practice, para 4.6 (my emphasis). Note the many examples given there of
    treatment that would not be justifiable.

3.5.6   Regulations may make provision for the purposes of s 5 as to the circumstances in which treatment is to be taken to be justified or not to be justified (s 5(6)). This power has been used to make regulations dealing with performance-related pay and agricultural wages. It has also been used to address questions arising under occupational pension schemes. This latter issue is returned to below, but at this point the regulations dealing with performance-related pay and agricultural wages will be explained.

Performance-related pay

3.5.7   Special provision is made by regulations for a justification defence under s 5 in relation to pay.[1] In this context, 'pay' means remuneration of any kind, including any benefit.[2] Less favourable treatment of a disabled person for a reason related to disability is to be taken to be justified if it results from the application to the disabled person of a term or practice under which the amount of a person's pay is wholly or partly dependent on that person's performance.[3] Thus employers are permitted to pay disabled employees according to performance (for example, by piece rates), including perform-ance as assessed by reference to any measure (whether relative or absolute) of output, efficiency or effectiveness in an employment.[4] But the term or practice in question must be one which is applied (1) to all the employer's employees, or (2) to all of a class of the employer's employees which includes the disabled person but which is not defined by reference to any disability.[5] The employer cannot choose to pay disabled employees by performance if fellow workers of the same class are being paid a fixed time rate.

---

1   Disability Discrimination (Employment) Regulations 1996, reg 3. See Employment Code of
    Practice, paras 5.28–5.29.
2   Ibid, reg 2. It suggested that the term 'benefit' should be construed widely in accordance with
    s 4(4) of the Act.
3   Ibid, reg 3(1)(a).

4   Ibid, reg 2. For the interaction of this provision with the s 6 duty to make adjustments, see **3.6.8**.
5   Ibid, reg 3(1)(b).

Agricultural wages

3.5.8   The Agricultural Wages Act 1948, s 5 and the Agricultural Wages (Scotland) Act 1949, s 5 allow the Agricultural Wages Board to issue a permit to a disabled individual incapable of earning the minimum wage set by the Board. The permit may set a lower minimum wage for that person and/or may vary other minimum terms and conditions (other than holidays) applicable to that worker. Paying such a worker a lower rate of pay might not be capable of justification under the 1995 Act simply by reason of the permit unless regulations so stipulated. Accordingly, special provision is made by regulations for the purposes of s 5 so that less favourable treatment of a disabled person is to be taken to be justified to the extent that it relates to (and accords with) a matter within the terms and conditions of a permit granted to incapacitated persons under the agricultural wages legislation.[1] This does not allow employers in the agricultural sector to discriminate against disabled persons in employment matters other than pay and terms and conditions covered by a permit.[2]

---

1   Disability Discrimination (Employment) Regulations 1996, reg 6(a). Failure to take a step otherwise required to comply with a s 6 duty to make reasonable adjustments is also to be taken to be justified if that step would relate to a matter within the terms and conditions of the permit but would exceed the requirements of those terms and conditions (reg 6(b)).
2   Employment Code of Practice, para 4.52.

3.6   DUTY TO MAKE REASONABLE ADJUSTMENTS

3.6.1   What distinguishes the disability discrimination legislation from existing discrimination law is the explicit duty which the 1995 Act places upon employers to make reasonable adjustments to work arrangements and the working environment so as to accommodate disabled persons (s 6). This duty is at best an example of legally mandated positive action. It is not a requirement of reverse discrimination or positive discrimination requiring an employer to treat disabled persons more favourably than others.

3.6.2   There is nothing in Part II of the Act to prevent employers voluntarily affording disabled persons preferential treatment.[1] However, s 6(7) appears to imply that the duty to make reasonable adjustments for disabled persons might be viewed erroneously as mandatory positive discrimination. This states that, subject to the duty upon employers to make adjustments within s 6, nothing in

Part II of the Act (the employment provisions) is to be taken to require an employer to treat a disabled person more favourably than the employer treats or would treat others. This subsection is capable of being misunderstood.

---

1   Subject to what is said about local government employers at **3.12**. See Employment Code of Practice, paras 2.2 and 5.26.

3.6.3   The duty to make reasonable adjustments is an essential part of the prohibition on disability-related discrimination. Without employers being required to adjust working practices or policies and to modify physical features of premises, disabled persons would face potentially indirect discrimination in the labour market. Employers' requirements and conditions will frequently represent barriers to equal opportunity and might have a disproportionate adverse impact upon disabled individuals. As in race and sex discrimination law, unless employers are required to re-examine norms and standards established by reference to the predominant society or culture (the so-called 'able-bodied world'), historic discrimination and inequality of opportunity is merely perpetuated.

When does the duty to make reasonable adjustments arise?

3.6.4   The duty upon an employer to make reasonable adjustments arises where: (a) any arrangements made by or on behalf of an employer; or (b) any physical features of premises occupied by the employer, place the disabled person concerned at a substantial disadvantage in comparison with persons who are not disabled (s 6(1)).[1] In these circumstances, it is the duty of the employer to take such steps as it is reasonable, in all the circumstances of the case, for *that* employer to have to take in order to prevent the arrangements or feature having that effect.[2]

---

1   A hypothetical comparison may be appropriate. Where a complainant is a disabled person by virtue of having had a disability in the past (within s 2(1)), the comparison called for in s 6(1) is with persons who are not disabled and who have not had a disability (s 2(2) and Sch 2, para 3).

2   See generally, Employment Code of Practice, paras 4.12–4.14.

3.6.5   The arrangements referred to in s 6(1) which might trigger a duty to make reasonable adjustments mean only: (a) arrangements for determining to whom employment should be offered; or (b) any term, condition or arrangements on which employment, promotion, transfer, training or any other benefit is offered or afforded (s 6(2)). Examples of such arrangements would include procedures for recruitment and selection or promotion (such as application forms, interviews or employment tests), and terms upon which employment opportunities are granted (such as insistence upon mobility or flexibility clauses or satisfaction of unreasonably high medical standards).[1]

1   See Employment Code of Practice, para 4.16 and see generally chapters 5–6 therein. The effect
    of s 6(2) would appear to be that the duty to make adjustments does not apply to dismissals as
    such. However, the examples of adjustments given in s 6(3) clearly encompass the processes
    that led to dismissal, while the use of the phrase 'arrangements on which employment . . . is . . .
    afforded in s 6(2)(b) is capable of a wide construction.

3.6.6   The term 'physical feature of premises' is not statutorily defined.
However, regulations made under s 6(8)(g)–(h) assist in the identification of
what is and what is not a relevant physical feature.[1] The following are to be
treated as physical features (whether permanent or temporary) of premises for
the purposes of s 6(1):

- any feature arising from the design or construction of a building on the
  premises;
- any feature on the premises of any approach to, exit from or access to
  such a building;
- any fixtures, fittings, furnishings, furniture, equipment or materials in or
  on the premises;
- any other physical element or quality of any land comprised in the
  premises.

For these purposes, a building means an erection or structure of any kind.[2]
Thus, the physical features of a building do not only include the physical fabric
and structure of a building. Features such as lighting, air conditioning,
building materials, fixtures and fittings, furniture and equipment are also
included.

It is clear, however, that it is only the physical features of 'premises occupied
by the employer' which are in scope.[3] The duty to make reasonable adjustments
in respect of the physical features of premises does not extend to a disabled
person's private house (for example, in the case of a homeworker) or to the
premises of another employer which a disabled employee might have to visit in
the course of employment (for example, a travelling sales executive visiting a
customer's premises).[4]

1   Disability Discrimination (Employment) Regulations 1996, reg 9. (Note also the Employment
    Code of Practice, para 4.15 and the example given at para 4.16.)
2   Ibid, reg 2.
3   Note the provisions of s 16 of and Sch 4, Part I to the Act which will apply where an employer
    occupies premises under a lease which prevents or hinders alterations being made in pursuit of
    a s 6 duty to make adjustments. These provisions are discussed in detail in Chapter 6.
4   HL Deb vol 566, col 184 (Lord Henley).

3.6.7   The duty to make reasonable adjustments arises only if the employment
arrangements or physical features in question place the disabled person
concerned 'at a *substantial* disadvantage in comparison with persons who are
not disabled' (s 6(1) with emphasis added). The duty to make reasonable
adjustments is an individualised duty. It arises only where the disabled person

in question suffers a comparative disadvantage. It does not necessarily arise generally or in respect of a class or group of disabled persons. Furthermore, the duty is imposed only following a comparative assessment of the adverse effect of the arrangement or physical feature upon the disabled person. The comparators are persons who are not disabled (and, in the case of a person with a past disability, who have not had a disability).[1]

---

1   See s 2(2) and Sch 2, para 3. See also Employment Code of Practice, para 4.13.

3.6.8 Moreover, the arrangements or physical features must place the disabled person at a 'substantial' disadvantage. The use of the word 'substantial' appears to create quite a high threshold for the operation of the duty to make reasonable adjustments. The problematic nature of this term has been discussed above.[1] However, the intention appears to be to ensure that minor and trivial disadvantages do not cause the duty to be imposed on employers and that only disadvantages of substance will call for accommodations.[2]

A term or practice under which the amount of a person's pay is wholly or partly dependent on that person's performance is not to be taken to place disabled persons at a substantial disadvantage.[3] But this does not affect the operation of s 6 where any arrangements or physical features of premises otherwise place the disabled person at a substantial disadvantage and thereby cause reduced performance by him or her.[4]

---

1   See **3.5.5**.
2   HC Deb Standing Committee E, col 196 (Mr J. Paice). This is confirmed by the Employment Code of Practice, para 4.17.
3   By virtue of the Disability Discrimination (Employment) Regulations 1996, reg 3(2).
4   Ibid, reg 3(3).

The duty illustrated

3.6.9   The following are examples listed in s 6(3) of the kinds of steps which an employer may have to take in relation to a disabled person in order to comply with the duty to make reasonable adjustments:[1]

- making adjustments to premises;
- allocating some of the disabled person's duties to another person;
- transferring the disabled person to fill an existing vacancy;
- altering the disabled person's working hours;
- assigning the disabled person to a different place of work;
- allowing the disabled person to be absent during working hours for rehabilitation, assessment or treatment;
- giving the disabled person, or arranging for him/her to be given, training;
- acquiring or modifying equipment;
- modifying instructions or reference manuals;
- modifying procedures for testing or assessment;

- providing a reader or interpreter;
- providing supervision.

This list is illustrative only of the types of adjustments that might be made and is not intended to be exhaustive. There is also a power to expand the duty in future, if necessary, by secondary legislation (s 6(10)). However, these examples do not exist in a vacuum. The duty to make such adjustments only arises where the conditions of s 6(1)–(2) are satisfied.[2]

---

1   Useful illustrations of what each of these adjustments might involve in practice are provided in the Employment Code of Practice, para 4.20 and throughout chapters 5–6 thereof.
2   See **3.6.4–3.6.8**.

3.6.10   During debate, the Minister confirmed that the examples of reasonable adjustments that might be undertaken could include the provision of a sign language interpreter, minicom facilities or alterations to working hours. Furthermore, a reasonable adjustment 'could be a modification to a working environment, to a term or condition of employment or to any similar matter relating to the employment'.[1] Where an employer has existing car parking facilities for employees, it might be a reasonable adjustment to allocate a dedicated car parking space to an employee with a mobility disability.[2]

Support for such initiatives might be sought by employers from funds available under the Government's Access to Work scheme. However, the Minister also indicated that the taxpayer would not be expected to meet all the costs of reasonable adjustments. Employers would have to take some financial responsibility, especially in respect of adjustments and costs relating to working hours and retraining.[3] Nevertheless, at the same time the Government has indicated that it does not intend to put a financial ceiling on the concept of reasonable adjustment,[4] but regulatory powers could be used if there was evidence that the statute was not working appropriately.[5]

---

1   HC Deb Standing Committee E, col 208 (Mr J. Paice).
2   HL Deb, vol 566, col 209 (Lord Henley). See Employment Code of Practice, para 6.7.
3   HC Deb Standing Committee E, col 209 (Mr J. Paice).
4   Although note s 6(4) discussed at **3.6.14**.
5   HC Deb Standing Committee E, cols 208–209 (Mr J. Paice). Note also the power to make regulations under s 6(8). Such regulations may, in particular circumstances, make provision by reference to the cost of taking the steps concerned in the duty to make reasonable adjustments (s 6(9)).

3.6.11   Nothing in the Act creates an obligation to provide disability leave[1] nor a requirement upon employers to retain newly disabled employees. However, an employee absent from work on account of disability might be entitled to the benefit of the s 6 duty upon employers to make adjustments, as well as the specific protection of unfair dismissal law. The combined effect of the new disability discrimination legislation and the existing unfair dismissal standards could be to produce an obligation upon employers to hesitate before dismissing an employee on the grounds of disability or incapacity. At the very least, such an employer will need to consider what reasonable adjustments might be made for the employee and this might have the effect of prolonging his or her employment tenure or of leading to redeployment.[2]

---

1   HC Deb Standing Committee E, col 220 (Mr J. Paice).
2   See Employment Code of Practice, paras 6.19–6.21.

What are reasonable steps to take?

3.6.12   The duty upon the employer is only to take such steps as, in the circumstances of the case, it is reasonable to take in order to prevent the arrangements or features having the adverse effect described in s 6(1). The employer is entitled to take account of all the circumstances when deciding what steps it would be reasonable to take. For example, it might be reasonable to weigh 'whether the benefit to the disabled person would be proportionate to the cost and the difficulty of the measures in question'.[1]

On the other hand, in deciding whether to make a reasonable adjustment, there is no compulsion upon an employer to take advice.[2] However, a failure to take advice or to seek assistance (for example, from an occupational medical adviser or disabled employment adviser) before determining whether or not to make a reasonable adjustment could be taken into account by an industrial tribunal in considering whether the employer had acted reasonably in the circumstances.[3] Equally, the test of reasonableness might need to take account of the extent to which the disabled person has co-operated with the employer who attempts to make a reasonable adjustment.

---

1   HC Deb Standing Committee E, col 196 (Mr J. Paice).
2   But see Employment Code of Practice, para 3.3.
3   HC Deb Standing Committee E, col 222 (Mr J. Paice).

3.6.13   For the purposes of the s 6 duty to make adjustments to premises occupied by an employer, it is *never* reasonable for an employer to have to take steps in relation to a disabled person to the extent that this would involve altering any physical characteristic (included within building works) which was adopted with a view to meeting the requirements for the time being of Part M of the building regulations[1] with regard to access and facilities for disabled people.[2] However, the physical characteristic in question must have met those requirements at the time the building works were carried out and must have continued substantially to meet those requirements which applied at the time the building works were carried out.[3] The latest version of Part M of the building regulations is now found in Sch 1 to the Building Regulations 1991.[4] In Scotland, the appropriate reference is to Part T of the Technical Standards for compliance with the Building Standards (Scotland) Regulations 1990[5] issued by the Scottish Office in 1990 and subsequently amended in July 1993 and July 1994.[6]

It might also be necessary to obtain statutory consents to an alteration (planning permission, listed building consent, etc) and an adjustment would not be a reasonable one to make if the occupier has applied for such consent and it has been refused. In such a case, the duty to make adjustments should take account of alternative ways of achieving a viable adjustment.[7]

---

1   Within the meaning of the Building Act 1984, s 122.
2   Disability Discrimination (Employment) Regulations 1996, reg 8(1)(a), and (2). (See further, Employment Code of Practice, paras 4.35–4.36.)
3   Ibid, reg 8(1)(b).
4   SI 1991/2768.
5   SI 1990/2179.
6   Disability Discrimination (Employment) Regulations 1996, reg 2. (See SI 1993/1457 and SI 1994/1266.)
7   Employment Code of Practice, paras 4.37–4.39.

3.6.14   Section 6(4) provides that, in determining whether it is reasonable for an employer to have to take a particular step in order to comply with the duty to make adjustments, regard is to be had, in particular, to the following matters:

- the extent to which taking the step would prevent the effect in question;[1]
- the extent to which it is practicable for the employer to take the step;[2]
- the financial and other costs which would be incurred by the employer in taking the step and the extent to which taking it would disrupt any of the employer's activities;[3]
- the extent of the employer's financial and other resources;[4]
- the availability to the employer of financial or other assistance with respect to taking the step.[5]

The Employment Code of Practice anticipates that other factors might be relevant, depending upon the circumstances, including the effect which an adjustment has upon other employees, any adjustments already made for other disabled employees, and the extent to which the disabled person is willing to co-operate with the employer's attempts to make an adjustment.[6] It may also be reasonable for an employer to have to make more than one adjustment.[7] However, regulations which may be made in the future under s 6(8) will be relevant when judging the reasonableness of requiring an employer to take a particular step in particular circumstances, including by reference to costs (s 6(9)).

---

1   That is, the effect of an arrangement or physical feature placing the disabled person at a substantial disadvantage in comparison with persons who are not disabled. See Employment Code of Practice, para 4.22.

2 See ibid, para 4.23.
3 See ibid, paras 4.24–4.27. The significance of the cost of a step may depend in part on the value of the employee's experience and expertise to the employer, including factors such as resources (for example training) already invested in the employee and the employee's length of service, level of skill and knowledge, quality of relationships with clients and level of pay: ibid, para 4.25.
4 See ibid, paras 4.28–4.30. It is more likely to be reasonable for an employer with substantial resources to have to make a significantly costly adjustment than it would be for an employer with fewer resources.
5 See ibid, para 4.31.
6 Ibid, para 4.32. See generally, para 4.21.
7 Ibid, para 4.33.

3.6.15 These matters listed in s 6(4) are the 'key criteria ... in no particular order of priority' by which the reasonableness of an adjustment will be judged.[1] For example, if the only possible adjustments that could be made to aid the output of a disabled worker could result in no more than a small improvement in productivity, but at a price of cost or disruption, the adjustments might not be reasonable.[2] Similarly, if after reasonable adjustments have been made a disabled worker's productivity is below normal, where the worker is paid according to performance an employer would not be expected to make further adjustments by compensating the worker for the loss of performance-related pay.[3]

1 HL Deb, vol 566, col 184 (Lord Henley).
2 HL Deb, vol 566, cols 184–185 (Lord Henley). See Employment Code of Practice, paras 4.22 and 4.23–4.27.
3 This is the effect of the interaction of s 6 of the Act with reg 3 of the Disability Discrimination (Employment) Regulations 1996. See the discussion at **3.5.7** and **3.6.8**. Note the Employment Code of Practice, paras 4.18, 4.22 and 5.28–5.29.

3.6.16 The Minister gave further illustrations.[1] It might not be reasonable for an employer (especially a small employer) needing an employee urgently to have to wait for an adjustment to be made to allow a disabled person to be employed.[2] An adjustment that would involve a breach of safety laws or fire regulations could not be reasonable.[3] The cost of the adjustment might also render it an unreasonable one to make, and cost will include use of staff and other resources, as well as direct monetary costs.[4]

The employer's resources must be taken into account and it might be more reasonable for an employer with considerable resources to make a significantly costly adjustment than for an employer with fewer resources.[5] Moreover, a step is not unreasonable if there is available compensatory help from an outside organisation or from the disabled person. For example, the employer might not be expected to purchase specialist computer equipment adapted for use by a person with a sight disability, but such equipment might be available under the Access to Work scheme or from a disability charity. It would also be a reasonable adjustment to allow a disabled worker to use his or her own auxiliary aids or equipment at work.[6]

---

1 HL Deb, vol 566, col 185 (Lord Henley).
2 See Employment Code of Practice, para 4.23.
3 See ibid, para 4.65.
4 See ibid, para 4.24.
5 See ibid, para 4.28.
6 See ibid, para 4.31.

To whom is the duty owed?

3.6.17 In respect of arrangements for determining to whom employment should be offered, the duty to make reasonable adjustments is only owed to a disabled person who is, or who has notified the employer that he or she may be, an applicant for that employment (s 6(5)(a)). The length of notice given by the disabled applicant to the employer might play a part in determining whether the employer has satisfied the duty to make reasonable adjustments. In any other case, the duty is owed to a disabled person who is an applicant for the employment concerned or who is an employee of the employer concerned (s 6(5)(b)).

3.6.18 More significantly still, s 6(6)(a) establishes that, in the case of an applicant or potential applicant for employment, the duty to make reasonable adjustments is not imposed upon any employer in relation to a disabled person *unless* the employer knows (or could reasonably be expected to know) that the disabled person concerned is, or may be, an applicant for the employment in question. In any case, the duty to make reasonable adjustments is not imposed upon any employer in relation to a disabled person *unless* the employer knows (or could reasonably be expected to know) that the disabled person concerned has (or has had) a disability and is likely to be placed at a substantial disadvantage in comparison with non-disabled persons because of any arrangements made by the employer or any physical features of premises occupied by the employer (s 6(6)(b) and Sch 2, para 4).

The Employment Code of Practice goes a little further than the Act. It suggests that an employer must do all that it could reasonably be expected to do to find out whether a person has a disability which is likely to place him or her at a substantial disadvantage.[1] This suggests that employers need to be proactive and that they will not necessarily escape liability by simply not asking whether a person has a disability and whether the effects of any disability call for an adjustment to be made.[2] As already noted, the Employment Code of Practice recommends that employers should only ask disability-related questions if disability is, or may be, relevant to the ability to do the job;[3] but, equally, employers should be positive in welcoming applications from disabled persons.[4] Asking about the effects of a disability is seen as a necessary part of the process of considering what reasonable adjustments might be made for a disabled person.[5] In any event, if a person asks for an adjustment to be made, the employer will be entitled to ask for evidence that the person has a disability such as to trigger the statutory duty.[6]

Moreover, because a reasonable adjustment may not work in practice without the co-operation of other employees, it may be necessary to reveal the fact of a person's disability (where otherwise not obvious) to some of that person's work colleagues (particularly a supervisor or manager) *in confidence* (for example, where special assistance may be needed).[7] This should be done on a selective and 'need to know' basis, but employers should be careful not to commit a separate act of discrimination by revealing such information without consulting the disabled person first or without a legitimate management purpose in doing so.[8]

---

1   Employment Code of Practice, para 4.57 and see the examples quoted there. Of course, if a disabled person chooses to conceal a disability, that will lessen the possibility that the employer should be expected to carry out a reasonable adjustment, unless the circumstances are such that it would be reasonable for the employer to be expected to know of the disability without the necessity for revelation: ibid, para 4.61.
2   The fact that the employer might not know of a person's disability will make no difference if, for example, a personnel officer, line manager, or occupational health officer employed by the employer has that information. The knowledge of an employee or agent of the employer is the vicarious knowledge of the employer itself: ibid, paras 4.62–4.63.
3   Ibid, para 5.20.
4   Ibid, para 5.10.
5   Ibid, paras 5.11 and 5.20.
6   Ibid, para 4.64.
7   Ibid, paras 4.58–4.59.
8   Ibid, para 4.60.

Discrimination, justification and reasonable adjustments

3.6.19   Section 6 sets out the extent of an employer's duty to make reasonable adjustments. By virtue of s 5(2), a failure, without justification, to comply with any duty imposed on an employer by s 6 in relation to a disabled person will amount to an act of discrimination by the employer. A failure to comply with a s 6 duty is justified under s 5(2) if, but only if, the reason for the failure is both material to the circumstances of the particular case and substantial (s 5(4)).[1]

---

1   Note the provisions of s 16 and Part I of Sch 4 to the Act which will apply where an employer occupies premises under a lease which prevents or hinders alterations being made in pursuit of a s 6 duty to make adjustments. These provisions are discussed in detail in Chapter 6.

3.6.20   A breach of s 6 is not otherwise an actionable breach of duty in itself but is merely an ingredient of the meaning of discrimination (s 6(12)). Given the structure of the Act, it would also seem logical that a disabled complainant will also have to anchor the discrimination to one of the categories of employment decisions or opportunities listed in s 4(1)–(2). In other words, a failure to make reasonable adjustments is only unlawful discrimination if it results, for example, in the disabled person being treated less favourably in recruitment and selection, employment terms, promotion, dismissal, etc.

3.6.21 Furthermore, where an employer has treated a disabled person less favourably for a reason which relates to disability (under s 5(1)), but has unjustifiably failed to comply with a s 6 duty to make reasonable adjustments, then the less favourable treatment cannot be justified under s 5(3) (that is, by reference to a material and substantial reason) unless the employer can show that it would have been justified even if the employer had complied with a s 6 duty to make a reasonable adjustment (s 5(5)).

So an employer cannot be liable for a justifiable non-performance of a duty to make reasonable adjustments under s 6 and a failure to make reasonable adjustments cannot be unlawful if the failure is justifiable.[1] In other words, before an employer can seek to justify the less favourable treatment of a disabled person for a reason related to disability it must first address its duty to make reasonable adjustments. The employer cannot rely upon a material and substantial reason for less favourable treatment if that reason could have been rendered immaterial or insubstantial by carrying out a reasonable adjustment.

---

1   HL Deb, vol 566, col 992 (Lord Henley). See the examples given in the Employment Code of Practice, para 4.7. See also paras 4.9 and 4.34.

3.7   OCCUPATIONAL PENSION SCHEMES

Employers' obligations

3.7.1 Section 4 of the 1995 Act (discrimination against applicants and employees) is capable of covering the actions of an employer who provides opportunities to employees for occupational pensions. In particular, s 4(2) outlaws discrimination against disabled persons in 'the terms of employment' and in the opportunities afforded for 'receiving any other benefit'. So, if an employer treated a disabled person less favourably than other employees in respect of access to or benefits from an occupational pension scheme (including the terms of membership), that might amount to an unlawful act of discrimination, unless capable of justification.

3.7.2 Special provision is made for benefits provided under an occupational pension scheme in respect of termination of service, retirement, old age, death, accident, injury, sickness or invalidity.[1] Where, by reason of the disabled person's disability (including any clinical prognosis flowing from the disability), the cost of providing any of the above benefits is likely to be substantially greater than it would be for a comparable person without that disability,[2] less favourable treatment of a disabled person is to be taken to be justified under s 5 if it results from applying the eligibility conditions set for receiving any such benefit or from determining the amount of any such benefit.[3] Employers should first satisfy themselves (at the time the disabled person is considered for admission to the scheme) of the likelihood of there being substantially greater costs and this will usually require a combination of actuarial advice and medical evidence.[4] Only the likelihood of a *substantial* additional cost should be regarded as a justification.[5]

1 Disability Discrimination (Employment) Regulations 1996, reg 4(3).
2 Ibid, reg 4(2).
3 Ibid, reg 4(1).
4 See Employment Code of Practice, paras 6.10–6.11. The justification defence cannot be applied to a disabled *member* of the scheme unless a term was imposed at the time of admission: ibid, para 6.12.
5 Ibid, para 6.14 which suggests that 'substantial' means more than minor or trivial.

3.7.3 Moreover, less favourable treatment is also *always* to be taken to be justified if an employer requires from a disabled person the same rate of contribution to an occupational pension scheme as the employer requires from its other employees (or from any class of employees which includes the disabled person but which is not defined by reference to any disability).[1] This is notwithstanding that the disabled person is not eligible under that scheme (for a reason related to his or her disability) to receive a benefit or to receive a benefit at the same rate as a comparable person (to whom the reason related to disability does not apply). This provision allows employers to maintain uniform rates of contributions to occupational pension schemes by requiring disabled employees to pay the same rate of contributions as other employees even if not eligible for some of the benefits.[2]

1 Disability Discrimination (Employment) Regulations 1996, reg 5.
2 Employment Code of Practice, para 6.15.

3.7.4 Does the duty to make reasonable adjustments apply to employers in respect of ensuring to disabled persons equal access to (and opportunities under) an occupational pension scheme? Section 6(11) disapplies the s 6 duty to make reasonable adjustments in respect of any benefit under an occu-pational pension scheme (including benefits in respect of termination of service, or retirement, old age or death, or accident, injury, sickness or invalidity). Future regulations may add to this list after consultation. So, for example, where a disabled person lawfully has been refused access to an occupational pension scheme (or denied the right to full benefits of the scheme) on actuarial grounds, there will be no obligation on the employer to adjust the terms of employment so as to compensate for the loss of the pension benefit by increasing the disabled employee's salary.[1]

---

1 Employment Code of Practice, para 6.16. Nor will an employer have to make an adjustment for a disabled employee receiving less benefit because that person justifiably receives a lower rate of pay (for example, because of a performance-related payment system).

Trustees of occupational pension schemes

3.7.5 Occupational pension schemes are run and managed by trustees, rather than by the employer. There would be nothing to prevent such schemes containing rules that discriminated against disabled persons or disabled employees (unless they were also caught by Part III of the Act). The Government was concerned that disabled persons might be unfairly denied access to an employer's pension scheme arrangements by the decisions of the scheme trustees (and not simply by the actions of employers).

To avoid this state of affairs or doubt, s 17(1) states that every occupational pension scheme shall be taken to include a provision to be referred to as 'a non-discrimination rule'. The effect of this implied non-discrimination rule relates to the terms on which persons become members of the scheme and the terms on which members of the scheme are treated (s 17(1)(a)). The non-discrimination rule also requires the trustees or managers of the occupational pension scheme to refrain from any act or omission which, if done in relation to a person by an employer, would amount to unlawful discrimination under Part II of the Act (s 17(1)(b)). Moreover, the 'other provisions of the scheme' are to have effect subject to the implied non-discrimination rule.

---

1 Note s 17(4) discussed below at **3.7.8**.

3.7.6 The effect of s 17 is to imply an 'overriding' rule of non-discrimination against disabled persons into the rules of occupational pension schemes.[1] 'This means that any discriminatory decision taken by trustees will be contrary to the rules of the scheme' and any disabled person affected by such a discriminatory decision 'will be able to seek redress through the dispute resolution mechanisms which already exist for pension schemes'.[2] Nevertheless, 'where a disabled applicant has a pre-existing medical condition which is likely to increase the risk of ill-health retirement or death in service', employers should be able to take that factor into account in the same way as they would do in respect of an applicant who was not disabled.[3] In the same breath, however, the Minister made it patent that such decisions must be based upon sound actuarial and medical evidence or advice. It must not be presumed that disability has a direct or inevitable effect upon life expectancy or risk of ill-health retirement. Disabled employees have a rebuttable right of access to employers' pension schemes.

1   The term occupational pension scheme has the same meaning as used under the Pension
    Schemes Act 1993 or the Pension Schemes (Northern Ireland) Act 1993.
2   HL Deb, vol 566, cols 994–995 (Lord Mackay of Ardbrecknish).
3   HL Deb, vol 566, col 995 (Lord Mackay of Ardbrecknish).

3.7.7   Section 17 effectively 'rides piggy-back' upon the provisions of ss 4–6 of
the Act and regs 4–5 of the Disability Discrimination (Employment) Regulations. The guidance contained in the Employment Code of Practice also
applies to trustees and managers of occupational pension schemes (with
appropriate modifications) as they do to employers.[1] Thus, trustees and
managers might incur liability,[2] or employ a justification defence,[3] in exactly
the same way as an employer might do so in respect of pensions. The exclusion
of the duty to make reasonable adjustments in this context is equally
applicable.[4] However, whereas the employer's liability might be tested in an
industrial tribunal, a complaint under s 17 against the trustees or managers of
an occupational pension scheme must be pursued through the appropriate
dispute resolution machinery for pension schemes. This is beyond the scope of
the present book.[5]

1   Employment Code of Practice, para 6.9 and see paras 6.10–6.16.
2   See **3.7.1**.
3   See **3.7.2–3.7.3**.
4   See **3.7.4**.
5   See the Occupational Pension Schemes (Internal Dispute Resolution Procedures) Regulations
    1996, SI 1996/1270 which come into force on 6 April 1997.

3.7.8   Without prejudice to the powers to make orders and regulations as set
out in s 67, s 17(3) permits regulations to be made under Part II of the Act in
respect of occupational pension schemes. Such regulations may make different
provisions affecting trustees or managers of occupational pension schemes to
those provisions which affect employers in relation to pension arrangements
(s 17(3)(a)). Alternatively, regulations may make provision modifying the
application to pension scheme managers or trustees of any regulations made
under Part II or of any provisions of Part II so far as they apply to employers
(s 17(3)(b)). In determining for the purposes of s 17(1)(b) whether an act or
omission would amount to unlawful discrimination if done by an employer, any
provision made in regulations under s 17(3) shall be applied as if they applied
in relation to the notional employer (s 17(4)). No regulations have been made
under s 17 at the time of writing.[1]

1   The only regulations that are relevant are the Disability Discrimination (Employment)
    Regulations, regs 4–5 made under s 5 of the Act. These have been discussed at **3.7.7**.

3.8 INSURANCE BENEFITS PROVIDED TO EMPLOYEES

3.8.1 Insurance benefits (such as private health insurance) offered to employees by an employer as an incident of a contract of employment are clearly within the scope of the prohibition on employment discrimination in s 4.[1] Section 4(2)(a)–(c) would seem particularly apposite. Section 18 makes special provision for the situation where an employer makes arrangements with an insurer for insurance-related benefits to be received by the employer's employees. This is designed to address discrimination by the insurance company as opposed to by the employer itself, and to the situation where the insurer treats disabled persons differently from others for non-actuarial reasons.

---

1   Subject to s 4(3) discussed at **3.3.10–3.3.11**. As to how the employment of a disabled person might affect the provision of liability insurance cover to the employer, see the Employment Code of Practice, para 6.18.

3.8.2 Section 18 applies in either of two circumstances. First, the section applies where a provider of insurance services enters into arrangements with an employer under which the employer's employees receive 'insurance services' provided by the insurer in question (s 18(1)(a)). Secondly, where the insurer enters into an arrangement with an employer under which the employer's employees are given an opportunity to receive insurance services provided by the insurer, the section is equally applicable (s 18(1)(b)). In both cases, it does not matter whether the employer–insurer arrangements cover all the employer's employees or only a class thereof.

3.8.3 Disability-related discrimination in respect of the provision of insurance benefits to employees under an employer–insurer arrangement is made unlawful by an awkward cross-reference to the provisions of Part III of the Act concerning the provision of goods, facilities or services.[1] Part III establishes that it is unlawful to discriminate against a disabled person for a reason related to disability in respect of the provision of goods, facilities or services to members of the public unless the discrimination is capable of justification (for example, by reference to actuarial evidence).

For the purposes of Part II of the Act, in the context of employment benefits, s 18(2) treats an insurer as having discriminated unlawfully against a disabled person who is a 'relevant employee' if the insurer acts in relation to the disabled employee in a way which would be unlawful discrimination under Part III.[2] In other words, s 18(2) looks to see whether the insurer would have committed an act of discrimination if the insurer was providing the service in question to members of the public and as if the insurance services in issue were being provided to the disabled person as a member of the public.

---

1   See ss 19–20 and Chapter 5. Account will be taken there of the insurance aspects of the Disability Discrimination (Services and Premises) Regulations 1996, SI 1996/1836.

2 A 'relevant employee' is determined by whether the employer–insurer arrangement is designed to benefit the employer's employees generally or only a class of employee (s 18(3)). It includes a person who has applied (or is contemplating applying) for employment by the employer (s 18(4)).

3.8.4 This is an unhappy piece of statutory drafting, not aided by being introduced into the draft legislation at the eleventh hour. The Minister attempted to explain its intended effect as follows:

> 'The insurance company will act unlawfully against a disabled person under [s 18] if it treats him in a way which would be an act of discrimination under Part III if done by the company with regard to a member of the public. That means that refusal to insure a disabled employee, or levying a higher premium, will be unlawful unless it is justified; for example, where there are reasonable grounds for supposing that the disabled person represents a higher risk than normal.'[1]

As will be seen in Chapter 5, the circumstances in which a service provider might justify less favourable treatment of a disabled person are more subjective and flexible than the test for justification in the employment context. In the final analysis, however, disabled persons who suspect that they have been discriminated against in the provision of occupational insurance benefits would be entitled to take both the employer and the insurer to an industrial tribunal.

1 HL Deb, vol 566, col 995 (Lord Mackay of Ardbrecknish). See further, Employment Code of Practice, para 6.17.

3.8.5 What 'insurances services' are covered by s 18? Section 18(3) indicates that future regulations will prescribe the description of insurance services caught by the section. No such regulations have been made at the time of writing. However, the subsection broadly indicates that, subject to further prescription, the prohibition on discrimination in relation to occupational insurance benefits will encompass the provision of benefits in respect of termination of service, retirement, old age, death, accident, injury, sickness or invalidity. The Minister confirmed that s 18 will apply to insurance services provided under a group scheme (such as permanent health insurance benefits).[1]

1 HL Deb, vol 566, col 1020 (Lord Mackay of Ardbrecknish) and see the Employment Code of Practice, para 6.17.

3.8.6 Of course, it might not be the insurer that has discriminated against the disabled employee. The employer might have refused admission to the insurance scheme, anticipating possible higher costs to itself if the benefits are to be bought for a disabled person. This might amount to discrimination under s 4 unless justifiable under s 5. Regulations may make provision for the purposes of s 5 as to the circumstances in which treatment is to be taken to be justified or not to be justified (s 5(6)). Particular provision may be made in such regulations by reference to the cost of affording any benefit (s 5(7)(a)). No such regulations have been made at the time of writing and the Government has given an assurance that it has in mind only serious or non-trivial costs as a ground for justifying less favourable treatment.[1]

---

1   HL Deb, vol 566, col 1000 (Lord Mackay of Ardbrecknish)

3.8.7   Moreover, ordinarily the employer cannot justify discrimination without first addressing the duty to make reasonable adjustments. Does this duty operate in respect of an employer in relation to occupational insurance benefits? By virtue of s 6(11), an employer has no s 6 duty to make reasonable adjustments to accommodate disabled persons in respect of occupational insurance benefits. The duty to make reasonable adjustments does not apply in relation to any of a number of benefits payable in money or money's worth under a scheme or arrangement for the benefit of employees. The benefits in question are those in respect of termination of service, retirement, old age, death, accident, injury, sickness or invalidity. Future regulations may add to this list after consultation.

3.9   DISCRIMINATION AGAINST CONTRACT WORKERS

3.9.1   Section 12 deals with discrimination by principals against contract workers in respect of the provision of contract work.[1] The terminology is defined in s 12(6). A 'principal' is a person (X) who makes work available ('contract work') for doing by individuals (Y) who are employed by another person (Z) who supplies them under a contract made with X.[2] A 'contract worker' is any individual (Y) who is supplied to the principal (X) under a contract made between X and Z for contract work to be done. Because of the expanded definition of 'employment' in s 68(1), it would seem logical that s 12 should apply to contract workers whether or not they are employees of Z or are self-employed but providing personal services under a contract with Z. However, that is not made explicit in the section.[3]

---

1   Similar provisions are to be found in the SDA 1975, s 9 and the RRA 1976, s 7. See generally, Employment Code of Practice, paras 7.1–7.8.
2   The existence of a contract between X (the principal) and Z (the contractor-employer) for the supply of Y's labour is crucial. In *Rice v Fon-A-Car* [1980] ICR 133, EAT, a taxi driver was not a contract worker simply because his services were supplied to customers through a central agency because the agency had no contractual relationship with the customers.
3   Doubts about the contractual status of such workers have been explored in the other discrimination jurisdictions. See *Construction Industry Training Board v Labour Force Ltd* [1970] 3 All ER 220; *Tanna v Post Office* [1981] ICR 374; *Mirror Group Newspapers v Gunning* [1986] ICR

145. See further *Daley v Allied Suppliers Ltd* [1983] ICR 90 (trainees engaged under contracts for training were not contract workers).

3.9.2 By s 12(1), it is unlawful for a principal, in relation to contract work done at an establishment in Great Britain,[1] to discriminate against a disabled person:

- in the terms on which the principal allows the disabled person to do that work;
- by not allowing the disabled person to do or continue to do the contract work;
- in the way the principal affords the disabled person access to any benefits or by refusing or deliberately omitting to afford the disabled person access to any benefits;
- by subjecting the disabled person to any other detriment.

These categories of unlawful acts are very similar to some of the categories contained in s 4 (discrimination against employment applicants and employees). However, they do not include discrimination in recruitment, selection, engagement and dismissal. Any disability-related discrimination in those areas will have been perpetrated by the employer rather than the principal for whom the contract work is to be done. A complainant would have a potential cause of action against the employer under ss 4–6.

1   The provisions of s 68 about the meaning of 'employment at an establishment in Great Britain' are modified accordingly (s 12(5)). Section 12 applies by extension to Northern Ireland by virtue of Sch 8, para 8.

3.9.3 As is the case in the parallel provisions of s 4(2)–(3), s 12(1) does not apply to benefits of any description if the principal is concerned with the provision (whether for payment or not) of benefits of that description to the public (or a section of the public including the contract worker) unless that provision differs in a material respect from the provision of the benefits by the principal to contract workers (s 12(2)). Benefits includes facilities or services (s 4(4)). In a case where s 12(1) does not apply to the provision of benefits, a contract worker might have a cause of action under Part III of the Act.

3.9.4 Section 12 outlaws disability discrimination against contract workers by applying the provisions on employment discrimination contained in ss 4–11 (except s 4(1)–(3)) to a principal in respect of contract work as if the principal were (or would be) the employer of the contract worker and as if any contract worker supplied to do work for the principal were an employee of the principal (s 12(3)).[1] In particular, the effect is that a principal may not discriminate against a contract worker for a reason related to disability in the way defined in s 5,[2] is subject to a duty to make adjustments under s 6, may take advantage of the defence of justification where it would be available to an employer in parallel circumstances, and may be exempted by the small business exception in s 7.

---

1 This 'piggyback' provision does not use s 4(1)–(3) because the circumstances of unlawful discrimination against contract workers are exhaustively set out in s 12(1).

2 Including victimisation within s 55. See s 12(4).

3.9.5 The intention behind s 12 is to protect disabled persons 'working under employment business arrangements if a hirer either refuses to hire the disabled person or discriminates against the disabled person once he has begun working for the hirer'.[1] Such persons will be generally protected by Part II of the Act in respect of their relationship with their employer (perhaps an employment agency or labour supplier), provided their employer employs 20 or more employees.[2] Section 12 extends that protection as against a third party during the period when their services have been hired or contracted to the third party, but again only if that third party (the so-called 'principal') employs 20 or more employees.[3]

---

1 HL Deb, vol 566, col 221 (Lord Henley).

2 See Employment Code of Practice, para 7.7.

3 These provisions also apply to severely disabled workers supplied by a local authority or voluntary organisation to a host employer under the Supported Placement Scheme: Employment Code of Practice, para 7.8.

Contract work and reasonable adjustments

3.9.6 If the principal is subject to s 12, then it will have a duty to make adjustments to accommodate disabled contract workers, including a duty to co-operate as far as is reasonable with adjustments already made for the worker by the employment business.[1] However, what will be a reasonable adjustment for a hirer to make will depend upon its individual circumstances and the rather limited, short-term nature of the labour hiring relationship. For example, it might be unreasonable for a principal to have to make adjustments if the disabled contract worker is to be seconded to the principal for only a short time.[2] Also, in practice, it might be reasonable for the principal to allow an adjustment to be made in respect of the disabled contract worker, but for the employer-supplier to provide or pay for the necessary adjustment.

---

1 HL Deb, vol 566, col 222 (Lord Henley); Employment Code of Practice, para 7.6

2 Employment Code of Practice, para 7.5. No indication is given of what would amount to a short period of time, although the example accompanying para 7.5 suggests that two weeks would certainly be such a period.

3.9.7   In a complex provision, regulations provide for the situation where a contract worker is likely to be placed at a similar substantial disadvantage (for the purposes of ss 6 and 12(3)) by arrangements made by or on behalf of all or most of the principals to whom he or she is or might be supplied.[1] This also covers the situation where a contract worker is likely to be placed at a similar substantial disadvantage by premises occupied by all or most of the principals to whom he or she is or might be supplied. In these situations, it is deemed to be reasonable for the contract worker's employer to have to take such steps as are within its power and as it would be reasonable for it to have to take if the arrangements were made by it (or on its behalf) or the premises were occupied by it (as the case may be).[2] In such a case, it is not reasonable for the principal to whom the contract worker is supplied in these situations to have to take any step which it is reasonable for the employer to have to take by virtue of this provision.[3]

This might be best explained by adopting and modifying an example provided in the Employment Code of Practice.[4] A disabled word-processor operator employed as a contract worker by a clerical agency requires a special keyboard as an adjustment for his or her disability. It can be anticipated that the contract worker will require such a keyboard wherever she or he is sent to work by the agency. It would be a reasonable step for the agency to supply the word-processor operator with the special keyboard and, so, it would not be reasonable to expect any firm to whom that contract worker's services are supplied to have to acquire a special keyboard for him or her. However, those firms would be under a separate duty to co-operate with the adjustment made by the agency (for example, by allowing the worker to carry and use the special keyboard at their premises). They might also have a residual duty to make a reasonable adjustment (for example, by ensuring that the keyboard can be made compatible with their computer systems, such as might be achieved by installing the appropriate driver software).

---

1   Disability Discrimination (Employment) Regulations 1996, reg 7(1).
2   Ibid, reg 7(2).
3   Ibid, reg 7(3).
4   Employment Code of Practice, para 7.6.

3.10   ENFORCEMENT, REMEDIES AND PROCEDURES

3.10.1   Section 8 sets out the enforcement procedure and remedies available when a claim of unlawful discrimination is made in respect of employment opportunities or contract work. A complaint of unlawful discrimination under Part II of the Act may be presented to an industrial tribunal under s 8(1) within three months of the act complained of (Sch 3, para 3). No other civil or criminal proceedings (except judicial review) may be brought (Sch 3, para 2). A conciliation process will normally follow (Sch 3, para 1). The usual remedy in a successful complaint will be compensation, including damages for injury to feelings and interest, but plaintiffs might also be entitled to seek a declaration as to their rights or a recommendation that the respondent should take reasonable action to obviate or reduce the adverse effect complained of (s 8 *passim*). An appeal from a decision of an industrial tribunal on a point of law will be to the Employment Appeal Tribunal.

3.10.2 Section 9 makes void any contract term or agreement which would contravene any part of Part II, limit or exclude the operation of any provision of Part II, or prevent any person from presenting a complaint to an industrial tribunal. An exception is made for settlements of claims by conciliation or through a compromise agreement following independent legal advice.

3.10.3 The question of enforcement, remedies and procedures in employment and contract work cases is considered in more detail in Chapter 10 (and see generally ss 8–9 and Sch 3, Part I). The failure to provide an institutional framework for the strategic enforcement of Part II of the Act is considered in Chapter 9.

3.11 DISABLED PERSONS (EMPLOYMENT) ACTS

3.11.1 Section 61(1) of the Disability Discrimination Act 1995 deals with the amendment of the Disabled Persons (Employment) Act 1944.[1] The 1944 Act has been the foundation stone of disabled employment rights for half a century.[2] However, the introduction of anti-discrimination legislation has led to a logical pruning and paring of the earlier statute.

---

1   The comparable amendments to the Disabled Persons (Employment) Act (Northern Ireland) 1945 are set out in a modified s 61 substituted by Sch 8, para 41. These will not be repeated here.

2   On the background, operation and ultimate failings of the 1944 legislation see House of Commons Employment Committee, *The Operation of the Disabled Persons (Employment) Act 1944* (HC Paper 389, April 1995) and the Government's reply to this report (HC Paper 667, July 1995).

3.11.2 From 2 December 1996, s 61(7) of the 1995 Act repeals the obligation upon employers of 20 or more employees to maintain a statutory three per cent quota of registered disabled persons (contained in ss 9–11 of the 1944 Act). The subsection also provides that the designated employment scheme for persons registered as handicapped by disablement (the so-called 'reserved occupations' provision of s 12 of the earlier statute) shall cease to have effect. The sections of the 1944 Act requiring employers to keep records in respect of quota compliance (s 14) and providing for proceedings in relation to criminal offences committed under that Act (s 19) will also cease to have effect by virtue of s 61(7).[1]

Notwithstanding the repeal of ss 9–12, 14 and 19 of the 1944 Act, certain saving and transitional provisions are contained in the Disability Discrimination Act 1995 (Commencement No 3 and Saving and Transitional Provisions) Order 1996, reg 3. Sections 9, 12 and 19 of the 1944 Act continue to have effect so as to allow prosecutions to be brought until 3 December 1997 in respect of alleged contraventions of ss 9(2), 9(5) or 12(2) of the 1944 Act prior to 2 December 1996. Section 14 of the 1944 Act and reg 9 of the Disabled Persons (General) Regulations 1945[2] continue to have effect so as to allow prosecutions to be brought until 3 December 1997 in respect of alleged contraventions of ss 9(2), 9(5) or 12(2). These transitional provisions also apply where it is alleged that contravention of s 14(6) or 14(7) hinder such prosecutions. As, in practice, prosecutions under these provisions have been rare, these transitional measures are of academic relevance only.

---

1   There are also further consequential repeals of s 13 (interpretation of earlier provisions which had been repealed by the 1944 Act itself) and s 21 (application of the 1944 Act as respects place of employment and nationality).
2   SR&O 1945/1558.

3.11.3   Consequent upon these repeals, the 1944 Act's definition of 'disabled person' and the register of disabled persons is redundant. Section 61(7) of the 1995 Act repeals ss 1 and 6–8 of the 1944 legislation accordingly. Any provision of existing subordinate legislation in which the term 'disabled person' is defined by reference to the DP(E)A 1944 definition will henceforth be construed by reference to the definition of this term contained in the 1995 Act (s 61(8)–(9)). Furthermore, as noted in Chapter 2, persons registered as disabled under the 1944 Act may be entitled, under certain conditions and for an interim period, to be deemed to satisfy the definition of disabled person for the purposes of the 1995 Act (Sch 1, para 7).

3.11.4   Section 15 of the 1944 Act gives the Secretary of State (in Northern Ireland, the Department of Economic Development) power to make arrangements for the provision of supported employment to provide job opportunities for severely disabled people unable or unlikely to obtain or retain work in open employment. Approximately 21,800 disabled persons presently benefit from supported employment and placement schemes operated by local authorities, voluntary organisations and Remploy Ltd.[1]

This power is retained but with consequential revisions occasioned by the 1995 Act. Similar consequential amendments are made to s 16 of the 1944 Act which gives preference under s 15 to ex-service men and women. These amendments or revisions are largely terminological and cosmetic and are not fully rehearsed here. One important change, however, is that in future the restriction under the 1944 Act preventing State funding for supported employment provision within companies that distribute profits may be lifted.[2] The Government does not believe that the entry of profit-making companies into the supported employment field will lead to the creaming off of less severely disabled workers by such companies or the exploitation of severely disabled workers by profit-oriented businesses.[3]

1 HL Deb, vol 565, col 708 (Lord Inglewood).
2 By virtue of s 61(3) amending s 15(2) of the 1944 Act.
3 HL Deb, vol 565, cols 708–709 (Lord Inglewood).

3.12 OTHER EMPLOYMENT LEGISLATION

3.12.1 The 1995 Act makes consequential amendments to (and repeals within) a small number of employment statutes or legislation affecting employment (s 70(4)–(5) and Schs 6–7).[1] These are largely designed to include appropriate cross-references to the Disability Discrimination Act 1995 in earlier legislation, to update the nomenclature of disability and to extend the new definition of disability and disabled person to other quarters. These amendments and repeals are not considered further in this context, with the following exception.

1 See also Sch 8, para 53 in respect of Northern Ireland. See also Employment Rights Act 1996, s 219, Sch 2, para 18 and Sch 3.

Employment in local government

3.12.2 A particular problem does arise in respect of local government employers. The Local Government and Housing Act 1989, s 7 requires all staff engaged by a local authority (or parish or community council) to be appointed on merit. Hitherto, this has been subject to the disabled quota provisions of the 1944 Act which allowed local government employers to ignore merit as an employment criterion in respect of persons registered as disabled under the 1944 legislation if the local authority in question was failing to meet the three per cent quota. As the 1995 Act abolishes the quota scheme, consequential amendments to the 1989 statute have been made by s 70(4), Sch 6, para 5 and Sch 7.

3.12.3 The effect of these amendments is to reinstate merit as an unchallenged employment criterion in local government. This casts doubt upon the ability of local authorities to discriminate positively in favour of disabled persons in employment policies where private sector employers would not be so prevented. For example, a local authority would be no longer enabled to give disabled persons priority interviews and make appointments before the remainder of the field. However, the amendments to the 1989 Act make it transparent that, while local authorities must appoint on merit, that is always subject to the duty to make reasonable adjustments under the 1995 Act.[1] It is equally clear that there remains a number of steps of positive action that local government employers might lawfully take in respect of disabled persons. These steps will include preferential training, special recruitment drives to encourage applications from disabled persons (either individually or in general) and guaranteed interviews for all suitable disabled applicants.[2]

---

1   Local Government and Housing Act 1989, s 7(2)(f) as inserted by para 5(c) of Sch 6 to the 1995 Act. See HC Deb, vol 265, col 120 (Mr J. Paice).
2   HC Deb, vol 265, cols 120–121 (Mr J. Paice). See also Employment Code of Practice, para 4.66.

Chapter 4

TRADE ORGANISATIONS

4.1 INTRODUCTION

4.1.1 Part II of the Act deals generally with discrimination against disabled persons in the field of employment. Chapter 3 examined discrimination against applicants and employees (ss 4–11) and discrimination against contract workers (s 12). Part II of the Act was amended at the Report stage in the House of Lords, largely at the prompting of the Trades Union Congress (TUC) and the Confederation of British Industry (CBI), to ensure that discrimination against disabled persons by trade organisations would be outlawed.[1]

---

1 Similar provisions are to be found in the Sex Discrimination Act 1975, s 12 and the Race Relations Act 1976, s 11.

4.1.2 Moving the amendments on behalf of the Government, Lord Henley explained that the effect of the amendments:

> 'means that trade unions, employers' associations and analogous bodies would be covered by this [Act] in their relationship with their members or prospective members who are disabled or who have had a disability. Such organisations are already covered in the [Act] to the extent that they are employers. However, they are not covered by the access to services right because they are not providing services to members of the general public – just to their members.'[1]

This is achieved in ss 13–15 of the Act. However, Lord Henley's analysis is correct only to a certain extent.

---

1 HL Deb, vol 566, cols 224–225 (Lord Henley, Minister of State, Department for Education and Employment).

4.1.3 A trade union or employers' association will be covered by ss 4–11 in Part II of the Act insofar as they employ persons within the meaning of the statute and insofar as they are not caught by the small employer exemption (which some smaller bodies could be). A full-time officer of a trade union or a clerical worker employed by a trade association, for example, will be employees (or would-be employees) protected from disability discrimination under Part II.

However, there is nothing in principle to prevent trade organisations of the kind described also being caught by Part III of the Act where they provide services to the public.[1] For example, a trade union which allows its premises to be used as a meeting place by groups other than those within the union's organisational structure or membership will be subject to the duties and non-discrimination requirements contained in ss 19–21. An illustration might include the use of a trade union's offices for a meeting of a local political party or community action group. Similarly, if a trade or professional organisation allows its facilities to be used for social purposes (such as wedding receptions), open to individuals unconnected with that organisation, it will need to consider its Part III obligations.[2]

---

1   See Chapter 5.
2   This is discussed in more detail in Chapter 5.

4.1.4   Nevertheless, the separate provision made in ss 13–15 of Part II of the Act in respect of discrimination by trade organisations against disabled members or disabled applicants for membership is important. Sections 13–15 contain largely self-contained measures and so warrant separate treatment in this chapter. These provisions are the subject of practical guidance and advice in a code of practice issued by the Secretary of State under s 53 of the Act (by virtue of s 53(8)).[1] Section 13 and parts of s 14 are effective from 2 December 1996.[2] However, ss 14(2), (4)–(5) and 15 (which relate to a trade organisation's duty to make reasonable adjustments) are not yet in force and no timetable for their implementation has been set.[3]

---

1   Trade organisations are dealt with as a separate part of the Employment Code of Practice (paras 7.9–7.13): *Code of Practice for the elimination of discrimination in the field of employment against disabled persons or persons who have had a disability* (1996, London: HMSO). A separate (but essentially identical) Employment Code of Practice covers Northern Ireland and reflects the different institutional context of the province. Both codes came into force on 2 December 1996.
2   By virtue of the Disability Discrimination Act 1995 (Commencement No 3 and Saving and Transitional Provisions) Order 1996.
3   See Employment Code of Practice, para 7.12.

4.2   MEANING OF 'TRADE ORGANISATION'

4.2.1   Sections 13–15 apply generally to discrimination by 'trade organisations' and to the associated duties of such bodies. The term 'trade organisation' is defined in s 13(4) and this definition is applicable for all the purposes of ss 13–15 by virtue of s 68(1). A trade organisation is 'an organisation of workers, an organisation of employers or any other organisation whose members carry on a particular profession or trade for the purposes of which the organisation exists' (s 13(4)). It is clear that ss 13–15 apply to three types of organisation.

Organisation of workers

4.2.2   First, 'an organisation of workers' is included. It is apparent from the parliamentary debates that the Government intended that trade unions should be subject to the Act in respect of rights of and to membership.[1] However, it is noteworthy that s 13(4) does not use the term 'trade union', but rather the term 'an organisation of workers' is employed. The words 'organisation' and 'workers' are not defined in the Act.

Some assistance might be gleaned from the definition of 'trade union' contained in the Trade Union and Labour Relations (Consolidation) Act 1992, s 1. That definition refers to a temporary or permanent organisation of workers whose principal purposes include the regulation of relations between workers and employers or employers' associations.[2] Note that the 1995 Act does not say what the purposes of an organisation of workers must be in order to qualify for coverage by s 13.

---

1   HL Deb, vol 566, cols 224–229 *passim.*
2   See generally *Harvey on Industrial Relations and Employment Law* (Butterworths) vol 2 Division M on which the following account draws.

4.2.3   A 'worker' for this purpose is a person who works (or seeks to work) under a contract of employment or under any other contract for the personal performance of any work or services (other than a professional and client relationship)[1] or in Crown employment (s 296 of the 1992 Act). This denotes that the term 'worker' is usually understood in a wider sense than the term 'employee' (although that term is already given a broad definition in s 68(1) of the 1995 Act).

However, police officers are not 'workers', but office-holders, so that the Police Federation would not be an organisation of workers,[2] while the position of the Prison Officers' Association is ambiguous.[3] Note that Part II of the Act does not apply to certain employments, including the police service and service as a prison officer (s 64(5)) and service in the armed forces (s 64(7)), so that this effectively overrides s 13.[4]

---

1   See *Writers' Guild of Great Britain v BBC* [1974] ICR 234; *Broadbent v Crisp* [1974] ICR 248; *Wiltshire Police Authority v Wynn* [1980] ICR 649.
2   *Home Office v Evans* (Divisional Court, 18 November 1993, unreported).
3   *Boddington v Lawton* [1994] ICR 478; but *cf* Criminal Justice and Public Order Act 1994, s 126.
4   See **9.4.8–9.4.9**.

4.2.4   Of more significance is the term 'organisation'. Borrowing again from the law of labour relations, it would appear that the term 'organisation' imports some notion of form, structure and stability, so that a mere loose association of workers would be insufficient.[1] It does not appear that the 1995 Act makes a distinction between permanent or temporary organisations of workers. As a result, any branch or other division of a trade union might constitute an organisation of workers, including unofficial workplace co-ordinating committees.

This was a particular concern of the TUC and Opposition members. In the House of Lords, Lord McCarthy stated that it was feared that ss 13–15:

> 'might render unions liable for any failure to make adjustments by an informal group of union members of whose existence the union's officers are unaware ... [including] groups of union members not recognising union rule books and with whom the national union does not communicate and who are given no powers or resources.'[2]

Lord Henley's response on behalf of the Government did not address Lord McCarthy's particular inquiry,[3] but it would seem that the TUC's concern is a real one given the wording of the Act and the lack of a definition of 'organisation of workers' in the statute.

---

1   *Conservative and Unionist Central Office v Burrell* [1982] 1 WLR 522; *cf Midland Cold Storage Ltd v Turner* [1972] ICR 230.
2   HL Deb, vol 566, cols 226–227.
3   HL Deb, vol 566, col 227.

Organisation of employers

4.2.5   Secondly, the Act embraces discrimination by 'an organisation of employers' (s 13(4)). Again, the statute clearly intends that 'employers' associations' should be within its purview, but that term is not utilised. Some assistance might be sought from the definition of 'employers' association' contained in s 122 of the 1992 Act (and see the definition of 'employer' in s 296 of that statute). Many of the same arguments and potential problems that have been visited in respect of trade unions will arise here and will not be rehearsed a second time.[1]

---

1   See **4.2.2–4.2.4**.

Other organisations

4.2.6   Thirdly, the legal regime contained in ss 13–15 applies equally to 'any other organisation whose members carry on a particular profession or trade for the purposes of which the organisation exists' (s 13(4)). The term 'profession' includes any vocation or occupation, while the term 'trade' encompasses any business (s 68(1)). It is suggested that this will capture professional bodies and trade associations which would not otherwise be classifiable as trade unions or employers' associations.[1]

For instance, The Law Society or Bar Council might be said to be an 'organisation whose members carry on a particular profession ... for the purposes of which the organisation exists' and the same can also be said of analogous organising bodies in other professions or professional spheres. Similarly, trade associations or organisations will be subject to the duties and restraints contained in this part of the legislation (even if they might also be simultaneously subject to other provisions in Parts II or III of the Act).

1 See Employment Code of Practice, para 7.9.

4.2.7 One area of some doubt concerns the position of bodies which issue qualifications or authorisations required for (or facilitating engagement in) a trade or profession.[1] Examples might include The Law Society, the Council of Legal Education or the General Medical Council. Such bodies might be excluded from Part III of the Act if they fall within the exclusions in respect of education contained in s 19(5)–(6).[2] However, if they are not so excluded, they might be caught by Part III insofar as they provide services to the public. Further or alternatively, they might be caught by ss 13–15 in Part II of the legislation insofar as they might be a professional or trade organisation as defined in s 13(4). This matter has not been clarified in the regulations issued under Part III of the Act.

1 See the remarks of Lord Henley at HL Deb, vol 566, col 226 and *cf* Sex Discrimination Act 1975, s 13 and Race Relations Act 1976, s 12.
2 See Chapters 5 and 7.

4.3 DISCRIMINATION BY TRADE ORGANISATIONS

4.3.1 Section 13 of the 1995 Act prohibits discrimination by trade unions, employers' organisations and analogous bodies for a reason related to disability in a similar way to the coverage of such discrimination on gender or racial grounds.[1] The section deals with discrimination in three forms: discrimination against applicants for membership, discrimination against existing members and discrimination by way of victimisation.[2] Discrimination is defined in s 14 and this is considered in more detail below.[3] Sections 13 and 14 are interdependent and must be read together. Section 14 determines whether an act of discrimination has occurred, while s 13 delineates what acts of discrimination are made unlawful.

1 Sex Discrimination Act 1975, s 12; Race Relations Act 1976, s 11.
2 See **4.4.6**.
3 See **4.4**.

Discrimination against applicants for membership of trade organisations

4.3.2 It is unlawful for a trade organisation (as defined in s 13(4)) to discriminate against a disabled person (as defined in Part I and Schs 1–2) 'in the terms on which it is prepared to admit him [or her] to membership of the organisation' (s 13(1)(a)). For example, a trade union which made it a condition of membership that a disabled person should pay a higher membership fee or joining fee than other applicants for membership would almost certainly transgress this provision. Similarly, a professional body that would only admit disabled persons to membership after a longer period of apprenticeship or practice in the profession than in the normal case might be in breach of s 13(1)(a).

4.3.3 Moreover, s 13(1)(b) provides that it is unlawful for a trade organisation to discriminate against a disabled person 'by refusing to accept, or deliberately not accepting, his [or her] application for membership'. A trade association which selectively or consistently refused membership of the association to disabled persons engaged in the relevant trade commits a *prima facie* breach of s 13. Similarly, a trade union which has received an application for membership from a disabled person, and *deliberately* fails to process that application, has committed a potential act of unlawful discrimination, even although it has not positively taken a step to reject the application. Its deliberate default in respect of the application might be tantamount to a non-acceptance.

Discrimination by trade organisations against existing members

4.3.4 Section 13(2) makes it unlawful for a trade organisation to discriminate against a disabled person who is a member of the organisation:

- in the way it affords him or her access to any benefits;
- by refusing him or her access to any benefits;
- by deliberately omitting to afford him or her access to any benefits;
- by depriving him or her of membership;
- by varying the terms on which he or she is a member;
- by subjecting him or her to any other detriment.

These are analogous to similar provisions in the Sex Discrimination Act 1975 and the Race Relations Act 1976. The term 'benefits' includes 'facilities and services' (s 4(4)).

The acts prohibited by s 13(2) are transparent and self-explanatory. In general, a trade organisation may not treat its disabled members as second-class members in respect of the rights and benefits of membership. This would include expulsion from membership where a non-disabled member would not be deprived of membership. The Employment Code of Practice warns trade organisations that they should not discriminate as regards training facilities, welfare or insurance schemes, invitations to attend events, processing of grievances, or assistance to members in their employers' disciplinary or dismissal procedures.[1] However, s 13(2) is not free-standing and must be considered in tandem with the meaning of discrimination set out in s 14. This is examined below.

---

1 Employment Code of Practice, para 7.10.

4.4 THE MEANING OF DISCRIMINATION BY TRADE ORGANISATIONS

4.4.1 The meaning of discrimination for the purposes of ss 13–15 is to be found in the self-contained definition in s 14. However, cases under Part III (ss 20 and 24) and s 5 in Part II are likely to be instructive.[1]

---

1 See the relevant treatment of these sections in Chapters 3, 5 and 6. See also the Employment Code of Practice, para 7.11

Less favourable treatment

4.4.2 For the purposes of s 13, a trade organisation discriminates against a disabled person if, for a reason which relates to the disabled person's disability, it treats him or her less favourably than it treats (or would treat) others to whom that reason does not (or would not) apply *and* it cannot show that the less favourable treatment is justified (s 14(1)). This is virtually identical to the definition of discrimination in the context of employment as contained in s 5(1). Many of the points made about that definition will apply here.[1]

The test of discrimination is a comparative one. How has the disabled person been treated by the trade organisation in comparison with a person to whom the reason relating to the disabled person's disability does not apply? This has been explored in some detail in the previous chapter and the analysis there is equally applicable here.[2]

---

1 See Chapter 3 and, in particular, **3.4**.
2 See **3.4.3–3.4.8**.

Reason related to disability

4.4.3 The important point to note is that discrimination by a trade organis-ation only arises if the organisation has treated a disabled member or would-be member differently from others 'for a reason which relates to the disabled person's disability' (s 14(1)(a)). In other words, the person's disability or a reason connected with that disability must have been a factor in the differential treatment. As in the comparable provisions in the pre-existing race and sex discrimination statutes, the fact that, for example, a trade union has provided a disabled member with poor representation or inadequate services is not enough.[1] The Act is not concerned with indifferent treatment as such, but with less favourable treatment connected with the prohibited ground, namely a person's disability.

1   See, for example, the race discrimination case of *Furniture, Timber and Allied Trades Union v Modgill* [1980] IRLR 142.

4.4.4   Similarly, if a trade union's rule book limits eligibility for membership of the union (for example, to workers working in a particular trade or industry or employed at a certain grade or level), a refusal to admit a disabled person to the union because he or she does not meet those eligibility conditions is not an act of prohibited discrimination.[1] A disabled nurse cannot seek to become a member of the National Union of Mineworkers and complain of disability discrimination when refused membership on eligibility grounds. That is, of course, subject to the proviso that a non-disabled person, similarly ineligible, was not or would not be admitted to membership of the organisation.

1   HL Deb, vol 566, col 226 (Lord McCarthy) and col 227 (Lord Henley).

Discrimination and the duty to make adjustments

4.4.5   For the purposes of ss 13–15, a trade organisation also discriminates against a disabled person if it fails to comply with a s 15 duty to make adjustments imposed on it in relation to the disabled person *and* it cannot show that its failure to comply with that duty is justified (s 14(2)). The s 15 duty to make adjustments is considered further below.[1]

1   See **4.5**. These provisions relating to the duty to make adjustments have not yet been brought into force.

Victimisation

4.4.6   Section 55(1) treats a person (X) as having discriminated against another person (Y) if X treats Y less favourably than X treats or would treat other persons whose circumstances are the same as Y's and X has done so for one of a number of statutory reasons contained in s 55(2). In essence, those statutory reasons relate to the fact, belief or suspicion that Y has exercised rights under the Act or assisted others to do so. This is victimisation and protects the rights of both disabled and non-disabled persons.[1]

An act of victimisation is treated as a discriminatory act and would provide the victimised person with a cause of action under ss 13–15 by virtue of s 13(3). For example, a trade union member (whether a disabled person or not) who was disciplined by his or her trade union because he or she gave evidence in legal proceedings against the union brought under the Act (for example, by a disabled person denied membership of the union for a reason allegedly related to disability) would have a separate right of complaint under s 13.

1 The ingredients of victimisation are explored in more detail in Chapter 10.

4.5 DUTY TO MAKE ADJUSTMENTS

4.5.1 When in force, s 15 will place trade organisations under a duty to make adjustments so as to accommodate disabled persons who are members or who are seeking membership.[1] This is not a general duty or a duty at large, but rather one which is owed to the particular disabled person concerned. Nevertheless, trade organisations will need to keep this duty in mind and ought to take steps to ensure and to anticipate that the rights of disabled persons in relation to the organisation are not compromised.

1 The marginal note to s 15 in the initial print run by HMSO of the Queen's Printer copy of the Act wrongly records the substance of s 15 (apparently confusing this section with s 38). This has been corrected subsequently.

4.5.2 Except within its own terms, the duty to make adjustments does not require trade organisations to treat disabled persons more favourably than they treat or would treat others (s 15(6)). Moreover, s 15 only imposes duties for the purpose of determining whether a trade organisation has discriminated against a disabled person. As we have seen,[1] s 14(2) treats an unjustified failure to comply with a s 15 duty as satisfying the meaning of discrimination for the purposes of the unlawful acts in s 13. A breach of a s 15 duty is not otherwise actionable as such (s 15(10)).

1 See **4.4.5**. But note that s 14(2) is not yet in force.

4.5.3 The s 15 duty to make adjustments is very similar to the parallel duty upon employers to make adjustments under s 6.[1] It is likely to be supplemented by regulations to be made under s 15(7)–(9). The duty contains two limbs, as the following analysis will demonstrate.

1 See Chapter 3 at **3.6**.

When does the duty arise?

4.5.4   First, where 'any arrangements' made by (or on behalf of) a trade organisation place the disabled person concerned 'at a substantial disadvantage in comparison with persons who are not disabled', the organisation is under a duty 'to take such steps as it is reasonable, in all the circumstances of the case, for it to have to take' in order to prevent the 'arrangements' having the effect of placing the disabled person at a comparative substantial disadvantage (s 15(1)(a)). The term 'any arrangements' applies only in relation to 'arrangements for determining who should become or remain a member of the organisation' and to any 'term, condition or arrangements on which membership or any benefit is offered or afforded' (s 15(2)).

4.5.5   Secondly, where 'any physical feature of premises occupied by the organisation' places the disabled person concerned 'at a substantial disadvantage in comparison with persons who are not disabled', the organisation is under a duty 'to take such steps as it is reasonable, in all the circumstances of the case, for it to have to take' in order to prevent the 'feature' having the effect of placing the disabled person at a comparative substantial disadvantage (s 15(1)(b)). The term 'physical feature of premises' is not statutorily defined, but this is expected to be the subject of clarification in regulations to be made under s 15(7).

4.5.6   Regulations under s 15(7) are also expected to provide as to the circumstances in which arrangements or physical features are to be taken (or are not to be taken) to have the effect of a comparative substantial disadvantage upon a disabled person as contemplated by s 15(1). No such regulations have been made at the present time.

To whom is the duty owed?

4.5.7   The duty to make reasonable adjustments is only owed to 'the disabled person concerned' (s 15(1)). In the case of arrangements for determining to whom membership should be offered, this means any disabled person who is an applicant for membership or who has notified the organisation that he or she may be an applicant for membership (s 15(4)(a)). In any other case, 'the disabled person concerned' is a disabled person who is an applicant for membership or who is already a member of the organisation (s 15(4)(b)).

Furthermore, an organisation cannot be placed under a s 15 duty to make adjustments if the organisation does not know (and could not reasonably be expected to know) that the disabled person in question (a) is (or may be) an applicant for membership, or (b) has a disability and is likely to be placed at a comparative substantial disadvantage by arrangements or physical features of premises (s 15(5)).

What are reasonable steps?

4.5.8   When a trade organisation is considering what steps it would be reasonable to take, in all the circumstances of the case, in order to prevent arrangements or physical features of premises placing a disabled person at a comparative substantial disadvantage, particular regard is to be had to a number of criteria. These criteria will also be used by a tribunal or court in judging whether a trade organisation has discharged its s 15 duty. Regulations yet to be made will provide as to the circumstances in which it is reasonable (or not reasonable) for a trade organisation to have to take steps of a prescribed description and as to what steps it is always (or never) reasonable for a trade organisation to have to take (s 15(7) by cross-reference to s 6(8)).

4.5.9 First, regard should be had to the extent to which taking a particular step would prevent the effect of substantial disadvantage (s 15(3)(a)). Trade organisations are not expected to make adjustments that would not have any real effect for the disabled person. Adjustments do not have to be made for their own sake if they would not ultimately accommodate the rights of the person affected.

Secondly, the organisation might consider the extent to which it is practicable for it to take the step in question (s 15(3)(b)). A step which is impracticable or impossible to take is not a reasonable adjustment.

4.5.10 Thirdly, regard must be had to the financial and other costs which would be incurred by the organisation in taking the step and the extent to which taking that step would disrupt any of its activities (s 15(3)(c)). Regulations to be made under s 15(7) may make provision by reference to the cost of taking the steps concerned (s 15(8)). Clearly, there might be a point where the costs of making an adjustment outweigh the benefits of doing so, and disruption to the activities of the organisation is part of that analysis.

4.5.11 Fourthly, account must be taken of the extent of the organisation's financial and other resources (s 15(3)(d)). The cost of making an adjustment might be more easily absorbed by a larger or wealthier organisation than it might be by a smaller or impecunious body. Account must also be taken of the availability to the organisation of financial or other assistance (for example, government funding) with respect to taking the step (s 15(3)(e)).

The duty illustrated

4.5.12 In contrast with the duty upon employers to make adjustments, there is no list (such as that contained in s 6(3) in relation to employment) of examples of steps that trade organisations might take when complying with their s 15 duty. When these provisions of the Act were being introduced by amendment in the House of Lords, the Minister illustrated the duty by the example of a trade union needing to ensure that, where it was reasonable, members with visual impairments could get union literature in braille form or members with hearing disabilities had access to signers at union meetings.[1]

A further example would be the need for trade organisations to ensure that the buildings which they occupy are physically accessible to members with disabilities, perhaps by widening doors, installing wheelchair ramps and considering the layout of meeting rooms.[2] These are good examples of the duty and may already represent best practice in many trade unions and other trade organisations. These examples are subject, of course, to the various tests of when the duty is owed and to whom, as discussed above.

---

1   HL Deb, vol 566, col 225 (Lord Henley).
2   Note the provisions of s 16 and Part I of Sch 4 to the Act which will apply where a trade organisation occupies premises under a lease which prevents or hinders alterations being made in pursuit of a s 15 duty to make adjustments. These provisions are discussed in detail in Chapter 6.

4.5.13   An interesting question concerns the overlap of the s 15 duty with the democratisation provisions in the recent reforms of trade union law now contained in the Trade Union and Labour Relations (Consolidation) Act 1992. Although s 59 of the 1995 Act states that nothing in the new legislation makes unlawful any act done in pursuance of any enactment, such as another statute, it is submitted that this does not prevent trade unions from being subject to the 1995 Act when discharging their obligations under the 1992 Act. In particular, trade unions will need to consider how to continue meeting the stringent requirements upon unions in respect of ballots and elections while also complying with the duty to make reasonable adjustments for their disabled members.

4.5.14   For example, Chapter IV of Part I of the 1992 Act requires elections to certain positions in the union to be conducted by secret postal ballot. Union members must not be unreasonably excluded from candidature (s 47 of the 1992 Act) and union members with a disability may be able to use s 15 of the 1995 Act to reinforce that right. The union is obliged to circulate election addresses for every candidate (s 48 of the 1992 Act) and s 15 of the 1992 Act might require a union to ensure that braille or large print versions of such addresses are made available. Similar requirements could also be made of the scrutineer's report and the publication of the results of the ballot at the conclusion of the election process.

4.5.15   Voting in the election is to be by means of a fully postal secret ballot (s 51 of the 1992 Act) and no other form of voting is acceptable. The system of fully postal voting actually works to the benefit of disabled members, some of whom might otherwise have been at a substantial disadvantage under a non-postal or partly postal voting system. However, a trade union might consider that the 1995 Act requires it to redesign the ballot paper so as to accommodate the needs of disabled members (especially those with visual or learning disabilities) while remaining within the form and content required by trade union law.

4.5.16   Similar considerations in respect of the rights of trade union members with disabilities might also arise in respect of other aspects of trade union law relating to administration, elections, ballots before industrial action, union discipline, political fund resolutions and ballots, and so on. Although employers' associations and trade or professional organisations are not subject to the same regulatory framework as trade unions, they too will need to consider how the 1995 Act impinges upon their democratic processes and their relations with disabled members.

4.6 DEFENCE OF JUSTIFICATION

4.6.1 The above discussion is subject to the defence of justification being available. Discrimination is defined in s 14(1) as being less favourable treatment of a disabled person for a reason which relates to that person's disability. Furthermore, discrimination comprises a failure to comply with a s 15 duty to make reasonable adjustments (s 14(2)). In both instances, a trade organisation has a defence of justification.

4.6.2 Less favourable treatment of a disabled person for a reason related to that person's disability is discriminatory if the trade organisation 'cannot show that the treatment in question is justified' (s 14(1)(b)). For this purpose, 'treatment is justified if, but only if, the reason for it is both material to the circumstances of the particular case and substantial' (s 14(3)). Regulations to be made in the future may provide as to the circumstances in which treatment is to be taken to be (or not to be) justified (s 14(6)).

4.6.3 However, if the trade organisation is under a s 15 duty to make adjustments in relation to the disabled person who has been less favourably treated for a disability-related reason, and has failed without justification to comply with that duty, it cannot justify its treatment of the disabled person under s 14(3) 'unless the treatment would have been justified even if the organisation had complied with the section 15 duty' (s 14(5)). Note that this provision (s 14(5)) is not yet in force.

In other words, before a trade organisation can seek to justify the less favourable treatment of a disabled person for a reason related to disability it must first address its duty to make reasonable adjustments. The trade organisation cannot rely upon a material and substantial reason for less favourable treatment if that reason could have been rendered immaterial or insubstantial by carrying out a reasonable adjustment. Regulations may provide as to the circumstances in which failure to comply with a s 15 duty is to be taken to be (or not to be) justified (s 14(6)).

4.6.4 A failure to comply with a s 15 duty to make adjustments is discriminatory if the trade organisation 'cannot show that its failure to comply with that duty is justified' (s 14(2)(b)). For this purpose, 'failure to comply with a section 15 duty is justified if, but only if, the reason for the failure is both material to the circumstances of the particular case and substantial' (s 14(4)). Neither s 14(2) nor s 14(4) are yet in force. Regulations may provide as to the circumstances in which failure to comply with a s 15 duty is to be taken to be (or not to be) justified (s 14(6)).

4.6.5 The defence of justification in respect of discrimination against disabled persons by trade organisations is closely related to the parallel defence available to employers in respect of discrimination against disabled employees and applicants for employment. The reader is referred to the fuller discussion of those provisions in Chapter 3 where the analysis is equally applicable to the present discussion.[1] During the legislative process, the Minister gave two examples of circumstances in which less favourable treatment of a disabled person by a trade organisation would be justified.[2]

---

1   See **3.5**.
2   HL Deb, vol 566, col 225 (Lord Henley). See also Employment Code of Practice, para 7.11.

4.6.6   First, a trade union delegation might be visiting inaccessible premises not controlled by the union. It might be necessary to omit from the delegation a member who is a wheelchair user because of the inaccessibility of the premises. The Minister suggested that the defence of justification would be available to the union if the disabled member raised a complaint of discrimination by the union under the 1995 legislation. It would also seem that the member in question would have no alternative cause of action under the Act against the controller of the inaccessible premises, unless the visit is to premises controlled by a service provider and the visit was for the purpose of being provided with goods or services or facilities within the meaning of Part III of the Act.

4.6.7   Secondly, the Minister stated that a disabled person could be excluded from membership of an employers' association (or trade association) for a particular trade if the disabled person does not work in that trade and is not qualified to do so. With respect, that is not a true example of the defence of justification in operation. If the disabled person has been excluded from membership of an employers' association or trade organisation because he or she does not work in that trade or is not qualified to do so, that is unlikely to be less favourable treatment for a reason related to the disabled person's disability and so would not be discrimination in the first place. The reason for the exclusionary treatment is that the person is not qualified for membership of the organisation and that is not a reason connected with disability, unless the conditions for qualification are indirectly discriminatory against disabled persons.

   If, on the other hand, the organisation did admit non-disabled persons regardless of whether they worked in the trade or were qualified to do so, that would be discrimination against the disabled applicant and it might be inferred easily that it was for a disability-related reason. However, it is unlikely (although possible) that the organisation could show that the differential treatment of the disabled person in those circumstances was for a material and substantial reason.

4.7   ENFORCEMENT AND REMEDIES

Discrimination by trade organisations contrary to ss 13–15 will be subject to the provisions on enforcement, procedure and remedies contained in ss 8–9. These sections provide a right of action in the industrial tribunal in like manner to actions alleging disability discrimination in connection with employment or contract work. The reader is referred to the summary of these provisions in the previous chapter.[1] This is discussed further in Chapter 10.

---

1   See **3.10**.

Chapter 5

GOODS, FACILITIES AND SERVICES

5.1 INTRODUCTION

5.1.1 The 1994 Green Paper promised that consultation would take place on extending the Building Regulations to ensure that physical barriers to access by disabled persons to public and domestic buildings would be removed or reduced. However, as the Green Paper acknowledges:

> 'removing physical impediments does nothing to banish the mental barriers of ignorance and prejudice. Making buildings easier to get into is of no avail if disabled people are kept outside because their appearance or behaviour is deemed too upsetting for other patrons or through misguided concern for their safety.'[1]

The Green Paper mooted a new right of access that would make it unlawful for providers of goods or services to treat an individual unfavourably because of that person's disability, except where there were physical barriers or genuine safety issues.

---

1   *A Consultation on Government Measures to Tackle Discrimination Against Disabled People* (July 1994) para 4.2 (referred to hereafter as 'Green Paper').

5.1.2 The 1995 White Paper took up this idea and proposed the introduction of a right of access to goods and services for disabled persons.[1] This would involve a prohibition upon discriminatory behaviour and would require reasonable and readily achievable positive action to overcome physical and communication barriers impeding access by disabled persons.

---

1   *Ending Discrimination Against Disabled People* (Cm 2729, January 1995) para 4.4 (referred to hereafter as 'White Paper').

5.1.3 The main features of this new right of access were stated to be as follows:

- refusing to serve disabled customers would be made unlawful unless it was essential for the provision of the goods or services concerned;
- policies, practices and procedures that directly discriminated against disabled persons would be prohibited unless they were fundamental to the nature of the business;
- auxiliary aids and services would be required to be provided where this is reasonable and readily achievable;
- in this context, account would be taken of the size, resources and nature of the business and any requirement would be subject to a statutory limit upon cost;

- physical barriers would have to be removed where reasonable and readily achievable, subject to a costs limitation and a phasing-in of the compliance requirement;
- alternatively, instead of removing barriers, a service provider might provide goods or services to disabled persons by alternative means;
- special provision would be made in respect of insurance services.

Exceptionally, the new right would not apply to transport vehicles or to educational establishments and would also not apply where the supply of the goods or services in question would pose a risk to the health and safety of the disabled person or others.[1]

---

1   White Paper para 4.6.

5.1.4   These novel rights of access prefaced in the Green Paper and proposed in the White Paper are set out in Part III of the Disability Discrimination Act 1995. Sections 19–21 of the Act establish a right of access for disabled persons to goods, facilities and services. These sections require service providers to adapt policies, procedures and practices, and to remove physical barriers and barriers to communication, so long as it is reasonable to do so. Sections 25–28 deal with enforcement of the new rights and related questions. Part III of the 1995 Act is broadly modelled after the comparable provisions of the Sex Discrimination Act 1975, ss 29–36 and the Race Relations Act 1976, ss 20–27 and decisions under these provisions may assist in the interpretation of the new legislation.

5.1.5   Part III of the Act has been brought partly into force at the time of writing. The Government intends to provide a long lead-in time for businesses to adapt to these new provisions. These measures are likely to be brought into force over a period as long as 10 years. However, the Minister indicated that the simple duty on service providers not to refuse service to a disabled person unreasonably was likely to be brought into force sooner rather than later, whereas the duty to remove physical barriers may not be effective for some time.[1] Accordingly, while much of ss 19–21 was brought into force on 2 December 1996,[2] the provisions relating to the duty to make reasonable adjustments (what are being referred to as the 'final rights of access') are not likely to be fully implemented before 2005.[3] However, the Act does not prevent service providers from treating disabled persons *more* favourably than non-disabled persons and there would be nothing to prevent service providers from voluntarily implementing some or all of the final rights of access in the absence of legal compulsion. There may be sound commercial reasons for so doing.

Those provisions of Part III which are in force are supported by the *Code of Practice: Rights of Access: Goods, Facilities, Services and Premises* (referred to hereafter as the 'Rights of Access Code of Practice') issued by the Secretary of State under s 51(2).[4] The Code gives practical advice on how to comply with the new legal duties in Part III and is designed to help disabled persons to understand the law. However, it does not impose legal obligations and is not an authoritative statement of the law. It may be used in evidence in legal proceedings and a court must take account of it where relevant.[5] Regulations under Part III have also been issued and will be considered at appropriate points in the text below.[6]

---

1 HL Deb, vol 566, col 1031 (Lord Mackay of Ardbrecknish).
2 By the Disability Discrimination Act 1995 (Commencement No 3 and Saving and Transitional Provisions) Order 1996. The regulation-making powers in ss 19(5)(c) and 20(6)–(8) were brought into effect on 6 June 1996.
3 The provisions are those in ss 19(1)(b), 20(2), (5), (9) and 21.
4 1996, London: HMSO. The Code was issued based on proposals made by the National Disability Council. A separate, but largely identical, Code of Practice has been issued in Northern Ireland.
5 See **9.2**, and see generally, Rights of Access Code of Practice, chapter 1.
6 Disability Discrimination (Services and Premises) Regulations 1996, SI 1996/1836 made under ss 19(5)(c), 20(7)–(8), 24(5), 67(2)–(3) and 68(1), and in force on 2 December 1996.

5.2 GENERAL PROHIBITION ON DISCRIMINATION IN RELATION TO GOODS, FACILITIES AND SERVICES

5.2.1 Section 19(1) of the Act makes it unlawful for 'a provider of services' to discriminate against a disabled person in a number of specified ways in relation to the provision of 'goods, facilities or services'. Although s 19 speaks of 'a provider of services' and refers throughout to the provision of a 'service', the section extends not only to the provision of services, but also includes the provision of any goods or facilities (s 19(2)(a)). It is also irrelevant whether the service, goods or facilities in question are provided on payment or without payment (s 19(2)(c)).

The meaning of 'a provider of services' is considered below,[1] as is the definition of 'goods, facilities and services'. It will also be necessary to revisit the meaning of 'discriminate' as used in this Part.[2] The question of who is a 'disabled person' for this purpose is answered by consideration of the provisions of ss 1–2 of and Schs 1–2 to the Act (together with any guidance and regulations to be issued).[3]

---

1 See **5.3**.
2 See **5.5**.
3 See Chapter 2.

Refusal to provide goods, facilities or services

5.2.2 First, it is an unlawful act for a service provider to discriminate against a disabled person in refusing to provide, or deliberately not providing, to a disabled person any service which the service provider provides, or is prepared to provide, to members of the public (s 19(1)(a)). For example, a theatre which refused to admit a person with cerebral palsy because of that individual's disability might be committing an unlawful act of discrimination.[1]

---

1   See further, Rights of Access Code of Practice, paras 3.3–3.5.

Failure to make reasonable adjustments

5.2.3   Secondly, it is an unlawful act for a service provider to discriminate against a disabled person by failing to comply with a duty imposed by s 21 of the Act to take such steps as are reasonable in order to make adjustments to practices, policies or procedures which make it impossible or unreasonably difficult for a disabled person to gain access to goods, facilities or services provided to other members of the public (s 19(1)(b)). This is a pivotal duty under the Act and calls for separate and detailed explication below.[1]

The point being made here is that a failure of a service provider to make reasonable adjustments (in order to allow disabled persons to enjoy a right of access to goods, facilities and services) is in itself potentially an unlawful act of discrimination if that failure has the effect of making it impossible or unreasonably difficult for the disabled person to make use of the goods, facilities or services in question.

---

1   See **5.7**. Note that this provision is not yet in force.

Standard or manner of service

5.2.4   Thirdly, it is an unlawful act for a service provider to discriminate against a disabled person in the 'standard of service' which the service provider provides to the disabled person or by virtue of the 'manner in which' the service provider provides that service to the disabled person (s 19(1)(c)). The 1994 Green Paper gives as an example of conduct that might be caught by this prohibition a restaurant that forced disabled customers to dine in a separate room unseen by other patrons.[1] A theatre which limited disabled patrons to matinee performances only might also fall foul of the Act, although there would be nothing to prevent a theatre arranging special matinee performances for disabled persons, provided they are also free to book seats for other times also.

---

1   Green Paper para 4.3. See also Rights of Access Code of Practice, paras 3.6–3.7.

5.2.5   Similarly, providing inferior goods or services to disabled persons should be caught, although it is recognised that what would amount to *inferior* goods or services might be difficult to measure. For example, requiring wheelchair-users to sit in a particular part of a theatre or restaurant when other customers or patrons have a comparatively free choice as to where they sit could be regarded as the provision of an inferior service.[1] Much will hinge upon the application of the defence of justification for the differential treatment in such cases,[2] but a service provider who adapted a deliberate policy to discourage disabled customers (for example, by deliberately surly, dilatory or inferior service) would have difficulty in justifying such discrimination.[3]

1   Green Paper para 4.4. See also Rights of Access Code of Practice, para 3.6.
2   See **5.6**.
3   HL Deb, vol 566, col 267 (Lord Mackay of Ardbrecknish).

Terms on which service is provided

5.2.6   Fourthly, it is an unlawful act for a service provider to discriminate against a disabled person in the terms on which the service provider provides a service (or goods or facilities) to the disabled person (s 19(1)(d)). An example of an act made unlawful by this provision would be a shop or entertainment outlet which charged higher prices for purchases by or admission to disabled persons in comparison with other customers.[1]

1   Green Paper para 4.3. See also Rights of Access Code of Practice, para 3.8.

5.3   PROVISION OF GOODS, FACILITIES AND SERVICES

5.3.1   As pointed out previously, although Part III of the Act consistently refers to the duties and liabilities of 'a provider of services' and generally to the provision of a 'service' or 'services', this is merely for the convenience of legislative drafting. Section 19(2)(a) makes it explicit that, for the purposes of ss 19–21, the provision of services includes the provision of 'any goods or facilities'. At the risk of repetition, it is also irrelevant whether any goods, facilities or services are provided on payment or without payment (s 19(2)(c)). The Rights of Access Code of Practice casts little further light on these questions.

Goods

5.3.2   The term 'goods' is not defined in the Act and no light is cast upon it by the legislative history of the 1995 Act. A literal definition of the term would suggest that the everyday meaning of 'goods' as chattels or moveable property is intended. In those circumstances, it is submitted, there is no cause to import a

definition of goods from any other statutory source and difficulties of
interpretation might then arise.

To take the obvious external source of a definition of goods, the Sale of
Goods Act 1979, s 61 defines goods as including 'all personal chattels other
than things in action and money', but goes on to exclude explicitly non-
physical property, such as choses in action (for example, company shares) and,
by implication, intellectual property (for example, copyrights, patents and
trade marks). A particular problem arises under the definition for the purposes
of a sale of goods governed by the 1979 Act in that, while crops or things severed
from, but previously attached to the land, are considered 'goods', land itself or
minerals forming part of the land are not regarded as 'goods'.

5.3.3 It would seem that either a literal or a purposive approach to the
meaning of 'goods' in the 1995 Act should produce a broad and all-embracing
interpretation. All other things being equal, a refusal on the grounds of a
person's disability to supply goods which are in the nature of personal or
moveable property will give rise to a cause of action. It is not thought that real
property, intellectual property or choses in action are intended to be within the
mischief of these provisions of the Act.[1]

---

1   But see Chapter 6 in respect of discrimination in relation to premises and the provisions of
    ss 22–24 discussed there.

Facilities

5.3.4 The term 'facilities' is again not defined within the Act. A literal
meaning of this term suggests that the statute is concerned with discrimination
in the provision or supply to disabled persons of equipment or physical means
for doing something. An example which readily suggests itself would concern a
service provider in the public telecommunications sector. The provision of a
telephone handset clearly involves the provision of 'goods'. The supply of a
telephone line link to the national network whereby a person can make and
receive telephone calls is the provision of a 'service'. The means by which the
service provider then bills that person for the provision of the goods and the
service, and the medium by which the customer may settle that account, would
amount to 'facilities'.

5.3.5 The distinction being sought to be made here is undoubtedly an
artificial one. It is probable, therefore, that the term 'facilities' is included in
the legislation to embrace any matter which is obviously neither goods nor
services and yet the refusal of which involves a denial of a legitimate right or
interest of the individual or persons generally. Furthermore, the distinction
may not matter, because the illustrations in the Act of what amounts to
'services' appear to encompass 'facilities' also.[1]

1   See **5.3.6**.

Services

5.3.6   We are on firmer ground in respect of 'services' because the Act provides in s 19(3) a non-exhaustive list of examples of services to which the legislation applies. These examples are as follows:

- access to and use of any place which members of the public are permitted to enter;
- access to and use of means of communication;
- access to and use of information services;
- accommodation in a hotel, boarding house or other similar establishment;
- facilities by way of banking or insurance or for grants, loans, credit or finance;
- facilities for entertainment, recreation or refreshment;
- facilities provided by employment agencies;
- facilities provided under s 2 of the Employment and Training Act 1973 or under ss 1–2 of the Employment and Training Act (Northern Ireland) 1950;[1]
- the services of any profession or trade, or any local or other public authority.

For example, a shop, restaurant, theatre, cinema or nightclub which refused access to a wheelchair-user or other disabled person would clearly fall within s 19(3).

1   See Sch 8, para 9(1).

5.3.7   However, it would seem that a private members' club (and organisations such as trade unions) would not be covered by Part III of the Act because of s 19(2)(b),[1] and such clubs (and organisations) would be free to discriminate against disabled persons seeking membership or access.[2] Nevertheless, even a private membership club will be subject to Part III obligations if it uses its premises to provide some services of a public nature. For example, a private golf club that provided facilities to non-members for wedding receptions could not lawfully discriminate against a disabled wedding guest.

1   See **5.3.11** and see Rights of Access Code of Practice, para 2.6.
2   See the case-law to like effect under the now repealed provisions of the Race Relations Act 1968: *Dockers Labour Club and Institute Ltd v Race Relations Board* [1976] AC 285; *Charter v Race Relations Board* [1973] AC 885. Cf Race Relations Act 1976, s 25 and *Applin v Race Relations Board* [1975] AC 259. Note that discrimination by trade organisations will be caught by ss 13–15.

5.3.8   The illustrative definition of services covered by Part III of the Act indicates that a wide range of establishments and businesses will be covered by the new right of access. Without intending to exhaust the possibilities, these will include hotels, restaurants, public houses, bars, cinemas, theatres, concert halls, sports stadia and facilities (such as public golf courses or bowling alleys), zoos, parks, amusement parks, museums, galleries, libraries, auditoria, convention or conference centres, shops, department stores, fast food outlets, shopping centres, showrooms, other retail or rental outlets, banks, post offices, service stations, hairdressers, hospitals, clinics and dental surgeries.

Also encompassed will be the offices of professionals providing services to the public (such as solicitors and accountants), the offices and facilities of local and public authorities (such as town halls or day care centres), public transport terminals or stations, and the services offered by public utilities (such as gas, electricity, water and telephone companies). Note, however, that it is not the businesses or establishments as such which trigger the Act's provisions, but rather the goods, facilities or services which are there provided. Furthermore, it is the public nature of the services provided that causes these businesses or establishments to be subject to the new order of accessibility.[1]

---

1   See Rights of Access Code of Practice, para 2.7.

5.3.9   Several unsuccessful attempts were made in the legislative process to add to the list of adumbrated services so as to include access to civic rights and duties, health services, broadcasting, the judicial system and legal proceedings, careers services, trade unions and employers' associations, trade and professional associations, and qualifying bodies.[1] The Minister explained that the Government's intention was:

> 'to provide a universal, all-embracing right of non-discrimination against disabled people that is applicable to all providers of goods, facilities and services to the general public ... [and that] service providers will be required to remove or alter physical or communication barriers and amend policies, procedures and practices that prevent disabled people using a service, and to provide auxiliary aids and services, where they are reasonably required.'[2]

In that light, the list of services contained in s 19(3) is not exhaustive.

---

1   Trade unions, employers' associations, trade associations and professional associations are the subject of ss 13–15 of Part II of the Act. See Chapter 4.
2   HC Deb Standing Committee E, cols 290–291 (Mr W. Hague, Minister for Disabled People).

5.3.10   The Minister confirmed that facilities for telecommunication, the judicial system and legal proceedings, and broadcasting services were intended to be covered,[1] as also are medical and health services.[2] So, for example, television companies will be expected to consider whether further teletext and subtitling services need to be introduced in the future.[3] In respect of careers services, this might be partly affected by the exclusion of education from the Act, although clearly training is within the statute's remit. In the House of Lords, the Minister explained what steps were being taken to make the justice system accessible to disabled persons, but confirmed that Part III does not apply to service as a juror or witness.[4] He also stated that Members of Parliament are within Part III in respect of their constituency duties.

---

1   HC Deb Standing Committee E, cols 292–293 (Mr W. Hague).
2   HL Deb, vol 564, col 1952 (Lord Mackay of Ardbrecknish).
3   Note the provisions of the Broadcasting Act 1990 in this regard and see also HL Deb, vol 566, cols 269–271 (Lord Mackay of Ardbrecknish).
4   HL Deb, vol 566, cols 259–262 (Lord Mackay of Ardbrecknish).

Provider of services

5.3.11   Section 19 (and, indeed, ss 19–21 in general) applies to 'a provider of services' and, as we have seen, this applies equally to a party who provides goods or facilities, whether on payment or without payment (ss 19(2)(a) and (c)). A person is 'a provider of services' only if that person is concerned with the provision of services 'to the public or to a section of the public' (s 19(2)(b)).[1] The relevant provision of services must also be one which is within the UK. The use of the word 'person' will include legal entities (such as companies or local authorities) as well as individuals or associations of individuals (such as trade unions or partnerships). It is clear, for example, that Part III will embrace the provision of services to the public or community by local and other public authorities.[2] Unlike in respect of the employment provisions in Part II, there is no exemption from Part III for small businesses.

---

1   As to how this might apply to private membership clubs, see **5.3.7**.
2   HL Deb, vol 565, col 672 (Lord Inglewood).

5.3.12   Part III of the Act plainly does not apply to manufacturers and producers unless they directly supply goods or services to members of the public.[1] While such persons might wish to consider how they might comply with the spirit of the legislation, they are not directly subject to its letter. There is no obligation upon manufacturers or producers of goods or services (who are not also direct suppliers to the public) to consider the accessibility of the design, labelling or packaging of those goods or services to disabled consumers. For example, there is no legal obligation upon manufacturers under the new law to include any user instructions bundled with goods or products in accessible formats (such as braille, large print or audio-visual medium) and there would appear to be no such duty placed upon the retail supplier either.[2]

---

1 HL Deb, vol 566, cols 241–242 (Lord Mackay of Ardbrecknish).
2 See, for example, the views of Lord Mackay of Ardbrecknish at HL Deb, vol 566, col 251.

To whom the service is provided

5.3.13 It is clear that Part III of the Act only addresses discrimination in the provision of goods, facilities or services to disabled persons as consumers themselves. It does not cover the provision of goods, facilities or services to a disabled person as a representative of another person (for example as parent, guardian or carer). Equally, it does not directly address discrimination against a person because of that individual's relationship to or association with a disabled person (perhaps as a spouse, parent or friend). Members of a family who are refused service in a restaurant because they are accompanied by a child with disabilities have no remedy under the Act (although the child will also have been discriminated against and will have a cause of action).

5.4 EXCLUSION OF EDUCATION, TRANSPORT AND OTHER PRESCRIBED SERVICES

5.4.1 Section 19(5) excludes education and transport from the scope of the anti-discrimination provisions in respect of the provision of goods, facilities or services contained in ss 19–21 of Part III of the Act. Instead, Part IV and Part V of the Act contain a number of provisions designed to improve and ensure the right of access of disabled persons to education and public transport. The scope of the exclusion of education and transport from Part III of the Act is considered in Chapters 7 and 8, where a discussion of the new standards and regulations on accessibility will also be found.

5.4.2 Section 19(5)(c) further provides that ss 19–21 of the Act do not apply to 'such other services' as may be prescribed by regulations made by the Secretary of State. The Disability Discrimination (Services and Premises) Regulations 1996, reg 9 is relevant here. The regulation provides that ss 19–21 do not apply to certain youth and community services provided by education authorities or voluntary organisations, to the provision of facilities for research in certain circumstances, and to some examination and assessment services. These exemptions are considered in more detail in Chapter 7.[1]

---

1 See also Rights of Access Code of Practice, para 2.9.

5.5 MEANING OF DISCRIMINATION

5.5.1 Section 19 makes it unlawful for a provider of services to 'discriminate' against a disabled person in a number respects in relation to goods, facilities and services. What does 'discriminate' mean for this purpose and in this context? The meaning of discrimination in the context of Part III of the Act is set out in s 20. Although the definition in s 20 is similar to the definition in ss 5 and 14, which has been previously explained,[1] the latter definitions are supplied for the purposes of Part II of the Act (discrimination in employment or by trade organisations). Decisions and judicial interpretation appertaining to ss 5 and 14 will be of assistance in applying the parallel definition in s 20, but care must be taken to ensure that in Part III cases relating to discrimination in the provision of goods, facilities or services direct reference is made to the wording of s 20 itself.

---

1   See Chapters 3–4.

Direct discrimination

5.5.2   A provider of services discriminates against a disabled person if, for a reason which relates to the disabled person's disability, the service provider treats the disabled person less favourably than the service provider treats or would treat others to whom the reason which relates to the disabled person's disability does not or would not apply, and the service provider cannot show that the less favourable treatment in question is justified (s 20(1)).[1]

---

1   See the example provided in Rights of Access Code of Practice, para 2.12.

5.5.3   Apart from the defence of justification, this is a definition of direct discrimination broadly comparable with the definition with which we are already familiar from the Sex Discrimination Act 1975 and the Race Relations Act 1976. However, the use of the phrase 'for a reason which relates to the disabled person's disability' in s 20(1)(a) suggests a more flexible test of discrimination than in those prior contexts. The Minister stated that this phraseology makes 'it clear that if a disabled person is refused service – for example, in a café – for a reason connected with his disability, where non-disabled people are happily served', that will be a *prima facie* case of discrimination, subject to any defence of justification.[1]

---

1   HL Deb, vol 566, col 120 (Lord Henley, Minister of State, Department for Education and Employment).

5.5.4   The concept of discrimination here proscribed clearly requires proof that the disabled person has been treated less favourably than other persons to whom the reason related to disability does not apply. This calls for a comparison of how the disabled person was treated relative to such other persons. The question is not merely whether the disabled person has experienced poor, inadequate or sub-standard provision in respect of goods, facilities or services.[1] Rather, the issue is whether there has been differential and unfavourable treatment of the disabled person in circumstances where other persons (to whom the reason related to disability does not apply) have not been so treated.

---

1   Rights of Access Code of Practice, para 2.14.

5.5.5   The comparator is another member of the public (or a hypothetical member of the public).[1] This might include a person with a disability of a different kind from the complainant because the wording of the Act does not appear to rule out the unlawfulness of differential treatment by service providers among disabled persons themselves. For example, if a group of variously disabled senior citizens sought to gain admission to a restaurant, but the restaurateur refused to allow admission to the one member of the party using a wheelchair, while admitting his or her disabled colleagues, that could be unlawful discrimination, all other things being equal. It would be no defence to argue that the restaurant had admitted disabled persons. The individual would have been less favourably treated in comparison with other members of the public.

---

1   Rights of Access Code of Practice, para 2.13.

5.5.6   The less favourable treatment must be related to the disabled person's disability. While the intention, purpose or motive with which the service provider acted is irrelevant, there must be a causal connection between the discriminatory action and the complainant's disability.[1] A disabled person who is refused admission to a cinema because he or she does not have the means to pay for entry, or who is refused service in a public house because he or she is drunk and disorderly, has not been discriminated against contrary to the Act.[2] The reason for the apparently less favourable treatment is not that person's disability, but rather a reason which is unrelated to disability. Indeed, in any event, in these illustrations it is doubtful whether there has been less favourable treatment at all, because the service provider might be able to show that any member of the public in like circumstances would have been treated in the same way.

1   Rights of Access Code of Practice, para 2.15.
2   Ibid, para 2.16.

5.5.7   Unlawful discrimination will have occurred if the above conditions are satisfied and the service provider cannot demonstrate that the less favourable treatment is justified. The defence of justification is a statutory one and is set out in s 20(3) of the Act. However, at this point, it should be noted that the defence of justification goes beyond the inherent defence, just discussed, of showing that the differential treatment was not informed by or connected with the disabled person's disability. The statutory defence of justification is discussed below.[1]

1   See **5.6**.

Indirect discrimination

5.5.8   A service provider who makes the provision of goods, facilities or services subject to a requirement or condition, which a smaller proportion of disabled persons than non-disabled persons can meet, could be said to have *indirectly* discriminated against disabled persons if they suffer a detriment as a result and the service provider cannot justify the imposition of the requirement or condition in issue. The Act does not contain an explicit prohibition on indirect discrimination in relation to goods, facilities and services, unlike the comparable provisions of the Sex Discrimination Act 1975 and the Race Relations Act 1976.

5.5.9   The 1994 Green Paper took the view that indirect discrimination would be 'more difficult to tackle effectively where disabled people are involved because disability occurs in many forms' and should not be the subject of legislation.[1] That view was reiterated in the 1995 White Paper which stated that 'a general prohibition of indirect discrimination ... could have unforeseen consequences which were unfairly burdensome for businesses'.[2] However, the Government accepted that certain practices, which had an indirect effect upon the right of disabled persons to access to goods, facilities or services, should be prevented.

The White Paper gives the specific example of a service provider banning animals from its premises and the disproportionate adverse effect this would have on persons with visual impairments who rely upon guide dogs. This would be a case that would clearly call for reasonable practical adjustments or modifications to be made by the service provider under s 21 of the Act.[3] While many incidents of indirect discrimination in relation to goods, facilities or services will be caught by the 'less favourable treatment' formula contained in s 20,[4] s 21 will assume even greater importance as a means to prevent (or to require the adjustment of) unjustifiable practices, rules, policies, requirements or conditions which have a harsh or adverse impact upon access by disabled persons.

---

1   Green Paper para 4.11.
2   White Paper para 4.5.
3   See **5.7**. Section 21 is not yet in force.
4   See **5.5.2**.

Failure to make reasonable adjustments

5.5.10   When in force, s 21 will place a duty on service providers to remove or alter physical and communication barriers; to amend policies, procedures and practices which prevent disabled persons using a service; and to provide auxiliary aids or services. This duty to make adjustments is the subject of more detailed exposition below.[1] However, for present purposes, it should be noted that a breach of this duty does not give rise to a cause of action in itself (s 21(10)), but is deemed to amount to discrimination against a disabled person in the absence of justification (s 20(2)). In other words, a failure to make reasonable adjustments will be a further category of disability discrimination prohibited by and actionable under the Act (by virtue of s 19(1)(b)).

---

1   See **5.7**.

Victimisation

5.5.11   Section 55 of the Act classifies 'victimisation' as unlawful discrimination for present purposes. This is dealt with further in Chapter 10. An act of victimisation contrary to s 55 will constitute an act of discrimination for the purposes of discrimination in relation to goods, facilities and services and will provide a cause of action, whether or not the person victimised is a disabled person. This is achieved on the face of ss 19–21 by virtue of s 19(4).

5.6   DEFENCE OF JUSTIFICATION

5.6.1   The justification defence in Part III of the Act differs significantly from the parallel defence in Part II of the statute (the employment provisions). The Government's view was that 'service providers often have to take very quick and perhaps less informed decisions when serving someone [so that] an opinion-based approach remains appropriate'.[1] The Part III defence also exhaustively identifies the key reasons that might justify less favourable treatment of a disabled person by a service provider.[2]

---

1 HL Deb, vol 566, col 119 (Lord Henley).
2 No other form of justification is available: Rights of Access Code of Practice, para 5.1.

5.6.2 A provider of services discriminates against a disabled person in the circumstances described by the Act if it cannot show that the discriminatory 'treatment in question is justified' (s 20(1)(b)). The discriminatory treatment of a disabled person will be justified *only if*, in the service provider's opinion, one or more statutory conditions are satisfied (s 20(3)(a)) *and* it is reasonable in all the circumstances of the case for the service provider to hold that opinion (s 20(3)(b)).[1] The justification defence in Part III of the Disability Discrimination Act is novel in at least three senses.

---

1 Future regulations may provide for circumstances in which it is reasonable (or not reasonable) for a service provider to hold a s 20(3)(a) opinion (s 20(6)).

5.6.3 First, existing anti-discrimination law in the fields of sex, race and equal pay discrimination (and fair employment legislation in Northern Ireland) does not contain an explicit justification defence to *direct* discrimination (as opposed to *indirect* discrimination). Given the Government's view that indirect discrimination against disabled persons would largely be caught by the prohibition on direct discrimination, the importing of a justification defence might be seen as regrettable, but inevitable.

5.6.4 Secondly, in any event, it might be argued that a justification defence is implicit in the principle of direct discrimination, in the sense that a respondent can always seek to show that the less favourable treatment complained of was not based upon the sex or race or protected characteristic of the plaintiff and, accordingly, was justifiable by reference to facially neutral factors (such as merit, ability, conduct, etc). However, properly understood, the justification defence is only truly relevant when the race or sex or protected characteristic of the plaintiff has played a part (usually unintentionally) in the resultant discrimination, but there are factors or criteria present which nevertheless excuse what would be otherwise discriminatory treatment, impacts or effects.

It is clear from the wording of s 20 that the defence of justification is only relevant where a disabled person has been treated less favourably 'for a reason which relates to the disabled person's disability' (s 20(1)(a)). In other words, a service provider may be allowed to justify discrimination in circumstances where the less favourable treatment has been informed by the complainant's disability.

5.6.5 Thirdly, in existing discrimination legislation, the justification defence available in instances of *indirect* discrimination is always the subject of an objective test, albeit one of variable quality in the decided cases. Part III of the Disability Discrimination Act 1995 bucks that trend and might be seen in some quarters as a worrying development.

Subjective opinion and objective reasonableness

5.6.6 The justification defence in Part III of the 1995 Act is in fact based upon a mixture of a subjective test and an objective test. While an opinion-based approach has been seen as appropriate, 'the proper degree of objectivity is imposed because the opinion must be shown to be reasonably held'.[1] The Rights of Access Code of Practice states that a service provider does not have to be an expert on disability, but is expected to take account of all the circumstances, including the information available to it, at the time.[2]

---

1   HL Deb, vol 566, col 119 (Lord Henley).
2   Rights of Access Code of Practice, para 5.2 and see the contrasting examples given there. The burden of proof of the justification defence is upon the service provider: ibid, para 5.3.

5.6.7 The service provider must be able to show that at the time of the act of discrimination it actually held the opinion that one of the statutory conditions for the operation of the defence was satisfied (a subjective test). The language and tense used in s 20(3)(a) makes it clear that it is the service provider's opinion at the time of the discriminatory treatment that matters. An *ex post facto* rationalisation of events will not be sufficient or permissible. Nevertheless, in practice, the subjective test of opinion will not be difficult to pass.

5.6.8 However, it must also be shown that it is reasonable, in all the circumstances of the case, for the service provider to hold that opinion (an objective test). Again, it would appear that the test of the reasonableness of the service provider's subjectively held opinion should be judged in the light of the circumstances of the case as known at the time of the discriminatory act (s 20(3)(b)).

5.6.9 The concept of reasonableness is one that the tribunals and courts are very experienced in applying. It will not be the reasonableness of the opinion itself that matters, however, but rather whether it was reasonable of the particular service provider to hold that opinion in the particular circumstances of the case and in respect of the particular disabled person who is the subject of the less favourable treatment. The wording of s 20(3)(b) does not appear to admit a test of reasonableness based upon what a reasonable service provider faced with similar circumstances might have opined, although undoubtedly that will be a useful starting point.

In applying the concept of reasonableness under s 20(3)(b) especial care must be taken to note that the subsection is judging whether it was reasonable for the service provider to hold the opinion and not whether the opinion itself was reasonable or whether the actions of the service provider were reasonable.

Conditions for justification defence

5.6.10 The conditions, one or more of which, in the service provider's reasonably held opinion, must be satisfied for the operation of the statutory defence of justification, are set out in s 20(4). Some of these conditions apply generally, but some apply only in the context of particular forms of discrimination in relation to goods, facilities or services. The Act contemplates five conditions or circumstances in which the justification defence might be operable.

Health or safety

5.6.11 First, in any case, disability discrimination might be justified where the less favourable treatment is 'necessary' (not merely reasonably necessary) in order not to endanger the health or safety of any person (s 20(4)(a)). This may include endangerment to the health or safety of the disabled person who is alleging discriminatory treatment. For example, a local authority recreation centre could be justified in refusing the use of its indoor climbing wall to a person with orthopaedic impairment, or in excluding a wheelchair-user from its basketball league, on the ground of a risk to the health and safety of the individual or other participants. A swimming instructor might be justified in excluding a disabled person from a beginners' swimming class if, by having to focus most attention on the disabled learner, the safety of other members of the class would be put at risk.[1]

---

1 HL Deb, vol 566, col 1025 (Lord Mackay of Ardbrecknish). See the further examples given in Rights of Access Code of Practice, para 5.5.

5.6.12 It remains to be seen how narrowly this defence of justification will be interpreted and applied in practice. Health or safety risk has been often relied upon by service providers as a blanket reason for excluding disabled persons from places of refreshment or entertainment (such as cinemas, theatres and restaurants). Reference is also frequently made to the requirements of fire regulations.[1] The use of the word 'necessary' in s 20(4)(a) will call for individual justification on the facts where a service provider seeks to rely upon health and safety as the grounds for compromising the civil rights of disabled citizens.[2]

---

1 Restrictions produced by genuine requirements of local fire regulations will excuse otherwise discriminatory treatment by virtue of s 59 (actions done in pursuance of a statutory authority).
2 See Rights of Access Code of Practice, paras 5.6–5.7.

Incapacity to contract

5.6.13 Secondly, in any case, the less favourable treatment of a disabled person can be justified if the disabled person is incapable of entering into an enforceable agreement, or of giving an informed consent, and for that reason the treatment is reasonable in that case (s 20(4)(b)). Regulations have been made under s 20(7) to disapply the effect of s 20(4)(b) in certain circumstances.[1] The deemed justification of treatment under s 20(4)(b) where a disabled person is incapable of entering into an enforceable agreement (or giving informed consent) does not apply where the disabled person is acting through another person by virtue of a power of attorney or functions conferred by or under Part VII of the Mental Health Act 1983. It also does not apply, in Scotland, in respect of powers exercisable in relation to the disabled person's property or affairs in consequence of the appointment of a curator bonis, tutor or judicial factor.

---

1   Disability Discrimination (Services and Premises) Regulations 1996, reg 8 and see Rights of Access Code of Practice, para 5.10.

5.6.14 Section 20(4)(b) generated some concern on behalf of persons with mental disabilities who, it was feared, might suffer discrimination in the provision of goods, facilities or services on the basis of a service provider's perception that they lacked full legal capacity to make a contract. The Government's view is that:

> 'If a service provider has a reasonably held belief that a contract with a disabled customer might be invalid, he must be allowed, under this measure, to refuse to enter into an agreement until it is reasonably clear that it would be enforceable, without the fear of being accused of discrimination'.[1]

That would allow a trader to refuse to sell goods to, or to enter into a consumer credit agreement with, a disabled person if the trader holds a reasonably held opinion that the customer lacks or might lack legal capacity (whether by virtue of age or mental incapacity).[2] The test here is whether it is reasonable to discriminate within the particular circumstances of the case.[3]

---

1   HC Deb Standing Committee E, col 349 (Mr W. Hague).
2   Rights of Access Code of Practice, paras 5.8–5.9. Unless there is clear evidence to the contrary, a service provider should assume that a disabled person is able to enter into a contract.
3   HC Deb, vol 257, col 893 (Mr W. Hague).

5.6.15 However, the Minister's view is that this exception or justification will only apply when the purchase of a product or service would normally be the subject of a written agreement or contract formality. It would thus apply in only a few cases (such as motor car hire purchase or consumer credit agreements).[1]

It remains to be seen whether such cases are few (but what of contracts for holidays, which are typically made on written standard form conditions, for example, or car rental agreements?). Furthermore, the Minister doubted whether it would be reasonable for a shopkeeper to rely upon this exception when someone is buying a newspaper or confectionery (as opposed to a luxury car).[2]

1   HC Deb, vol 257, col 350 (Mr W. Hague).
2   HC Deb, vol 257, col 893 (Mr W. Hague).

Providing the service

5.6.16   Thirdly, where disability discrimination takes the form of a refusal or deliberate omission to provide to a disabled person any goods, facilities or services provided to members of the public,[1] such less favourable treatment might be justified if it is 'necessary' (not merely reasonably necessary) because the service provider would otherwise be unable to provide the goods, facilities or services in issue to members of the public (s 20(4)(c)). The 1995 White Paper gave as an example that it would no longer be possible to bar disabled persons from places of entertainment, but a coach training champion athletes would still be able to exclude the majority of the population from coaching classes.[2]

1   Under s 19(1)(a) as discussed at **5.2.2**.
2   White Paper para 4.4. See also the example given in Rights of Access Code of Practice, para 5.11.

5.6.17   The Government believes that it has introduced a strict test for the application of this defence. The Minister for Disabled People stated that s 20(4)(c) 'applies only in circumstances in which, if a service provider were to serve a particular disabled person, he would not be able to continue to provide his service at all'.[1] The Minister could not think of a meaningful example of when this provision would be applicable and his opinion was that it would only apply in extreme and rare circumstances.

It would not be enough, for example, that a disabled person had caused an inconvenient queue of other customers to form behind him or her in a department store because he or she had a communication difficulty which caused delay in advising the sales assistant of his or her requirements. The service provider might be irritated by that, but could not use this as a reason to justify refusing to continue serving that disabled person.[2] Similarly, a public house could not refuse to serve a party of customers with visible disabilities because other customers might object to their presence. The preferences of other customers is not a justification for discrimination.

1   HC Deb Standing Committee E, col 354 (Mr W. Hague).
2   See Rights of Access Code of Practice, para 5.13.

Standard of service

5.6.18   Fourthly, in a case where the discriminatory treatment arises in the standard of service provided to disabled persons, or the manner in which or terms on which the service provider provides goods, facilities or services to disabled persons,[1] that treatment may be justifiable if it is 'necessary' (not merely reasonably necessary) in order for the service provider to be able to provide the service to the disabled person or to other members of the public (s 20(4)(d)). This is clearly linked to the third condition above and is likely to apply in exactly the same way, if at all.

By way of illustration, a cinema which reserves seats at the end of rows for persons with mobility disabilities might rely upon this provision to justify what might amount to a differential standard or manner or service. Without making such arrangements, the cinema might argue that it could not admit such a disabled person at all without infringing fire regulations or would otherwise cause greater inconvenience to other customers. Similarly, a museum which provides a daily guided tour of its exhibits might be justified in rostering a guide with sign language skills to assist deaf visitors only on specified days of the week.[2]

1   Under s 19(1)(c)–(d) as discussed at **5.2.4–5.2.6**.
2   See the further example in Rights of Access Code of Practice, para 5.12.

Greater expense

5.6.19   Fifthly, if the service provider has discriminated in the terms on which goods, facilities or services are provided to a disabled person,[1] that discrimination is capable of being justified where the difference in such terms as between that disabled person and other members of the public 'reflects the greater cost' to the service provider in providing the goods, facilities or services to the disabled person (s 20(4)(e)).

The Minister for Disabled People indicated that this measure is aimed at small businesses in particular, and gave as an example a shoe maker asked to make a shoe for a disabled person to an unusual design or in an unusual fabric.[2] If that task would involve greater labour or special equipment and materials, it might be reasonable for the shoe maker to charge the disabled customer a premium to reflect that.

1   Under s 19(1)(d) as discussed at **5.2.5–5.2.6**.

2   HC Deb Standing Committee E, col 357 (Mr W. Hague). See also the similar example given by Lord Mackay of Ardbrecknish: HL Deb, vol 564, col 2009. See further the example given in Rights of Access Code of Practice, para 5.14.

5.6.20   Taken literally, however, this last condition in s 20(4)(e) might justify a hotelier charging a disabled person a room supplement for providing him or her with a room adapted to take a wheelchair or with an audio-visual fire alarm. It might also justify a services supplier charging blind consumers for the additional cost of providing braille or tape formats of sales literature and so on.

Nevertheless, the Government has clarified this point by stating that a service provider who attempts to pass on the costs of compliance with the Act to disabled persons (as opposed to spreading those costs across all customers or clients) would not be facilitated in doing so by s 20(4)(e).[1] An assurance was given that the Act does not permit surcharges upon disabled persons for extra expenses or opportunity costs incurred by service providers in complying with the new legislation.

1   HC Deb Standing Committee E, col 357 (Mr W. Hague).

5.6.21   Moreover, s 20(5) provides that any increase in the cost of providing a service (or goods or facilities) to a disabled person, which results from the service provider's compliance with a s 21 duty to make reasonable adjustments, is to be disregarded for the purposes of s 20(4)(e). Service providers will thus not be able directly to pass on to disabled customers the costs of complying with their duties under the new legislation.[1]

1   HL Deb, vol 564, cols 2009–2010 (Lord Mackay of Ardbrecknish); HL Deb, vol 566, col 119 (Lord Henley). Section 21 is not yet in force.

Insurance services

5.6.22   The Act contemplates that regulations might be made under s 20(8) so as to provide for other circumstances in which less favourable treatment of a disabled person for a reason relating to disability could be deemed to be justified for the purposes of s 20. Regulations address the circumstances where, for a reason which relates to a disabled person's disability, a provider of insurance services (in connection with an insurance business[1] carried on by it) has treated a disabled person less favourably than it treats or would treat others to whom that reason does not or would not apply.[2] That treatment is to be taken as justified under s 20 if it is based upon information which is relevant to the assessment of the risk to be insured and if it is reasonable having regard to the information relied upon and any other relevant factors.[3] The information, which might include actuarial or statistical data or a medical report, must be from a source upon which it is reasonable to rely.[4]

This provision recognises that insurers may need to distinguish between individuals on the basis of the risks against which they seek to insure.[5] The burden of proof will be upon the insurer to show that there was an additional risk associated with the disabled person which arises from his or her disability. Transitional provision is made for existing policies of insurance.[6] In effect, any treatment in relation to an insurance policy which existed before the regulations came into force on 2 December 1996 is automatically taken to be justified until it falls for renewal or review on or after 2 December 1996,[7] after which time it falls to be treated under s 20 and reg 2. Transitional provisions are also made in respect of cover documents and master policies.[8]

---

1 Within the meaning of the Insurance Companies Act 1982.
2 Disability Discrimination (Services and Premises) Regulations 1996, regs 1(2), 2(1) and 2(2)(a).
3 Ibid, regs 2(1) and 2(2)(b)–(c).
4 Ibid, reg 2(2)(b).
5 Rights of Access Code of Practice, para 5.19.
6 Disability Discrimination (Services and Premises) Regulations 1996, reg 3. An existing policy of insurance is one that incepted before 2 December 1996 (ie the time when the liability to risk of the insurer or insurance company under the policy of insurance commenced): regs 1(2) and 3(4); and see Insurance Companies Act 1982, s 96.
7 Ibid, reg 3(2). A review of an existing policy as part of a general reassessment of the pricing structure for a group of policies is not a review for this purpose: reg 3(3).
8 Ibid, reg 4.

Guarantees and deposits

5.6.23 Regulations made under s 20(8) deal with guarantees where, for a reason which relates to a disabled person's disability, a service provider treats that person less favourably in respect of a guarantee than it treats or would treat others to whom that reason does not or would not apply.[1] The guarantee, whether legally enforceable or not, must have been provided by the service provider. It must guarantee that the purchase price of services provided will be refunded if not of satisfactory quality or that services in the form of goods provided will be replaced or repaired if not of satisfactory quality.[2] The service provider must have refused to provide a replacement, repair or refund under the guarantee because damage (above the level at which the guarantee would normally be honoured) has occurred for a reason which relates to the disabled person's disability.[3] It must be reasonable in all the circumstances of the case for the service provider to refuse to provide a replacement, repair or refund under the guarantee.[4] If all these conditions are satisfied, the less favourable treatment is deemed to be automatically justified under s 20.[5] Accordingly, this provision deals with situations where a disabled person's disability results in higher than average wear and tear to goods or services supplied and where it would not be reasonable to expect service providers to honour a guarantee.[6]

Section 20(8) regulations also deal with the question of deposits in respect of goods and facilities.[7] The circumstances in which this special provision operates are as follows. Goods or facilities have been provided to a disabled person for which that person is required to provide a deposit which is refundable if the goods or facilities are returned undamaged.[8] The service provider has refused to refund some or all of the deposit because damage has occurred to the goods or facilities for a reason which relates to the disabled person's disability.[9] That damage is above the level at which the provider would normally refund the deposit in full.[10] If it is reasonable in all the circumstances of the case for the service provider to refuse to repay the deposit in full,[11] then that less favourable treatment (for a reason related to disability) is deemed to be justified for the purposes of s 20.[12]

1 Disability Discrimination (Services and Premises) Regulations 1996, reg 5(1).
2 Ibid, reg 5(2)(a). A guarantee includes any document which has the effect referred to in reg 5(2)(a), whether or not so described: reg 5(3).
3 Ibid, reg 5(2)(b).
4 Ibid, reg 5(2)(c).
5 Ibid, reg 5(1).
6 Rights of Access Code of Practice, para 5.20.
7 Disability Discrimination (Services and Premises) Regulations 1996, reg 6.
8 Ibid, reg 6(2)(a).
9 Ibid, reg 6(2)(b).
10 Ibid, reg 6(2)(b).
11 Ibid, reg 6(2)(c).
12 Ibid, reg 6(1).

Justification and the duty to make adjustments

5.6.24 Where a service provider has subjected a disabled person to an act amounting to less favourable treatment and is itself also subject to the duty to make reasonable adjustments under s 21, the act of discrimination is nevertheless capable of being excused by an application of the justification defence in accordance with s 20. However, s 20(2) makes it clear that a service provider also discriminates against a disabled person for the purposes of s 19 if it fails to comply with a duty to make reasonable adjustments, unless the service provider can show that the failure to comply with that duty is justified. That is a quite separate form of discrimination from mere less favourable treatment.[1]

1 These provisions are not yet in force.

5.6.25 What is not immediately clear from the drafting of s 20 is what is the test of justification in the case of discrimination arising from a failure to comply with a s 21 duty to make reasonable adjustments? This lack of clarity is the product of the radical redrafting of the justification defence during the passage of the Bill in the House of Lords. Section 20(3) defines the circumstances in which 'treatment' might be justified by reference to the conditions in s 20(4).[1] However, the need to justify 'treatment' can only logically arise in cases of discrimination falling under s 20(1). Section 20(2) defines discrimination by reference to a failure to comply with a s 21 duty to make reasonable adjustments and the term 'treatment' is not used in that context.

---

1 See **5.6.10–5.6.23**.

5.6.26 It is suggested that s 20 has to be read as a whole. The commonsense interpretation of this section would suggest two conclusions. First, in cases of less favourable treatment discrimination, a service provider should not be able to justify discrimination without first demonstrating compliance or attempted compliance with a s 21 duty to make reasonable adjustments. Secondly, discrimination in the form of a failure to comply with the statutory duty to make reasonable adjustments may be justifiable if the service provider reasonably holds the opinion that one of the statutory conditions for the justification defence are satisfied.[1] This interpretation accords with the literal wording of the section. Section 20(9) states that in subsections (3), (4) and (8) 'treatment' includes a failure to comply with a s 21 duty.

---

1 Applying the test of justification in s 20(3) to cases falling under s 20(2) and cross-referring to the conditions in s 20(4).

5.7   DUTY TO MAKE REASONABLE ADJUSTMENTS

5.7.1 The keystone to the new rights of access contained in Part III of the Act is the statutory duty placed upon service providers by s 21 to make reasonable adjustments to allow disabled persons meaningful access to the provision of goods, facilities and services provided to the public. A breach of the duty to make reasonable adjustments is not actionable in itself (s 21(10)). Accordingly, a failure to observe the duty on the part of a service provider does not give an aggrieved disabled person a common law right in tort to sue for breach of a statutory duty. Nevertheless, the duty to make reasonable adjustments, as defined in s 21, is important for determining whether a service provider has discriminated against a disabled person (s 21(10)) and a failure to comply with the statutory duty is treated as amounting to discrimination against the disabled person (s 20(2)). Such a failure is potentially an unlawful act of discrimination (s 19(1)(b)). At the time of writing, the provisions on the duty to make reasonable adjustments have not been brought into force.

5.7.2 The 1995 White Paper proposed that it would not be enough simply to prohibit discriminatory behaviour. Legislation would also require 'positive action which is reasonable and readily achievable to overcome the physical and communication barriers that impede disabled people's access'.[1] This would mean that policies, practices and procedures which discriminated against disabled persons would have to be prohibited, unless fundamental to the nature of the business. Auxiliary aids and services (such as information on tape for blind customers or induction loops in places of entertainment for individuals with hearing disabilities) would have to be provided, if this was reasonable and readily achievable. Physical barriers might also have to be removed or alternative means of access be provided.

---

1   White Paper para 4.4.

General duty of providers of services to make adjustments

5.7.3   Section 21 of the Act places a general duty on service providers to amend policies, procedures and practices which prevent disabled persons using a service; to remove or alter physical and communication barriers; and to provide auxiliary aids or services. The detail of this duty is now revealed. It is clear that the general duty contains three aspects, as discussed below.

Practices, policies or procedures

5.7.4   First, the duty to make reasonable adjustments applies in the circumstances described by s 21(1). This duty will potentially apply where a provider of goods, facilities or services has a 'practice, policy or procedure' which makes it 'impossible or unreasonably difficult' for disabled persons to make use of goods, facilities or services which the service provider provides or is prepared to provide to other members of the public. In such a case, it is the duty of the service provider 'to take such steps as it is reasonable, in all the circumstances of the case', for the service provider to have to take 'in order to change' the policy, practice or procedure in question so that 'it no longer has' the effect described (that is, impossible or unreasonably difficult access for disabled persons to the goods, facilities or services in point).

Regulations may make provision, for these purposes, as to the circumstances in which it is reasonable (or alternatively, not reasonable) for a service provider to have to take steps of a prescribed description (s 21(5)(a)–(b)). Moreover, such regulations may prescribe what is to be included or not included within the meaning of a 'practice, policy or procedure' (s 21(5)(c)–(d)). No such regulations have been made at the time of writing.

5.7.5   Apart from the promised regulations, the Act provides no further guidance or interpretation as to the meaning of the duty in s 21(1) or its component parts. Neither the 1994 Green Paper nor the 1995 White Paper cast further light on this duty. The parliamentary debates on the draft legislation are also unhelpful. However, it is plain that the duty does not require the service provider to take any steps which are unreasonable or which do not achieve the effect of providing access in any event. It is also true that steps need not be taken if they would fundamentally alter the nature of the goods, facilities or services in question or which would alter the nature of the trade, profession or business that the service provider runs or owns (s 21(6)).

For example, a shop might be reasonably expected to provide a telephone ordering service, but only if it also provides a delivery service as part of its normal business. A high street retailer would not be expected to provide a mail order service if it has not previously done so. In contrast, a catalogue shopping company, which already offers telephone ordering facilities, might in future be reasonably expected to offer a Minicom-type service for deaf customers.

5.7.6 Equally, the duty will be subject to a costs limitation and the duty will not require the service provider to take any steps which would cause expenditure to be incurred exceeding a maximum sum yet to be prescribed by regulations (s 21(7)). These regulations, when made, may provide for the prescribed maximum to be calculated by reference to any of the following criteria:

- aggregate amounts of expenditure incurred in relation to different cases;
- prescribed periods;
- services of a prescribed description;
- premises of a prescribed description;
- such other criteria as may be prescribed.[1]

The regulations may also provide for expenditure incurred by one service provider to be treated as incurred by another (s 21(9)).

Consultation is to take place before the maximum sum is to be determined, but this power is seen as 'fundamental to keep control of the costs that businesses will face and to retain support for the new rights'.[2] The Minister is considering a number of formulae by which the maximum costs might be set. One would be to set the costs ceiling as a percentage of a business's rateable value; another would be to set different limits for different categories of service provider; a third would be to have one, simple, overall limit of universal application.

---

1   In all these cases by virtue of s 21(8).
2   HC Deb Standing Committee E, col 359 (Mr W. Hague).

5.7.7 The wording of s 21(1) is relatively unambiguous and the duty to make reasonable adjustments set out there is not likely to give rise to many disputes of legal interpretation. The key to the section is how the courts will interpret the central terms, namely:

- a practice, policy or procedure;
- impossibility or unreasonable difficulty in relation to the use of a service;
- the taking of reasonable steps to change the practice, policy or procedure so as to remove the adverse effect.

What will prove to be of most interest, however, is how this duty will be applied in practice by service providers and in what ways it will be illustrated by the subsequent body of reported cases.

5.7.8 One obvious example that will be caught by s 21(1) is the policy or practice of shops or places of entertainment which exclude access to dogs accompanied by their owners. Such a policy or practice will need to be revisited and exception made (as is often the voluntary position already) for guide dogs accompanied by a visually impaired person. Similarly, cinemas or restaurants which refuse or limit access to wheelchair users will have to rethink this practice in the light of s 21(1). A transport provider or theatre which requires tickets to be booked in person might have to reconsider whether that policy militates against disabled persons and whether a telephone or other remote booking facility ought not to be introduced. Public utilities might have to consider requests for alternative billing or accounts arrangements (for example, quarterly statements in braille).

Physical features

5.7.9 Secondly, s 21(2) applies where a physical feature makes it impossible or unreasonably difficult for disabled persons to make use of goods, facilities or services which a service provider provides or is prepared to provide to other members of the public. By way of example in the statute itself, a 'physical feature' refers to a feature 'arising from the design or construction of a building or the approach or access to premises' (s 21(2)). Regulations may be made which will make provision for the purposes of this subsection as to things which are to be treated, or which are not to be treated, as physical features (s 21(5)(e)–(f)).

5.7.10 The 1994 Green Paper referred to the fact that disabled persons cannot take access to non-domestic buildings for granted and pointed out that high steps, narrow doorways, and absence of lift access and aids to communication constituted typical physical barriers.[1] Where a physical feature of this kind has the effect described, then s 21(2) places a duty upon the service provider 'to take such steps as it is reasonable, in all the circumstances of the case', for the service provider to have to take in order to:

- 'remove the feature';
- 'alter it so that it no longer has that effect';
- 'provide a reasonable means of avoiding the feature';
- 'provide a reasonable alternative method of making the service in question available to disabled persons'.

Regulations yet to be enacted may prescribe matters which are to be taken into account in determining whether the providing of means to avoid a physical feature or the providing of an alternative method of making the service available to disabled persons is 'reasonable' (s 21(3)(a)).

1   Green Paper para 3.3.

5.7.11   It is worth noting that s 21(2) leaves the choice of steps to be taken to overcome the adverse effects of a physical feature to the service provider. The subsection does not require the service provider to remove or alter the physical feature as a priority. Somewhat controversially, the effect of this provision is not wholly integrationist and it permits a 'separate but equal' or segregated approach to the provision of goods, facilities or services to disabled persons.

5.7.12   For example, if access to a museum is by a front entrance which could not be made accessible to wheelchair-users without rebuilding or physical alteration, it might be reasonable for the museum trustees to provide a wheelchair-accessible entrance at the side or back of the building. However, such alternative means of access to the building might not be reasonable where the disabled visitor has to negotiate rubbish bins or other obstacles in the process.[1] In such a case, physical alterations to the main entrance might be the only reasonable solution. Moreover, while cinemas will have to make reasonable provision to allow access to wheelchair-users, that does not mean that all seats in the cinema will have to be removable to accommodate disabled patrons.[2]

The Minister also gave the illustration of a café with a dining area covering two rooms. In one room, 80 per cent of the tables can accommodate a blind person with a guide dog; in the other room, in which entertainment by a pianist is provided to diners, no tables can accommodate diners accompanied by guide dogs. In these circumstances, the café owner will be unable to argue that the premises are accessible to disabled customers with guide dogs. A reasonable adjustment in respect of the whole dining facilities is called for so that blind customers can use the service in full.[3]

1   HL Deb, vol 564, cols 2022–2023 (Lord Inglewood).
2   HL Deb, vol 566, col 266 (Lord Mackay of Ardbrecknish).
3   HL Deb, vol 566, col 267 (Lord Mackay of Ardbrecknish).

5.7.13   Regulations may also exempt categories of service providers from the duty to make reasonable adjustments in respect of physical features only (s 21(3)(b)). The Government has indicated that it does not intend to use this power widely or often, but wishes to safeguard certain groups of service providers who might otherwise be faced with a disproportionately heavy burden under s 21(2) or for whom it would not be possible or sensible to make physical alterations.[1]

It is apparently intended that the exclusionary power will be used sparingly and might be applied, for example, to a service provider whose business is conducted from within a listed building (such as a stately home or working industrial revolution era mill open to the public) and would face particular difficulty in making alterations or adjustments to physical features of the building.[2] Nevertheless, the Government has made it clear that there is no general or automatic exemption from the Act for listed buildings and that service providers occupying such premises would be expected to seek the necessary consents for physical alterations where this would be reasonable to comply with the new duties towards disabled persons.[3]

1   HC Deb Standing Committee E, cols 358–359 (Mr W. Hague).
2   Occupiers of listed buildings might be generally protected by s 59 (acts done in compliance with existing enactments, such as listed buildings regulations).
3   HL Deb, vol 564, cols 2021–2024 (Lord Inglewood).

5.7.14   An important question will be how the duty to make reasonable adjustments in respect of physical features applies to a physical feature of a building (or an extension to a building) if the building regulations applied to the erection of the building (or the extension). What if the building (or extension) has been erected in compliance with any requirement of the building regulations which related to the provision of access and facilities for disabled persons?

5.7.15   As the 1995 White Paper explained,[1] the building regulations require all newly built and most extended public buildings and places of employment to be accessible to disabled persons. The Government has promised wide consultation on proposals to extend the building regulations to include new measures to help disabled persons gain access to and within new *domestic* dwellings.[2] Otherwise, the Government envisages that over time the public built environment (that is, non-domestic buildings) will become more accessible to disabled persons as existing public buildings (such as shops, offices and places of entertainment) are replaced or extended.

In the meanwhile, it might be assumed that the building regulations make sufficient provision for questions of disabled access to new or recently extended buildings. That does not mean, however, that service providers occupying such buildings will not be expected to take further *reasonable* steps to adjust, alter or remove physical features to aid access to disabled persons.

1   White Paper para 4.2.
2   White Paper para 8.1.

5.7.16   As is the case in respect of other aspects of the duty to make reasonable adjustments, it is implicit that the duty to adjust, alter or remove a physical feature does not require the service provider to take any steps which are unreasonable or which do not achieve the effect of providing access in any event. It is also the case that steps need not be taken if they would fundamentally alter the nature of the goods, facilities or services in question or which would alter the nature of the trade, profession or business that the service provider runs or owns (s 21(6)). Furthermore, the duty in respect of physical features will also be the subject of a costs limitation yet to be formulated (s 21(7)–(9)).[1]

---

1 See the discussion at **5.7.6**.

5.7.17   Nevertheless, it is likely that this aspect of the duty to make reasonable adjustments will call for some imagination from service providers. For example, a supermarket might be reasonably expected to consider whether the aisles between shelves or between the check-out tills are sufficiently wide to accommodate wheelchair-users. A restaurant may need to consider how its seating arrangements are designed, while an art gallery may need to consider the height at which exhibits are hung, in both cases so as to accommodate diners or art lovers who are wheelchair-users.

Signage in public buildings might also be counted as physical features and is often poorly designed or sited, without the needs of disabled persons in mind. The height and design of points of sale or service in stores, banks or post offices also frequently cause physical barriers between disabled customers and sales assistants. Lighting and ventilation in buildings might also be regarded as a 'physical feature', so that the needs of persons with vision or respiratory impairments might call for reasonable adjustments to be made in these areas.

5.7.18   Often very little effort or modification is required to remove or ameliorate the ill-effects of physical barriers. Installing simple ramps or repositioning fixtures and fittings can often make a lot of difference for little or no expense. Other alterations might involve some cost, but with attendant benefits for all, as well as increased custom for the service provider. These might include widening entrance doors or installing two-way door hinges to assist wheelchair-users, creating designated parking spaces for disabled customers or removing high pile, low density carpeting to aid the mobility of customers using a prosthesis or walking aid.

Alternative methods of providing goods or services might also be considered. For example, a self-service petrol pump might not be reasonably capable of being redesigned or modified for use by a person with disabilities, but it might then be reasonable to expect the service station to provide an attendant service, without extra charge. A multi-screen cinema might find it impracticable or too costly to make all screening theatres accessible to disabled patrons, but might instead ensure that film schedules rotate so that all films are accessible at some time during the weekly season.

5.7.19   Note that s 27 makes special provision where a service provider occupies its premises under lease. Where the lease or the lessor prevents or hinders the occupier in making adjustments to the premises so as to comply with a s 21 duty, s 27 (and Part II of Sch 4) modifies the effect of the lease and places duties upon the lessor. This is a complex provision warranting detailed analysis. Section 27 is discussed further in Chapter 6.

Auxiliary aids and services

5.7.20 Thirdly, s 21(4) applies where: (a) an 'auxiliary aid or service' would enable disabled persons to make use of goods, facilities or services which a service provider provides or is prepared to provide to members of the public; or (b) an 'auxiliary aid or service' would facilitate the use by disabled persons of such goods, facilities or services. In such a case, it is the duty of the service provider 'to take such steps as it is reasonable, in all the circumstances of the case', for the service provider to have to take in order to provide the auxiliary aid or service in question. A failure to comply with this duty is an act of unlawful discrimination if its effect is to make it impossible or unreasonably difficult for the disabled person to make use of any goods, facilities or services (s 19(1)(b)).

5.7.21 The term 'auxiliary aid or service' is exemplified in the subsection by reference to the provision of information on audio tape or the provision of a sign language interpreter (s 21(4)). Further illustrations would include the provision of induction loops in theatres or cinemas, large print point of sales literature in shops or audio-visual telephones in hotel rooms for individuals with sensory impairments. However, in many cases, an auxiliary aid or service might amount to no more than the allocating of a particular member of staff to provide requested assistance to a disabled customer. For example, a blind customer in a self-service store might reasonably request that a store assistant should locate a particular item for purchase or should read out loud the description of goods from any product packaging.

5.7.22 Therefore, a training or conference company organising a seminar on the new Disability Discrimination Act would have to take reasonable steps to accommodate the known needs of disabled delegates attending the seminar (such as by providing a sign interpreter or an induction loop system). It would need to choose the seminar location in a hotel or conference centre that was reasonably physically accessible for delegates with mobility disabilities.

How far such a company would have to go, however, would be subject to the reasonableness test (and the costs limitation noted below).[1] This might not extend so far as requiring the seminar notes or handouts to be prepared in braille as well as in ordinary print. It might be sufficient to arrange for a tape recording of proceedings to be made for later use by a delegate with a sensory impairment. Nevertheless, each case will have to be treated on its merits and it is impossible to be dogmatic about what would or would not be reasonable in particular situations.

---

1   See **5.7.23**.

5.7.23 Regulations may be made which will make provision for the purposes of s 21(4) as to things which are to be treated, or which are not to be treated, as auxiliary aids or services (s 21(5)(g)–(h)). As previously noted, it is plain that the duty to provide auxiliary aids or services does not require the service provider to take any steps which are unreasonable or which do not achieve the effect of providing access in any event. For example, a museum might not be expected to provide a sign language interpreter for deaf visitors, provided it has adequate written descriptions or a guide book.

It is also the case that steps need not be taken if they would fundamentally alter the nature of the goods, facilities or services in question or which would alter the nature of the trade, profession or business that the service provider runs or owns (s 21(6)). Furthermore, the duty to provide auxiliary aids or services will also be the subject of an expenditure cap yet to be formulated (s 21(7)–(9)).

5.7.24 The 1995 White Paper envisaged that auxiliary aids and services will have to be provided where this is reasonable and readily achievable 'given the size, resources and the nature of the business'.[1] The words in quotation marks do not appear in the statutory language, but they provide an obvious indicator of the kinds of factors that will be relevant in judging what is reasonable in any particular case. It is suggested that this indicates that the Government's intention is that reasonableness will be judged more by reference to the identity and status of the service provider than by the needs and circumstances of the disabled person, but the language of the statute nevertheless appears to require the reasonableness test to take account of all the circumstances of the case. What is reasonable must be judged in the round and the interests of both parties are required to be weighed in the balance. These remarks will apply equally to the application of the reasonableness test with reference to the duty to make reasonable adjustments in relation to policies, practices and procedures, and in respect of physical features.

---

1   White Paper para 4.4.

Defence of justification and duty to make adjustments

5.7.25 As we have seen, an unjustifiable breach of the duty to make reasonable adjustments may be treated as an act of discrimination against a disabled person (s 20(2)) and that might be an actionable act of discrimination under s 19(1)(b). How does the statutory defence of justification available under s 20(1)(b) and (2)(b) apply where the discrimination in question arises from a failure to observe a duty to make reasonable adjustments? The interaction of s 21 with the justification defences in s 20 has been considered above.[1]

---

1   See **5.6.24–5.6.26**.

5.8 ENFORCEMENT, REMEDIES AND PROCEDURES

5.8.1 Section 25 sets out the enforcement procedure and remedies available when a claim of unlawful discrimination is made in respect of the provision of goods, facilities or services. A claim of unlawful discrimination in relation to the provision of goods, facilities or services under Part III of the Act is to be the subject of civil proceedings for tort in the county court (in England and Wales or Northern Ireland) or in reparation for breach of a statutory duty in the sheriff court (in Scotland).[1] The usual remedy will be damages (including damages for injury to feelings),[2] subject to an upper limit to be prescribed,[3] but a plaintiff might also be entitled to seek a declaration or an injunction.[4] The question of enforcement procedures and remedies is considered in more detail in Chapter 10 (and see generally s 25 and Sch 3, Part II).

---

1   See s 25(1), (3) and (4). The modification of s 25 for Northern Ireland is achieved in Sch 8, para 12.
2   By virtue of s 25(2).
3   Under Sch 3, para 7.
4. This is the effect of s 25(5).

5.8.2 Section 26 makes void any contract term which would contravene, limit or exclude any provision relating to the right of access to goods, facilities and services. An exception is made for settlements of claims. A court may remove or modify any such void term. This provision is dealt with in more detail in Chapter 10.

5.8.3 Section 28 provides for the establishment of a conciliation service to provide advice and support to individuals alleging discrimination by those providing goods and services. This is to encourage the promotion of settlements of disputes without recourse to litigation in the courts. We shall return to this measure in Chapter 10.

Chapter 6

PROPERTY, PREMISES AND LEASES

6.1 INTRODUCTION

6.1.1 Sections 22–24 of the 1995 Act make it unlawful for landlords and other persons who are disposing of or selling property to discriminate against a disabled person. These provisions mirror similar measures in the Sex Discrimination Act 1975 and the Race Relations Act 1976,[1] although they are not in identical terms. While it is not thought that discrimination against disabled persons is as widespread as racial discrimination once was in the property market, the Minister felt sufficiently moved by at least one case of landlord discrimination against a disabled person to introduce an amendment to the Act during its progress as a Bill.[2]

---

1 SDA 1975, ss 30–32; RRA 1976, ss 21–24.
2 HC Deb Standing Committee E, col 453 (Mr W. Hague, Minister for Disabled People).

6.1.2 As the provisions on discrimination in relation to premises are a free-standing part of Part III of the Act, they warrant separate treatment in this chapter. However, much of the terminology used in ss 22–24 echoes many of the concepts used elsewhere in the Act. Accordingly, decisions reached and precedents made in respect of other sections will be influential and of assistance in the interpretation of the new law on discrimination in respect of premises.

6.1.3 At a late stage in the passage of the legislation, the Government also made provision for the position where employers, trade organisations and service providers occupy premises under the terms of a lease. It was recognised that such parties might find it difficult to discharge a duty to make reasonable adjustments for disabled persons (under ss 6, 15 and 21 respectively), especially in respect of the physical features of premises, where the lease or the landlord prevented or hindered such adjustments. Accordingly, s 16 (in respect of employers and trade organisations) and s 27 (in respect of service providers) adjust the respective rights of the landlord and tenant to a commercial lease so as to accommodate the new duties to make adjustments to premises. Sections 16 and 27 are supplemented by Sch 4. These provisions affect property interests and so are logically dealt with in this chapter.

6.2 DISCRIMINATION IN RELATION TO PREMISES

6.2.1 Section 22(1) of the Act makes it unlawful for 'a person with power to dispose of any premises' to discriminate against a disabled person in one of a number of ways, while s 22(3) makes it unlawful for 'a person managing any premises' to discriminate against a disabled person 'occupying those premises' in similar fashion. Section 22(4) deals with discrimination by the withholding of a licence or consent required for the disposal of premises to a disabled person. A 'disabled person' for these purposes means a disabled person (including a person who has had a disability in the past) as defined in ss 1–2 of and Schs 1–2 to the Act.[1] The meaning of discrimination in this context is set out in s 24. Sections 22–24 came into force on 2 December 1996, with the exception of the regulation-making power in s 24(5), which came into effect on 6 June 1996.[2] The regulation-making power has been used to produce one relevant regulation,[3] which will be referred to below. These measures are supported by the new Rights of Access Code of Practice,[4] to which reference will be made at appropriate points.

1 As discussed in Chapter 2.
2 See the Disability Discrimination Act 1995 (Commencement No 3 and Saving and Transitional Provisions) Order 1996.
3 See the Disability Discrimination (Services and Premises) Regulations 1996, reg 7 (on when less favourable treatment is justified in connection with deposits in respect of premises).
4 *Code of Practice: Rights of Access: Goods, Facilities, Services and Premises* (1996, London: HMSO). See in particular, paras 2.8, 2.10–2.11, 4.1–4.15, 5.5–5.10 and 5.15–5.17. Arguably, the Rights of Access Code of Practice fails to deal adequately with discrimination in the disposal and management of premises, concentrating as it does on the provision of goods, facilities and services. It is regrettable that a separate code of practice covering premises has not been devised.

Unlawful acts of discrimination

6.2.2 First, it is unlawful to discriminate 'in the terms' on which a person with power to dispose of premises offers to dispose of those premises to a disabled person (s 22(1)(a)). For example, a landlord cannot seek to charge a higher rent for premises to a disabled tenant than the landlord would otherwise charge to a non-disabled lessee.[1]

1 See also Rights of Access Code of Practice, para 4.10.

6.2.3 Secondly, it is unlawful to discriminate where a person with power to dispose of premises refuses to dispose of those premises to a disabled person (s 22(1)(b)). This is a self-evident measure designed to prevent disabled persons from being denied the rights to own a legal interest in property solely because of their disability. It is analogous with the illegitimacy of a property owner's action in refusing to sell or lease property to a member of an ethnic minority. It does not prevent the property owner from refusing to dispose of the property to a disabled person for reasons unconnected with that person's disability (for example, their inability to meet the purchase price or evidence that as a tenant they would be a bad credit risk).[1]

1   See also Rights of Access Code of Practice, para 4.11.

6.2.4   Thirdly, it is unlawful for a person with power to dispose of any premises to discriminate against a disabled person in his or her 'treatment' of that disabled person 'in relation to any list of persons in need of premises of that description' (s 22(1)(c)). This prohibition most obviously addresses discrimination against disabled persons in relation to local authority housing lists. For example, a refusal to include a disabled person on a housing list or the removal of that person from such a list or a failure to accord that person proper priority in accordance with their ranking on the list might all be acts of unlawful discrimination. Similarly, allocating less desirable property to a disabled person on a housing list where a non-disabled person is more favourably treated would constitute a likely act of discrimination.[1]

1   See also Rights of Access Code of Practice, para 4.12. However, the Act does not prohibit more favourable treatment or positive action in respect of disabled persons and housing lists: ibid, para 4.15

6.2.5   Fourthly, it is unlawful for a person managing any premises to discriminate against a disabled person occupying those premises 'in the way' the person managing the premises 'permits the disabled person to make use of any benefits or facilities' (s 22(3)(a)). The terms 'benefits or facilities' are not defined and there is no express intention to include 'services' within these terms. Section 68(1) apparently does not permit a cross-reference to the definition used in s 4(4) for the purposes of Part II of the Act.[1]

Inclusion of a person managing any premises clearly broadens the scope of s 22 which is not solely concerned with discrimination by property owners. A property management agency, housekeeper, estate agent or rent collection service could all constitute parties who might be liable under this provision (and those provisions mentioned below).[2]

1   The Rights of Access Code of Practice illustrates benefits and facilities as including laundry facilities, access to a garden and parking facilities (para 4.9).
2   The Rights of Access Code of Practice also mentions accommodation agencies (para 4.8).

6.2.6   Fifthly, it is unlawful for a person managing any premises to discriminate against a disabled person occupying those premises by 'refusing or deliberately omitting' to permit the disabled person to make use of any benefits or facilities (s 22(3)(b)). For example, a property management agency, managing a residential block of flats on behalf of a landlord, may not discriminate by refusing a disabled tenant access to benefits or facilities, such as common garden or recreational areas.[1]

1   See also Rights of Access Code of Practice, para 4.13.

6.2.7   Sixthly, it is unlawful for a person managing any premises to discrimi-nate against a disabled person occupying those premises by 'evicting' the disabled person (s 22(3)(c)). This paragraph of the subsection does not seek to prohibit the eviction of disabled tenants in accordance with a lawful process where, for example, the disabled person has failed to pay rent or has breached the terms of the tenancy. Instead, it provides a disabled tenant, who has been evicted by a manager of premises because of a reason related to disability, an additional cause of action apart from any available under the law of landlord and tenant.

6.2.8   Seventhly, it is unlawful for a person managing any premises to discriminate against a disabled person occupying those premises by 'subjecting him [or her] to any other detriment' (s 22(3)(c)). This measure most obviously addresses harassment of a disabled tenant by the person managing the premises.[1]

1   See also Rights of Access Code of Practice, para 4.14.

6.2.9   Finally, it is unlawful for any person 'whose licence or consent is required' for the disposal of any premises 'comprised in ... a tenancy' to discriminate against a disabled person by withholding that licence or consent for the disposal of the premises to the disabled person (s 22(4)). In Scotland, this prohibition applies in respect of the disposal of any premises 'the subject of' a tenancy. This subsection applies to tenancies created before or after the passing of the Act (s 22(5)).

Meaning of 'a person with power to dispose of any premises'

6.2.10   The phrase 'a person with power to dispose of any premises', as used in s 22(1), is not defined in the Act. However, the word 'dispose' is defined in s 22(6) and, by this circuitous route, some light can be cast upon the class of person whose potentially unlawful actions constitute the mischief at which ss 22–24 of the Act are aimed.[1]

1   The Rights of Access Code of Practice simply explains that disposing of premises includes selling and letting premises (para 4.7).

6.2.11   A person with the power to dispose of premises includes a person who has the power to grant a right to occupy the premises (s 22(6)). Where the premises are comprised in or the subject of a tenancy, the relevant party will be the person with the power to assign the tenancy or to sub-let or part with possession of the premises or any part of them (s 22(6)). The Act thus covers both the sale and lease of premises and, by implication, any other form of legal disposal (for example, by licence). *Quaere* whether the statute is also concerned with the disposal of premises by the operation of the law of succession or insolvency law?[1]

---

1   However, it is doubtful whether ss 22–24 covers the hire of premises or rooms booked in hotels and guest houses. These situations will be covered by Part III of the Act: Rights of Access Code of Practice, para 4.7.

6.2.12   The Act does not automatically apply to private occupiers disposing of premises by private agreement or transaction.[1] This is because s 22(2) states that the provisions in s 22(1) preventing discrimination against disabled persons by a person with a power to dispose of premises do not apply to 'a person who owns an estate or interest in premises *and wholly occupies them*' (emphasis added), unless further conditions are satisfied. So the statute does not make any discrimination against a disabled person unlawful where a person with the power to dispose of premises is the owner (or owns a legal interest in the premises), wholly occupies the premises, and disposes of the premises by private agreement.

---

1   Note also the exception for small dwellings contained in s 23 and discussed at **6.2.16**.

6.2.13   However, the statutory prohibitions in s 22(1) will still apply if such a person uses the services of an estate agent or publishes an advertisement (or causes an advertisement to be published) for the purpose of disposing of the premises (s 22(2)). These are the further conditions referred to above.[1] That would cease to be a disposal by a purely private agreement.

An 'estate agent' for this purpose is a person carrying on the trade or profession of providing services 'for the purpose of finding premises for persons seeking to acquire them or assisting in the disposal of premises' (s 22(6)). That definition would appear to be wide enough to include not only an estate agent per se, but also an accommodation bureau or agency. An 'advertisement' includes every form of advertisement or notice, whether to the public or not (s 22(6)). So the circulation to a small or select number of persons of the details of premises for disposal would constitute an advertisement of the premises and would trigger the provisions in s 22(1) prohibiting discrimination against disabled persons in the subsequent disposal.

---

1   See **6.2.12**.

Meaning of 'premises' and 'tenancy'

6.2.14   Again, the term 'premises' is not statutorily defined, except to the extent that s 68(1) indicates that premises include land of any description and s 22(8) makes it clear that the Act is only concerned with premises in the UK. Nevertheless, the ordinary, literal meaning of the word 'premises' suggests that the Act is concerned with legal and equitable interests in houses, lands, tenements and buildings, while the Act makes no apparent distinction between commercial and non-commercial (or domestic) property. Thus the Act would appear to cover, for example, dwelling-houses, office blocks, flats, bed-sits, factory premises, industrial or commercial sites, agricultural land and so on – in other words, real property of any description.[1]

---

1   See further, Rights of Access Code of Practice, para 2.8. But note the exemption for small dwellings contained in s 23 and discussed at **6.2.16**.

6.2.15   The Act clearly impinges upon the law of landlord and tenant, as s 22 obviously and expressly applies to the granting of tenancies, their assignment and the right to sub-let. A 'tenancy' is defined in s 22(6) as meaning a tenancy created by a lease or sub-lease, by an agreement for a lease or sub-lease, by a tenancy agreement or in pursuance of any 'enactment', as defined in s 68 (eg a statutory tenancy).[1]

---

1   Note that the Disability Discrimination (Sub-leases and Sub-tenancies) Regulations 1996, SI 1996/1333 do not apply to ss 22–24 and are not relevant in the present context.

Exemption for small dwellings

6.2.16   Where certain statutory conditions are satisfied, the prohibitions concerning discrimination against disabled persons in the disposal or management of premises (s 22(1) and (3)) or by the withholding of a licence or consent for the disposal of premises (s 22(4)) do not apply by virtue of s 23(1). In essence, s 23 provides an exemption for small dwellings from these provisions of the legislation.[1] The conditions referred to in s 23(1) are set out in s 23(2). These conditions are cumulative rather than alternatives. In other words, all the conditions must be satisfied in order to obtain the statutory exemption.

---

1   See the brief attempt to summarise these complex provisions in the Rights of Access Code of Practice, para 2.10.

6.2.17   First, the relevant occupier must reside, and must intend to continue to reside, on the premises (s 23(2)(a)). The use of the word 'reside' indicates that this exemption is only enjoyed in respect of dwelling-houses or other residential property and does not apply to commercial or industrial premises. A 'relevant occupier' means a person with the power to dispose of the premises in a case where s 22(1) would otherwise apply (discrimination in relation to the disposal of premises) or, in any case where s 22(4) would otherwise apply (discrimination by withholding a licence or consent for the disposal of tenancy premises), the person whose licence or consent is required for the disposal of the premises (s 23(6)).

In both cases, the relevant occupier will include 'a near relative' and this term is exhaustively defined by s 23(7) to mean a person's spouse, partner, child, grandparent, grandchild, or brother or sister (whether of full or half blood or by affinity). As the Minister explained:

> 'The need to identify whether someone is or is not a partner arises only if the "relevant occupier" is not actually present on the premises at the point in time when discrimination is alleged: for example, where he or she was temporarily away on business.'[1]

The word 'partner' as used here means the other member of a couple consisting of a man and a woman who are not married to each other but are living together as husband and wife (s 23(7)).

---

1   HL Deb, vol 564, col 2029 (Lord Inglewood).

6.2.18 Secondly, the relevant occupier (as previously defined) must be sharing accommodation on the premises with persons who reside on the premises and who are not members of the relevant occupier's household (s 23(2)(b)). This condition appears to contemplate a multi-occupancy residential building with shared accommodation. For example, this might include a large house, sub-divided into individually let bed-sits, with a resident landlord and shared accommodation, such as communal kitchens or bathrooms.

6.2.19 Thirdly, the shared accommodation in question must not be storage accommodation or a means of access (s 23(2)(c)). This underlines the last observation illustrating the notion of shared accommodation. It indicates that it is not enough that there is a common entrance door or passageway. Equally, the premises would not include shared accommodation only by virtue of there being a garage or cellar in which the tenants or occupiers may store their personal effects.

6.2.20 Finally, the premises must be 'small premises' (s 23(2)(d)). Premises are 'small premises' by virtue of s 23(3) if they fall within s 23(5). Under s 23(5) premises are 'small premises' if there is not normally residential accommodation on the premises for more than six persons in addition to the relevant occupier and any members of the relevant occupier's household. A householder who has converted part of his or her dwelling-house into bed-sit accommodation would fall outside this exemption if such accommodation embraced more than six tenants.

6.2.21   Alternatively, premises are 'small premises' if they fall within s 23(4). Premises fall within that subsection if they satisfy four conditions. First, only the relevant occupier and members of his or her household reside in the accommodation occupied by him or her (s 23(4)(a)). Secondly, in addition to the accommodation occupied by the relevant occupier, the premises must comprise residential accommodation for at least one other household (s 23(4)(b)). Thirdly, the residential accommodation for each other household must be let (or available for letting) on a separate tenancy or similar agreement (s 23(4)(c)). Finally, there must not normally be more than two such other households (s 23(4)(d)).

A large house where, for example, the basement and an annex have been converted into self-contained residential dwellings or flats would satisfy these conditions if the owner also resides on the premises and there is an element of shared accommodation (other than for storage or access purposes).

Meaning of discrimination

6.2.22   As in Part II and the goods, facilities and services provisions of Part III of the Act, ss 22–24 dealing with discrimination in relation to premises include a self-contained definition of discrimination in s 24. While case-law on the meaning of discrimination as used elsewhere in the statute will be instructive, care must be taken to ensure that an action for alleged discrimination in the disposal or management of premises satisfies the definition of discrimination in s 24. Nevertheless, the reader is referred to the detailed discussion of the meaning of discrimination in Chapters 3 and 5.

6.2.23   Note also that s 24 does not create a free-standing right to complain of discrimination. It will be necessary to show that discrimination has occurred under s 24 in a way made unlawful under s 22. The two sections are interdependent, as the opening words of s 24(1) clarify.[1]

---

1   'For the purposes of section 22 ...' (s 24(1)).

Less favourable treatment

6.2.24   A person discriminates against a disabled person if, for a reason related to the disabled person's disability, that person treats the disabled person less favourably than that person treats (or would treat) others to whom that reason does not or would not apply (s 24(1)(a)). Such less favourable treatment for a reason related to disability will amount to potential discrimination for the purposes of s 22 if the alleged discriminator cannot show that the treatment in question is justified (s 24(1)(b)).

Justification defence

6.2.25 The justification defence can only be made out if the criteria contained in s 24(2) are met. First, the alleged discriminator must hold the opinion that one or more statutory conditions are satisfied (s 24(2)(a)). Secondly, it must be reasonable, in all the circumstances of the case, for that person to hold that opinion (s 24(2)(b)). Regulations yet to be made may amplify the circumstances in which it is reasonable (or not reasonable) for a person to hold the opinion that one or more of the statutory conditions are satisfied (s 24(4)).

6.2.26 Section 24(3) lists four possible statutory conditions about the satisfaction of which the alleged discriminator must hold a reasonably held opinion. The conditions listed in s 24(3) are very similar to the parallel conditions for the operation of the justification defence in respect of discrimination arising in the context of goods, facilities or services (s 20(4)).[1]

---

1 The justification defence in relation to disability-related discrimination in the disposal or management of premises raises similar issues to those already considered in respect of discrimination affecting the provision of goods, facilities or services. The reader is referred to Chapter 5 for a more considered analysis of these issues.

6.2.27 First, in any case, the alleged discriminator may be able to justify less favourable treatment by showing that he or she reasonably believed that the treatment was necessary in order not to endanger the health or safety of any person, including the disabled complainant (s 24(3)(a)).[1] Secondly, in any case, less favourable treatment might be justified by reference to a reasonably held opinion that the disabled person was incapable of entering into an enforceable agreement or of giving an informed consent (s 24(3)(b)).[2] In this instance, however, it is also necessary to show that for that reason the treatment was reasonable in the particular case.

Thirdly, in a case falling within s 22(3)(a),[3] the alleged discriminator might be able to show a reasonably held opinion that the discriminatory treatment was necessary in order for the disabled occupier of premises (or occupiers of other premises forming part of the building) to make use of a benefit or facility (s 24(3)(c)). Finally, in a case falling under s 22(3)(b),[4] less favourable treatment might be justified by demonstrating a reasonably held opinion that the treatment was necessary in order for the occupiers of other premises forming part of the building to make use of the benefit or facility (s 24(3)(d)).

---

1 See further, Rights of Access Code of Practice, paras 5.5–5.7.
2 See further, Rights of Access Code of Practice, paras 5.8–5.10. Note that the provisions on powers of attorney, etc contained in the Disability Discrimination (Services and Premises)

142 *Disability Discrimination*

Regulations 1996, reg 8 do not apply to s 24 as they do to s 20 in the context of goods, facilities and services (see **5.6.13**).

3 That is, a case where a person managing premises has treated a disabled occupier less favourably in the way in which the disabled person is allowed to make use of any benefits or facilities. See Rights of Access Code of Practice, paras 5.15–5.17.

4 That is, a case where a person managing premises has treated a disabled occupier less favourably by refusing or deliberately omitting to permit the disabled person to make use of any benefits or facilities. See Rights of Access Code of Practice, paras 5.15–5.17.

6.2.28 Section 24(5) empowers the Minister to make regulations to provide for additional circumstances in which less favourable treatment of a disabled person is to be taken to be justified. The Disability Discrimination (Services and Premises) Regulations 1996, reg 7 provides for one such circumstance to date. This relates to deposits in respect of premises.

The regulation applies where a person with power to dispose of any premises (referred to as 'the provider') grants a disabled person a right to occupy the premises.[1] It does not matter whether this is by means of a formal tenancy agreement or otherwise. The provider may have required the disabled person, in respect of his or her occupation of the premises, to provide a deposit which is refundable at the end of the occupation, provided that the premises and contents are not damaged.[2] The regulation is then triggered if the provider refuses to refund some or all of the deposit because the premises or contents have been damaged for a reason which relates to the disabled person's disability.[3] If the damage is above the level at which the provider would normally refund the deposit in full,[4] and if it is reasonable in all the circumstances of the case for the provider to refuse to refund the deposit in full,[5] then that apparently less favourable treatment of the disabled person for a reason relating to his or her disability is deemed to be justified for the purposes of s 24.[6]

1 Disability Discrimination (Services and Premises) Regulations 1996, reg 7(2)(a).
2 Ibid, reg 7(2)(b).
3 Ibid, reg 7(2)(c).
4 Ibid, reg 7(2)(c).
5 Ibid, reg 7(2)(d).
6 Ibid, reg 7(1). That assumes, of course, that the provider treats (or would treat) others to whom the disability-related reason does not (or would not) apply more favourably than the disabled person, for otherwise there is no discrimination that needs to be justified.

Duty to make reasonable adjustments

6.2.29 There is no explicit duty to make reasonable adjustments for disabled persons in the context of the disposal or management of premises. It remains to be seen whether judicial interpretation of the meaning of discrimination under s 24(1) (discussed above) will give rise to an implicit duty of this nature.[1]

---

1   The Rights of Access Code of Practice suggests not (para 4.4).

Enforcement and remedies

6.2.30   The provisions in respect of disability-informed discrimination in the disposal or management of premises are enforced (and remedies are sought) in exactly the same way as complaints of discrimination in respect of the provision of goods, facilities and services. The relevant provisions are contained in ss 25–28 and Sch 3, Part II. Further discussion is pursued in Chapter 10.

Victimisation

6.2.31   For the purposes of ss 22–24 (as for Part II as a whole) a person (X) discriminates against another person (Y) if X treats Y less favourably than X treats (or would treat) other persons whose circumstances are the same as Y's, and X does so for one of a number of statutory reasons (s 55(1)). Those statutory reasons relate to the fact that Y has exercised (or is believed or suspected by X as having exercised or as intending to exercise) rights under the 1995 Act (s 55(2)). For example, Y may have brought proceedings against X or given evidence in respect of such proceedings. This is victimisation and it is explained in more detail in Chapter 10.[1]

---

1   See also Rights of Access Code of Practice, paras 6.1–6.2.

6.2.32   Section 22(7) states that an act of victimisation amounts to discrimination for the purposes of ss 22–24. It will allow a disabled person or a non-disabled person to have a cause of action for any of the unlawful acts outlined in s 22. By way of illustration, if Y was employed by local authority X and brought a complaint of disability-related employment discrimination against X, it would be an act of discrimination if X then victimised Y by removing Y from the local authority's housing waiting list. In these particular circumstances, it is not strictly necessary that Y should be a disabled person. It is sufficient that he or she has been victimised within the meaning of s 55 for doing something in relation to the Act and has suffered a discriminatory act within s 22. Section 22 thus also provides rights to non-disabled persons in this narrow context (by virtue of s 22(7)).

6.3   ALTERATIONS TO PREMISES OCCUPIED UNDER LEASES

6.3.1   For the sake of convenience, consideration must be given in the context of the current chapter to the provisions of ss 16 and 27. These sections have the effect, in certain circumstances, of providing a remedy where a duty to make reasonable adjustments involving an alteration to premises is in potential conflict with the terms of a lease and the rights of the landlord. Section 16 applies to employers and trade organisations, while s 27 applies to providers of services. At the time of writing, s 27 (and Sch 4 Part II which supports it) is not yet in force because the duty to make adjustments in respect of goods, facilities and services (the final rights of access under ss 20(2) and 21) have not yet been implemented. The provisions of s 16 (and Sch 4 Part I which underpins it) were brought into force at various times and are fully effective from 2 December 1996.[1]

---

1 See **1.3.3–1.3.4**. The statutory provisions are amplified by the Disability Discrimination (Employment) Regulations 1996, SI 1996/1456, regs 8–15 (effective 2 December 1996) and the Disability Discrimination (Sub-leases and Sub-tenancies) Regulations 1996, SI 1996/1333 (effective 7 June 1996). See also Disability Discrimination (Employment) Regulations (Northern Ireland) 1996, SR 1996/419 and Disability Discrimination (Sub-leases and Sub-tenancies) Regulations (Northern Ireland) 1996, SR 1996/420. The Employment Code of Practice, paras 4.35–4.48 will also be relevant in employment cases. The Rights of Access Code of Practice does not yet deal with these provisions.

Duty to make reasonable adjustments and physical features of premises

6.3.2 Where any physical features of premises occupied by an employer place a disabled person at a substantial disadvantage in comparison with non-disabled persons, it is the duty of the employer to take such steps as it is reasonable in all the circumstances of the case to take in order to prevent the physical feature in question having that effect (s 6(1)(b)). That duty might require the employer to make adjustments to the premises (s 6(3)(a)), subject to considerations such as practicability, cost and resources (s 6(4)). An unjustifiable failure to consider or discharge that duty can amount to an act of unlawful discrimination under s 5. The detail of this duty has been considered in Chapter 3.

6.3.3 A similar duty to make reasonable adjustments to any physical feature of premises occupied by a trade organisation is imposed upon such an organisation under s 15, although not yet in force. This has also been discussed in an earlier section (see Chapter 4).

6.3.4 In respect of Part III of the Act, a detailed duty to make reasonable adjustments is also placed upon service providers (see Chapter 5). When in force, s 21 will establish that, where a physical feature of a building makes it impossible or unreasonably difficult for disabled persons to make use of a service provided to the public by a service provider, it is the duty of the service provider to make reasonable adjustments. That duty involves taking such steps as it is reasonable in all the circumstances of the case to take in order to remove the physical feature or to alter it so that it no longer has the adverse effect referred to. Alternatively, the service provider might provide a reasonable means of avoiding the feature or provide a reasonable alternative method of making the service available to disabled persons (s 21(2)). As with employers and trade organisations, a service provider's unjustified failure to discharge a duty to make reasonable adjustments to its premises in these ways is a potential act of discrimination under s 20 (when s 20(2) is in force).

The problem of leases

6.3.5 The duty to make reasonable adjustments to premises is primarily imposed upon the employer, trade organisation or service provider that occupies the premises in issue. Where that person owns the premises there can be no question that the person has a right to make alterations to the premises, subject only to planning and environmental considerations. In such a case, if there is a duty to make an adjustment, and if an alteration to the fabric or a physical feature of the premises would otherwise be a reasonable adjustment to make, then the Act will expect the occupier to take such steps, all other things being equal.

6.3.6 Nevertheless, many parties who would be subject to the Act occupy premises, not as outright legal owners, but in the relationship of landlord and tenant under a commercial lease. A term or covenant in that lease might often forbid or restrict alterations to the property or might only permit such alterations with the prior consent of the landlord. In that latter case, consent under the lease might not be forthcoming if the landlord reasonably or unreasonably withholds permission. In these circumstances, the employer, trade organisation or service provider might be in breach of its duty to a disabled person to make reasonable adjustments. This could amount to an act of disability discrimination contrary to the Act, although the restriction in the lease or the landlord's refusal to countenance an alteration to the occupied premises might bring a justification defence into play.

6.3.7 The Government was concerned to clarify the relation between these conflicting legal obligations of discrimination law and the law of landlord and tenant. Reliance might have been placed upon ss 9 and 26 which invalidate terms of any agreement which require a person to contravene the Act or which serve to exclude or limit the operation of the statute. Arguably, those sections could have been used to remove or modify restrictive clauses or covenants in commercial leases that prevented a tenant subject to the Act from prosecuting an alteration to the leased premises in pursuit of a duty to make reasonable adjustments for disabled persons. The Minister felt unable to rely upon that mechanism.[1]

Equally, the Government was unwilling to allow a situation whereby landlords of commercial or industrial premises could thwart or undermine the objectives of the new legislation. The Government's solution to this problem is contained in ss 16 and 27 of and in Sch 4 to the Act.

---

1 HL Deb, vol 566, col 1016 (Lord Henley).

The effect of the Act upon premises occupied under leases

6.3.8 Where an employer, trade organisation or provider of services ('the occupier') occupies premises under a 'lease' ss 16 and 27 potentially apply (ss 16(1)(a) and 27(1)(a)). A lease for this purpose includes a tenancy, sub-lease or sub-tenancy, and an agreement for a lease, tenancy, sub-lease or sub-tenancy (ss 16(3) and 27(3)). The Act provides that regulations may further define the meaning of these terms.[1] Accordingly, for the purposes of s 16, 'sub-lease' means any sub-term created out of or deriving from a leasehold interest and 'sub-tenancy' means any tenancy created out of or deriving from a superior tenancy.[2] Regulations may also supplement or modify the provisions of ss 16 and 27 or Sch 4 in relation to cases where the occupier occupies premises under a sub-lease or sub-tenancy.[3] The effect is largely that where there are references in s 16 and Sch 4, para 1 to a 'lessor', in cases of an occupier occupying premises under a sub-lease or sub-tenancy that reference is to be taken as referring to the lessor who is the occupier's immediate landlord.[4]

---

1 By virtue of ss 16(3) and 27(3).
2 Disability Discrimination (Sub-leases and Sub-tenancies) Regulations 1996, reg 3.
3 By virtue of Sch 4, paras 4 and 9.
4 Disability Discrimination (Sub-leases and Sub-tenancies) Regulations 1996, reg 4(a). Further modifications are made to s 16 and Sch 4 by reg 4, and these are referred to in the text below.

6.3.9 If the effect of the lease would otherwise be that the occupier would not be entitled to make a particular alteration to the premises (ss 16(1)(b) and 27(1)(b)), and if the alteration is one which the occupier proposes to make in order to comply with a s 6 or s 15 or s 21 duty to make reasonable adjustments (ss 16(1)(c) and 27(1)(c)), then the remaining provisions of s 16 or s 27 apply.

If the terms and conditions of a lease impose conditions which are to apply if the occupier alters the premises, then the occupier is treated for the purposes of ss 16(1)(b) and 27(1)(b) as not being entitled to make the alteration (ss 16(4)(a) and 27(4)(a)). Similarly, the occupier is to be treated for the purposes of ss 16(1)(b) and 27(1)(b) as otherwise not being entitled to make the alteration if the terms and conditions of the lease entitle the lessor to impose conditions when giving any consent to the occupier's altering the premises (ss 16(4)(b) and 27(4)(b)).

6.3.10 If the conditions in ss 16(1) or 27(1) are satisfied, ss 16(2)(a) and 27(2)(a) provide that the lease shall have effect as if it provided for the occupier to be entitled to make the alteration with the written consent of the lessor. In other words, the new law implies a statutory term into the lease or agreement at issue. Moreover, that statutory term would first require the occupier to make a written application to the lessor for such consent if the occupier wishes to make an alteration to the premises (ss 16(2)(b) and 27(2)(b)). Furthermore, the Act affects the rights of the lessor under the lease by implying into its terms a requirement that, if a written application for consent is made by the occupier, the lessor will not withhold consent unreasonably (ss 16(2)(c) and 27(2)(c)).

In turn, however, the lessor is deemed to be entitled to make any consent the subject of reasonable conditions (ss 16(2)(d) and 27(2)(d)).

Where the occupier occupies premises under a sub-lease or sub-tenancy, any superior lease under which the premises are held has effect (except to the extent to which it expressly so provides) in relation to the lessor and lessee who are parties to the superior lease as if it provided for the lessee to have to make a written application to the lessor for consent to the alteration.[1] If such an application is made, the superior lease has effect as if it provided for the lessor not to withhold its consent unreasonably and for the lessor to be entitled to make its consent subject to reasonable conditions.[2]

Rather puzzlingly, however, the opening words of ss 16(2), 16(2A) and 27(2) appear to restrict the vigour of this otherwise quite far-reaching adjustment of the rights of commercial landlord and tenant. This makes it apparent that a lease shall have effect as modified by the statutory implied terms contained in ss 16(2) and 27(2), 'except to the extent to which it [that is, the lease or superior lease] expressly so provides'. This suggests that the landlord might impose express terms in the lease that have the intent and effect of thwarting the implications made in the lease by ss 16(2) or 16(2A) or 27(2). If that is right, then it may be that such express terms would have to surmount the test of an invalid agreement in ss 9 or 26. The author does not believe that is the intention of these words which may be simply stating the obvious: namely, that these statutory measures are irrelevant where the lease or superior lease already makes such comparable provision.[3]

---

1 Section 16(2A)(i) inserted by the Disability Discrimination (Sub-leases and Sub-tenancies) Regulations 1996, reg 4(b).
2 Section 16(2A)(ii)–(iii) inserted by the Disability Discrimination (Sub-leases and Sub-tenancies) Regulations 1996, reg 4(b). In employment cases, see Employment Code of Practice, para 4.47.
3 That seems to be the interpretation offered by the Employment Code of Practice, para 4.40.

6.3.11 In employment cases, it is *not* reasonable for an employer to have to take a step in relation to premises occupied by it which would otherwise be required in order to comply with a s 6 duty to make reasonable adjustments, and which is contrary to the terms of any lease under which the employer occupies the premises, if:

- the employer has applied to the lessor in writing to take the step;
- the employer has indicated in writing that it proposes to take the step, subject to the lessor's consent, in order to comply with s 6;
- the lessor has withheld that consent; and
- the occupier (employer) has informed the disabled person that it has applied for the consent of the lessor and that the lessor has withheld that consent.[1]

For the purposes of the duty to make reasonable adjustments under s 6, the regulations also provide that where, under any binding obligation, an employer is required to obtain the consent of any person to any alteration of the premises occupied by the employer, it is *always* reasonable for the employer to have to take steps (*not* including an application to a court or tribunal) to obtain that consent and it is *never* reasonable for the employer to have to make that alteration before that consent is obtained.[2] In this context, a binding obligation means a legally binding obligation (not contained in a lease) in relation to the premises (whether arising from an agreement or otherwise).[3] An example of such an obligation would include a mortgage or a charge or, in Scotland, a feu disposition.[4]

---

1 Disability Discrimination (Employment) Regulations 1996, reg 15. See further, Employment Code of Practice, para 4.41.
2 Ibid, reg 10. See further, Employment Code of Practice, para 4.48. Note also the possible effect of building regulations and statutory consents (see **3.6.13**).
3 Ibid, reg 2.
4 Employment Code of Practice, para 4.48.

6.3.12 It is implied that the lessor will not withhold consent unreasonably (s 16(2)(c)), although the landlord is entitled to make any consent the subject of reasonable conditions (s 16(2)(d)).[1] In employment cases, a lessor is to be taken to have withheld consent to an alteration where the lessor has received a written application by or on behalf of the occupier (employer) for consent to make the alteration and the lessor has failed within a period of 21 days (or such longer period as is reasonable) either:

- to reply consenting to or refusing the application; or
- to reply consenting to the application subject to obtaining the consent of another person required under a superior lease or binding obligation (such as a mortgage or charge or, in Scotland, a feu disposition); and
- seeks that consent.[2]

If the lessor belatedly meets the above requirements, it shall be taken to have withheld its consent from the date of the failure to meet the requirements on time, but then shall be treated as having not withheld its consent from the time when it belatedly met the requirements.[3] A lessor is treated as not having sought the consent of another person (if so required) unless the lessor has applied in writing to that person indicating that the lessor's consent to the alteration has been applied for in order to comply with a s 6 duty and that the lessor has given its consent conditionally upon obtaining the other person's consent.[4]

---

1 In which case, the occupier must carry out the alteration subject to that condition: Employment Code of Practice, para 4.42. As to when it would be reasonable or unreasonable to withhold consent, see ibid, paras 4.43–4.45. See further, **6.3.13**. The question of what is a reasonable condition to consent is discussed at **6.3.13**. See further, Employment Code of Practice, para 4.46.
2 Disability Discrimination (Employment) Regulations 1996, reg 11(1)–(2) made under Sch 4, para 3 for the purposes of s 16 (and Sch 4 Part I). The period of 21 days begins with the day on which the application is received. See further, Employment Code of Practice, para 4.48.

6.3.13   In employment cases, a lessor is deemed to have withheld consent *unreasonably* where the lease provides that consent shall or will be given to an alteration of the kind in question.[1] Consent is also taken to be withheld *unreasonably* where the lease provides that consent shall or will be given to an alteration of the kind in question if the consent is sought in a particular way and that has been complied with.[2] Moreover, a lessor is deemed to have withheld consent *unreasonably* where the lessor is to be taken to have withheld consent by virtue of reg 11 (as discussed at **6.3.12**).[3]

On the other hand, in employment cases, a lessor is to be taken to have acted *reasonably* in withholding consent where there is a binding obligation (for example a mortgage or charge) requiring the consent of a third party to an alteration, the lessor has taken steps to seek that consent, and that consent has not been given or has been given subject to a condition making it reasonable for the lessor to withhold consent.[4] Alternatively, a lessor is to be taken to have acted *reasonably* in withholding consent where the lessor is bound by an agreement which allows the lessor to consent to the alteration in question subject to a condition that the lessor makes a payment and that condition does not permit the lessor to make its consent subject to a condition that the occupier (employer) reimburse the lessor the payment.[5] If it would be *reasonable* for the lessor to withhold consent, but consent has nevertheless been given, it would be *reasonable* to impose a condition on that consent that upon expiry of the lease the occupier (employer) or any assignee or successor must reinstate any relevant part of the premises which is to be altered to its state before the alteration was made.[6]

Where (in employment cases) the lessor gives consent to an alteration but subject to a condition, such a condition is to be taken to be *reasonable* in all the circumstances if it is any of the following conditions (or a condition to a similar effect). The first is a condition that the occupier (employer) must obtain any necessary planning permission (and any other consent or permission) required by or under any enactment.[7] The second is that the occupier must submit any plans or specifications for the alteration to the lessor for approval (provided the condition binds the lessor not to withhold approval unreasonably) and that the work is carried out in accordance with such plans or specifications.[8] The third is that the lessor must be permitted a reasonable opportunity to inspect the work when complete.[9] The fourth and final example of a reasonable condition is that the occupier (employer) must repay to the lessor the costs reasonably incurred in connection with the giving of the consent.[10]

1   Disability Discrimination (Employment) Regulations 1996, reg 12(a).
2   Ibid, reg 12(b).
3   Ibid, reg 12(c).
4   Ibid, reg 13(1). See further, Employment Code of Practice, para 4.48.

5   Ibid, reg 13(2).
6   Ibid, reg 14(2).
7   Ibid, reg 14(1)(a).
8   Ibid, reg 14(1)(b).
9   Ibid, reg 14(1)(c).
10 Ibid, reg 14(1)(d).

Employment and trade organisation cases

6.3.14   In employment cases (and, when fully in force, cases of discrimination by trade organisations), Part I of Sch 4 to the Act supplements s 16 and provides for remedies in cases covered by these provisions (s 16(5)). Where an industrial tribunal is considering a complaint of unlawful discrimination by an employer or trade organisation under s 8, Sch 4, para 1 deals with a failure by an occupier to obtain consent to the alteration. This applies where any question arises as to whether an employer or trade organisation occupying premises under a lease has failed to comply with a s 6 or s 15 duty to make reasonable adjustments by failing to make a particular alteration to premises. In answering that question, the tribunal must ignore any constraint attributable to the fact that the employer or trade organisation occupies the premises under lease unless the occupier has applied to the lessor in writing for consent to make the alteration.

6.3.15   The effect of Sch 4, para 1 is to deny a respondent employer or trade organisation recourse to a justification defence based upon the restrictive terms or covenants of a lease unless and until it has sought to obtain the landlord's consent to the making of the alteration despite that restriction. In other words, the occupier of the premises cannot plead justification by pointing to the negative terms of a lease alone.[1] The occupier is expected to rely upon the provisions of s 16 and to seek the landlord's consent to the alteration by means of written application.

1   Employment Code of Practice, para 4.41.

6.3.16   The sting in the tail of this provision, however, is that in industrial tribunal proceedings where a question arises about a duty to make a reasonable adjustment by an alteration to premises occupied under a lease, either the complainant or the occupier may request the tribunal to join (in Scotland, sist) the lessor as a party to the proceedings (Sch 4, para 2(1)).[1] The tribunal must grant such a request if it is made before the hearing commences (Sch 4, para 2(2)), otherwise the granting of such a request is at the tribunal's discretion (Sch 4, para 2(3)). Such a request to join the lessor to proceedings cannot be made once the tribunal has determined the complaint (Sch 4, para 2(4)).

1   In the case of sub-tenancies and sub-leases, the lessor will include a superior landlord: Disability Discrimination (Sub-leases and Sub-tenancies) Regulations 1996, reg 4(c).

6.3.17 If the lessor (or superior landlord) has been joined (or sisted) as a party to the industrial tribunal proceedings under Sch 4, para 2, then the tribunal has certain powers in relation to the lessor if certain conditions are satisfied. The tribunal may determine whether the lessor has refused consent to the alteration or consented subject to one or more conditions (Sch 4, para 2(5)(a)). If so, the tribunal may then determine whether the refusal or any of the conditions was unreasonable (Sch 4, para 2(5)(b)).[1] Where the tribunal has so determined, it may take one or more steps (Sch 4, para 2(6)).

The tribunal may make such a declaration as it considers appropriate (Sch 4, para 2(6)(a)) or make an order authorising the occupier to make an alteration specified in the order (Sch 4, para 2(6)(b)). This latter power is quite novel and is likely to prove important in practice. An order made under this power may require the occupier to comply with any conditions specified in the order (Sch 4, para 2(7)). Alternatively or additionally, the tribunal may order the lessor to pay compensation to the complainant (Sch 4, para 2(6)(c)).

Any step taken by the tribunal above may be in substitution for or in addition to any step taken by the tribunal under s 8(2) (remedies available against the respondent occupier-employer or trade organisation). However, if the tribunal decides to order the lessor to pay compensation to the complainant, it may not make a parallel compensation order under s 8(2) against the occupier-respondent (Sch 4, para 2(9)).

---

1   The provisions of the Disability Discrimination (Employment) Regulations 1996, regs 10–15 will be relevant to this exercise. See the discussion at **6.3.11** et seq.

Non-employment cases

6.3.18 Similar, but slightly different, enforcement provisions are made by Part II of Sch 4 in respect of a duty to make alterations to premises by providers of services. These provisions are not yet in force. Where any question arises as to whether a service provider occupying premises under a lease has failed to comply with a duty to make reasonable adjustments by failing to make a particular alteration to premises, any constraint attributable to the fact that the service provider occupies the premises under lease must be ignored unless the occupier has applied to the lessor in writing for consent to make the alteration (Sch 4, para 5). This is a similar principle to that in employment cases.[1]

---

1   See **6.3.14**.

6.3.19 Schedule 4, para 6(1) provides for a reference to be made to the court where the lessor has refused consent for such an alteration to be made by the occupier. A reference may also be made where the lessor has given consent to the alteration but has made the consent subject to one or more conditions. In both cases, the occupier must have first applied in writing to the lessor for the necessary consent. In these circumstances, the occupier or a disabled person (who has an interest in the proposed alteration to the premises being made) may refer the matter to the county court.[1]

The wording of Sch 4, para 6 does not seem to contemplate that such a reference can only be made where legal proceedings under s 25 have been commenced. These provisions would appear to provide for a preliminary clarification of the rights of the parties concerned by the court, even where litigation based upon a complaint of unlawful disability discrimination has not been initiated or contemplated. This distinguishes non-employment cases from employment cases.

---

1   In Scotland, the sheriff court. See Sch 4, para 6(2).

6.3.20   Where the matter has been referred to the court in the manner envisaged by Sch 4, para 6(1), the court shall determine whether the lessor's refusal was unreasonable or whether any conditions imposed upon consent are unreasonable (Sch 4, para 6(3)).[1] If the court decides that the lessor's refusal of consent to the alteration (or any conditions imposed upon the consent) was unreasonable then the court may make an appropriate declaration at its discretion. It may also make an order authorising the occupier to make an alteration specified in the order (Sch 4, para 6(4)). Such an order may require the occupier to comply with specified conditions (Sch 4, para 6(5)).

---

1   Regulations to be made under Sch 4, para 8 will assist here. No regulations have been made at
    the time of writing.

6.3.21   If litigation has been commenced under s 25, then in any court proceedings where a question arises about a duty to make a reasonable adjustment by an alteration to premises occupied under a lease, either the plaintiff (in Scotland, the pursuer) or the occupier may ask the court to join (in Scotland, sist) the lessor as a party to the proceedings (Sch 4, para 7(1)). The court must grant such a request if it is made before the hearing commences (Sch 4, para 7(2)), otherwise the granting of such a request is at the court's discretion (Sch 4, para 7(3)). Such a request to join the lessor to proceedings cannot be made once the court has determined the claim (Sch 4, para 7(4)). If the lessor has been joined (or sisted) as a party to the proceedings, then the court has certain powers in relation to the lessor if certain conditions are satisfied.

6.3.22   The court may determine whether the lessor has refused consent to the alteration at issue (Sch 4, para 7(5)(a)(i)) or whether the lessor has consented to the alteration but subject to one or more conditions (Sch 4, para 7(5)(a)(ii)). If so, in either case, the tribunal may then determine whether the refusal (or any of the conditions) was unreasonable (Sch 4, para 7(5)(b)).[1] Where such a finding has been made, the court may make such a declaration as it considers appropriate (Sch 4, para 7(6)(a)) or order the lessor to pay compensation to the plaintiff or pursuer (Sch 4, para 7(6)(c)). Although this is not made explicit, it seems logical that any such remedy against the lessor may be made in addition to or instead of any remedy that the court would be able to make against the occupier-defendant to the proceedings. However, if the court decides to order the lessor to pay compensation to the plaintiff or pursuer, it may not make a parallel compensation order against the occupier-defendant (Sch 4, para 7(8)).

Moreover, the court is also given an additional or alternative power which might prove quite radical in practice. If the court has determined that the lessor's refusal of consent to (or conditions imposed upon) an alteration was unreasonable, it may make an order authorising the occupier to make an alteration specified in the order (Sch 4, para 7(6)(b)). Such an order may require the occupier to comply with any conditions specified in the order (Sch 4, para 7(7)).

---

1   Any regulations made under Sch 4, para 8 will be relevant to this exercise. No regulations have been made at the time of writing.

Management and disposal of premises

6.3.23   The provisions of s 27 and Sch 4 do not apply to discrimination against disabled persons in relation to the disposal and management of premises under ss 22–24. This is because there is no parallel duty to make reasonable adjustments in that area as there is in respect of employment, goods, facilities or services. There is no duty upon a private or domestic landlord to make or consent to changes or alterations to the property when a disabled person is seeking to become a tenant.[1] However, the provisions of s 26 may act to invalidate any prejudicial term within a main tenancy agreement, such as one seeking to prevent the tenant sub-letting the rented property to disabled persons.

---

1   HL Deb, vol 566, col 1016 (Lord Henley).

Chapter 7

EDUCATION

7.1 INTRODUCTION

7.1.1 Controversially, the Act excludes access to education from the scope of the prohibition on discrimination in the provision of goods, facilities and services in ss 19–21 of Part III of the Act (s 19(5)).[1] This exclusion is subject to any provision to the contrary that may be made by regulations made by the Secretary of State (proviso to s 19(5)). At the time of writing, no such regulations have been made.[2]

---

1 This is in contrast to the position under sex or race discrimination law. See Part III of the Sex Discrimination Act 1975 and the Race Relations Act 1976.
2 The Secretary of State is empowered to exclude such other services as may be prescribed by regulations (s 19(5)(c)). This power has been used and will be referred to below.

7.1.2 The controversial aspect of this exclusion is that education is recognised as crucial to the aspirations of disabled persons to enjoy full and equal opportunities. In many respects, the new right to freedom from discrimination in employment (discussed in Chapter 3) will be undermined if educational opportunities are not equally available to disabled persons to enable them to compete with a well-qualified labour force as they seek to enter the competitive labour market.

Nevertheless, the Disability Discrimination Act 1995 does address the question of access to education by means other than the utilisation of the anti-discrimination framework contained in Part III of the statute. This is achieved in Part IV of the Act.

7.2 EDUCATION AND THE ANTI-DISCRIMINATION PRINCIPLE

7.2.1 The 1994 Green Paper anticipated that the new right of access to goods and services would not apply to educational facilities.[1] This is because provision for disabled pupils and students was already the subject of other legislation.[2] This disapplication of the new right of access was confirmed by the 1995 White Paper, which went on to promise fresh initiatives in respect of educational opportunities for disabled persons.[3] The exclusion of access to education from the new right not to be discriminated against as a disabled person in relation to the provision of goods, facilities and services is set out in s 19(5)(a) of the 1995 Act.

1   A *Consultation on Government Measures to Tackle Discrimination Against Disabled People* (July 1994) para 4.9.
2   See, for example, in England and Wales the Further and Higher Education Act 1992, the Education Act 1993, Part III and the *Code of Practice on the Identification and Assessment of Special Educational Needs.*
3   *Ending Discrimination Against Disabled People* (Cm 2729: January 1995) para 4.6 and Chapter 6.

7.2.2   First, ss 19–21 of the Act do not apply to education which is funded or secured by a 'relevant body' (s 19(5)(a)). A relevant body is one defined in s 19(6) and means:

- a local education authority in England and Wales;
- an education authority in Scotland;
- the Funding Agency for Schools;
- the Schools Funding Council for Wales;
- the Further Education Funding Council for England;
- the Further Education Funding Council for Wales;
- the Higher Education Funding Council for England;
- the Scottish Higher Education Funding Council;
- the Higher Education Funding Council for Wales;
- the Teacher Training Agency;
- a voluntary organisation;
- a body of a prescribed kind;[1]
- an education and library board in Northern Ireland.[2]

1   That is, one prescribed by regulations under the Act.
2   By virtue of Sch 8, para 9(3).

7.2.3   Secondly, ss 19–21 of the Act do not apply to education 'provided at an establishment which is funded by' one of the relevant bodies listed above or which is funded by a Minister of the Crown (including the Treasury) or by the Department of Education for Northern Ireland (s 19(5)(a)(i) and Sch 8, para 9(2)).

7.2.4   Thirdly, according to s 19(5)(a)(ii), ss 19–21 of the Act do not apply to education provided at 'any other establishment which is a school' as defined in the Further and Higher Education Act 1992, s 14(5) or the Education (Scotland) Act 1980, s 135(1) or the Education and Libraries (Northern Ireland) Order 1986 (this latter by virtue of Sch 8, para 9(2)). This exclusion ensures that private educational establishments are treated on an equal footing with those in the public sector and the maintained sector.

7.2.5   This is a comprehensive list of exclusions which will apply to schools, colleges and universities in the public sector or which are in receipt of public funds or which are wholly in the private sector. The effect of these provisions is to exclude education in pre-school institutions, primary schools, secondary schools, colleges and universities from the new rights of access provided by Part

III of the Disability Discrimination Act 1995. Education does not count as goods, facilities or services for the purposes of the principle of non-discrimination.

7.2.6 While employment in educational establishments will be within the prohibition on disability discrimination contained in Part II of the Act, the new legislation does not touch upon educational opportunities or the rights of disabled pupils or students within such educational establishments. In particular, the aspirations of disabled children to mainstream education rather than segregated education are not addressed by the 1995 Act, nor is the right of disabled children or adults to physical access to and reasonable accommodation within educational institutions. The question of disability rights in the field of education is engaged beyond the provisions of Part III of the Act, although note the provisions in Part IV (discussed below).

7.2.7 There is one lacuna in the Government's exclusion of education from the anti-discrimination measures in the Act. The exclusion clearly applies only to 'education' per se. Although the term 'education' is not defined in the Act, it clearly does not extend to non-educational facilities or services which an educational establishment happens to provide alongside its curricular activities. For example, many schools and colleges allow the public to use their sporting facilities (such as swimming pools, playing fields and racquet sports arenas) with or without payment and outside the core scholastic timetable. It is arguable that such provision involves the public provision of facilities or services which would not be caught by the exclusion of education.

Schools are also often used as polling stations during local and central government elections, and it is possible that access to such buildings for this purpose would involve the provision of a facility to the public.[1] Of course, in both examples, it would be necessary to identify who the provider of the facilities or services was – but it would not matter whether it was the school authority itself or whether it was some other legal person merely using the educational premises under a licence or other legal relationship (and note s 19(3)(h)).

---

1 Local authorities are, in any event, under a duty to review arrangements for polling stations, including disabled access, by virtue of the Representation of the People Act 1983, s 18. See also the comments of Lord Mackay of Ardbrecknish at HL Deb, vol 564, cols 2005–2006.

7.2.8 However, the Secretary of State has moved by regulation to exempt certain educational services from ss 19–21.[1] In so doing, the regulations may have plugged some of the gaps in the attempted exclusion of education from Part III identified at **7.2.7**. The intention is to exclude from Part III of the 1995 Act coverage of certain youth and community services provided by education authorities or voluntary organisations, the provision of facilities for research in certain circumstances, and some examination and assessment services.

1 Insofar as they do not already fall within s 19(5)(a) at **7.2.2–7.2.4**. See the Disability
   Discrimination (Services and Premises) Regulations 1996, SI 1996/1836, reg 9 (in force 2
   December 1996) made under s 19(5)(c).

7.2.9 First, ss 19–21 do not apply to services provided by a local educational
authority (LEA) in carrying out its functions under the Education Act 1944,
ss 41 or 53,[1] and, in Scotland, by an education authority in carrying out its
functions under the Education (Scotland) Act 1980, s 1(3). Section 41(1) of
the 1944 Act places a duty on every LEA to secure the provision for its area of
adequate facilities for further education. Further education means full-time
and part-time education suitable for the requirements of persons over
compulsory school age (including vocational, social, physical and recreational
training) and organised leisure-time occupation[2] provided in connection with
the provision of such education.[3] LEAs must give particular attention to
persons with learning difficulties when exercising these functions.[4] Section
53(1) of the 1944 Act places a duty on LEAs to secure that the facilities for
further education include adequate facilities for recreation and social and
physical training. LEAs may establish, maintain and manage camps, holiday
classes, playing fields, play centres and other places (including playgrounds,
gymnasiums and swimming baths) for this purpose, and may organise games,
expeditions and other activities.

1 Disability Discrimination (Services and Premises) Regulations 1996, reg 9(1)(a). Section 41 was
   substituted by the Further and Higher Education Act 1992, s 11. Section 53 was amended by the
   Education (Miscellaneous Provisions) Act 1948, Sch 1 Part I; the Education Act 1980, Sch 7; and
   the Education Reform Act 1988, Sch 12, para 54.
2 That is, leisure-time occupation, in such organised cultural training and recreative activities as
   are suited to their requirements, for any persons over compulsory school age who are able and
   willing to profit by facilities provided for that purpose: Education Act 1944, s 41(5).
3 Education Act 1944, s 41(3). See to like effect the Education (Scotland) Act 1980, s 1(3).
4 Education Act 1944, s 41(8).

7.2.10 Secondly, ss 19–21 of the 1995 Act will not apply to the provision by a
voluntary organisation of social, cultural and recreational activities and
facilities for physical education and training where such activities are designed
to promote the personal or educational development of persons taking part in
them.[1]

Thirdly, the provision of facilities for research (including the supervision of
or guidance of research) at a relevant establishment will not be covered by Part
III of the Act.[2] A 'relevant establishment' means an establishment funded by
one of the bodies listed in **7.2.2** (except a body of a prescribed kind or, in
Northern Ireland, an education and library board) or by a Minister of the
Crown,[3] or any other establishment which is a school as defined in the Further
and Higher Education Act 1992, s 14(5) or the Education (Scotland) Act 1980,
s 135(1).[4]

Fourthly, ss 19–21 of the 1995 Act will no longer embrace the assessment at a relevant establishment (as explained immediately above) of pupils or students in connection with education provided to them by the establishment or by another relevant establishment.[5] This also excludes the assessment at a relevant establishment of pupils or students to whom education has not been provided by the establishment where the assessment is undertaken.[6]

1   Disability Discrimination (Services and Premises) Regulations 1996, reg 9(1)(b).
2   Ibid, reg 9(1)(c).
3   Ibid, reg 9(2)(a) which cross-refers to s 19(6) of the 1995 Act.
4   Ibid, reg 9(2)(b) which cross-refers to s 19(5)(a)(ii) of the 1995 Act. See **7.2.4**.
5   Ibid, reg 9(1)(d)(i) and see reg 9(2).
6   Ibid, reg 9(1)(d)(ii).

7.2.11   These are complex provisions and it remains to be seen how far the regulations operate wholly to exclude these services which are closely connected with the provision of education. However, it is suggested that these regulations are not wide enough to exclude from the scope of Part III a whole raft of services, facilities and activities which may be provided on school, college or university premises. In addition to the examples already given (at **7.2.7**), student unions would not seem to be excluded from ss 19–21,[1] while many colleges and universities allow their halls of residence to be used for conferences and self-catering holiday facilities open to the public during vacations and would thus seem to be subject to the Act. At the time of writing, it is understood that the Government is considering how these incidental or ancillary services allied to education might be partly exempted from the Act and, in particular, excluded from any duties to make reasonable adjustments under s 21.

1   Unless it can be suggested that they are caught by the Disability Discrimination (Services and Premises) Regulations 1996, reg 9(1)(b) discussed at **7.2.10**.

7.3   EDUCATION AND PART IV OF THE ACT

7.3.1   Although the provision of education is not subject to the anti-discrimination principles of the new legislation, Part IV of the Act amends the Education Act 1993 and the Further and Higher Education Act 1992 to encourage policy-making and action by educational institutions to promote the integration of disabled pupils and students. These provisions, which are contained in ss 29–31, apply to schools, colleges and universities. They do not apply in Northern Ireland,[1] although extension might be made by order at some future time. At the time of writing, Part IV of the Act has yet to be brought fully into force.

Schools

7.3.2 In respect of primary and secondary education, Part III of the Education Act 1993 is concerned with children with special educational needs (SEN). A child has SEN if he or she has a learning difficulty which calls for special educational provision to be made for him or her.[1] A child has a learning difficulty in the following circumstances:

- if the child has a significantly greater difficulty in learning than the majority of children of that age; or
- if the child has a disability which prevents or hinders him or her from using educational facilities of the kind generally provided for children of that age in schools within the local education authority's area; or
- if the child is under the age of five years and is likely to fall within either of the above categories once he or she reaches the age of five years.[2]

1   Education Act 1993, s 156(1) and see s 156(4) (meaning of 'special educational provision').
    See also *Code of Practice on the Identification and Assessment of Special Educational Needs* (1994).
2   Education Act 1993, s 156(2).

7.3.3 The Secretary of State is obliged to publish a code of practice to give advice to local education authorities and school governing bodies in the discharge of their duties in respect of children with SEN.[1] Under s 159 of the 1993 Act, local education authorities are required to keep under review their arrangements for special educational provision, while s 160 imposed a qualified duty to secure the education of children with SEN in mainstream schools rather than in special schools.

1   Education Act 1993, ss 157–158.

7.3.4 The Disability Discrimination Act 1995 approaches the task of improving educational opportunities and access for disabled pupils by amending the Education Act 1993, s 161(5) from a date yet to be announced. That subsection is part of a provision setting out the duties of governing bodies (in the case of county, voluntary or grant-maintained schools) and local education authorities (in the case of maintained nursery schools) in relation to pupils with SEN. The Education Act 1993, s 161(5) requires information relating to pupils with SEN to be included in annual reporting mechanisms.[1]

1   Disability Discrimination Act 1995, s 29(1). See *School Prospectuses and Governors' Annual Reports* (DfEE Circulars 11/96 (primary schools) and 12/96 (secondary schools)). In October 1996 the DfEE also issued draft guidance to schools and local education authorities in respect of their duties under the 1995 Act.

7.3.5 The Government explained its intentions as follows:

> 'One of the major themes in the Education Act 1993 was that mainstream schools should play their full part in providing for pupils with special needs at every stage; and that a school's duties should be clarified through the code of practice for the identification and assessment of such children ... Local accountability is ensured through the requirement on schools to formulate and publish information about their policy for children with special needs, keeping parents and prospective parents informed. The publication of SEN policies will help to prevent the possibility that parents could feel inclined to send their child to a special school on the basis that they did not know enough about the SEN provision in local mainstream schools.'[1]

The 1995 reforms are intended to build upon that foundation.

---

1   HL Deb, vol 564, cols 1993–1994 (Lord Mackay of Ardbrecknish).

7.3.6 From 1 January 1997, the 'annual report' for each county, voluntary or grant-maintained school will be required to include a report containing information as to:

- the arrangements for admission of disabled pupils;
- the steps taken to prevent disabled pupils from being treated less favourably than other pupils;
- the facilities provided to assist access to school by disabled pupils.[1]

The 'annual report' in question is a reference to the report to parents required to be prepared under the articles of government for the school.[2] This gloss upon the existing obligations of schools' governing bodies applies only in respect of pupils who are disabled persons within the meaning of the 1995 legislation,[3] whether or not they have a SEN statement prepared under s 168 of the 1993 legislation.

---

1   Education Act 1993, s 161(6) as inserted by the Disability Discrimination Act 1995, s 29(2). It is intended to extend this provision to Northern Ireland in an appropriate education order: HL Deb, vol 565, col 742 (Lord Inglewood). See *School Prospectuses and Governors' Annual Reports* (DfEE Circulars 11/96 (primary schools) and 12/96 (secondary schools)).
2   In accordance with the Education (No 2) Act 1986, s 30 or the Education Act 1993, Sch 6, para 8. The cross-reference is made in the Education Act 1993, s 161(7) as inserted by the Disability Discrimination Act 1995, s 29(2).
3   Education Act 1993, s 161(7) as inserted by the Disability Discrimination Act 1995, s 29(2).

7.3.7 In the Minister's assessment, these amendments will require schools that are inaccessible to disabled children to admit it and to consider how they might be made accessible in a cost-effective way.[1] This might be done by local budget prudence or, in the case of grant-maintained schools, by application for capital grants from the funding authorities. The Government believes that its reforms will also strengthen parental rights by giving dissatisfied parents a means to voice concerns about a school's non-compliance with its own stated policies through the existing local admissions appeals arrangements. Moreover, the Minister was confident that these measures will encourage genuine and full integration of disabled pupils in mainstream education 'as far as possible'.[2]

---

1   HL Deb, vol 564, col 1994 (Lord Mackay of Ardbrecknish).
2   HL Deb, vol 564, cols 1994–1995 (Lord Mackay of Ardbrecknish).

7.3.8   Further amendment is made to the Education Act 1994, s 1 which establishes the Teacher Training Agency, the body which has responsibility for funding institutions providing teacher training. In exercising its functions under the Education Act 1994, the Teacher Training Agency must have regard to the requirements of disabled persons.[1] Although this is not made clear, it is arguable that this will cover the needs of disabled persons entering the teaching profession as well as the training of teachers in respect of the needs of disabled pupils.

---

1   Education Act 1994, s 1(4) as inserted by the Disability Discrimination Act 1995, s 29(3) with
    effect from 31 July 1996 by virtue of the Disability Discrimination Act 1995 (Commencement
    No 3 and Saving and Transitional Provisions) Order 1996, SI 1996/1474, Sch, Part II.

Further education colleges and institutions

7.3.9   In justifying the exclusion of further and higher education from the goods, facilities and services sections of the Act, the Minister stated that the Government placed a high priority on widening access to colleges and universities.[1] However, the Government wished to consider the practical effects of inclusion and sought to avoid undermining the strategic role which the further and higher education funding councils play. In particular, Lord Mackay opined that:

> 'Each institution would have to consider adaptations without regard to provision elsewhere. That would inevitably lead to piecemeal arrangements and a dissipation of scarce resources.'[2]

The Government elected for what it regarded as a coherent programme for encouraging access, enforceable through the existing complaints procedures rather than by litigation.[3]

---

1   HL Deb, vol 564, col 1989 (Lord Mackay of Ardbrecknish).
2   Ibid.
3   HL Deb, vol 564, col 1990 (Lord Mackay of Ardbrecknish).

7.3.10 Nevertheless, the Government recognised that there was a genuine problem in guaranteeing access for disabled persons to educational opportunities in colleges and universities. Its preferred solution, and the one contained within the Act, is to amend the provisions of the Further and Higher Education Act 1992 which sets out the framework for further and higher education for disabled students (including those with learning disabilities) in England and Wales. The amendments contained in the 1995 Act apply only to England and Wales and not to Scotland. Legislation already requires Scottish colleges to submit development plans including information on provisions made for disabled students.[1] It is intended that similar requirements will be laid down in future legislation providing for the incorporation of further education colleges in Northern Ireland.[2]

1 Further and Higher Education (Scotland) Act 1992, s 22.
2 HL Deb, vol 564, cols 1991–1992 (Lord Mackay of Ardbrecknish).

7.3.11 The 1992 statute 'requires the further education funding councils to act in a strategic manner to secure sufficient and adequate provision of further education'.[1] The councils must take particular account of the needs of the population in terms of location, equipment, aptitudes and abilities, and they have especial responsibilities in respect of disabled students. To those ends, the Further Education Funding Council for England (FEFCE) requires colleges to submit strategic plans, including analysis of local needs, and its funding methodology takes into account the needs of disabled students. Moreover, the FEFCE's inspectorate 'includes a specialist team with specific responsibilities for reporting on the quality of provision for disabled students' in the further education sector.[2]

1 HL Deb, vol 564, col 1990 (Lord Mackay of Ardbrecknish).
2 HL Deb, vol 564, col 1990 (Lord Mackay of Ardbrecknish). The Minister reported (at col 1991) that the FEFCE had adjusted recurrent funding methods for the 1995–96 academic year to enable colleges to claim up to 8,800 per student to cover the extra costs involved in educating students requiring additional support.

7.3.12 Part IV of the Disability Discrimination Act 1995 seeks to build upon the existing strategy by amending the Further and Higher Education Act 1992 with effect from 31 July 1996.[1] The funding councils for further education institutions and colleges are now required to place conditions upon the financial support they give to such educational establishments under the Further and Higher Education Act 1992, s 5. In particular, the Disability Discrimination Act 1995, s 30(2) amends the Further and Higher Education Act 1992, s 5(6)(b) so as to make the administration of funds by further education funding councils subject to a new s 5(7A) set of conditions for financial support given to further education colleges.[2] These new conditions are expressly without prejudice to the funding councils' existing powers to impose conditions on the granting of such financial support (contained in s 5(6)(b) of the 1992 legislation).

---

1 By virtue of the Disability Discrimination Act 1995, s 30(1) and the Disability Discrimination Act 1995 (Commencement No 3 and Saving and Transitional Provisions) Order 1996, Sch, Part II.
2 Disability Discrimination Act 1995, s 30(2).

7.3.13   Those additional specific conditions:

- require the governing body to publish 'disability statements' containing information about the provision of facilities for education made by the institution in respect of 'disabled persons'; and
- may include conditions relating to the provision made (or to be made) by the institution with respect to 'disabled persons'.[1]

The phrase 'disabled persons' as used here means only such persons as satisfy the definition of 'disabled person' in the Disability Discrimination Act 1993, ss 1–2 and Schs 1–2 (see Chapter 2).[2]

---

1 Further and Higher Education Act 1992, s 5(7A) as inserted by the Disability Discrimination Act 1992, s 30(3).
2 Further and Higher Education Act 1992, s 5(7B) as inserted by the Disability Discrimination Act 1992, s 30(3).

7.3.14   The information to be contained in a disability statement about the provision of facilities made by further education institutions in England and Wales in respect of disabled persons is prescribed by the Education (Disability Statements for Further Education Institutions) Regulations 1996.[1] A disability statement must cover the following matters:[2]

- the policies of the institution relating to the provision of facilities for education;
- the names of a member or members of the staff with special responsibility for disabled persons;
- admission arrangements;
- educational facilities and support, including academic and curriculum support, relevant staff expertise, and technology and equipment available;
- additional support or special arrangements during examinations and assessments;
- facilities and support associated with educational facilities and support, including counselling and welfare arrangements;
- physical access to educational and other facilities.

The statement should also contain information about arrangements for handling complaints and (where applicable) appeals in respect of admission arrangements, educational facilities and support, additional support or special arrangements during examinations and assessments, facilities and support associated with educational facilities and support (including counselling and welfare arrangements), and physical access to educational and other facilities.

If on or before 1 August 1996 a further education funding council sets a condition of financial support requiring the governing body of a further education institution to publish a disability statement, the institution in question must publish the disability statement by 1 December 1996.[3] If the condition date is after 1 August 1996, then the disability statement must be published by 1 October in the financial year following the financial year in which the condition date fell.[4] Thereafter, subsequent disability statements must be published by 1 October in the following year.[5]

---

1 SI 1996/1664 made under ss 5(7A)–(7B) and 89(4) of the Further and Higher Education Act 1992. Section 5(7A)–(7B) was inserted by the Disability Discrimination Act 1995, s 30. The Regulations came into force on 31 July 1996.
2 Education (Disability Statements for Further Education Institutions) Regulations 1996, reg 2.
3 Ibid, reg 3(1)(a).
4 Ibid, reg 3(1)(b). The term 'financial year' means the period from 1 April to 31 March in any year: reg 3(3).
5 Ibid, reg 3(2). The term 'year' as used here appears to mean a calendar year (1 January to 31 December). So if an institution had to publish its first disability statement by 1 December 1996, its second disability statement should be published by 1 October 1997 and so on.

7.3.15 Explaining these amendments to the further education legislation, Lord Mackay of Ardbrecknish stated that the new provisions:

'would place a duty on the funding councils to require individual colleges to produce, as a condition of grant, information on their facilities for education for students with disabilities. We envisage further consultation with the councils prior to prescribing the frequency and content of the statements in the regulations. Information is likely to include physical access, the provision of specialist equipment, facilities which may help students with particular disabilities, admission policies, counselling and welfare arrangements.'[1]

The Minister envisaged that the new measures would highlight good practice, would encourage colleges to emulate good practice and would assist disabled students to make informed choices.

These provisions do not give disabled students directly enforceable rights as such, but they will 'be able to seek redress from the councils on the rare occasions when provision fails to meet expectations raised by the information' contained in a statutory disability statement. It would seem that ultimately a funding council could demand repayment of a grant paid to a college which fails to meet the new legislative requirements.[2]

---

1 HL Deb, vol 564, col 1991 (Lord Mackay of Ardbrecknish).
2 Ibid.

7.3.16 Further amendments to the 1992 legislation build upon the strategic role of the further education funding councils. The funding councils are now required to make an annual report in writing to the Secretary of State on:

- the progress made during the previous year in the provision of further education for disabled students in their area; and
- their plans for future provision of further education for disabled students.[1]

The Government envisages that the funding councils will draw on existing review and planning mechanisms as well as new information generated from the disability statements produced by colleges and the evidence gathered by the FEFCE's committee on education and disability (the Tomlinson Committee).[2]

---

1 Further and Higher Education Act 1992, s 8(6) as added by the Disability Discrimination Act 1995, s 30(4) and in force 31 July 1996.
2 HL Deb, vol 564, col 1991 (Lord Mackay of Ardbrecknish).

7.3.17 The term 'disabled students' as used here refers only to students who are disabled persons for the purposes of the Disability Discrimination Act 1995.[1] The obligation to make a written annual report of the kind described arises as soon as is reasonably practicable after the end of a funding council's financial year. This means the period of 12 months ending with 31 March 1997 and each successive period of 12 months.[2].

---

1 Further and Higher Education Act 1992, s 8(7) as added by the Disability Discrimination Act 1995, s 30(4).
2 Further and Higher Education Act 1992, s 8(6)–(7) as added by the Disability Discrimination Act 1995, s 30(4).

7.3.18 The Disability Discrimination Act 1995 also amends (from a date to be determined) the functions of local education authorities (LEAs) in respect of further education in order to underpin the new duties of colleges and funding councils. This is achieved by s 30(7) amending the Education Act 1944, s 41. Local education authorities will be placed under a new duty to publish disability statements at prescribed intervals.[1] Such statements must contain information (to be prescribed by regulations) about the provision of facilities for further education made by the LEA in respect of disabled persons within the meaning of the 1995 Act.[2] The intention is to ensure that courses provided by LEAs enjoyed 'parity of esteem' with FEFC-funded courses and that disabled students should be better informed about such locally provided courses.[3] These provisions are not yet in force.

1 Education Act 1944, s 41(2A) as added by the Disability Discrimination Act 1995, s 30(8). The prescribed intervals will be dealt with in regulations (Education Act 1944, s 41(2B)).
2 Education Act 1944, s 41(2B) as added by the Disability Discrimination Act 1995, s 30(8).
3 HL Deb, vol 566, cols 1032–1033 (Lord Henley).

Universities and higher education institutions

7.3.19 Prior to the Disability Discrimination Act 1995, the Secretary of State provided mere guidance to the higher education funding councils that they should have regard to the needs of disabled students in universities and institutions of higher education. It might have been thought sufficient to have amended the Further and Higher Education Act 1992 to make parallel provisions for the university sector to those adopted in further education, as described above.

7.3.20 Such a proposal generated much debate in academic circles because s 68(3) of the 1992 Act prevents the Government from making grants to higher education establishments conditional by reference to courses, staff and admissions. This subsection is regarded as a bulwark of academic freedom and proposals to require universities to promulgate disability statements generated concern in higher education circles that this would result in interference with course and curriculum design.[1] As a result, the amendments of the 1992 statute by the 1995 Act in respect of higher education take a slightly different course from that in respect of further education.

1 The essence of that concern is captured in the contributions to the legislative debate of Lord Beloff and Earl Russell: HL Deb, vol 564, cols 874–876 and 1983–1986 respectively.

7.3.21 The higher education funding councils for England and Wales will henceforth be required to have regard to the requirements of disabled persons when exercising their statutory functions.[1] Parallel provision is made for Scotland by s 31(1) of the 1995 Act.[2] In both cases, the new statutory duty applies only in respect of disabled persons within the meaning of the 1995 Act.[3]

1 Further and Higher Education Act 1992, s 62(7A) as inserted by the Disability Discrimination Act 1995, s 30(5). Section 62 of the 1992 Act is concerned with the establishment of higher education funding councils in England and Wales.
2 Further and Higher Education (Scotland) Act 1992, s 37(4A) as inserted by the Disability Discrimination Act 1992, s 31(2).
3 Further and Higher Education Act 1992, s 62(7B) as inserted by the Disability Discrimination Act 1995, s 30(5); Further and Higher Education (Scotland) Act 1992, s 37(4B) as inserted by the Disability Discrimination Act 1995, s 31(2).

7.3.22 The higher education funding councils are then empowered to make grants, loans or other payments to the governing body of a university or higher education institution conditional upon a requirement that the governing body should publish 'disability statements' at specified intervals.[1] This is without prejudice to the existing powers of the funding councils to impose conditions on governing bodies, but the language of the new subsections makes it clear that the requirement to publish periodic disability statements is mandatory. A disability statement for this purpose is a statement containing information (to be specified in the conditions subject to which grants, loans or other payments are made by a council) about the provision of facilities for education and research made by the university or institution in respect of disabled persons (as defined in the 1995 Act).[2]

---

1   Further and Higher Education Act 1992, s 65(4A) as inserted by the Disability Discrimination Act 1995, s 30(6); Further and Higher Education (Scotland) Act 1992, s 40(5) as inserted by the Disability Discrimination Act 1995, s 31(3). The word 'specified' in the context of specified intervals means specified in the conditions subject to which grants, loans or other payments are made by a council: Further and Higher Education Act 1992, s 65(4B) as inserted by the Disability Discrimination Act 1995, s 30(6); Further and Higher Education (Scotland) Act 1992, s 40(6) as inserted by the Disability Discrimination Act 1995, s 31(3).
2   Further and Higher Education Act 1992, s 65(4B) as inserted by the Disability Discrimination Act 1995, s 30(6); Further and Higher Education (Scotland) Act 1992, s 40(6) as inserted by the Disability Discrimination Act 1995, s 31(3). It is clear that the 'facilities' referred to do not merely include *physical* facilities: HL Deb, vol 566, cols 278–279 (Lord Henley).

7.3.23   The amendments to the powers of the higher education funding councils in respect of the administration of funds are designed to achieve the:

> 'intention that the [disability] statements would assist disabled students and funding councils generally in understanding the provision available for education and research in the particular institution ... The statements would thus go wider than simply including information about physical facilities. It will be a matter for the funding councils, in consultation, to determine how to specify the information needed in the statements to achieve that in a viable and cost-effective way. I should stress that the provision of information will not *ipso facto* require any changes in the nature of the facilities offered by the institution.'[1]

This is apparently achieved without compromising the guarantees of academic freedom inherent in the 1992 legislation.

The Minister stated the Government's view that there was nothing in the Act that might require a university to change admissions arrangements, modify course structures or alter assessment programmes in order to meet the needs of disabled students. Moreover, nothing in a disability statement is intended to be used to pressurise universities or funding councils to change curriculum and admissions policies.[2] It would seem, however, that the Government hopes that disability statements will concentrate the minds of universities and will encourage them to be receptive to the needs of disabled students.

---

1   HL Deb, vol 564, col 1993 (Lord Mackay of Ardbrecknish).
2   HL Deb, vol 566, col 1036 (Lord Henley).

7.3.24 These provisions came into force on 31 July 1996. Following consultations,[1] the Higher Education Funding Council for England (HEFCE) and its Welsh and Scottish counterparts (HEFCW and SHEFC) have each issued a specification for disability statements required from institutions funded by each Council,[2] but the analysis that follows will use the HEFCE specification as an exemplar (although there are subtle differences between each Council's specifications). The account below is a summary of the required content of a disability statement for a HEFCE institution and reference should be made to the specifications themselves for the detail of that requirement in any particular case. It is anticipated that a disability statement will be produced every three years, but should be updated and resubmitted where there have been significant changes.[3] Statements should be published and may be referred to in other publications (such as prospectuses).[4] The HEFCE requires its funded institutions to submit statements covering 1996–97 to 1998–99 by January 1997.

1 See HEFCE Consultation Paper CP3/95 (December 1995); HEFCW Circular W96/20HE (March 1996); SHEFC Consultation Paper 01/96 (February 1996).
2 See HEFCE Circular 8/96 (May 1996); HEFCW Circular W96/43HE (June 1996).
3 HEFCE Circular 8/96, para 18.
4 Ibid, paras 20–21. The Internet or World Wide Web might be used for dissemination purposes and the Careers Advisory Network on Disability Opportunities (CANDO) at Lancaster University has proposed co-ordinating this (see http://www.comp.lancs.ac.uk/uniservices/careers/cando).

7.3.25 While a disability statement should describe facilities for education and research offered by a higher education institution to disabled persons, it is also designed to inform the funding council about such provision and to highlight good practice.[1] Although institutions are free to decide what facilities should be offered, they are encouraged to consider provision for disabled students and 'to plan strategically for future developments'.[2] Statements should be 'concise, informative and developmental' (perhaps 4–8 pages long), may if necessary make reference to *accessible* secondary sources, and may need to be produced in alternative formats or media.[3] Statements should be structured so as to provide information under the headings of current policy, current provision, and future activity and policy development.

1 HEFCE Circular 8/96, para 8.
2 Ibid, para 9.
3 Ibid, para 10.

7.3.26 As far as current policy is concerned, the statement should contain general information on policies and procedures relating to disabled students for:[1]

- equal opportunities;
- access and admissions;
- examinations and assessments;
- quality assessment, and monitoring and evaluation of support services;
- staff development and training programmes;
- provision of financial assistance to disabled students;
- charging students for certain facilities.

If an institution does not have policies for the above areas, it should give an overview of its policies affecting disabled students. In connection with current provision, the statement should describe the nature and range of provision for disabled students, including:[2]

- names and titles (and contact details) of the co-ordinator and member of senior management responsible for disabled students;
- examples of the types of information, advice, services and materials available, and a broad picture of how the institution provides support;[3]
- academic services and support arrangements (for example special provision for examinations and marking);
- information technology provision;
- a general description of the physical environment;
- specific information on medical facilities, transport, religious and spiritual worship, external services, and award ceremonies.

The statement should indicate any restrictions on services and facilities, and an indication of the number of disabled students at the institution.[4] Finally, the statement should outline plans for policy development and improvements to provision in the short to long term, covering at least the next three years.[5]

---

1 HEFCE Circular 8/96, paras 12–13. The date on which the policy or procedure became effective should also be stated. The HEFCW also includes complaints and appeals procedures in the list of existing policy: HEFCW Circular W96/43HE, para 8.
2 HEFCE Circular 8/96, para 14.
3 The circular suggests a number of questions that might be addressed: ibid, para 14.b.
4 Ibid, paras 15–16.
5 Ibid, para 17.

Chapter 8

PUBLIC TRANSPORT

8.1 INTRODUCTION

8.1.1 The 1994 Green Paper considered whether the new right of access proposed in general should be extended to facilities for transport or travel.[1] It was anticipated that the new right would not require modifications to transport systems where otherwise existing physical barriers prevented access. The 1995 White Paper confirmed that the new right would not apply to transport vehicles but would apply to stations.[2] It suggested that further initiatives would take place outside the framework of the proposed disability discrimination legislation. In the event, the initiatives are taken in Part V of the Disability Discrimination Act 1995. Part V is not yet in force at the time of writing.

---

1 *A Consultation on Government Measures to Tackle Discrimination Against Disabled People* (July 1994) para 4.5.
2 *Ending Discrimination Against Disabled People* (Cm 2729: January 1995) para 4.6.

Transport services and Part III of the Act

8.1.2 Transport services are not generally or unconditionally subject to the anti-discrimination principles contained in Part III of the Act. Subject to any provision to the contrary in future regulations, ss 19–21 do not apply to any service 'so far as it consists of the use of any means of transport' (s 19(5)(b)). This appears to mean that the right of access to goods, facilities or services contained in s 19 will require transport providers to make some (but not all) of their facilities or services accessible without discrimination to disabled people (subject to the remaining provisions of Part III).

For example, facilities and services such as timetables, ticketing arrangements, booking facilities, waiting areas, toilet facilities, platforms and other public areas will be subject to the anti-discrimination provisions of the Act and transport providers will need to consider what reasonable adjustments might be made in order to ensure that disabled passengers enjoy effective access to such facilities or services (at least, when s 21 is brought into force). However, ss 19–21 do not require buses, taxis, trains, aeroplanes or other forms of public transport (including heritage vehicles) to be accessible in themselves without discrimination or to be accommodating of the needs of disabled passengers.[1]

---

1 HL Deb, vol 566, col 463 (Lord Mackay of Ardbrecknish).

8.1.3 Of course, there may be other legal or extra-legal sources which assist disabled persons to achieve a right of access in respect of transport vehicles. For example, some local authorities already make the accessibility of taxis the subject of licensing conditions. Nevertheless, the 1995 Act does not create a general right of transport accessibility.

Transport employers and Part II of the Act

8.1.4 The exclusion of transport services from Part III of the Act does not prevent disabled persons from enjoying a right to equal employment opportunity under Part II of the statute in respect of transport employers from 2 December 1996 onwards. By way of illustration, a disabled bus driver would be entitled not to be discriminated against by the transport provider in its guise as employer. Ironically, that might call for modifications to be made to a vehicle if that would be a reasonable adjustment within the meaning of s 6.[1] For example, a driver with impaired hearing might be entitled to the installation of a simple audio-visual signalling system that indicated when a passenger wished to alight.

---

1 See Chapter 3.

Public transport and Part V of the Act

8.1.5 Although transport systems are not fully covered by the anti-discrimination measures in the Act, the new legislation does empower the Government to enact new accessibility standards for public transport at some future date. These accessibility standards will apply to taxis, public service vehicles and rail vehicles. They apply only to land-based transport services and so will not apply to aircraft or ferries. These are the measures set out in Part V of the Act which provides a statutory framework for future regulations. Part V of the Act has not been brought into force as yet and cannot be effective in any event unless and until the necessary accessibility regulations are promulgated. Each of the methods of transport covered by Part V are now examined in turn and the new framework for devising accessibility standards is described.

8.2 TAXIS

8.2.1 While many local authorities have attempted to improve the accessibility of taxis to disabled passengers through licensing conditions, the Government took the view during the passage of the Disability Discrimination Act that such a piecemeal approach had been tried and failed. The Government did express its 'clear intention' to introduce 'provisions to require that, from days to be determined, taxis newly licensed must, as a condition of licence, be accessible to all disabled people, including those who use wheelchairs'.[1] However, in the same breath, the Minister also made it 'absolutely clear that we are not talking about a universal requirement for the current purpose-built taxi design', while accepting that there had been criticism of the current models of wheelchair-accessible taxis.[2]

1 HL Deb, vol 564, col 2034 (Lord Mackay of Ardbrecknish). A date for the implementation of the taxi accessibility standards has not been indicated: HL Deb, vol 566, cols 453–454.
2 HL Deb, vol 564, cols 2034–2035 (Lord Mackay of Ardbrecknish).

Taxi accessibility regulations

8.2.2 The Secretary of State is given power by s 32(1) of the 1995 Act to make 'taxi accessibility regulations' for the purpose of securing that it is possible:

- for disabled persons to get into and out of taxis in safety;
- for disabled persons to be carried in taxis in safety and in reasonable comfort;
- for disabled persons in wheelchairs to be conveyed in safety into and out of taxis while remaining in their wheelchairs;
- for disabled persons in wheelchairs to be carried in taxis in safety and in reasonable comfort while remaining in their wheelchairs.

In the Minister's view, the regulations 'will focus clearly on the needs of all disabled people and will be drawn up in close consultation with the Disabled Persons Transport Advisory Committee' (DPTAC).[1] Design parameters will be defined based on research and experience to provide 'optimum levels of accessibility' and manufacturers will be expected to meet the new market demand so created.[2]

1 HL Deb, vol 564, col 2035 (Lord Mackay of Ardbrecknish).
2 Ibid.

8.2.3 Such 'taxi accessibility regulations' made under s 32(1) may, in particular, require 'regulated taxis' to conform with regulations as to the size of door openings for passenger use, the floor area of 'passenger compartments',[1] the amount of headroom in passenger compartments and the fitting of restraining devices designed to ensure the stability of a wheelchair while the taxi is moving (s 32(2)(a)). Moreover, the regulations may require drivers of regulated taxis plying for hire (or under hire) to comply with regulations as to the carrying of ramps or other devices designed to facilitate the loading and unloading of wheelchairs (s 32(2)(b)). The regulations might also require the driver of a regulated taxi, in which a disabled person in a wheelchair is being carried (while remaining in the wheelchair), to comply with regulations as to the position in which the wheelchair is to be secured (s 32(2)(c)).

1 The meaning of this term is to be prescribed in future regulations (s 32(5)).

8.2.4 Section 32(2) establishes the requirement that taxi drivers must recognise their duty to carry disabled customers. It would not be lawful for drivers to refuse to pick up a disabled passenger in a wheelchair 'on the pretext ... that they are not carrying the ramps'.[1] A failure to comply with such accessibility regulations by a driver plying for hire (or under hire) will be a criminal offence (s 32(3)). On summary conviction, a person guilty of such an offence will be liable to a fine not exceeding level 3 on the standard scale (s 32(4)).

---

1   HL Deb, vol 564, col 2035 (Lord Mackay of Ardbrecknish).

8.2.5 To what taxis will these new regulations and duties apply? The s 32 regulations will define which taxis are to be regulated for these purposes. However, s 32(5) makes it explicit that the regulations can only apply to a 'taxi' as narrowly defined. A 'taxi' for this purpose means only a vehicle licensed under the Town Police Clauses Act 1847, s 37 or the Metropolitan Public Carriage Act 1869, s 6.[1] It does not include a taxi which is drawn by a horse or other animal.

The effect is that the new accessibility standards for taxis will apply only to hackney cabs or so-called 'black cabs' and will not apply to private hire cars or 'minicabs'.[2] At the same time, it is not intended that the taxi trade will in future be expected to make universal use of the London-style black cab or that the new legislation will produce a universal purpose-built taxi design.[3]

---

1   In Northern Ireland, a taxi is a vehicle licensed to stand or ply for hire under the Road Traffic (Northern Ireland) Order 1981, art 61 and which seats not more than 8 passengers in addition to the driver (para 16(2) of Sch 8 to the 1995 Act).
2   HL Deb, vol 566, col 451 (Lord Mackay of Ardbrecknish).
3   HL Deb, vol 566, col 453 (Lord Mackay of Ardbrecknish).

8.2.6 The Government was concerned 'to ensure an orderly transition to the new requirements without damaging the viability of the taxi trade'.[1] Accordingly, by virtue of s 34(1), taxi licensing authorities[2] shall not grant a taxi licence unless the taxi conforms with the relevant taxi accessibility regulations, but the effect of s 34(2) is to ensure that the licensing requirements by reference to any taxi accessibility regulations only apply to newly licensed taxis, as opposed to taxis with existing licences and seeking renewal.[3] Section 34(2) is an awkwardly worded subsection:

> 'Subsection (1) does not apply if such a licence was in force with respect to the vehicle at any time during the period of 28 days immediately before the day on which the licence is granted.'

Its intention is to regulate only new entrants to the taxi trade (or newly acquired taxis). It does not prevent the re-licensing of non-accessible taxis provided that, subject to 28 days' grace, the new licence comes into force immediately on the expiry of the previous licence.[4]

---

1 HL Deb, vol 564, col 2035 (Lord Mackay of Ardbrecknish).
2 See s 68(1) as to the meaning of this term.
3 The provisions of s 34 are applied to Northern Ireland with appropriate substitutions: Sch 8, para 18.
4 HL Deb, vol 566, cols 440–441 (Lord Mackay of Ardbrecknish).

8.2.7 This is best explained in the Minister's own words:

> 'Subsection (1) provides that a licensing authority may, after a certain date, only license taxis which comply with the construction requirements that will be set out in the regulations ... We are also mindful of the need to protect the interests of the cab trade, much of which comprises small businesses. While it is reasonable to expect new taxis to be fully accessible, it would ... be unreasonable to require someone who had recently purchased and licensed a new non-accessible vehicle to dispose of it prematurely.'[1]

However, it is not intended that this exceptional treatment should continue indefinitely.

---

1 HL Deb, vol 564, col 2035 (Lord Mackay of Ardbrecknish).

8.2.8 The Secretary of State may provide by order that the s 34(2) exemption shall cease to have effect on a specified date (s 34(3)). The effect of such an order may be varied for different areas or localities (s 34(4)).[1] Thus it is contemplated that there will be a future date beyond which no non-accessible vehicle can be re-licensed as a taxi. That date is to be the subject of consultation with the trade. This might affect cities such as London, Edinburgh, Liverpool and Manchester that have already set dates by which all taxis must be accessible.

---

1 By virtue of s 67(7), this is without prejudice to the generality of the powers to make regulations or orders by statutory instrument conferred by s 67(2)–(3).

8.2.9 The Government hopes that these provisions will open up new markets for the taxi trade, but acknowledges that compliance with the new standards could create difficulties. This is recognised in s 35(1). The Secretary of State may make 'exemption regulations' to enable taxi licensing authorities[1] to apply for an order to be exempt from the s 34 licensing provisions if the licensing authority believes that, having regard to 'circumstances prevailing in its area', the application of the licensing conditions would be 'inappropriate' and if their application would result in 'an unacceptable reduction in the number of taxis' in that area (s 35(3)).

The exemption regulations may make particular provision and prescriptions requiring a licensing authority proposing to apply for a s 35 exemption order to carry out consultations,[2] to publish its proposal, to consider any represen-tations made about the proposal (before it applies for an order) and to make its application in a prescribed form (s 35(2)). Section 35 does not apply in Northern Ireland.[3]

---

1   That is, a licensing authority responsible for licensing taxis in any area of England and Wales other than the area to which the Metropolitan Public Carriage Act 1869 applies (s 35(7)).
2   Including 'as a matter of course, disabled people and the taxi trade' (HL Deb, vol 564, col 2036 (Lord Mackay of Ardbrecknish)).
3   Sch 8, para 19.

8.2.10   Section 35 'is a recognition of the enormously wide variations in types of area and of taxi use in this country'. The Minister expressed that the 'strong presumption must be that, whatever the area, there will be now, or may be in the future, disabled people whose mobility would be enhanced by the availability of accessible vehicles'. However, at the same time he recognised the possibility that Part V of the Act 'could jeopardise the viability of the trade in a particular area to the point at which there ceased to be taxi provision for anyone'. The Government wished to avoid that result.[1]

---

1   See generally HL Deb, vol 564, col 2036 (Lord Mackay of Ardbrecknish).

8.2.11   The Secretary of State must consider any application for an exemption order and consult the DPTAC (and any other persons the Secretary of State considers appropriate). Then the Secretary of State may make an exemption order (in the terms applied for or in such other terms as the Secretary of State considers appropriate) or refuse to make such an order (s 35(4)).

8.2.12   Even if a taxi is exempted from the taxi accessibility regulations, the Government will still have power to require an 'exempt taxi' to comply with 'swivel seat regulations' as to the fitting and use of swivel seats in the taxi. The Secretary of State is given a power to make 'swivel seat regulations' requiring any 'exempt taxi' plying for hire in an area in respect of which an exemption order (made under s 35) is in force to conform with provisions as to the fitting and use of 'swivel seats' (s 35(5)).[1]

An 'exempt taxi' is a taxi in relation to which s 34(1) would apply if there was not a s 35 exemption order in force (s 35(7)). The term 'swivel seats' will be defined in regulations (s 35(7)). No further light on these proposed regu-lations is cast by the parliamentary debates on the legislation.[2]

1   Note s 35(6) which cross-refers to s 34.
2   Although see HL Deb, vol 566, cols 1042–1043 (Lord Mackay of Ardbrecknish).

Duties of taxi drivers towards disabled passengers

8.2.13   Drivers of regulated taxis are placed under new duties by s 36 of the Act in respect of a taxi which has been hired by or for a disabled person in a wheelchair; or by a person who wishes to be accompanied by a disabled person in a wheelchair (s 36(1)). These duties are:

- to carry in the taxi the passenger while he or she remains in the wheelchair;
- not to make any additional charge for doing so;
- to carry the wheelchair in the taxi if the passenger chooses to sit in a passenger seat;
- to take such steps as are necessary to ensure that the passenger is carried in the taxi in safety and in reasonable comfort.[1]

1   Section 36(3)(a)–(d). The term 'the passenger' means the disabled person concerned and 'carry' means carry in the taxi concerned (s 36(2)).

8.2.14   In addition, it will be the driver's statutory duty to give such assistance as may be reasonably required:

- to enable the passenger to get into or out of the taxi;
- to enable the passenger to be conveyed into and out of the taxi while in the wheelchair if the passenger wishes to remain in the wheelchair;
- to load the passenger's luggage into or out of the taxi;
- to load the wheelchair into or out of the taxi if the passenger does not wish to remain in the wheelchair.[1]

1   Section 36(3)(e).

8.2.15   A failure to comply with any of these duties without lawful excuse will be a criminal offence punishable upon summary conviction by a fine not exceeding level 3 on the standard scale (s 36(5)). However, there are certain defences and exemptions contained within s 36 (discussed below).

8.2.16   Section 36 does not require the driver of a taxi to carry more than one person in a wheelchair, or more than one wheelchair, on any one journey (s 36(4)(a)).[1] Nothing in s 36 requires a taxi driver to carry any person in circumstances in which it would otherwise be lawful for the driver to refuse to carry that person (s 36(4)(b)). For example, a taxi driver could not be required to carry a disabled passenger where the taxi is already exceeding the number of passengers who may be carried in accordance with its licence. It will also be a defence to show that, even although the taxi conformed with any taxi accessibility regulations made under s 32, it would not have been possible for the wheelchair of the disabled passenger concerned to be carried in safety in the taxi (s 36(6)).

1   The subsection contemplates an exception in the case of a taxi of a prescribed description, but no such prescription has been made at the time of writing.

8.2.17   Section 36 also makes provision for the exemption of taxi drivers from these new statutory duties on medical grounds. A taxi licensing authority shall issue a driver with a certificate of exemption from the s 36 duties if it is satisfied that it is appropriate to exempt the driver on medical grounds (s 36(7)(a)).[1] An exemption certificate may also be issued on the ground that the driver's physical condition makes it impossible or unreasonably difficult for him or her to comply with a taxi driver's duties imposed under s 36 (s 36(7)(b)). The Government felt that this exception was important, especially for taxi drivers who themselves had a disability.[2] Provision is made in s 38 for an appeal against a refusal to grant an exemption certificate.

1   In Northern Ireland, this power lies with the Department of the Environment (Sch 8, para 20). Provision is made in s 49 for criminal offences committed in connection with exemption certificates (for example, forgery or the making of false statements).
2   HL Deb, vol 564, col 2036 (Lord Mackay of Ardbrecknish).

8.2.18   The currency of the certificate of exemption shall be for such period as the licensing authority specifies in the certificate when issued (s 36(8)). Once an exemption certificate has been issued to a taxi driver under s 36(7), and so long as it remains in force, the driver is exempt from the duties imposed under s 36(3), provided an exemption notice (in a prescribed form and in a prescribed manner) is exhibited on the taxi (s 36(9)).[1]

1   The necessary prescriptions have yet to be made.

8.2.19   In order to address the problem of persons with sensory impairments, who use guide or hearing dogs, being refused access to taxis because they wish to be accompanied by their animal, s 37 imposes additional duties on taxi drivers. These duties arise where the taxi has been hired by or for a disabled person ('the passenger') accompanied by a guide dog or hearing dog (s 37(1)(a) and (2)). The duties also apply where the taxi has been hired by a person who wishes to be accompanied in the taxi by a disabled person ('the passenger') accompanied by a guide or hearing dog (s 37(1)(b) and (2)). A guide dog is a dog trained to guide a blind person, while a hearing dog is a dog trained to assist a deaf person (s 37(11)).[1] It is noteworthy that these duties apply to all taxis and not just to regulated taxis.

---

1 Section 37 might also be applied in future by regulations to any other category of dog trained to assist a disabled person with a prescribed disability (s 37(9)–(10) and Sch 8, para 21(3)). No such regulations or prescription have been made at the present.

8.2.20 The duties of a taxi driver in the above situations are to carry the disabled passenger's dog, allowing it to remain with the passenger in the taxi, and not to make any additional charge for so doing (s 37(3)). A breach of these duties is a criminal offence punishable on summary conviction by a fine not exceeding level 3 on the standard scale (s 37(4)).

8.2.21 However, in like manner to the exemption from duties under s 36 (carrying of passengers in wheelchairs),[1] a licensing authority may exempt a driver from the s 37 duties by means of an exemption certificate if it is satisfied that such exemption is appropriate on medical grounds (s 37(5)).[2] In deciding that question, the authority must have particular regard to the physical characteristics of the taxi in question (s 37(6)). For example, this exemption might cover a driver who has a medical condition that is aggravated by dogs, such as an asthmatic condition or an allergy.[3] Provision is made in s 38 for an appeal against a refusal to grant an exemption certificate.

---

1 Similar provisions are also made as to the issue and currency of a s 37 exemption certificate and the display of such certificate in the taxi (s 37(7)–(8)).
2 In Northern Ireland, this power lies with the Department of the Environment (Sch 8, para 21). Provision is made in s 49 for criminal offences committed in connection with exemption certificates (for example, forgery or the making of false statements).
3 HL Deb, vol 564, col 2037 (Lord Mackay of Ardbrecknish).

8.2.22 Any person who is aggrieved by a refusal of a licensing authority to issue an exemption certificate under s 36 or s 37 may appeal under s 38(1) to the local magistrates' court (or, in Northern Ireland, a court of summary jurisdiction) for the petty sessions area in which the licensing authority has its principal office (s 38(3)). An appeal must be made within 28 days of the refusal (s 38(1)). If the court allows such an appeal, it may direct the licensing authority to issue an exemption certificate and may specify the period of the currency of the exemption (s 38(2)).

Taxi accessibility at designated transport facilities

8.2.23 The Secretary of State may by regulations provide for the application of any provision of the 1995 Act relating to taxis or taxi drivers (that is, those described above) to be extended to vehicles (or their drivers) used for the provision of services under 'a franchise agreement' (s 33(2) as read with s 33(4)).[1] These regulations may apply any such taxi provisions with such modifications as the Secretary of State considers appropriate (s 33(3)).

---

1 This power also applies to the potential extension of regulations made in pursuance of the Civic Government (Scotland) Act 1982, s 20(2A).

8.2.24 A 'franchise agreement' is a contract entered into by the 'operator' of a 'designated transport facility' for the provision by the other party to the contract of 'hire car' services for members of the public using any part of the transport facility and which involves vehicles entering any part of that facility (s 33(1)). A 'designated transport facility' means any premises which form part of any port, airport, railway station or bus station which has been designated for the purposes of s 33 by an order made by the Secretary of State (s 33(4)). The 'operator' of such a facility means any person who is concerned with the management or operation of the facility (s 33(4)). The definition of 'hire car' will be prescribed by regulations (s 33(4)).

8.2.25 The intention of s 33, when brought into force, is to ensure that 'taxis' (using that term here in the popular, loose sense) that ply for hire at airports, railway stations and other transport termini could be brought within the accessibility regime for taxis created by ss 32–39. Section 33 is not designed to capture those taxis that already fall within the definition of a taxi regulated for any of the purposes of those sections. They will be already subject to the new duties and standards. Instead, it is intended to embrace those taxis that are private hire cars or mini-cabs and which are entitled to provide car hire services to passengers under a monopoly contract or franchise with the operator of the transport terminus in question (such as, for example, the British Airports Authority at London Gatwick Airport).[1]

---

1 HC Deb, vol 265, cols 159–160 (Mr S. Norris, Minister for Transport in London).

Application to Scotland and Northern Ireland

8.2.26 On the face of the Act, the new duties and framework contained in ss 32–38 apply only in England and Wales. However, s 39 will amend the Civic Government (Scotland) Act 1982 so as to enable the provisions of ss 32–38 to be extended to Scotland by means of regulatory powers. These new provisions also apply to Northern Ireland with the appropriate modifications contained in Sch 8, paras 16–23.

8.3 PUBLIC SERVICE VEHICLES

8.3.1 Introducing the clauses that subsequently became ss 40–48 of the Act (access to buses, coaches and rail services) Lord Mackay of Ardbrecknish stated that they 'add up to a very significant change in the field of transport'.[1] His Lordship acknowledged that the transport industry had worked closely with the Department of Transport for many years 'to promote and encourage the introduction of better designs and operating practices to meet the needs of disabled people'.[2]

Nevertheless, the Government believed that legislation was necessary to continue progress towards an accessible transport system. At the same time, however, these new statutory measures are not retrospective and, when brought into force, will apply only to new vehicles.[3] It was intended to provide a legal framework compatible with existing transport requirements, but flexible enough to allow the introduction of new requirements that are workable and viable in a technical, operational and economic sense.

---

1 HL Deb, vol 565, col 714.
2 HL Deb, vol 565, col 715.
3 HL Deb, vol 566, col 463 (Lord Mackay of Ardbrecknish). Heritage and replica vehicles are thus implicitly outside the new regime.

8.3.2 Sections 40–45 apply to 'public service vehicles' or PSVs. A PSV is a vehicle adapted to carry more than eight passengers (in addition to the driver) and which is in public service.[1] These provisions will apply to buses and coaches of the required capacity offering a public transport service. They are not yet in force.

---

1 See Disability Discrimination Act 1995, s 40(5) and Sch 8, para 24(2). See also the provisions of the Public Passenger Vehicles Act 1981 and the Road Traffic (Northern Ireland) Order 1981.

PSV accessibility regulations

8.3.3 After due consultation with the DPTAC and other representative organisations (s 40(7) and Sch 8, para 24(3)), the Secretary of State is empowered to make 'PSV accessibility regulations' under s 40(1).[1] The purpose of such regulations is to secure that it is possible for disabled persons to get on to and off 'regulated public service vehicles' in safety and without unreasonable difficulty. In the case of disabled persons in wheelchairs, the regulations will seek to achieve this purpose while a disabled person remains in his or her wheelchair (s 40(1)(a)). Furthermore, the regulations will attempt to secure that it is possible for disabled persons to be carried in 'regulated public service vehicles' in safety and reasonable comfort (s 40(1)(b)).

---

1 Section 40 is not yet in force and no PSV accessibility regulations have been laid. The power to make such regulations in Northern Ireland is vested with the Department of the Environment (Sch 8, para 24(1)).

8.3.4 As used in this context, a 'regulated public service vehicle' means a PSV to which the PSV accessibility regulations are expressed to apply (s 40(5)). This implies that the Secretary of State will have discretion in defining which vehicles or kinds of public service are covered by the accessibility regulations. Moreover, s 40(6) provides that the regulations may make different provision as respects different classes or descriptions of vehicle and as respects the same class or description of vehicle in different circumstances.[1] For example, in the case of full-size single deck buses, an access solution might be low floors, whereas, in the case of coaches, a lift might be appropriate.[2] Local and regional variations might also be necessary, as might flexibility of timescales for implementation.

1 By virtue of s 67(7), this is without prejudice to the generality of the powers to make regulations or orders by statutory instrument conferred by s 67(2)–(3).
2 HL Deb, vol 565, col 716 (Lord Mackay of Ardbrecknish).

8.3.5 The PSV accessibility regulations may, in particular, make provision as to the construction, use and maintenance of regulated PSVs (s 40(2)). Such provision may include provision as to:

- the fitting of equipment to vehicles;
- equipment to be carried by vehicles;
- the design of such equipment;
- the fitting and use of restraining devices designed to ensure the stability of wheelchairs while vehicles are moving;
- the position in which wheelchairs are to be secured while vehicles are moving.

It is not intended that this list should be exhaustive.[1]

1 HL Deb, vol 565, col 716 (Lord Mackay of Ardbrecknish).

8.3.6 While s 40 makes frequent reference to the needs of wheelchair-users, the accessibility regulations are intended to make provision for the needs of other disabled travellers, including those with sensory impairments (for example, by the use of colour contrast on handrails and seating and improved lighting levels).[1] The general power to make codes of practice under the Act might also be used to give guidance to transport staff on assistance to disabled persons (for example, in respect of audible announcements).[2]

1 HL Deb, vol 566, cols 459–460 (Lord Mackay of Ardbrecknish).
2 See the existing code of practice issued by the rail regulator (*Meeting the Needs of Disabled Passengers*). See also the Public Vehicles (Conduct of Drivers, Inspectors, Conductors and Passengers) Regulations 1990 which make provision in respect of guide dogs on PSVs.

8.3.7 A regulated PSV shall not be used on the road unless it conforms with the provisions of any PSV accessibility regulations (s 40(3)(b)). To do otherwise is a criminal offence punishable on summary conviction by a fine not exceeding level 4 on the standard scale (s 40(4)). It is also a criminal offence of like weight to contravene or fail to comply with any provision of the PSV accessibility regulations (s 40(3)(a)) or to cause or permit a regulated PSV to be used on a road in non-conformity with such regulations (s 40(3)(c)).

8.3.8 Section 48 makes provision for offences committed under s 40 by a body corporate. If such an offence is committed with the consent or connivance of a director,[1] manager, secretary or other similar officer, then there is joint liability for the offence (s 48(1)). Joint liability may also arise where the offence is attributable to any neglect on the part of any such officers. The position is also the same where the offence is committed with the consent or connivance (or is attributable to any neglect on the part) of a person purporting to act in such a capacity. In addition, in Scotland only, a s 40 offence committed by a partnership or other unincorporated association in the above circumstances can lead to a partner or a person concerned in the management or control of the association incurring joint criminal liability (s 48(3)).

---

1 Where the affairs of a body corporate are managed by its members, a director will include any such member (s 48(2)).

Accessibility certificates

8.3.9 Without prejudice to the generality of the restraints and offences created in s 40, s 41(1)(a) requires that a regulated PSV shall not be used on a road unless a vehicle examiner appointed under the Road Traffic Act 1988, s 66A has issued an 'accessibility certificate'.[1] An 'accessibility certificate' is a certificate which certifies that the prescribed provisions of the PSV accessibility regulations have been satisfied in respect of the vehicle in question.[2]

This will parallel the existing initial roadworthiness certification procedure for PSVs and it is envisaged that accessibility certificates will be issued at the same time as certificates of initial fitness.[3] A fee may be payable on application or issue (s 45(1)(b)). Subject to s 41(1)(b) and the provisions of s 42,[4] if a regulated PSV is used on a road without an accessibility certificate the operator of the vehicle is guilty of an offence and is liable on summary conviction to a fine not exceeding level 4 on the standard scale (s 41(3)).[5]

---

1 Provision is made for appeal to the Secretary of State against the refusal of a vehicle examiner to issue an accessibility certificate (s 44(3)–(6)). A fee may be charged for such an appeal (s 45).
2 Provision is made in s 49 for criminal offences committed in connection with accessibility certificates (for example, forgery or the making of false statements).
3 HL Deb, vol 565, col 716 and vol 566, col 463 (Lord Mackay of Ardbrecknish).

4   See **8.3.11**.
5   By virtue of s 41(4) the term 'operator' has the same meaning as in the Public Passenger
    Vehicles Act 1981. The appropriate modification of s 41(3)–(4) for Northern Ireland is made
    by Sch 8, para 25(2).

8.3.10   After due consultation (s 40(7)), the Secretary of State (in Northern Ireland, the Department of the Environment) may make further regulations with respect to applications for accessibility certificates and their issue (s 41(2) and Sch 8, para 25(1)). Such regulations may also provide for the examination of vehicles in respect of which applications have been made and in respect of copies of certificates which have been lost or destroyed. At the time of writing, s 41 is not in force and no accessibility certificate regulations have been made.

8.3.11   Where the Secretary of State (in Northern Ireland, the Department of the Environment) is satisfied that prescribed provisions of the PSV accessibility regulations for the purposes of s 41 accessibility certificates have been satisfied in respect of a particular vehicle, that vehicle may be given s 42 approval on application and payment of a fee (ss 42(1) and 45(1)(a)).[1] A vehicle approved in this manner is referred to as a 'type vehicle' (s 42(2)) and this provision will clearly apply to vehicles produced in large numbers. The Secretary of State may at any time withdraw approval of a type vehicle (s 42(6)).

1   In accordance with s 42(5)(a), the Secretary of State may make regulations with respect to
    applications for (and grants of) approval under s 42(1). Note the Northern Ireland
    modifications to s 42 contained in Sch 8, para 26.

8.3.12   If the Secretary of State refuses an application for the approval of a vehicle under s 42(1), provision is made for a review of that decision (s 44). A request for review must be made before the end of a period to be prescribed by regulations (s 44(1)) and the applicant for review must pay any fee fixed under s 45 (no such fee has been prescribed at this moment). In reviewing the original decision, the Secretary of State must consider any written representations made by the applicant before the end of the prescribed period (s 44(2)).[1]

1   The provisions appertaining to reviews, appeals and fees generally under ss 44–45 are modified
    for the purposes of Northern Ireland by Sch 8, paras 28–29.

Type approval certificates

8.3.13   If a person authorised by the Secretary of State has made a declaration in the prescribed form that a particular vehicle conforms in design, construction and equipment with a type vehicle, then a vehicle examiner may issue 'an approval certificate' to the effect that subsequent individual vehicles conform to the type vehicle (s 42(3), (4) and (8)).[1] The vehicle examiner may issue such an approval certificate after examining the vehicle to which the statutory declaration applies, if he or she thinks fit (s 42(4)).[2] However, s 42 is clearly designed to avoid the need for each vehicle of the same type to be individually inspected.[3]

---

1 Regulations may make general provision in respect of approval certificates (s 42(5)). Note the consultations requirements of s 40(7)). Provision is made in s 49 for criminal offences committed in connection with approval certificates (for example, forgery or the making of false statements).
2 Provision is made for appeal to the Secretary of State against the refusal of a vehicle examiner to issue an approval certificate (s 44(3)–(6)). A fee may be charged for such an appeal (s 45).
3 HL Deb, vol 565, col 717 (Lord Mackay of Ardbrecknish).

8.3.14 If the Secretary of State withdraws approval of a type vehicle (under s 42(6)), then a vehicle examiner may not issue any further approval certificates by reference to the type vehicle (s 42(7)(a)). However, any approval certificate issued by reference to the type vehicle before such withdrawal of approval shall continue to have effect for s 41 purposes (s 42(7)(b)).

Offences and exemptions

8.3.15 A regulated PSV vehicle shall not be used on a road unless it has a s 41 accessibility certificate or unless alternatively a s 42 approval certificate has been issued in respect of the vehicle (s 41(1)). Use of a regulated PSV in contravention of these alternative conditions is a criminal offence punishable on summary conviction by a fine not exceeding level 4 on the standard scale (s 41(3)).

8.3.16 Sections 40–42 do not prevent the use of a regulated PSV on the road if the Secretary of State has by order authorised its use by reference to the class or description of the vehicle or by explicit specification (s 43(1)).[1] This allows special operating authorisation for vehicles which do not comply with the PSV accessibility regulations and for which an accessibility or approval certificate is not in force.

The Government recognised that there might be circumstances in which an individual vehicle or class of vehicles could not reasonably be expected to meet the full requirements of the new vehicle accessibility standards.[2] Such circumstances might be used to recognise the difficulty or undesirably of attempting to make vintage or heritage vehicles fully accessible.[3] Special authorisation under s 43 may be given subject to specified restrictions or conditions (s 43(2)) and even an order authorising the use of a vehicle in these circumstances may require it to conform with certain aspects of the PSV accessibility regulations, with specified modifications or exceptions (s 43(3)).

1 In Northern Ireland the s 43 powers are vested in the Department of the Environment (Sch 8, para 27).
2 HL Deb, vol 565, col 717 (Lord Mackay of Ardbrecknish).
3 HL Deb, vol 566, col 463 (Lord Mackay of Ardbrecknish).

8.3.17 Ordinarily, where the Secretary of State is given a power under the Act to make an order, that power is exercisable by statutory instrument (s 67(1)). An exception is provided for under s 67(6) in respect of an order under s 43 by which the Secretary of State has authorised the use on roads of a regulated PSV which does not comply with the PSV accessibility regulations or which does not possess an accessibility or approval certificate under ss 40–42 of the Act. Such an authorisation order need not be made by statutory instrument if it applies only to a specified vehicle or to vehicles of a specified person. Nevertheless, such an order is capable of being amended or revoked as if it was an order made by statutory instrument (s 67(6)).

8.4 RAIL VEHICLES

8.4.1 Although provision has already been made in railways legislation to ensure that rail transport operators have a duty to have regard to the needs of disabled passengers, the Government regarded the provision of accessible rail services as 'a key link in the transport chain'.[1] Sections 46–47 of the Disability Discrimination Act 1995 are intended to strengthen the existing legislative framework by addressing access to rail services, including light rapid transit and tram systems. They are not yet in force.

1 HL Deb, vol 565, col 717 (Lord Mackay of Ardbrecknish).

Rail vehicle accessibility regulations

8.4.2 The Secretary of State is empowered by s 46(1) to make 'rail vehicle accessibility regulations' after appropriate consultations (s 46(11) and Sch 8, para 30(4)).[1] At the time of writing, s 46 is not in force and no regulations have been made.

The purpose of the regulations when made will be to secure that it is possible for disabled persons to get on to and off 'regulated rail vehicles' in safety and without unreasonable difficulty, and to be carried in such vehicles in safety and in reasonable comfort (s 46(1)(a)). Moreover, the regulations will make provision for securing that it is possible for disabled persons in wheelchairs to get on to and off 'regulated rail vehicles' in safety and without unreasonable difficulty while remaining in their wheelchairs, as well as to be carried in such vehicles in safety and reasonable comfort while remaining in their wheelchairs (s 46(1)(b)).

---

1   In Northern Ireland the s 46 powers are vested in the Department of the Environment (Sch 8, para 30(1)).

8.4.3   Particular provision may be made in any future rail vehicle accessibility regulations as to the construction, use and maintenance of 'regulated rail vehicles' (s 46(2)). Especial provision may be made in the regulations as to:

- the fitting of equipment to rail vehicles;
- equipment to be carried by rail vehicles;
- the design of equipment to be fitted to or carried by rail vehicles;
- the use of equipment fitted to or carried by rail vehicles;
- the toilet facilities to be provided in rail vehicles;
- the location and floor area of the wheelchair accommodation to be provided in rail vehicles;[1]
- assistance to be given to disabled persons.[2]

While s 46 makes frequent reference to the needs of wheelchair-users, the accessibility regulations are intended to make provision for the needs of other disabled travellers, including those with sensory impairments (for example, by the use of colour contrast on handrails and seating and improved lighting levels).[3]

---

1   The meaning of the term 'wheelchair accommodation' will be defined by regulations (s 46(6)).
2   Section 46(2)(a)–(g).
3   HL Deb, vol 566, cols 459–460 (Lord Mackay of Ardbrecknish).

8.4.4   On the other hand, different provisions may be made in any regulations so as to differentiate between different classes or descriptions of rail vehicles (s 46(5)(a) and as respects different 'networks' (s 46(5)(c)).[1] Similarly, different provisions may be made in the rail vehicle accessibility regulations as respects the same class or description of rail vehicle in different circumstances (s 46(5)(b)). By virtue of s 67(7), these powers are without prejudice to the generality of the powers to make regulations or orders by statutory instrument conferred by s 67(2)–(3).

This apparently recognises that 'the design and use of rail vehicles will vary according to a range of factors' including locality, systems and uses. It seems to be intended that there should be flexibility so that the 'accessibility regulations do not undermine the historic character of heritage railways'.[2] In addition, different provisions might be made to reflect the different operating conditions and vehicle design on different parts of the London Underground railway (for example, those lines that use tubes rather than orthodox tunnels to carry rail vehicles).

---

1   The term 'network' means any permanent way or other means of guiding or supporting rail vehicles or any section of such a network (s 46(6)).
2   HL Deb, vol 565, col 718 (Lord Mackay of Ardbrecknish).

Offences

8.4.5   If a 'regulated rail vehicle' is used for carriage while not conforming with any appropriate provisions of the rail vehicle accessibility regulations the 'operator'[1] commits a criminal offence punishable on summary conviction by a fine not exceeding level 4 on the standard scale (s 46(3)–(4)). A person uses a rail vehicle for carriage if that person uses it for the carriage of members of the public for hire or reward at separate fares (s 46(10)).

---

1   The person having the management of that vehicle (s 46(6)).

8.4.6   Section 48 makes provision for offences committed under s 46 by a body corporate. If such an offence is committed with the consent or connivance of a director,[1] manager, secretary or other similar officer, then there is joint liability for the offence (s 48(1)). Joint liability may also arise where the offence is attributable to any neglect on the part of any such officers. The position is also the same where the offence is committed with the consent or connivance (or is attributable to any neglect on the part) of a person purporting to act in such a capacity. In addition, in Scotland only, a s 46 offence committed by a partnership or other unincorporated association in the above circumstances can lead to a partner or a person concerned in the management or control of the association incurring joint criminal liability (s 48(3)).

---

1   Where the affairs of a body corporate are managed by its members, a director will include any such member (s 48(2)).

Regulated rail vehicles

8.4.7   The key to an understanding of these new access provisions when brought into force will be appreciation of which rail vehicles are to be covered by any regulations. The rail vehicle accessibility regulations will apply only to the 'regulated rail vehicles' as defined in s 46(6). This indicates that the scope of the new regulations will be determined in the accessibility regulations themselves as the term 'regulated rail vehicle' is said to be 'any rail vehicle to which the rail vehicle accessibility regulations are expressed to apply' (s 46(6)).

It is clear that the Secretary of State will have maximum flexibility to determine which rail vehicles are to be included or excluded from the new access requirements.

8.4.8 However, it is equally plain that the new regulations can only apply to modes of passenger transport that satisfy the root definition of a 'rail vehicle'. Section 46 will only apply to a vehicle constructed or adapted to carry passengers on any railways, tramway or 'prescribed system' (s 46(6)).[1] Except in Northern Ireland,[2] the terms 'railway' and 'tramway' have the same meaning as in the Transport and Works Act 1992 and the use of the term 'prescribed system' means a transport system using a prescribed mode of guided transport within the meaning of the 1992 Act (s 46(7)).

---

1   In Northern Ireland the term 'rail vehicle' means a vehicle constructed or adapted to carry passengers by rail (Sch 8, para 30(2)).
2   See Sch 8, para 30(3).

8.4.9   Yet, however the term 'rail vehicle' is defined, it is also clear that the new accessibility standards will not apply to any rail vehicle (or class of rail vehicle) first brought into use on or before 31 December 1998 (s 46(6)).[1] The Government made it clear in debate that it intended to use the regulation-making powers in s 46 only in respect of new railway rolling stock and that there was no intention to require modifications to any existing rolling stock.[2]

---

1   The time at which a rail vehicle or class of rail vehicle is to be treated for s 46 purposes as first brought into use may be determined by regulations made under s 46(8). Such regulations may provide for the disregarding of periods of testing or other prescribed periods of use (s 46(9)).
2   HL Deb, vol 565, col 717 (Lord Mackay of Ardbrecknish).

Exemptions

8.4.10   Section 47 makes general provision for exemptions from the rail vehicle accessibility regulations. After due consideration and consultation (s 47(3)), the Secretary of State (in Northern Ireland, the Department of the Environment) may make exemption orders under s 47(1) to authorise the use for carriage of any regulated rail vehicle of a specified description (or in specified circumstances) even although that vehicle does not conform with the appropriate provisions of applicable rail vehicle accessibility regulations. An exemption order may be made subject to specified restrictions or conditions (s 47(4)–(5)). The regulations may provide for procedural issues in respect of the application for, granting of, currency of or revocation of exemption orders (s 47(2)). Section 47 is not currently in force, but the Government does not envisage that the s 47 powers of exemption will be widely used.[1]

---

1   HL Deb, vol 565, col 718 (Lord Mackay of Ardbrecknish).

Chapter 9

INSTITUTIONAL FRAMEWORK

9.1 NATIONAL DISABILITY COUNCIL

9.1.1 Part VI of the Act deals with the establishment of a National Disability Council (NDC) and related issues (ss 50–52). A separate Northern Ireland Disability Council (NIDC) is also established by modifications to Part VI of the Act introduced by Sch 8, paras 33–35. References below to the NDC should be treated as including references to the NIDC with appropriate modifications. The statutory provisions relating to the NDC (ss 50–52 and Sch 5) were brought into force on 1 January 1996 and the Council was established from that date.[1]

---

1   Disability Discrimination Act 1995 (Commencement No 1) Order 1995, SI 1995/3330. The statutory provisions establishing the NIDC (ss 50–52 and Sch 5 as modified by Sch 8) were implemented by the Disability Discrimination Act 1995 (Commencement No 1) Order (Northern Ireland) 1996, SR 1996/1.

9.1.2 The NDC is established under s 50(1) of the Act. The remaining provisions of s 50 set out the duties and functions of the Council, while Sch 5 deals with questions of the status of the Council and matters relating to its procedure (s 50(8)).[1] Schedule 5 also deals with the membership of the Council, as well as the terms of office and remuneration of Council members. Provision is made for the staffing of the Council, its supplementary regulation-making powers and its annual reports.

---

1   In respect of Northern Ireland, Sch 5 is modified as it applies to the NIDC by Sch 8, para 52.

9.1.3 The Council is a body corporate (Sch 5, para 1(1)). It is not to be treated as a servant or agent of the Crown and does not enjoy any status, immunity or privilege of the Crown (Sch 5, para 1(2)). The Council has the power to regulate its own procedure, including the power to determine its own quorum (Sch 5, para 2).

Membership of the National Disability Council

9.1.4 The NDC may consist of a minimum of 10 members and a maximum of 20 members (Sch 5, para 3(1)), including a chairman and deputy chairman. Council members are appointed by the Secretary of State,[1] as is the chairman and deputy chairman of the Council, both of whom are members of the Council (Sch 5, para 3(3)–(4)). A member of the NDC or NIDC will be disqualified from sitting as a member of the House of Commons or the Northern Ireland Assembly.[2]

The first chairman on the NDC is David Grayson (Director, Business in the Community). As originally constituted, the NDC consists of 17 council members, excluding the chairman but including the chairman of the NIDC (Harry McConnell, Director of Human Resources, Queen's University, Belfast).

---

1   In Northern Ireland, appointments will be made by the Department of Health and Social Services.
2   By virtue of s 70(7) of the 1995 Act amending the House of Commons Disqualification Act 1975, Sch 1 Part II and the Northern Ireland Assembly Disqualification Act 1975, Sch 1 Part II.

9.1.5   Council members are appointed from among persons who, in the opinion of the Secretary of State, satisfy one of the following criteria (Sch 5, para 3(5)):

- they are persons who have knowledge or experience of the needs of disabled persons or the needs of a particular group or groups of disabled persons;
- they are persons who have knowledge or experience of the needs of persons who have had a disability or the needs of a particular group or groups of such persons;
- they are persons who are members or representatives of professional bodies or bodies which represent industry or other business interests.

9.1.6   The Secretary of State is obliged to consult such persons as he or she considers appropriate before appointing a Council member (Sch 5, para 3(6)). This does not explicitly include organisations of and for disabled persons, although the Minister of Disabled People has given such an assurance.[1] It is also anticipated that the Council will be representative of the regions, of women and of ethnic minorities.

---

1   HC Deb Standing Committee E, col 404 (Mr W. Hague).

9.1.7   It is intended that the power of appointment will be used to 'try to secure that at all times at least half' the Council members consist of disabled persons, persons who have had a disability or the parents or guardians of disabled persons (Sch 5, para 3(7)).[1] During the passage of the Act, unsuccessful attempts were made to raise this proportion from a half to three-quarters. The Minister for Disabled People has indicated that half the Council seats will be set aside for disabled persons or their representatives, but that the functioning of the Council should not become unconstitutional simply because of a temporary imbalance in membership proportions caused by an unforeseen resignation — hence the word 'try' in the subsection.[2]

1   The statutory implication is that such persons must meet the definitions contained in ss 1–2 and
    Schs 1–2 as discussed in Chapter 2. Of the 19 members of the NDC as originally constituted
    (including the chairman), 11 were either a disabled person or the parent or guardian of a
    person with disabilities.
2   HC Deb Standing Committee E, col 403 (Mr W. Hague).

9.1.8   The term of office of a Council member shall not exceed five years, but
otherwise a member shall hold and vacate office in accordance with the terms
of his or her appointment (Sch 5, para 4(1)), subject to a right to resign office
by written notice to the Secretary of State (Sch 5, para 4(3)). There is nothing to
prevent a member from serving more than one term of appointment on the
Council, whether consecutively or after an interruption of service (Sch 5, para
4(2)). Regulations made under Sch 5, para 4(4) provide that the Secretary of
State may remove a member of the Council from office in one of three
circumstances.[1] First, removal may occur where a Council member has failed to
attend meetings of the Council, without the Council's consent, throughout a
continuous period of six months ending not earlier than three months before
the date on which the removal takes effect. Secondly, if a Council member is an
undischarged bankrupt, or is otherwise unable to pay his or her debts, he or she
may be removed from office. Thirdly, a Council member may be deprived of
membership if incapable of discharging the functions of office or if guilty of
misbehaviour.

1   National Disability Council Regulations 1996, SI 1996/11, reg 2 in force 29 January 1996. See to
    like effect: Northern Ireland Disability Council Regulations (Northern Ireland) 1996, SR
    1996/13, reg 2 in force 19 February 1996.

9.1.9   The Act intends that Council members should be remunerated while in
office. Schedule 5, para 5 provides that, subject to the approval of the Treasury,[1]
the Secretary of State may pay such remuneration or expenses to any member
of the Council as is considered appropriate.[2] The Act also provides for
appropriate staffing of the Council (Sch 5, para 6).

1   In Northern Ireland, the Department of Finance and Personnel.
2   See further, National Disability Council Regulations 1996, reg 3 and Northern Ireland
    Disability Council Regulations (Northern Ireland) 1996, reg 3.

Duties and functions of the National Disability Council

9.1.10   The primary duty of the Council is set out in s 50(2) and is to advise the
Secretary of State on its own initiative or at the request of the Secretary of State
on the following matters:

- matters relevant to the elimination of discrimination against disabled persons and persons who have had a disability;
- measures which are likely to reduce or eliminate such discrimination;
- matters related to the operation of the Act or of provisions made under the Act (ie orders, regulations, codes of practice and guidance).

These duties would appear broad enough to allow (although not require) the Council to review any pre-existing legislation (such as fire or safety regulations) which is apparently inconsistent with the objectives or spirit of the 1995 Act.[1]

The Secretary of State may by order confer additional functions on the Council (s 50(3)),[2] but this will not include any functions with respect to the investigation of complaints which might be the subject of proceedings under the new legislation (s 50(4)). This distinguishes the NDC from the Equal Opportunities Commission (EOC) and the Commission for Racial Equality (CRE). It is clear that the Council is a purely advisory body, enabled only to make recommendations in respect of the matters or measures listed above.

---

1   The Government's view on this point is a little equivocal. See HL Deb, vol 565, cols 665–666 (Lord Mackay of Ardbrecknish).
2   No such order shall be made unless a draft of the statutory instrument containing the order has been laid before Parliament and approved by a resolution of each House (s 67(4)).

9.1.11   The Council's power to give advice on its own initiative on matters relevant to the elimination of disability discrimination, or measures likely to reduce or eliminate such discrimination, does not include a power to give advice in respect of any matter relating to the operation of provisions of (or arrangements made under) the Disabled Persons (Employment) Acts 1944 and 1958, the Employment and Training Act 1973, the Employment Rights Act 1996 or the Enterprise and New Towns (Scotland) Act 1990, s 2(3).[1]

The Council is also not empowered to give advice on its own initiative on matters related to the operation of the 1995 Act (or of provisions made under it) insofar as those matters or provisions arise under Part II of the Act (discrimination in the employment field) or under ss 53–54 (codes of practice prepared by the Secretary of State) or under s 56 (statutory discrimination questionnaire in employment cases) or under s 61 (arrangements for the provision of supported employment).[2]

---

1   By virtue of s 50(9)(a) of the 1995 Act (as amended). In Northern Ireland, this constraint applies in respect of the Disabled Persons (Employment) Act (Northern Ireland) 1945, the Contracts of Employment and Redundancy Payments Act (Northern Ireland) 1965, the Employment and Training Act (Northern Ireland) 1950 and the Employment Rights (Northern Ireland) Order 1996 (Sch 8, para 33(5)).
2   By virtue of s 50(9)(b) of the 1995 Act.

9.1.12 However, all these restrictions on the Council's power to give advice on its own initiative do not have effect at any time when there is in existence neither the National Advisory Council on the Employment of Disabled People (NACEDP),[1] nor any person appointed by the Secretary of State under s 60(1) of the Act to advise or assist him or her generally in connection with matters relating to the employment of disabled persons and persons who have had a disability (s 50(10)). Their responsibilities would then pass automatically to the NDC. The existence, remit and constitution of the NACEDP is to be reviewed by the Government in 1997.[2]

The intention of these restrictions, therefore, is to ensure separate spheres of responsibility between the NDC and the pre-existing advisory bodies, and to avoid duplication between the work of the NDC and the NACEDP. The Minister for Disabled People has opined that the NDC would not 'be precluded from considering the adequacy of anti-discrimination provisions in employment where that is appropriate as an aspect of its broad overview of anti-discrimination measures'.[3]

---

1 Established under the Disabled Persons (Employment) Act 1944, s 17(1)(a). In Northern Ireland, the appropriate cross-reference is to committees established under the Disabled Persons (Employment) Act (Northern Ireland) 1945, s 17.
2 HL Deb, vol 565, cols 638–639 (Lord Mackay of Ardbrecknish).
3 HC Deb Standing Committee E, col 397 (Mr W. Hague) and see also HL Deb, vol 565, cols 637–638 (Lord Mackay of Ardbrecknish).

9.1.13 The Council is further limited in discharging its primary duties under the Act by s 50(5). This ensures that, in carrying out the duties referred to above, the Council must have particular regard to the extent and nature of the benefits which would be likely to result from the implementation of any recommendations which it makes. Moreover, it must also consider the likely cost of implementing any such recommendations. To that extent, the Council is required when making recommendations, if reasonably practicable, to assess the likely cost of implementation and the likely financial benefits which would result from the implementation of its recommendations (s 50(6)).

9.1.14 In exercising its primary advisory functions, and before giving the Secretary of State advice on any matter, the Council is obliged to consult and have regard to any representations made to it as a result of such consultations (s 50(7) and especially s 50(7)(c)). There would appear to be nothing to prevent the Council from consulting widely and to issue a public invitation to individuals, voluntary organisations and businesses to submit evidence to it in respect of matters which it has under consideration.[1] Indeed, s 50(7)(b) expects the Council to consult with such persons as it considers appropriate. However, s 50(7)(a) particularly requires the Council to consult with any body:

• established by any enactment for the purpose of giving advice in relation to disability or any aspect of disability;

- established by a Minister for the purpose of giving advice in relation to disability or any aspect of disability;
- having functions in relation to the matter to which the advice relates.

This will include specialist bodies such as the NACEDP, the Disabled Persons Transport Advisory Committee (DPTAC) and the Health and Safety Commission. It might include (although this is not made explicit) voluntary organisations of and for disabled persons.[2]

---

1   HL Deb, vol 566, col 987 (Lord Mackay of Ardbrecknish).
2   HL Deb, vol 565, col 656 (Lord Mackay of Ardbrecknish).

9.1.15   Apart from its primary duties and functions adumbrated above, the Council also has a duty, when asked to do so by the Secretary of State, to prepare proposals for a code of practice dealing with matters referred to it by the Secretary of State (s 51(1)(a)).[1] In similar circumstances, it may be asked to review a code of practice and, if it considers it appropriate, propose alterations to the code (s 51(1)(b)).

The Council does not have the power to issue codes of practice on its own initiative. It merely has the power to prepare or to review them when asked to do so by the Secretary of State. The power to issue such codes of practice prepared by the NDC is vested in the Secretary of State under s 52 of the Act (s 51(2)), although the Council might suggest to the Secretary of State that he or she instruct it to prepare a code of practice where it has identified such a need. Where the Council has been involved in the preparation or review of codes of practice, the Secretary of State *may* issue those codes of practice under s 52 in response to the Council's proposals made under s 51(1). Codes of practice are considered in further detail below.[2]

---

1   In Northern Ireland, the appropriate request would come from any Northern Ireland Department and textual references in ss 51–52 to 'the Secretary of State' must be read accordingly (Sch 8, paras 34–35).
2   See **9.2**. The NDC was involved in early 1996 with the preparation of the Rights of Access Code of Practice made under Part III of the Act.

9.1.16   It is clear that the NDC is not a sibling of the EOC or the CRE. The NDC is not a rights agency to which individual complaints of discrimination may be submitted. It is a purely advisory body with a limited remit and no powers of enforcement. In particular, unlike the pre-existing Commissions, the Council lacks the power to provide assistance or advice to complainants, to conduct formal investigations into suspected acts or patterns of discrimination or to bring proceedings to enforce the Act on behalf of complainants or in its own name. It also lacks a general power to monitor and review the operation of the legislation. The Government rejected arguments for the creation of a disability rights commission, contending that such a commission would not work, might create a risk of a backlash against disability rights and would not fit the social context of the late 1990s.[1]

The Government has indicated that it expects the NDC 'to work with industry on issues which cannot be dealt with under rights-based legislation such as the design and labelling of products' and to consider other legislation which has a constraining effect upon the spirit of the new disability discrimination legislation.[2] It will be no part of the NDC's functions to provide advice directly to disabled people or to firms (except through its codes of practice).

---

1 HL Deb, vol 565, cols 639–642 and vol 566, cols 408–410 (Lord Mackay of Ardbrecknish).
2 HL Deb, vol 565, col 636 and vol 566, col 987 (Lord Mackay of Ardbrecknish).

Annual reports

9.1.17   The NDC must make an annual report to the Secretary of State as soon as is practicable after the end of each financial year (Sch 5, para 8(1)).[1] The annual report is designed to inform the Secretary of State as to the Council's activities during the preceding financial year. The annual report is to be laid before Parliament,[2] and it is anticipated that the report will be published and available in the public domain (Sch 5, para 8(2)). It is the Government's intention that the Council should publish its annual report in formats accessible to persons with various disabilities (such as in signed and subtitled video format, audio cassette and braille).[3] In any event, the Council will be subject to the provisions of Part III of the Act and, as a provider of goods, facilities or services, would be legally obliged to produce the report in alternative formats as far as reasonably possible.[4] The NDC published its first annual report in July 1996.[5]

---

1 In Northern Ireland, the NIDC will make its annual report to the Department of Health and Social Services (Sch 8, para 52).
2 In Northern Ireland, the appropriate reference is to the Northern Ireland Assembly.
3 HC Deb Standing Committee E, cols 407–408 (Mr W. Hague).
4 See Chapter 5.
5 See National Disability Council, *Annual Report 1995–1996* HC Paper 564 (1996, London: HMSO). The NDC has also established a home page on the World Wide Web (http://www.open.gov.uk/ndc/ndchome.htm).

Supplementary powers of the Council

9.1.18   Schedule 5, para 7 anticipates that the Council may be granted additional powers or functions. The Secretary of State is empowered to make supplementary regulations to address further provisions. These include the provision of information by the Secretary of State to the Council and the

Disability Discrimination

commissioning of research to be undertaken on behalf of the Council.[1]
The regulations also provide as to the circumstances in which (and the
conditions subject to which) the Council may appoint advisers.[2]

---

1 See National Disability Council (No 2) Regulations 1996, SI 1996/1410, reg 2 (on the
commissioning of research).
2 See ibid, reg 3.

9.2 CODES OF PRACTICE

Codes of practice prepared by the National Disability Council

9.2.1 As has already been noted above,[1] when asked to do so by the Secretary
of State, the NDC has a duty to prepare proposals for a code of practice dealing
with matters referred to it by the Secretary of State (s 51(1)).[2] In similar
circumstances, the Council may be asked to review an existing code of practice
and, where appropriate, propose alterations to the code. However, the Council
does not have the power to issue codes of practice of its own initiative and may
only prepare or review a code if asked to do so by the Secretary of State.

Nevertheless, as part of its advisory functions or in its annual report, the
Council might suggest to the Secretary of State that he or she instruct it to
prepare a code of practice where it has identified a need for a code of practice
or for the revision of an existing code.[3] The Minister suggested that the Council
will always be able to express its opinion about the operation of a code of
practice, but will not be able to undertake the revision or detailed redrafting it
believes necessary unless invited to do so by the Secretary of State.[4]

---

1 See **9.1.15**.
2 In Northern Ireland, the NIDC has a parallel duty under s 51 at the behest of any department.
3 HC Deb Standing Committee E, col 411 (Mr W. Hague).
4 HC Deb Standing Committee E, col 416 (Mr W. Hague).

9.2.2 In preparing a proposal for an original or amended code of practice,
s 52 requires the Council to consult any persons specified by the Secretary of
State when requesting the Council to act (s 52(2)(a)).[1] The NDC shall also
consult 'such other persons (if any) as the Council considers appropriate'
(s 52(2)(b)). Prior to making its proposal, the Council must publish the new or
revised code in draft form so that interested parties may consider the substance
of what the Council intends to propose. Section 52(3) anticipates that the
Council will receive submissions from such parties, as the subsection requires
the NDC to consider any representations made to it concerning the draft code.
If the Council thinks it appropriate, it shall modify its proposal in the light of

any of those representations. Only then is the proposal forwarded to the Secretary of State.

---

1   The modification of s 52 for the purposes of Northern Ireland is set out in Sch 8, para 35.

9.2.3   The power to issue any codes of practice which have been prepared or reviewed by the NDC lies in the hands of the Secretary of State alone under s 52 of the Act (s 51(2)). The Council has no code-issuing powers of its own. Where the Council has been involved in the preparation or review of codes of practice, the Secretary of State *may* issue those codes of practice under s 52 in response to the Council's proposals made under s 51(1). However, the Secretary of State must first decide what action to take on the NDC's proposal.

The Secretary of State may approve the proposal or approve it subject to such modifications as he or she considers appropriate. Alternatively, the Secretary of State may refuse to approve the proposal. There would appear to be no mechanism whereby an original or revised code of practice proposed by the NDC but disapproved of by the Secretary of State can be resurrected unless the Secretary of State makes a fresh request to the Council within the terms of s 51(1).[1] However, the Secretary of State must give the Council a written statement of his or her reasons for refusing to approve the proposed code (s 52(10)).

---

1   See **9.2.1**.

9.2.4   If the Secretary of State approves the proposal, with or without modifications, the code may then be issued by the Secretary of State in accordance with a statutory procedure. The statutory procedure whereby the Secretary of State may issue an original or revised code of practice as a result of proposals made by the NDC is laid down in the remaining provisions of s 52.

9.2.5   The first step is to prepare a draft of the proposed code (or revised code) and to lay it before each House of Parliament (s 52(5)).[1] The second step is to allow Parliament a 40-day period in which to consider the draft code and to determine whether to resolve not to approve it.[2] Parliament is not required to take any positive steps to approve the draft code, but it requires a negative resolution of either House to disapprove of the code. In such a case, the code falls and the Secretary of State shall take no further steps in relation to the proposed code (s 52(6)). This would not appear to prevent a new draft of the proposed code from being laid before Parliament on a future occasion (s 52(9)).

---

1   In Northern Ireland, the Northern Ireland Assembly (Sch 8, para 35) although, as the Assembly is presently dissolved, power has reverted to Westminster.

2   As to the calculation of the 40-day period, see s 52(12). In Northern Ireland, the relevant statutory period is defined by the Interpretation Act (Northern Ireland) 1954, s 41(2). See para 35 of Sch 8 to the 1995 Act.

9.2.6   The third step is taken only if within the 40-day period neither House of Parliament resolves not to approve the draft code. If both Houses remain silent, the Secretary of State is thereby mandated to issue the code in the form laid before Parliament (s 52(7)). The code of practice will then come into force on a date appointed by ministerial order (s 52(8)) and will remain in force unless and until it is revoked by the Secretary of State by order (s 52(11)). It is intended that codes of practice will either be issued free of charge or will be made available at charge through bookshops. In the latter case, free copies of a code would be made available to interested organisations, including those of and for disabled persons.[1]

1   HC Deb Standing Committee E, col 421 (Mr W. Hague).

9.2.7   The way in which the NDC may prepare or amend codes of practice to be issued by the Secretary of State is not so dissimilar from the power of the EOC or the CRE to issue codes of practice under the sex or race discrimination statutes.[1] All three bodies do not have the autonomous power to issue codes of practice and must first submit their proposals for the approval of the Secretary of State and Parliament. The noticeable difference, however, is that, unlike the EOC and the CRE, the NDC may not take the initiative to propose a draft code of practice and may only act at the request of the Secretary of State. Furthermore, under the 1995 Act, it is the Government which issues any codes of practice and not the NDC (cf the powers of the EOC and CRE).

1   See SDA 1975, s 56A and RRA 1976, s 47. See further the EOC's *Code of Practice for the Elimination of Discrimination on the Grounds of Sex and Marriage and the Promotion of Equality of Opportunity in Employment* (1985) and the CRE's *Code of Practice for the Elimination of Racial Discrimination and the Promotion of Equality of Opportunity in Employment* (1984).

9.2.8   The first code of practice to be issued under ss 51–52 is the *Code of Practice: Rights of Access: Goods, Facilities, Services and Premises* (the Rights of Access Code of Practice) issued by the Secretary of State under s 51(2).[1] This is referred to in detail in the context of Chapters 5–6. The Code was issued based upon proposals made by the National Disability Council and following a consultation process throughout the second quarter of 1996.[2]

1   1996, London: HMSO. A separate, but largely identical, Code of Practice has been issued in Northern Ireland.
2   See the description of this process and an account of the genesis of the Rights of Access Code of Practice in National Disability Council, *Annual Report 1995–1996* HC Paper 564 (1996, London:

HMSO), 6–7. See also, National Disability Council, *Code of Practice: Rights of Access: Goods, Facilities, Services and Premises: Analysis of Consultation Responses* (1996, London: NDC).

Codes of practice prepared by the Secretary of State

9.2.9 In the sex and race discrimination field, the statutory commissions alone have the power to prepare and issue codes of practice, albeit only with the necessary intervening ministerial and parliamentary approval. In employment law generally, the Advisory, Conciliation and Arbitration Service (ACAS) has the power (dating back to 1974) to prepare and issue codes of practice for the purpose of promoting the improvement of industrial relations.[1] ACAS codes of practice also require ministerial and parliamentary approval. Since 1980, however, the Secretary of State has also had statutory power to issue codes of practice in the employment and industrial relations field.[2] The extension of that power into one area of employment discrimination law is countenanced by the 1995 Act (s 53).

---

1 The power is now contained in the Trade Union and Labour Relations (Consolidation) Act 1992, ss 199–202.
2 The power is now contained in the Trade Union and Labour Relations (Consolidation) Act 1992, ss 203–208.

9.2.10 Under s 53 of the Disability Discrimination Act 1995, the Secretary of State may issue codes of practice containing such 'practical guidance' as he or she considers appropriate with a view to 'eliminating discrimination' against disabled persons (and persons who have had a disability) in the field of employment or 'encouraging good practice' in relation to the employment of disabled persons (and persons who have had a disability).[1] This power is contained in s 53(1). It clearly extends not simply to the making of a code of practice to address discrimination in the employment field, but also (by virtue of s 53(8)) to embrace practical guidance in respect of discrimination against contract workers and by trade organisations contrary to ss 12–13. Under s 53(1) the Secretary of State has the power to revise and reissue such codes of practice (see also s 53(7)). One code of practice has been prepared and issued under s 53(1) – the Employment Code of Practice.[2] It provides guidance and assistance to employers in respect of their new obligations under Part II. The Employment Code of Practice was the subject of wide consultation during late 1995 and early 1996.[3]

---

1 By virtue of s 53(9), employment includes contract work as defined by s 12(6). In Northern Ireland, the s 53 powers are vested in the Department of Economic Development (Sch 8, para 36).
2 *Code of Practice for the elimination of discrimination in the field of employment against disabled persons or persons who have had a disability* (1996, London: HMSO). The Employment Code of Practice came into force on 2 December 1996 by virtue of the Disability Discrimination (Guidance and

Code of Practice) (Appointed Day) Order 1996, SI 1996/1996, para 3. A separate (but essentially identical) Employment Code of Practice covers Northern Ireland and reflects the different institutional context of the province. Both codes came into force on 2 December 1996.

3   See *Consultation on the Employment Code of Practice, Guidance on Definition of Disability and Related Regulations: An Analysis of the Responses* (1996, London: Department for Education and Employment).

9.2.11   It would seem that the NDC's limited power to prepare codes of practice is likely to be restricted to the scope of the non-employment provisions of the Act. It is probable that code-making authority in respect of disability-related employment discrimination will be exercised by the Secretary of State in tandem with the NACEDP and any other statutory employment advisers appointed under s 60(1). This reading of the NDC's powers would seem to follow from the combination of ss 50(9) and 53(1) of the Act.[1]

1   This is confirmed by the Under-Secretary of State for Employment (Mr J. Paice) at HC Deb Standing Committee E, col 423. See also **9.1.11–9.1.12**.

9.2.12   The objectives of any code of practice issued under s 53 are said to be the elimination of discrimination against, and the encouragement of good practice in relation to, disabled persons in the employment field. While the effect of those objectives may result in the promotion of equality of opportunity for disabled persons in the employment field,[1] that latter objective is not made explicit. Interestingly, the Employment Code of Practice issued in July 1996 is expressly stated to have been issued by the Secretary of State under s 53(1)(a) and not s 53(1) in general.[2] This means that the Code contains only practical guidance 'with a view to ... eliminating discrimination in the field of employment' (s 53(1)(a)), but does not extend to 'encouraging good practice in relation to the employment of disabled persons ...' (s 53(1)(b)).[3] Prior to the 1995 Act, there was an existing *voluntary* code of practice in respect of the employment of disabled persons which did encourage best practice.[4] As a non-statutory code, strictly this has not been superseded by the s 53 Employment Code of Practice, although it is clearly dated and is unlikely to be reissued by the Employment Service.

1   Cf SDA 1975, s 56A(1)(b) and RRA 1976, s 47(1)(b).
2   Employment Code of Practice, para 1.1.
3   Nevertheless, it does contain a chapter (Chapter 3) containing general guidance to help avoid discrimination which does appear to encourage policy-making by employers and many of the examples given in the body of the Code clearly represent good practice. See also paras 4.55 et seq setting up management systems to help avoid discrimination.
4   See the Employment Service's *Code of Practice on the Employment of Disabled People* (revised March 1993).

9.2.13   A code of practice issued under s 53 may include practical guidance as to certain express matters (s 53(3)), but this is without prejudice to the generality of the power contained in s 53(1). For example, the code might encourage (but not require) employers to monitor and record the participation of disabled persons in their workforces, especially once the register of disabled persons under the 1944 Act is abolished.[1] Indeed, the Government intends to monitor the position of disabled people in the labour market itself through the Labour Force Surveys and other research, and to monitor its own position as an employer of disabled staff.[2] Nevertheless, s 53(3) anticipates that practical guidance will be given to employers generally on two particular questions.

---

1 HL Deb, vol 565, col 696 (Lord Inglewood). See Employment Code of Practice, para 3.5.
2 HL Deb, vol 565, col 697 (Lord Inglewood) and vol 566, cols 432–433 (Lord Henley).

9.2.14 First, a code of practice may give practical guidance as to the circumstances in which it would be reasonable, having regard to the costs involved, for an employer (or other person) to be expected to make adjustments in favour of disabled persons and persons who have had a disability (s 53(3)(a)). The Employment Code of Practice addresses this issue.[1] This will be of assistance to employers (and to tribunals) in coming to terms with the duty under ss 4(2) and 6 to make reasonable adjustments in respect of employment arrangements and physical features of the workplace which place disabled persons at a substantial disadvantage in access to employment opportunities.[2] Such practical guidance supplements the regulations made under s 6(8) to amplify that duty to make reasonable adjustments.[3]

---

1 See paras 4.21–4.32.
2 See Chapter 3 above. See also s 15 in relation to adjustments to be made by trade organisations and s 12(3) in relation to contract workers.
3 See the Disability Discrimination (Employment) Regulations 1996 in general.

9.2.15 Secondly, a code of practice may give practical guidance as to what steps it is reasonably practicable for employers to take for the purpose of preventing their employees from doing in the course of their employment (or contract work) anything which is made unlawful by the new statute (s 53(3)(b)). Section 58(1) provides that an employer is vicariously liable for anything done by an employee in the course of employment, whether or not it was done with the employer's knowledge or approval. However, s 58(5) gives the employer a possible defence in such a case of potential vicarious liability if the employer can prove that it took reasonably practicable steps to prevent the employee from committing unlawful acts.[1] So the power to issue a code of practice may be used to explain and illustrate how this defence might operate in practice.[2]

---

1 Section 58 is discussed in more detail in Chapter 10.

2   See Employment Code of Practice, paras 4.11, 4.55–4.56, 4.58–4.59 and 4.62–4.63.

9.2.16   The procedure whereby the Secretary of State may prepare and issue (or revise and reissue) codes of practice under s 53 is outlined in s 54.[1] It is implicit that the Secretary of State must first prepare the code in draft form. It is explicit that he or she should then consult appropriate organisations representing the interests of employers or of disabled persons (s 54(1)). This might include consultation with the NDC and NACEDP.[2] The obligation to consult is not as tightly drawn as it might have been.

---

1   Section 54 is modified for Northern Ireland by Sch 8, para 37.
2   HL Deb, vol 565, cols 667–669 (Lord Inglewood).

9.2.17   First, the appropriateness of the organisations which the Secretary of State chooses to consult is a matter for his or her consideration, although presumably, if the Secretary of State exercised his or her discretion in this matter too narrowly, the consultation might be challengeable by judicial review. Secondly, there would appear to be no obligation to consult both employers' organisations *and* organisations representing disabled persons. The wording of the subsection suggests that the Secretary of State could, if he or she so decides, consult employers but not disabled persons and vice versa. Again, such a decision could be reviewable in judicial proceedings. Thirdly, there is no obligation to consult organisations of employees or trade unions per se, although the provision anticipates that the relevant organisations will be those representing the interests of disabled persons in employment or seeking employment. That would suggest that trade unions, as well as organisations of and for disabled persons, will have a stake in the consultation exercise.

9.2.18   Apart from the statutory consultation exercise, the Secretary of State must in addition publish a draft of any code which he or she proposes to issue (s 54(2)). This allows interested parties to make representations concerning the draft code. The Secretary of State must consider any representations so made and, if he or she thinks it appropriate, modify the proposed code in the light of those representations.

9.2.19   Following the consultation and representations stages, if it is decided to proceed with the issue of a code of practice, a draft of the code is to be laid before each House of Parliament by the Secretary of State (s 54(3)).[1] As with codes of practice prepared by the NDC, Parliament has 40 days within which to consider the draft code prepared by the Secretary of State.[2] If, within that period, either House resolves not to approve the code, no further steps may be taken in relation to it (s 54(4)). However, this does not prevent a new draft of the proposed code being laid before Parliament on a later occasion (s 54(7)).

If, within the 40-day period, neither House resolves to disapprove the draft code, the Secretary of State is then authorised to issue the code in the form represented by the draft (s 54(5)). The code will only come into force on a date appointed by ministerial order (s 54(6)). The Secretary of State may subsequently determine to revoke the code of practice and the revocation is to be effected by order (s 54(8)).

---

1 In Northern Ireland, the draft code will be laid before the Northern Ireland Assembly (Sch 8, para 37). In practice, power has reverted to Westminster while the Assembly is dissolved.
2 The calculation of the 40-day period is made in accordance with s 54(9). In Northern Ireland, by virtue of Sch 8, para 37, the relevant statutory period is defined in the Interpretation Act (Northern Ireland) 1954, s 41(2).

Legal effect of codes of practice

9.2.20 Whether a code of practice made under the 1995 Act is prepared by the NDC or by the Secretary of State, once issued the legal effect of a code of practice is the same. A failure on the part of any person to observe any provision of a code of practice does not of itself make that person liable to any legal proceedings (ss 51(3) and 53(4)). However, the code is admissible in evidence in any proceedings under the Act before an industrial tribunal, county court or sheriff court (ss 51(4) and 53(5)). A provision of the code is to be taken into account by a tribunal or court if it appears to be relevant to any question arising in legal proceedings (ss 51(5) and 53(6)).

Thus, while breach of a provision of a code of practice will not be sufficient to found liability, that evidence, taken with a substantive provision of the Act, might assist a court or tribunal to reach an adverse conclusion or to draw adverse inferences, especially where the legal test of liability involves questions of 'reasonableness' or what is 'practicable'.

9.3 SECTION 3 GUIDANCE

9.3.1 Under s 3 of the Act the Secretary of State is empowered to issue guidance about the matters which a court or tribunal ought to take into account when determining whether an impairment has a substantial adverse effect on a person's ability to carry out normal day-to-day activities or whether such an impairment has a long-term adverse effect (s 3(1)).[1] A court or tribunal addressing these questions, for any purpose of the legislation, is obliged to take account of any guidance issued by the Secretary of State under s 3 which appears to it to be relevant (s 3(3) and s 3(12)). If any s 3 guidance has been issued, the Secretary of State may from time to time revise the whole or any part of such guidance and reissue it (s 3(11)(a)). The Secretary of State also has authority to revoke any guidance by order (s 3(11)(b)).

1	In Northern Ireland, the power to issue s 3 guidance is vested in the Department of Economic Development (Sch 8, para 2).

9.3.2 The power to issue guidance under s 3 is at large, but s 3(2) makes it clear that such guidance may give examples in four particular circumstances and in relation to particular activities:

- effects which it would be reasonable to regard as substantial adverse effects;
- effects which it would not be reasonable to regard as substantial adverse effects;
- substantial adverse effects which it would be reasonable to regard as long term;
- substantial adverse effects which it would not be reasonable to regard as long term.

Further interpretative assistance is to be found in Sch 1 to the Act and in the discussion of the concept of 'disability' in Chapter 2.

9.3.3 The Minister for Disabled People gave an assurance in Committee that the guidance powers will not be used to weaken the definition of disability or to exclude particular impairments.[1] The guidance is intended to illustrate and exemplify rather than to exclude or limit the statutory definitions. The Secretary of State has issued s 3 guidance which came into force on 31 July 1996.[2] The substance of this guidance has been considered in Chapter 2.[3]

1	HC Deb Standing Committee E, col 124 (Mr W. Hague).
2	*Guidance on matters to be taken into account in determining questions relating to the definition of disability* (1996, London: HMSO). The Guidance came into force on 31 July 1996 by virtue of the Disability Discrimination (Guidance and Code of Practice) (Appointed Day) Order 1996, SI 1996/1996, para 2. In Northern Ireland, the power to issue s 3 guidance is vested in the Department of Economic Development (Sch 8, para 2(1)) and a separate edition of the Guidance has been issued there.
3	See also: *Consultation on the Employment Code of Practice, Guidance on Definition of Disability and Related Regulations: An Analysis of the Responses* (1996, London: Department for Education and Employment).

9.3.4 In preparing a draft of any guidance (or revised guidance) under s 3, the Secretary of State is required to consult such persons as he or she considers appropriate (s 3(4)). If the Secretary of State proposes to issue any s 3 guidance (or to reissue any revised guidance), he or she must first publish a draft of it, consider any representations that are made about the draft and, if the Secretary of State thinks it appropriate, may modify the proposals in the light of any of those representations (s 3(5)).

9.3.5 During the legislative process, concerns were expressed about parliamentary scrutiny of any guidance to be issued or reissued by the Secretary of State under s 3. The Government conceded that there was a strong case for making such guidance subject to the same parliamentary scrutiny as applied to codes of practice prepared under the Act, namely the negative resolution procedure.[1]

---

1   HL Deb, vol 566, cols 122–123 (Lord Mackay of Ardbrecknish).

9.3.6   Accordingly, if the Secretary of State decides to proceed with any proposed guidance (or revised guidance), he or she shall lay a draft of it before each House of Parliament (s 3(6)).[1] If either House resolves not to approve the draft guidance within the next 40 days (calculated in accordance with s 3(12)), the Secretary of State shall take no further steps in relation to the proposed guidance (s 3(7)), although a new draft of the proposed guidance may be subsequently laid before Parliament (s 3(10)). If no such resolution is made within the 40-day period, the Secretary of State shall issue the guidance in the form of the draft proposal (s 3(8)) and the guidance shall come into force on a date to be appointed by order (s 3(9)).

---

1   In Northern Ireland, the Department of Economic Development shall lay any guidance before the Northern Ireland Assembly (Sch 8, para 2). Because the Assembly is dissolved at present, power has reverted to Westminster.

9.3.7   In Northern Ireland, the power to issue s 3 guidance is in the hands of the Department of Economic Development. A modified procedure for obtaining approval by the Northern Ireland Assembly of any s 3 guidance issued by the Department of Economic Development in Northern Ireland is set out in para 2 of Sch 8 to the Act. As the Assembly has been dissolved for some time, this provision is robbed of significance and the default powers have reverted to Westminster.

9.4   MISCELLANEOUS ISSUES

9.4.1   Part VI of the Act contains a number of miscellaneous provisions that might be conveniently dealt with here. Appropriate cross-references to other parts of this account are made here and elsewhere.

Employment advisers to the Secretary of State

9.4.2   Section 60 permits the Secretary of State to appoint such persons as are thought fit to advise or assist him or her in connection with matters relating to the employment (and self-employment) of disabled persons and persons who have had a disability (s 60(1) and (5)). These advisers may be appointed to act generally or in relation to a particular area or locality (s 60(2)) and, subject to Treasury approval, the advisers may be paid appropriate allowances and compensation for loss of earnings (s 60(3)–(4)). In Northern Ireland, the respective duties or powers of the Secretary of State and the Treasury under s 60 are exercisable by the Department of Economic Development and the Department of Finance and Personnel (Sch 8, para 40).

9.4.3   It would seem that s 60 lays the ground for the review of the National Advisory Council on the Employment of Disabled People (NACEDP) and its local advisory committees which is due to be carried out in 1997.[1] Section 60(6) empowers the Secretary of State to disestablish the NACEDP and the local advisory committees by ministerial order.[2] The suggestion here is that the NACEDP might be replaced by individual advisers appointed by the Secretary of State, whether or not the functions of the NACEDP will be transferred to the newly established NDC.[3] In the meanwhile, the functions of the existing NACEDP are extended to embrace disabled persons and persons who have had a disability as defined in the 1995 Act.[4]

1   See **9.1.12**.
2   This would involve the repeal of DP(E)A 1944, s 17 and Sch 2 and the parallel provisions under the DP(E)A (Northern Ireland) 1945 (by virtue of Sch 8, para 40(3)) by ministerial order. This appears to be the only example of a so-called 'Henry VIII' clause in the 1995 Act (although note s 7(2) of the Act and see **9.4.19**).
3   See generally **9.1**.
4   This is achieved by s 60(7) of the 1995 Act amending s 17 of the 1944 Act and s 60(8) of the 1995 Act amending the Chronically Sick and Disabled Persons Act 1970, s 16 (which extended the functions of the NACEDP). This provision is extended to Northern Ireland with the appropriate modifications, except that the 1970 Act does not apply in the province (Sch 8, para 40(4)–(5)).

Amendment of the Disabled Persons (Employment) Act 1944

9.4.4   Section 61 amends the DP(E)A 1944, ss 15–16 in a number of respects.[1] These are the provisions which give the Secretary of State power to make arrangements for supported employment of disabled persons. Section 61 also repeals a number of sections of the 1944 Act and makes consequential provision. The effect of these amendments and repeals of the existing law relating to disabled employment rights has been discussed in Chapter 3.[2]

1   The Disabled Persons (Employment) Act (Northern Ireland) 1945 is amended by Sch 8, para 41 which modifies the effect of s 61 in the Northern Ireland context. Section 61 came into force on 2 December 1996.
2   At **3.11**.

Application of the 1995 Act to the Crown

9.4.5   The 1995 Act applies to any act or deliberate omission done by or for the purposes of a Minister of the Crown or government department in exactly the same way as it would apply to an act or omission done by a private person (s 64(1)(a)). It also applies in like manner to an act or deliberate omission done on behalf of the Crown by a statutory body or a person holding a statutory office (s 64(1)(b)). In short, the new legislation applies to both the public and private sector.[1] Section 64 came into force on 2 December 1996.

---

1   Similar provisions are to be found in the SDA 1975, s 85 and RRA 1976, s 75. In Northern Ireland, s 64 is modified by the terms of Sch 8, para 44.

9.4.6 Section 64(2) further clarifies that Part II of the Act (outlawing discrimination against disabled persons in the employment field) applies to service for the purposes of a Minister of the Crown or government department (other than service of a person holding a statutory office) or on behalf of the Crown for the purposes of a person holding a statutory office or the purposes of a statutory body.[1] A 'statutory body' is one set up by or under an enactment and a 'statutory office' is construed accordingly (s 64(8)). The effect of s 64(2) is to provide that civil servants are to be regarded as employees, but not a person holding a statutory office.[2] The kinds of office holders who might be thus excluded will include justices of the peace, by way of example, but a person employed by such an office holder is within the statute.

---

1   Service for the purposes of a Minister of the Crown or government department does not include service in any office mentioned in the House of Commons Disqualification Act 1975, Sch 2 (ie ministerial offices) or service as the head of a Northern Ireland department (s 64(8) and Sch 8, para 44).
2   HC Deb Standing Committee E, cols 441–442 (Mr J. Paice, Under-Secretary of State for Employment).

9.4.7 However, a statutory office holder is not entirely excluded from the Act's protection. This is because s 66(2) provides that, when making an appointment of a statutory office holder, the Minister or government department concerned must not act in a way which would contravene the employment provisions in Part II of the Act, as if the Minister or government department were acting as an employer. So, in respect of an appointment of a person by a Minister or government department to an office or post, which would not otherwise be an employment within the meaning of Part II and s 64(2)(a), the anti-discriminatory principles of the Act will apply (s 66(1)). However, regulations may prescribe that certain public appointments are to be outside this extended protection (s 66(3)). No such regulations have been made to date, although s 66 came into force on 2 December 1996.

9.4.8 The Act explicitly excludes service as a prison officer (with the exception of custody officers or prison custody officers),[1] a fire fighting member of a fire brigade,[2] and service in the naval, military or air forces from protection under Part II of the legislation (discrimination in employment). This is achieved by s 64(5)–(7) and Sch 8, para 44(3). The meaning of such service is amplified in s 64(8) and Sch 8, para 44(4). The rationale for these exceptions is said to be that they involve positions calling for unusually demanding all-round requirements for fitness and stamina. The physical and mental capacity of recruits to these services is a matter of judgement for the recruiting authorities to make, without being hindered by the Act.[3]

---

1 Within the meaning of the Criminal Justice and Public Order Act 1994, s 127 and the Prison Act (Northern Ireland) 1953, s 2(2).
2 Maintained in pursuance of the Fire Services Act 1947 or as defined in the Fire Services (Northern Ireland) Order 1984.
3 HC Deb, vol 257, cols 894–895 (Mr J. Paice).

9.4.9 Police officers are implicitly outside the scope of the Act as they are neither employees under a contract of service nor are they Crown servants within the meaning of s 64 of the statute. In any event, s 64(5) makes it explicit that Part II does not apply to service in the Ministry of Defence Police,[1] the British Transport Police,[2] the Royal Parks Constabulary,[3] or the United Kingdom Atomic Energy Authority Constabulary.[4]

---

1 Established under the Ministry of Defence Police Act 1987, s 1.
2 Established under the British Transport Commission Act 1949, s 53.
3 Established under the Parks Regulation Act 1872.
4 That is, the special constables nominated by the Authority under the Special Constables Act 1923, s 3.

9.4.10 Parts II to V of the Crown Proceedings Act 1947 apply to proceedings against the Crown brought under the 1995 Act as they apply to Crown proceedings in England and Wales, in Northern Ireland and in Scotland under s 23 of the 1947 Act (s 64(3)–(4) and Sch 8, para 44(1) and (4)(b)). However, ss 20 and 44 of the 1947 Act (dealing with the removal of proceedings from the county court to the High Court or from the sheriff court to the Court of Session) are disapplied for this present purpose.

Application of the 1995 Act to Parliament

9.4.11 The effect of s 65(1) of the 1995 Act is that the new disability discrimination legislation applies to an act (or deliberate omission) done by (or for the purposes of) the House of Lords or the House of Commons.[1] In other words, the Act is equally applicable to Parliament as it would be to a private person. Nothing in any rule of law or the law or practice of Parliament prevents proceedings being instituted under the Disability Discrimination Act 1995 against either of the Houses of Parliament in an industrial tribunal or a court. Otherwise, parliamentary privilege would dictate that the new law would not apply to the legislature itself.[2]

1 Section 65 does not apply to Northern Ireland (Sch 8, para 45). It came into force on 2 December 1996.
2 HL Deb, vol 565, col 725 (Lord Mackay of Ardbrecknish).

9.4.12 As far as the employment discrimination provisions of Part II of the Act are concerned, s 65(2) provides that the Corporate Officer of the House of Commons is to be treated as the employer of any person who is (or would be) a relevant member of the House of Commons staff.[1] There are similar concessions made under the sex and race discrimination legislation.[2]

1 For the purposes of the Employment Rights Act 1996, s 195.
2 Sex Discrimination Act 1975, ss 85A–85B; Race Relations Act 1976, ss 75A–75B.

9.4.13 In respect of discrimination in relation to the provision of goods, facilities or services to members of the public under ss 16–18 of the Act, the relevant provider of any services in question would be the Corporate Officer of the House of Commons and the Corporate Officer of the House of Lords respectively (s 65(3)). The two Houses provide a number of obvious services to visitors, such as refreshment facilities and information services. However, where the service at issue is the access to and use of any place in the Palace of Westminster which members of the public are permitted to enter (such as the public galleries in the debating chambers), the Corporate Officers of both Houses are treated as joint providers of such a service (s 65(4)). This makes it plain that physical access to the political process of the legislature itself is a matter that can be addressed and redressed when the provisions of the new law come into force.

Regulations and orders

9.4.14 The Act makes provision in several places for the subsequent enactment of regulations and orders which will amplify the substantive provisions of the new legislation. Section 67 sets out the Government's powers and the procedural requirements needed to make regulations and orders.[1] The section came into force on 17 May 1996.

1 Section 67 is modified in the Northern Ireland context by Sch 8, para 40 and here any power to make regulations or orders under the 1995 Act is exercisable by statutory rule for the purposes of the Statutory Rules (Northern Ireland) Order 1979.

9.4.15 Any power under the Act to make regulations or orders is to be exercised by statutory instrument (s 67(1)).[1] The term 'regulations' means regulations made by the Secretary of State (s 68(1)). Any such power may be exercised to make different provision for different cases, including different provision for different areas (s 67(2)). The power to make regulations and orders under the Act includes the power to make incidental, supplemental, consequential or transitional provisions (s 67(3)(a)). That power is exercised by the Secretary of State as appears to him or her as expedient. The power to make regulations and orders may also provide for a person to exercise a discretion in dealing with any matter (s 67(3)(b)). Nothing in s 34(4) (licensing of taxis in compliance with taxi accessibility regulations) or s 40(6) (public service vehicle accessibility regulations) or s 46(5) (rail vehicle accessibility regulations) affects the powers conferred by s 67(2) or (3) above.[2]

---

1 An exception is provided for under s 67(6) in respect of an order under s 43 by which the Secretary of State may authorise the use on roads of a regulated public service vehicle (PSV) which does not comply with the PSV accessibility regulations or which does not possess an accessibility or approval certificate under ss 40–42 of the Act. See **8.3.16–8.3.17**.
2 See Chapter 8.

9.4.16 Under s 50(3), the Secretary of State may by order confer additional functions on the National Disability Council.[1] However, no such order shall be made unless a draft of the statutory instrument containing the order has been laid before Parliament and approved by a resolution of each House (s 67(4)).

---

1 See **9.1.10**.

9.4.17 A statutory instrument made under the Act is subject to annulment by a resolution of either House of Parliament (s 67(5)). However, that annulment procedure does not apply to a statutory instrument made under s 3(9) (an order appointing the date on which any s 3 guidance as to the meaning of disability is to come into force) or ss 52(8) or 54(6) (an order appointing the date when a code of practice shall come into force) or under s 70(3) (an order appointing the date when the provisions of the Act come into force).

9.4.18 The Government has stated that it does not intend to use its power to make regulations and orders in such a way as to exempt whole categories of occupations from the Act's protection, although consideration may be given to excluding seasonal workers from the scope of Part II.[1] Nevertheless, concern might be expressed at the extent to which the Act gives the relevant Government ministers extensive powers to amplify or restrict the application of the statute's substantive principles by means of regulations or orders.

---

1 HC Deb, vol 257, col 896 (Mr J. Paice). No such exclusion has been made to date.

9.4.19 The majority of these powers are subject to the negative resolution procedure, but the House of Lords Select Committee on the Scrutiny of Delegated Powers was satisfied that most of these powers did not require to be drawn to the attention of the House.[1] Thus, while in many respects the Act is enabling legislation, requiring further regulations to make it work, it is not a mere skeleton statute.

The one power the Select Committee hesitated over was the power in s 7(2) to redefine the meaning of small business for the purpose of the small employer exemption from Part II of the Act (discrimination in the employment field).[2] The Secretary of State has the power to substitute a lower threshold of employees in the definition of the exempted businesses. This is a form of 'Henry VIII' clause (a clause allowing a Minister in effect to amend primary legislation by secondary legislation) and is only subject to the negative resolution procedure. The Select Committee considered that because the s 7(2) power can only be used to reduce the number of employers enjoying the exemption it was not objectionable in principle.

---

1   See the Committee's 7th Report for Session 1994–95 (HL Paper 63) paras 14–19.
2   See **3.2.9–3.2.11**.

Chapter 10

ENFORCEMENT, REMEDIES AND PROCEDURE

10.1 CAUSES OF ACTION AND LEGAL LIABILITY

10.1.1 The Disability Discrimination Act 1995 creates a number of causes of action and bases of legal liability which have already been referred to in the discussion of the substantive provisions of the new statute in earlier chapters of this book. It may be helpful to collect and revisit that information here.

Discrimination

10.1.2 The Act broadly creates six new causes of action based upon unlawful discrimination against disabled persons.

10.1.3 First, s 4(1) of the Act makes it unlawful for an employer to discriminate against a disabled person in the field of recruitment, selection and employment offers. Section 4(2) of the Act also makes it unlawful for an employer to discriminate against a disabled person employed by the employer where the discrimination relates to employment terms and opportunities, dismissal or the subjecting of the disabled person to any other detriment. The ingredients of the unlawful actions or omissions which constitute these first two causes of action are spelt out in the remaining subsections of s 4, in the provisions of ss 5–7 and by Part II of the Act generally.[1]

Sections 17–18 of the Act extend this liability to trustees and managers of occupational pension schemes and providers of insurance services in the circumstances explained there.[2] As will be explained below, liability might also arise in relation to the lessor of premises occupied under a lease (s 16 and Sch 4).

---

1   See Chapter 3.
2   See Chapter 3.

10.1.4 Secondly, s 12(1) of the Act makes it unlawful for a principal to discriminate against a disabled person in relation to contract work in terms very similar to (but not identical with) those applicable to employers under s 4. Section 12 relies in general upon the provisions of Part II of the Act to amplify this liability.[1]

---

1   See Chapter 3.

10.1.5 Thirdly, s 13 provides that it is unlawful for a trade organisation to discriminate against a disabled person in access to membership (s 13(1)) and in respect of the rights of membership (s 13(2)). Section 13 is supplemented by ss 14–16 and Sch 4.[1]

---

1 See Chapter 4.

10.1.6 Fourthly, s 19(1) of the Act makes it unlawful for a person to discriminate against a disabled person in relation to the provision of goods, facilities or services. This cause of action is amplified in the remaining subsections of s 19 and in the provisions of ss 20–21 and of Part III of the Act in general.[1] The provisions of s 27 and Sch 4 will also be relevant where the service provider occupies premises under lease.

---

1 See Chapter 5.

10.1.7 Fifthly, s 22(1) of the Act provides that it is unlawful for a person with the power to dispose of any premises to discriminate against a disabled person in relation to the disposal or terms of disposal of premises or in the treatment of disabled persons in relation to waiting lists for premises. Section 22(3) of the Act also makes it unlawful for a person managing any premises to discriminate against a disabled person occupying those premises in relation to the way in which a disabled person is permitted or not permitted to use any benefits or facilities in relation to those premises, or by evicting the disabled person or subjecting him or her to any other detriment. It is also unlawful for any person whose licence or consent is required for the disposal of any premises comprised in or the subject of a tenancy to discriminate against a disabled person by withholding the licence or consent for the disposal of the premises to the disabled person (s 22(4)). These causes of action are amplified by the remaining provisions of s 22, by ss 23–24 and by Part III generally.[1]

---

1 See Chapter 6.

10.1.8 Finally, s 55 provides that, for the purposes of Part II or Part III of the Act, a person has a cause of action if he or she is victimised by another person in connection with the exercise of any rights contained within the Act. A cause of action is supplied here by cross-referencing s 55 with ss 4, 12, 13, 19 and 22.[1] Victimisation is dealt with in detail immediately below.

---

1 By virtue of ss 4(5), 12(4), 13(3), 19(4) and 22(5).

Victimisation

10.1.9 The concept of liability arising from the victimisation of a person because they sought to exercise statutory rights is one which is established in discrimination law and in employment law generally.[1] The victimisation provisions in the 1995 Act are drafted in a slightly different way from the existing models, but it is likely that the case-law under the comparable sections of the SDA 1975 and the RRA 1976 will be informative.[2]

---

1 See the Sex Discrimination Act 1975 (SDA 1975), s 4; the Race Relations Act 1976, (RRA 1976), s 2; Employment Rights Act 1996, s 104.
2 This would appear to be the tenor of the explanation of s 55 supplied by the Under-Secretary of State for Employment. See HC Deb Standing Committee E, cols 425–426 (Mr J. Paice).

10.1.10 Section 55(1) provides that a person (A) discriminates against another person (B) if A treats B less favourably than A treats or would treat other persons whose circumstances are the same as B's and A does so for one of a number of reasons. Section 55(2) sets out those alternative reasons as follows:

- B has brought proceedings against A or any other person (C) under the Act;
- B has given evidence or information in connection with proceedings brought by a person (D) against A or C under the Act;
- B has otherwise done anything under the Act in relation to A or any other person (C);
- B has alleged (expressly or impliedly) that A or C has contravened the Act;
- A believes or suspects that B has done or intends to do any of the above things.

However, victimisation of B by A in any of these circumstances is not made unlawful solely by virtue of s 55(1) if the less favourable treatment of B by A is because of an allegation made by B which was false and not made in good faith (s 55(4)).

10.1.11 The effect of s 55 is to treat the listed forms of victimisation as amounting to acts of discrimination for the purposes of Part II or Part III of the Act. Section 55 came into force on 2 December 1996 and will apply to acts of victimisation on or after that date. Where B brings an action alleging unlawful discrimination by dint of victimisation in employment (or contract work) or by a trade organisation or in the provision of goods, facilities and services or in respect of the disposal (or management) of premises, it does not matter whether B is or is not a disabled person within the meaning of the Act (ss 4(5), 12(4), 13(3), 19(4) and s 22(7)).

Unlike the sex and race discrimination statutes, the 1995 Act is asymmetrical. That is to say, it does not make unlawful any act of reverse discrimination against non-disabled persons or more favourable treatment of disabled persons.[1] Similarly, it does not directly outlaw discriminatory treatment of a person because of his or her association or relationship with a disabled person. So s 55(1) provides the only basis for a cause of action under the Act for a person who either does not satisfy the definition of a disabled person in Part I or who is not a disabled person at all.

---

1   But note the position of local government employers discussed at **3.12**.

10.1.12   If the person being victimised (B) is a disabled person or a person who has had a disability, the disability in question is to be disregarded when comparing B's circumstances with that of any other person who is the comparator for judging A's less favourable treatment of B (s 55(3)). It is also clear that a tribunal or court could determine how B has been treated in comparison with a hypothetical comparator.[1]

---

1   HC Deb Standing Committee E, col 426 (Mr J. Paice).

10.1.13   Section 55 will or should catch the following illustrations:[1]

- B, a disabled person, is dismissed by A (his or her employer) because B took A to an industrial tribunal under the Act for refusing him or her access to a training opportunity or a promotion.
- B, a non-disabled person, is demoted and receives a cut in pay because he or she gave evidence in court proceedings brought under the Act against A (B's employer) by C (a disabled person) who had been refused service in A's restaurant because C was a wheelchair-user.
- B, a disabled tenant of A (a local authority landlord), is evicted from his or her rented flat or removed from the housing list by A because B wrote to the local press complaining that A was failing to make provision under the Act to allow disabled persons physical access to the local community centre.
- B, a non-disabled activist on disability rights is refused entry to A's cinema because B had picketed the cinema alleging that it was physically inaccessible to disabled persons contrary to the new legislation.

However, judicial interpretation of the victimisation provisions of the SDA 1975 and RRA 1976 demonstrate that not all forms of apparent victimisation will be caught.[2]

---

1   See also Employment Code of Practice, paras 4.53–4.54 and the Rights of Access Code of Practice, paras 6.1–6.2.
2   See, for example, *British Airways Engine Overhaul Ltd v Francis* [1981] IRLR 9, EAT (there must be a connection between B's actions, A's actions and the provisions of the Act); *Aziz v Trinity Street Taxis Ltd* [1988] IRLR 204, CA (there must be a causal link between the victimisation and a protected act). See also, *Cornelius v University College of Swansea* [1987] IRLR 141, CA; *Kirby v Manpower Services Commission* [1980] IRLR 229, EAT; *Nagarajan v Agnew* [1994] IRLR 61, EAT.

Aiding unlawful acts

10.1.14   A person who knowingly aids another person to do an act made unlawful by the 1995 Act is treated for the purposes of the legislation as having done the same kind of unlawful act in his or her own right (s 57(1)). This is modelled after like provisions in the other discrimination statutes.[1] Section 57 came into force on 2 December 1996.

---

1   SDA 1975, s 42 and RRA 1976, s 33.

10.1.15   The effect of s 57 is that a person can become liable for a discriminatory act committed contrary to the new legislation merely by aiding and abetting the person who is primarily responsible for the discriminatory conduct. For example, if a company's personnel officer knowingly or deliberately discriminates against disabled applicants for employment, the company will be primarily responsible under the principle of statutory vicarious liability contained in s 58 (see **10.1.19**), but the personnel officer may also be liable under s 57, having aided the company to commit the discrimination in question.[1]

---

1   See also the example given in Rights of Access Code of Practice, para 6.3.

10.1.16   However, it is not commonplace for complainants to seek to make employees or officers of a company, which has discriminated in the above circumstances, jointly or individually liable in legal proceedings for their part in the act of discrimination. This is because of the difficulty of proving that such a person 'knowingly' aided an unlawful act. The mental element of knowledge or intention is crucial. Furthermore, there may be little to be gained in terms of remedies.

10.1.17   A person faced with an allegation of aiding another person to commit a discriminatory act made unlawful by the legislation has an explicit defence under s 57(3). For the purposes of s 57, a person does not knowingly aid another to do an unlawful act if he or she acts in reliance on a statement made to him or her by that other person. The statement must be to the effect that the discriminatory act would not be unlawful because of any provision of the Act and it must be reasonable to rely upon that statement. That other person is guilty of a criminal offence if he or she knowingly or recklessly makes such a statement which is false or misleading in a material respect (s 57(4)). A person guilty of that offence is liable upon summary conviction to a fine not exceeding level 5 on the standard scale (s 57(5)). An employer or principal cannot be made vicariously liable for such an offence committed by an employee or agent (s 58(4)).

Liability of employers and principals

10.1.18   Anything done by a person in the course of his or her employment is treated by s 58(1), for the purposes of the Act, as also done by his or her employer, whether or not it was done with the employer's knowledge or approval. This statutory principle of vicarious liability is an important inclusion because, for example, the Act speaks of unlawful acts committed by 'an employer' (s 3), 'a provider of services' (s 19) and 'a person with power to dispose of any premises' (s 22). It reflects similar provisions in other discrimination statutes.[1] Vicarious liability cannot extend to an offence committed under s 57(4) by virtue of s 58(4).[2]

---

1   SDA 1975, s 41; RRA 1976, s 32.
2   See **10.1.17**.

10.1.19   The effect of s 58 (from 2 December 1996) is to make the employer vicariously liable for the discriminatory actions of an employee during the course of employment. However, both the employer and the employee remain potentially liable, because the employee may have knowingly aided the employer in the commission of an unlawful act of discrimination.[1] Section 58 does not release the employee from any individual liability that might arise. So, even although the employee might not be capable of committing an act of discrimination made unlawful by the Act, he or she may be deemed to have aided the employer's unlawful act. This is because s 57(2) provides that an employee for whose act the employer is liable under s 58 shall be taken to have aided the employer to do the act.[2]

---

1   See under the SDA 1975: *Enterprise Glass Co Ltd v Miles* [1990] ICR 787, EAT. See generally, Employment Code of Practice, paras 4.11, 4.55–4.59 and 4.62–4.63; Rights of Access Code of Practice, paras 6.4–6.5.
2   For an illustration of this under the SDA 1975, see *Read v Tiverton District Council* [1977] **IRLR** 202, IT.

10.1.20   The meaning of 'in the course of employment' is established in a long line of case-law and common law precedents will be relevant.[1] It is insufficient that the act was done while on duty or that the occasion to commit the act was provided in the context of employment. However, it is enough that the act that gave rise to the discriminatory conduct was authorised by the employer, although carried out in an unauthorised or prohibited fashion.[2]

---

1   See, for example, *Irving and Irving v Post Office* [1987] IRLR 289, CA.
2   *Aldred v Nacanco* [1987] IRLR 292, CA; *Heasmans v Clarity Cleaning Co Ltd* [1987] IRLR 286, CA.

10.1.21 In a case of vicarious liability under s 58, an employer has a possible defence. Section 58(5) invites the employer to escape vicarious liability (but not, of course, any liability faced in its own right) by proving that it took such steps as were reasonably practicable to prevent the employee from doing the act complained of or doing acts of the same description in the course of employment. It may be sufficient to avoid vicarious liability by showing, for example, that the employer was unaware of the discriminatory acts being perpetrated by the employee and that there was proper and adequate staff supervision, including appropriate training and the dissemination of an anti-discrimination or equal opportunities policy.[1] The burden of proof will be upon the employer.

---

1   *Balgobin and Francis v London Borough of Tower Hamlets* [1987] IRLR 401, EAT, a sex discrimination case under comparable provisions.

10.1.22 Section 58 also applies in part to the relationship of principal and agent. Anything done by a person as agent for a principal, and with the principal's express or implied authority, is treated for the purposes of the Act as also done by the agent, whether the authority was given before or after the act in question (s 58(2)–(3)). Once again, this means that the principal is vicariously liable for the discriminatory actions of the agent and is jointly liable with the agent. The agent will be treated as having aided the principal to commit the unlawful act by virtue of s 57(2). There is no defence available to the principal under s 58(5) as there would be to an employer in a case of vicarious liability.

Exceptions for statutory authority or national security

10.1.23 There are a number of exceptions within the Act whereby an act or omission that would otherwise amount to discrimination related to disability is treated as not being unlawful. In Part II of the Act, for example, discrimination by an employer in relation to employment at an establishment outside the UK is not made unlawful (s 3(6)), while s 10 contains exceptions from the employment provisions for charities and bodies that provide supported employment for disabled persons.

Further examples of exceptional treatment are to be found in Part III of the Act, which applies only to the provision of services within the UK (s 19(2)(b)) and, broadly speaking, does not apply to the provision of services in education and transport (s 19(5)). In respect of premises, s 22 only applies to premises within the UK (s 22(8)) and s 23 provides a general exemption for small dwellings.

10.1.24 Section 59 of the Act contains a number of exceptions in respect of statutory authority, national security and other matters with effect from 17 May 1996.[1] By virtue of s 59(1), nothing in the 1995 legislation causes an act or deliberate omission to be made unlawful where that act or omission is done in any of the following circumstances:

- in pursuance of any 'enactment';
- in pursuance of any 'instrument' made by a Minister of the Crown under any 'enactment';
- to comply with any condition or requirement imposed by a Minister of the Crown (whether before or after the passing of the Act) by virtue of any 'enactment'.[2]

An 'enactment' for this purpose will include an Act of Parliament, subordinate legislation[3] (such as a statutory instrument) and any Order in Council (s 68(1)),[4] whether passed or made before or after the date the Disability Discrimination Act 1995 received Royal Assent (s 59(2)), namely 8 November 1995. An 'instrument' clearly refers to subordinate legislation made by a Minister under statutory delegated authority, whether made before or after the passing of the 1995 Act (s 59(2)).

---

1   Section 59 contains exceptions which are broadly similar in scope to the exceptions contained in RRA 1976, ss 41–42 and, to a lesser extent, SDA 1975, ss 51A–52 .
2   In Northern Ireland, the relevant functions of a Minister of the Crown referred to in s 59 will be those of a Northern Ireland department (Sch 8, para 39).
3   See s 68(1) which cross-refers to the Interpretation Act 1978, s 21.
4   Including, by virtue of Sch 8, para 47(1), any statutory provision within the meaning of the Interpretation Act (Northern Ireland) 1954, s 1(f).

10.1.25   In any proceedings under s 8 of the Act (that is, in respect of discrimination in employment or contract work or by a trade organisation), a certificate signed by or on behalf of a Minister of the Crown (or a Northern Ireland department) which certifies that any conditions or requirements specified in the certificate were imposed by a Minister (or that department), and were in operation at or throughout a specified time, shall be conclusive evidence of the matters certified (Sch 3, para 4(1)(a) and Sch 8, para 50(2)). A document purporting to be such a certificate shall be received in evidence and, unless the contrary is proved, is deemed to be such a certificate (Sch 3, para 4(2)). Identical provision is made by Sch 3, paras 8(1)(a) and 8(2) in respect of proceedings under s 25 of the Act (proceedings under Part III of the Act in respect of goods, facilities, services and premises).[1]

---

1   The modification of this provision in the context of Northern Ireland is set out in Sch 8, para 50(4).

10.1.26   An example was of how these exceptions might operate was given by the Minister for Disabled People in Committee:

'Under s 12 of the Health and Safety at Work etc Act 1974, the Secretary of State is given the power to give the Health and Safety Commission directions about ways in which it carries out its functions. If one of those functions, in the Secretary of State's opinion, required the Commission to do something which adversely affected disabled people, it would not be unlawful and could not be challenged under the provisions of the Bill.[1]

The Minister also made it clear that it was important that the exception should apply to both existing and future enactments. He illustrated this point by referring to the hypothetical possibility that a future safety legislative provision might require employers to modify equipment for the protection of employee operators. As a result of that modification, a disabled person might find it no longer physically possible to operate the equipment. The exception ensures that, by refusing to remove or alter the modification, the employer would not be in breach of the duty to accommodate disabled persons under the 1995 Act. The new safety law would override the disability discrimination legislation to that extent alone, although other forms of reasonable adjustment might remain appropriate for the employee.[2]

---

1 HC Deb Standing Committee E, col 428 (Mr W. Hague). See also the examples in respect of alterations to the highway or to listed buildings given by Lord Inglewood at HL Deb, vol 565, col 673.
2 There would be nothing to prevent a future enactment being made expressly subject to the 1995 Act. See also Employment Code of Practice, para 4.65; Rights of Access Code of Practice, para 5.18.

10.1.27 The use of the phrase 'in pursuance of' in s 59(1)(a) and (b) would appear to be deliberate (indeed, the Bill was deliberately amended at the Government's motion to include the phrase). In the comparable provisions of the Race Relations Act 1976, the draftsman also used the term 'in pursuance of' any enactment or instrument rather than 'under' any enactment or instrument. This has led to a narrow interpretation of the exception by the courts to the effect that the exemption applies only to actions reasonably necessary to comply with a statutory obligation and not to acts done in exercise of a power of discretion conferred by the enactment or instrument.[1]

The use of the word 'under' (contained originally in the Bill) may well have had the effect of inviting a wider interpretation of the exemptions in s 59(1) of the 1995 Act. The result may have been that these exceptions would have applied to anything done under statutory authority, whether of a discretionary nature or not, and that would have gone some way towards undermining the objectives of the 1995 legislation. That possibility has apparently been excluded.

---

1 *Hampson v Department of Education and Science* [1990] IRLR 302, HL.

10.1.28 Section 59(3) further provides that nothing in the 1995 statute makes unlawful any act done for the purpose of safeguarding national security. In proceedings under Part II before an industrial tribunal or under Part III before a court, a certificate signed by or on behalf of a Minister of the Crown which certifies that an act specified in the certificate was done for the purpose of safeguarding national security is to be conclusive evidence of the matter certified (Sch 3, paras 4(1)(b) and 8(1)(b)).[1] A document purporting to be such a certificate shall be received in evidence and, unless the contrary is proved, is deemed to be such a certificate (Sch 3, paras 4(2) and 8(2)).

---

1   In Northern Ireland, the relevant certificate must be signed by the Secretary of State (Sch 8, para 50(2)).

10.2   ADVICE AND ASSISTANCE

Statutory questionnaire in employment cases

10.2.1   Section 56 makes provision for help for persons suffering disability discrimination in relation to employment. The section applies to a person ('the complainant') who considers that he or she may have been discriminated against by another person ('the respondent') in contravention of Part II of the Act and against whom the complainant may decide to make a complaint or has already done so (s 56(1)).

10.2.2   The Secretary of State is mandated by s 56(2) to prescribe by order forms by which the complainant may question the respondent on the respondent's reasons for doing any relevant act or on any other matter which is or may be relevant.[1] This power has not been used at the time of writing. It is clear from the wording of s 56(1) that these questionnaire forms may be used either before or after proceedings have been commenced. Forms may also be prescribed by which the respondent may (if the respondent so wishes) reply to any questions. The power to prescribe such forms is to be taken with a view to helping the complainant to decide whether, in the first place, to make a complaint against the respondent, and, in the second place, to formulate and present the case in the most effective manner.

The Secretary of State may also prescribe the period within which any questionnaire must be served on the respondent employer (at least, if it is to have the effect described in **10.2.4**) and the manner in which the questionnaire (and any reply) must be served (s 56(4)). In the existing discrimination questionnaire procedure,[2] the questions may be served on a potential respondent any time before proceedings are brought (but within three months of the alleged act of discrimination) or up to 21 days after making an originating application or thereafter with the leave of the tribunal.

---

1   In Northern Ireland, the Secretary of State's powers under s 56 are exercised by the Department of Economic Development (Sch 8, para 38).
2   See **10.2.3**.

10.2.3 Section 56 is modelled after similar provisions for assisting aggrieved persons to obtain information in cases of potential sex or race discrimination.[1] The questionnaire procedure has proved to be a useful device for assisting complainants in potential race or sex discrimination complaints in deciding whether to pursue proceedings and how best to frame the presentation of the complaint. It is likely to prove equally effective in disability discrimination cases.

---

1   SDA 1975, s 74; RRA 1976, s 65. The relevant provisions and forms in these jurisdictions are to be found in the Sex Discrimination (Questions and Replies) Order 1975, SI 1975/2048 (amended by SI 1977/844) and the Race Relations (Questions and Replies) Order 1977, SI 1977/842.

10.2.4 A respondent employer faced with a statutory discrimination questionnaire must consider very carefully how to reply to the questions, because the question and any reply by the respondent is admissible in evidence in any subsequent tribunal proceedings under Part II of the Act (s 56(3)(a)). It does not appear to matter whether the respondent's reply is in accordance with the prescribed forms or not.

However, the provisions of s 56 take effect subject to any enactment or rule of law regulating the admissibility of evidence in tribunal proceedings (s 56(5)). While the rules of evidence are not strictly applied in industrial tribunals, the credibility of and compelling nature of evidence in such proceedings does depend upon the tribunal weighing and assessing such evidence in the light of those rules.

10.2.5 If, in the view of an industrial tribunal in subsequent proceedings under Part II of the Act, the respondent deliberately omitted to reply to the questionnaire within a reasonable period without reasonable excuse, the tribunal may draw any inference which it considers it is just and equitable to draw (s 56(3)(b)(i)).[1] This might include an inference that an unlawful act of disability discrimination contrary to Part II of the Act has been committed by the respondent.[2] Similar adverse inferences may be drawn if the tribunal takes the view that the respondent's reply to a questionnaire is evasive or equivocal (s 56(3)(b)(ii)).[3]

---

1   On the general power of tribunals to draw inferences of discrimination, see *King v The Great Britain-China Centre* [1991] IRLR 513, CA.
2   See, for example, the race discrimination case of *Virdee v ECC Quarries Ltd* [1978] IRLR 295, IT.
3   See, for example, the sex discrimination case of *Carrington v Helix Lighting Ltd* [1990] IRLR 6, EAT.

10.2.6 The questionnaire procedure is without prejudice to any other enactment or rule of law regulating interlocutory and preliminary matters in proceedings before an industrial tribunal (s 56(5)). This means that the ability to administer a statutory questionnaire to elicit replies to specific questions from a respondent is in addition to the tribunal's procedural powers in respect of further and better particulars, interrogatories and discovery.[1]

---

1   *Oxford v Department of Health and Social Security* [1977] IRLR 225, EAT.

10.3   ENFORCEMENT AND PROCEDURE IN EMPLOYMENT CASES

Industrial tribunal proceedings

10.3.1   A complaint by any person that another person has unlawfully discriminated against him or her contrary to Part II of the Act (the employment provisions contained in ss 4–7 and 11, the contract worker provisions in s 12 or the provisions touching trade organisations in ss 13–15) may be presented to an industrial tribunal under s 8(1). The term 'person' includes an individual, a body corporate and unincorporated associations.[1]

---

1   Interpretation Act 1978, Sch 1.

10.3.2   The industrial tribunals will also have jurisdiction under s 8(1) to hear complaints where the complainant alleges that another person is to be treated as having discriminated against him or her contrary to Part II of the Act. This expressly includes actions against a person who knowingly aids another to do an unlawful act contrary to Part II (under s 57). It also embraces actions based upon an act done by a person in the course of employment and which is to be treated, by virtue of s 58, as also done by that person's employer. Furthermore, an act done by an agent with the authority of another person (the principal) is treated as being the act of the principal (under s 58) and will be equally actionable under s 8(1). The provisions of ss 57–58 have been considered in detail above.[1]

---

1   See **10.1.14–10.1.22**.

10.3.3   Section 8(1) is largely modelled after the similar provisions in the Sex Discrimination Act 1975, s 63(1) and the Race Relations Act 1976, s 54(1). It is expressly provided that a complaint of employment discrimination contrary to Part II of the Act can only be brought via industrial tribunal proceedings under s 8 of the Act. The unlawfulness of any act by virtue of Part II of the statute does not give rise to any other civil or criminal proceedings (Sch 3, para 2(1)). However, this does not prevent the possibility of an application for judicial review being made in respect of an act made unlawful by the new legislation (Sch 3, para 2(2)).

10.3.4 The proceedings of industrial tribunals are governed by the Industrial Tribunals (Constitution and Rules of Procedure) Regulations 1993, SI 1993/2687.[1] It is not intended to rehearse the constitution and procedures of the industrial tribunals here. It is sufficient to note that proceedings are commenced by presenting an originating application to the Central Office of Industrial Tribunals within the statutory time-limits and that a respondent may then present a defence in the form of a notice of appearance. Decisions of an industrial tribunal are made unanimously or by a majority. An appeal from a decision of an industrial tribunal may be made to the Employment Appeal Tribunal, on a point of law, and from there to the Court of Appeal and the House of Lords.

---

1 In Scotland, see Industrial Tribunals (Constitution and Rules of Procedure) (Scotland) Regulations 1993, SI 1993/2688. Both Rules of Procedure have been amended. In England and Wales, see SI 1994/536 and SI 1996/1757; in Scotland, see SI 1994/538 and SI 1996/1758.

10.3.5 Part I of Sch 3 to the 1995 Act contains detailed further provisions concerning enforcement and procedures in respect of employment cases (s 8(8)). These provisions do merit further attention here. It might be noted first, however, that the industrial tribunals are themselves subject to the Act and will be covered by the new right of access to goods, facilities and services contained in Part II of the Act (see Chapter 5).[1]

---

1 HC Deb Standing Committee E, col 279. Legal aid is not generally available in industrial tribunal proceedings.

10.3.6 An industrial tribunal shall not consider a complaint under s 8 of the 1995 Act unless it is presented before the end of the period of three months beginning when the act complained of was done (Sch 3, para 3(1)).[1] An 'act' includes a deliberate omission (s 68(1)). The three-month time-limit for the presentation of a complaint is important as it goes to the question of the jurisdiction of the industrial tribunal to hear the complaint at all. The tribunal cannot be seised of jurisdiction, in any event, in respect of an act of disability discrimination which occurred before 2 December 1996 (unless its effects are continuing ones).

---

1 This mirrors the identical provisions in the SDA 1975, s 76(1) and the RRA 1976, s 68(1). The case-law under those Acts will be instructive here and is referred to in the notes below.

10.3.7 Some confusion might arise as to when the three-month time period begins to run.[1] In the case of an isolated act of disability discrimination, the presumption will be that time starts to run from the date of the act or the omission itself. Schedule 3, para 3(3)(c) makes it plain that a deliberate omission is to be treated as done when the person in question decided upon it. Subject to rebutting evidence, a person is treated as having decided upon an omission when he or she does an act inconsistent with doing the omitted act or, in the absence of such inconsistent behaviour, when the period expires within which he or she might reasonably have been expected to do the omitted act if it was to be done (Sch 3, para 3(4)).[2]

However, in other cases, there is more flexibility in measuring the date upon which time starts to run. In the case of any act or omission which extends over a period of time, the three months' limitation provision will not start to run until the end of the period in question (Sch 3, para 3(3)(b)).[3] Moreover, where the alleged unlawful act of discrimination is attributable to a term in a contract, time does not start to expire until the end of the contract. The unlawful act is said to extend throughout the duration of the contract (Sch 3, para 3(3)(a)).

---

1 Compare the provisions of the SDA 1975, s 76(6) and the RRA 1976, s 68(7).
2 See, for example, *Swithland Motors plc v Clarke* [1994] ICR 231, EAT.
3 See *Amies v Inner London Education Authority* [1977] ICR 308, EAT and *Sougrin v Haringey Health Authority* [1991] ICR 791, EAT (distinguishes between continuing acts and continuing consequences); *Calder v James Finlay Corporation Ltd* [1989] IRLR 55, EAT (refusal of access to employment benefit throughout employment construed as continuing act of discrimination); *Littlewoods Organisation plc v Traynor* [1993] IRLR 154, EAT (a failure to remedy a discriminatory situation can be a continuing act of discrimination). On continuing acts of discrimination generally, see *Barclays Bank plc v Kapur* [1991] ICR 208, HL.

10.3.8 Even where a complaint has been presented out of time, an industrial tribunal may nevertheless entertain it if, in all the circumstances of the case, 'it considers that it is just and equitable to do so' (Sch 3, para 3(2)). This allows industrial tribunals considerable discretion to admit late applications under the Act.[1] Tribunal decisions to extend the time-limit in such cases are rarely challengeable on appeal.[2] In the first year or so of the new Act being in force, tribunals are likely to allow late complaints to proceed where the applicant was unaware of a cause of action or the time-limits governing it.[3]

---

1 Compare the similar provision in the SDA 1975, s 76(5) and the RRA 1976, s 68(6). Contrast the more restrictive provision in unfair dismissal cases under the Employment Rights Act 1996, s 111.
2 *Hutchinson v Westward Television Ltd* [1977] ICR 279, EAT.
3 See, for example, *Foster v South Glamorgan Health Authority* [1988] ICR 526, EAT.

Conciliation

10.3.9 As is already the case in respect of sex and race discrimination and unfair dismissal actions,[1] it is anticipated that there will be an attempt to reach a conciliated settlement between the parties before a complaint under s 8 of the Act proceeds to a hearing by the tribunal. What was Sch 3, para 1 (1) of the 1995 Act (what is now the Industrial Tribunals Act 1996, s 18(1)(c), (2)) provides that a copy of a complaint of disability discrimination under s 8 of the Act shall be sent to a conciliation officer of the Advisory Conciliation and Arbitration Service (ACAS)[2] or, in Northern Ireland, the Labour Relations Agency.[3]

---

1 Industrial Tribunals Act 1996, s 18.
2 See s 68(1) which refers to a conciliation officer as a person designated under the Trade Union and Labour Relations (Consolidation) Act 1992, s 211. Note the Industrial Tribunals Act 1996, s 42(1). Note also the provisions of rules 2(3) and 20(7) in Sch 1 to the Industrial Tribunals (Constitution and Rules of Procedure) Regulations 1993, SI 1993/2687 relating to conciliation.
3 Schedule 8, para 50(1). But see now the Industrial Tribunals (Northern Ireland) Order 1996, SI 1996/1921.

10.3.10 In such a case, the conciliation officer must try to promote a settlement of the complaint, without a tribunal hearing, if requested to do so by both parties or if the conciliation officer considers that there is a reasonable prospect of a successful attempt to promote a settlement being made (Industrial Tribunals Act 1996, s 18(2)). This latter provision allows the conciliation officer to be proactive, even if only one of the parties has requested a conciliatory intervention. Moreover, where a complaint has yet to be presented to an industrial tribunal, but a person is contemplating presenting such a complaint, the conciliation officer shall try to promote a settlement if asked to do so by the potential complainant or potential respondent (Industrial Tribunals Act 1996, s 18(3)).

10.3.11 ACAS conciliation is a well-established and often successful method of alternative dispute resolution in cases of individual disputes in employment law. Insight into how the conciliation process operates in discrimination and employment cases generally can be gleaned from the ACAS Annual Reports and from the numerous advisory booklets and publications issued by the Service. Regional offices of ACAS will be a helpful source in this regard. There is an existing body of case-law concerning conciliated settlements which it is not proposed to revisit here.[1]

---

1 See generally, *Harvey on Industrial Relations and Employment Law* (Butterworths).

10.3.12 Two points about the conciliation stage are worth making here. First, the conciliation officer must consider the desirability of encouraging the parties to resolve the complaint by the use of appropriate available procedures for the settlement of grievances (Industrial Tribunals Act 1996, s 18(6)). This is particularly so in cases which have not yet resulted in an originating application, and where the complainant is in employment. A complaint might be more easily resolved by utilising the employer's internal grievance procedure, if any. Many employers have already adopted such procedures, either as an adjunct to disciplinary rules and practices, or as part of an equal opportunities policy or statement. Secondly, anything communicated to the conciliation officer during the course of the conciliation process is inadmissible in evidence in any subsequent proceedings before the industrial tribunal, unless with the consent of the person who communicated that matter (Industrial Tribunals Act 1996, s 18(7)).

10.3.13 If a conciliated settlement has been agreed with the assistance of an ACAS conciliation officer,[1] the agreement will usually be recorded in writing using form COT3. An oral agreement would be equally valid,[2] although obviously less certain. A conciliated settlement will be a valid agreement and will not be avoided by the provisions of s 9(1) of the 1995 Act if it merely records an agreement not to institute proceedings or an agreement to discontinue proceedings before an industrial tribunal (s 9(2)(a)). Unless the conciliated settlement is otherwise challengeable or invalid, the industrial tribunal will then have no jurisdiction to hear the complaint which is the subject of the conciliation. Even if a respondent reneges on an ACAS-brokered settlement, the complainant must sue on the agreement rather than seek to reopen the complaint.

---

1 In Northern Ireland, an officer of the Labour Relations Agency.
2 *Gilbert v Kembridge Fibres Ltd* [1984] ICR 188, EAT.

Compromises or settlements

10.3.14 Apart from a settlement produced as a result of individual conciliation under the auspices of ACAS, what other possibilities arise to settle or to compromise a complaint under the 1995 Act without proceeding to an industrial tribunal hearing? Section 9 of the Act treats as void any term of an agreement which purports to prevent any person from presenting a complaint to an industrial tribunal under Part II of the Act (s 9(1)(c)). However, that does not apply expressly to an agreement to discontinue or not to institute proceedings if that agreement is the product of ACAS conciliation (s 9(2)(a)). A settlement or compromise agreement is also valid under s 9(2)(b) if certain conditions are satisfied.[1]

---

1 Similar, but not identical, provisions are to be found in relation to 'compromise agreements' introduced by the Trade Union Reform and Employment Rights Act 1993, s 39 in the SDA 1975, s 77; the RRA 1976, s 72; the Trade Union and Labour Relations (Consolidation) Act 1992, s 288; and the Employment Rights Act 1996, s 203.

10.3.15   First, the complainant must have received 'independent' legal advice from a 'qualified lawyer' as to the terms and effect of the proposed agreement not to institute proceedings or to discontinue existing proceedings before the industrial tribunal (s 9(3)(a)). The legal advice in question must highlight in particular the effect of such agreement upon the complainant's ability to pursue the complaint before an industrial tribunal. In other words, the advice must have made it clear that the settlement will generally prevent the complainant resurrecting the complaint by seeking a hearing of the tribunal.

10.3.16   Legal advice given to a complainant is 'independent' if it is given by a lawyer who is not acting for the other party or for a person who is connected with that other party (s 9(4)). For this purpose, a person will be treated as connected to the other party to the discrimination complaint if one is a company which the other person controls directly or indirectly, or both persons are companies controlled directly or indirectly by a third person (s 9(5)). It would seem that the legal advice is only truly independent if the lawyer in question is not acting for the respondent (or a connected person) at all as opposed to not acting for the respondent in the particular matter at hand.[1]

The independent legal advice must have been received from a qualified lawyer. This means that the lawyer must be a barrister (or, in Scotland, an advocate) in private practice or otherwise employed to give legal advice (for example, as a member of a neighbourhood law centre or trade union legal department) or a solicitor holding a practising certificate.

---

1   Cf the wording of the Employment Rights Act 1996, s 203(3), (4).

10.3.17   Secondly, at the time when the advice was given to the complainant, there must have been in force a policy of insurance covering the risk of a claim by the complainant in respect of any loss that might arise as a consequence of the advice (s 9(3)(b)). This is designed to protect the complainant from the consequences of negligent professional advice and provides the complainant with a secure alternative cause of action against the negligent adviser. There has been some doubt as to whether the professional indemnity arrangements for solicitors satisfy this requirement, although the question remains untested.

10.3.18   Finally, the compromise or settlement agreement must be in writing, relate to the particular complaint, identify the legal adviser and state that the conditions above have been satisfied (s 9(3)(c)).

Restriction on publicity

10.3.19   As a result of a commitment given during the passage of the legislation,[1] where evidence of a personal nature is likely to be heard by the industrial tribunal hearing a complaint of disability discrimination under s 8 of the 1995 Act, special provision is made for the restriction of publicity.[2] This provision was originally made in s 62(1) of the 1995 Act but is now contained in the Industrial Tribunals Act 1996, s 12(1).[3] Evidence of a personal nature means any evidence of a medical or other intimate nature which might reasonably be assumed to be likely to cause significant embarrassment to the complainant if reported.[4] The Secretary of State is empowered to make regulations with respect to the procedure of industrial tribunals so as to achieve this objective.[5]

1   HL Deb, vol 566, col 428 (Lord Mackay of Ardbrecknish).
2   Similar provision is made for the restriction of publicity in the Employment Appeal Tribunal: see Disability Discrimination Act 1995, s 63 and the Industrial Tribunals Act 1996, s 32 and Sch 2, para 7(7)–(8) and Sch 3. This is not considered in further detail here.
3   Section 62 of the 1995 Act is repealed by Sch 3 to the 1996 Act and replaced by s 12 of the 1996 Act. Part II of Sch 2 to the Industrial Tribunals Act 1996 makes transitional provisions because, while ss 62(1)–(2) and 62(7) of the 1995 Act came into force on 17 May 1996, the remaining parts of s 62 were not in force when the 1996 Act became effective on 22 August 1996 and, at the time of writing, were still not in force. See the Industrial Tribunals Act 1996, Sch 2, para 7.
4   Disability Discrimination Act 1995, s 62(7); Industrial Tribunals Act 1996, s 12(7).
5   Disability Discrimination Act 1995, s 62(2); Industrial Tribunals Act 1996, s 12(2).

10.3.20   The regulations take the form of amendments to the tribunal procedure regulations.[1] A new rule 14(1A) provides that, in proceedings under s 8 of the Disability Discrimination Act 1995 in which evidence of a personal nature is likely to be heard by the tribunal, at any time before promulgation of its decision, the tribunal may make a 'restricted reporting order' on the application of the complainant or of its own motion.[2] A 'restricted reporting order' is an order made in exercise of the regulation-making powers.[3] It has the effect of prohibiting the publication in Great Britain of 'identifying matter' in a written publication (such as a newspaper or magazine, but also including a film, a soundtrack and any other record in a permanent form) available to the public. Such an order will also have the effect of prohibiting the inclusion of any 'identifying matter' in a relevant radio or television programme (within the meaning of the Broadcasting Act 1990) for reception in Great Britain.[4] This will effectively restrain the press and broadcast media from reporting any 'identifying matter' about the case which is likely to lead members of the public to identify the complainant or any other persons named in the restricted reporting order.[5]

1   Similar powers to make restricted reporting orders in respect of allegations of sexual misconduct already exist (now under the Industrial Tribunals Act 1996, s 11). See the Industrial Tribunals (Constitution and Rules of Procedure) Regulations 1993, SI 1993/2687 (Sch 1, r 14); Industrial Tribunals (Constitution and Rules of Procedure) (Scotland) Regulations 1993, SI 1993/2688 (Sch 1, r 14).

2 The new rule 14(1A) is introduced into the respective Rules of Procedure by SI 1996/1757, para 15 and SI 1996/1758, para 13. If the complaint is being dealt with together with any other proceedings, the tribunal may also direct that the order applies in whole or in part in relation to those other proceedings (r 14(1B)).
3 Disability Discrimination Act 1995, s 62(7); Industrial Tribunals Act 1996, s 12(7).
4 But not including an indictment or other document prepared for use in particular legal proceedings: Disability Discrimination Act 1995, s 62(7); Industrial Tribunals Act 1996, s 12(7).
5 Similar provisions also apply to Northern Ireland with the necessary modifications.

10.3.21 Once made, a restricted reporting order has effect until the promulgation of the tribunal's decision in the case, unless the order is revoked earlier.[1] If the restricted reporting order is broken by a newspaper or periodical, the proprietor, editor or publisher of the newspaper or periodical is guilty of a summary offence punishable by a fine not exceeding level 5 on the standard scale.[2] Where the order is breached in a publication in any other form, the publisher of the matter shall be so liable.[3] Where the identifying matter is published in breach of a restricted reporting order by a radio or television broadcaster, the broadcast company and the programme editor (or his or her equivalent) face criminal liability as before.[4]

1 Disability Discrimination Act 1995, s 62(2)(a); Industrial Tribunals Act 1996, s 12(2)(a).
2 Disability Discrimination Act 1995, s 62(3)(a); Industrial Tribunals Act 1996, s 12(3)(a).
3 Disability Discrimination Act 1995, s 62(3)(b); Industrial Tribunals Act 1996, s 12(3)(b).
4 Disability Discrimination Act 1995, s 62(3)(c); Industrial Tribunals Act 1996, s 12(3)(c).

10.3.22 If a person is charged with an offence arising out of a breach of a restricted reporting order,[1] it is a defence to prove that at the time of the alleged offence that person was not aware (and neither suspected nor had reason to suspect) that the publication or programme in question was of (or included) the matter in question.[2] Offences committed by a body corporate with the consent or connivance of (or attributable neglect of) a director, manager, secretary or other similar officer (including a person purporting to act in such capacity) are to be treated as offences of joint liability.[3]

1 Under the Disability Discrimination Act 1995, s 62(3); Industrial Tribunals Act 1996, s 12(3).
2 Disability Discrimination Act 1995, s 62(4); Industrial Tribunals Act 1996, s 12(4).
3 Disability Discrimination Act 1995, s 62(5)–(6); Industrial Tribunals Act 1996, s 12(5)–(6).

The hearing and decision

10.3.23 This is not the place to rehearse the practice and procedure of an industrial tribunal hearing. The reader is referred to the usual sources. It is worth noting, however, that whereas a tribunal will usually give its written reasons for its decision in summary form, unless a party requests reasons in

extended form, in race and sex discrimination cases the tribunal must give
extended reasons. This principle has also been applied to reasons for decisions
in disability discrimination cases.[1]

---

1   Industrial Tribunals (Constitution and Rules of Procedure) Regulations 1993, Sch 1, r 10 (as
    amended).

10.4   REMEDIES IN EMPLOYMENT CASES

10.4.1   Where an industrial tribunal finds that a complaint of unlawful
disability discrimination in the employment field contrary to Part II of the Act is
well-founded, 'it shall take such of the following steps as it considers just and
equitable' (s 8(2)):

• 	make a declaration as to the rights of the complainant and the
	respondent in relation to the matters to which the complaint relates;
• 	order the respondent to pay compensation to the complainant;
• 	recommend that the respondent take, within a specified period, action
	appearing to the tribunal to be reasonable, in all the circumstances of the
	case, for the purpose of obviating or reducing the adverse effect on the
	complainant of any matter to which the complaint relates.

This reflects the almost identical powers of industrial tribunals in sex and race
discrimination cases in relation to employment opportunities and rights.[1] Note
also the possibility of a complainant having rights to compensation against a
commercial landlord where an employer or trade organisation has been
unable to comply with a s 6 or s 15 duty to make adjustments to premises (s 16
and Sch 4).[2]

---

1   SDA 1975, s 65; RRA 1976, s 56.
2   This has been discussed in Chapter 6.

Declaration of rights

10.4.2   Where a complainant has successfully brought a disability discrimination application against a respondent employer, the very least that the
disabled person will be entitled to is a declaration under s 8(2)(a) that he or
she has suffered unlawful discrimination in certain particulars or that his or her
rights have been unlawfully transgressed. A declaration of the complainant's
rights alone is likely to be appropriate in those cases where the complainant has
suffered no measurable loss or where there is a point of principle involved. A
tribunal might occasionally use its declaratory powers to encourage the
employer to take some positive step towards the successful complainant (ie

offer employment to or reinstate him or her), although the legal effect of such a declaration is of doubtful value.

Compensation and interest

10.4.3 In the existing employment discrimination jurisdictions, compensation is frequently regarded as the primary remedy. Given the 1995 Act's emphasis upon employers' duties to make reasonable adjustments to accommodate disabled workers, it remains to be seen whether there will be a shift under the new legislation away from first reliance upon compensatory remedies and towards recommendations of positive action.

10.4.4 Where a tribunal orders compensation to be paid in an employment discrimination case under s 8(2)(b), the amount of the compensation is calculated according to the principles applicable to the calculation of damages in claims in tort or, in Scotland, in reparation for breach of a statutory duty (s 8(3)). In other words, disability discrimination compensation will be assessed like any claim for damages in tort and according to common law principles. Case-law under the parallel provisions of the SDA 1975 and the RRA 1976 will be instructive. Like those statutes as amended,[1] there is no limit on the maximum amount of compensation that can be awarded for a breach of Part II of the 1995 Act.

---

1   For that reason, sex or race discrimination cases decided before the coming into effect of the Sex Discrimination and Equal Pay (Remedies) Regulations 1993, SI 1993/2798 (22 November 1993) and the Race Relations (Remedies) Act 1994 (3 July 1994) will not adequately reflect the true measure of damages to be awarded in such cases. Until those dates, tribunals could not award discrimination compensation exceeding 11,000.

10.4.5   A successful applicant will be entitled to be compensated for any actual financial or pecuniary loss up to the date of the tribunal decision, provided that it is caused by or attributable to the discriminatory act or omission. The tribunal may also be invited to calculate future or continuing losses within the award. The main head of damages is likely to be present or future loss of earnings which have resulted as a consequence of the act of discrimination. This will include loss of basic wages or salary together with any fringe benefits (such as a bonus, commission, company car, private health insurance, pension entitlements, and so on) to which the individual would have been entitled but for the discriminatory action. The complainant will be subject, of course, to a duty to mitigate any loss.

10.4.6   The quantum of compensation may also include compensation for injury to feelings, whether or not the award includes compensation under any other head (s 8(4)). It is suggested that such an element of damages will be appropriate (and easily implied without pleading) in most cases unless exceptional.[1]

In race and sex discrimination cases, the amount of appropriate awards in respect of injuries to feelings is currently undergoing something of a radical review in the tribunals. This is because the level of damages awarded under this heading was previously influenced by the fact that the maximum amount of a total award of damages in these cases was set at 11,000. Awards in the region of 500 to 3,000 in respect of injury to feelings were seen as being the appropriate range.[2] With the removal of the cap on damages, it may now be appropriate for tribunals to reflect injury to feelings more generously in compensation.

1   *Murray v Powertech (Scotland) Ltd* [1992] IRLR 257, EAT.
2   The general principles can be gleaned from the following cases: *Alexander v Home Office* [1988] IRLR 190, CA; *Noone v North West Thames Regional Health Authority* [1988] IRLR 195, CA; *Sharifi v Strathclyde Regional Council* [1992] IRLR 259, EAT; *Deane v London Borough of Ealing* [1993] IRLR 209, EAT; *Ministry of Defence v Sullivan* [1994] ICR 193, EAT.

10.4.7   Aggravated damages may be awarded in exceptional cases where a respondent has acted in a high-handed, malicious, insulting or oppressive manner, but exemplary damages are now almost certainly not appropriate in disability discrimination claims because of recent developments in common law.[1]

1   See the thread of principle which has developed through the following cases: *Alexander v Home Office* [1988] IRLR 190, CA; *City of Bradford Metropolitan Borough Council v Arora* [1991] IRLR 165, CA; *AB v South Western Water Services Ltd* [1993] 1 All ER 609, CA; *Deane v Ealing London Borough Council* [1993] IRLR 209, EAT.

10.4.8   It is expected that tribunals will be empowered and required (subject to its discretion) to include an element of interest in the award of any compensation ordered to be paid. That is currently the position in the sex and race discrimination jurisdictions.[1] The 1995 Act provides for regulations to be made to give tribunals the power to award interest upon compensation and to specify how that interest is to be determined (s 8(6)).[2]

1   See the Sex Discrimination and Equal Pay (Remedies) Regulations 1993, SI 1993/2798 and the Race Relations (Remedies) Act 1994 which will provide an example of how interest is likely to be awarded in disability discrimination cases.
2   Consequential amendment will also have to be made to any order made under the Industrial Tribunals Act 1996, s 14 (power to make provision as to interest on sums payable in pursuance of industrial tribunal decisions) by virtue of s 8(7) of the 1995 Act. See the Industrial Tribunal (Interest) Order 1990, SI 1990/479.

Recommendations

10.4.9   Under s 8(2)(c), where the industrial tribunal has upheld a complaint of disability discrimination in employment, it may recommend that the respondent take, within a specified period, action appearing to the tribunal to be 'reasonable', in all the circumstances of the case, for the purpose of obviating or reducing the adverse effect on the complainant of any 'matter' to which the complaint relates. This mirrors the similar powers contained in sex and race discrimination statutes, except that here the action to be recommended must be 'reasonable' action, whereas in sex and race cases the action must be 'practicable'.[1] How the tribunals will interpret that difference of terminology, and what real effect it will have, remains to be seen.

---

1   SDA 1975, s 65(1)(c); RRA 1976, s 56(1)(c). Note also the use of the term 'act of discrimination' in these statutes where the simple word 'matter' appears in the 1995 Act. There does not appear to be any obvious consequence of this change in wording.

10.4.10   It is clear that the power to make recommendations may only be used by the tribunal to attempt to obviate or reduce the adverse effects of the discrimination on the complainant. This does not give the tribunal broader powers to effect changes for the benefit of a wider class of persons who are not party to the proceedings. The recommendation must be directed towards an individualised remedy rather than a class-based remedy. So the respondent employer cannot be ordered to review the wider effect of the discriminatory act nor to cease committing such an act in the future.

The tribunal's attention must be entirely focused upon making a recommendation which will counteract or reduce the discriminatory effect upon the complainant. This might include, for example, a recommendation that the employer should consider the complainant for the next available suitable vacancy or reconsider the training opportunities or career development of a disabled complainant already in the respondent's employment. It might also include a recommendation that the employer take steps that would amount to the making of reasonable adjustments to arrangements or the physical features of premises if this would be within that employer's duty under s 6 and directed towards preventing a substantial disadvantage to the disabled complainant created by those unadjusted arrangements or physical features.

10.4.11   It is a moot point whether the industrial tribunal's powers under s 8(2)(c) allow it to recommend that the disabled complainant should actually be engaged for or promoted to the next available suitable vacancy. Such a power was clearly not within the letter or spirit of the SDA 1975 or the RRA 1976 because the employer, in obeying such a recommendation, might then commit an act of unlawful positive or reverse discrimination.[1] That does not appear to be a problem under the 1995 Act because the legislation is asymmetrical. The Act does not prohibit (but neither does it require) positive discrimination in favour of disabled persons, and a non-disabled person treated less favourably than a disabled person has no cause of action under the new legislation.

---

1   *Noone v North West Thames Regional Health Authority (No 2)* [1988] IRLR 530, CA; *British Gas plc v Sharma* [1991] IRLR 101, EAT.

10.4.12 If the respondent fails 'without reasonable justification' to comply with a recommendation made by an industrial tribunal under s 8(2)(c) the tribunal may, if it thinks it just and equitable, order the payment of compensation or increase the amount of a compensation order already made (s 8(5)). What will amount to 'reasonable justification' will clearly be a question of fact and will vary from case to case.[1] For example, if a recommendation has been made to the effect that the complainant should be considered for promotion, but in the meanwhile he or she has lost their employment due to a genuine redundancy exercise, that would probably amount to a reasonable justification for the failure to accord with the recommendation. It is unlikely that justification could be advanced by reference to factors which are themselves made unlawful under the Act. So, for example, if the complainant was only selected as a redundancy candidate because he or she was a disabled person, that would not be a justifying reason.

---

1   *Nelson v Tyne and Wear Passenger Transport Executive* [1978] ICR 1183, EAT.

10.5   ENFORCEMENT, PROCEDURES AND REMEDIES IN NON-EMPLOYMENT CASES

10.5.1 Section 25 deals with claims of disability discrimination arising under Part III of the Act in respect of goods, facilities, services and premises. Such claims are to be the subject of civil proceedings in the same way as any other claim in tort or, in Scotland, in reparation for breach of a statutory duty (s 25(1)). Proceedings in England and Wales, and in Northern Ireland, may be brought only in the county court (s 25(3) and Sch 8, para 12). In Scotland, proceedings may be brought only in a sheriff court (s 25(4)). Except as provided by s 25, no civil or criminal proceedings may be brought in respect of an act merely because the act is made unlawful under the provisions of Part III of the statute (Sch 3, para 5(1)). This does not prevent proceedings for judicial review arising in respect of any decision taken in relation to Part III (Sch 3, para 5(2)).

10.5.2 The limitation period for Part III claims brought under s 25 is six months. A county court or sheriff court shall not consider a claim under s 25 unless proceedings in respect of it have been instituted before the end of the period of six months beginning when the act complained of was done (Sch 3, para 6(1)).[1] This is subject to one exception in Sch 3, para 6(2) considered below.[2]

---

1   An 'act' includes a deliberate omission (s 68(1)).
2   See **10.5.9**.

10.5.3 Similar questions about the operation of this limitation period are likely to arise as those in respect of the comparable provisions affecting employment cases.[1] In particular, in the case of an isolated act of disability discrimination, the presumption will be that time starts to run from the date of the act or the omission itself. Schedule 3, para 6(4)(c) makes it plain that a deliberate omission is to be treated as done when the person in question decided upon it. Subject to rebutting evidence, a person is treated as having decided upon an omission when he or she does an act inconsistent with doing the omitted act or, in the absence of such inconsistent behaviour, when the period expires within which he or she might reasonably have been expected to do the omitted act if it was to be done (Sch 3, para 6(5)).

However, in other cases, there is more flexibility in measuring the date upon which time starts to run. In the case of any act or omission which extends over a period of time, the six-months limitation provision will not start to run until the end of the period in question (Sch 3, para 6(4)(b)). Moreover, where the alleged unlawful act of discrimination is attributable to a term in a contract, time does not start to expire until the end of the contract. The unlawful act is said to extend throughout the duration of the contract (Sch 3, para 6(3)(a)).

---

1   See **10.3.6–10.3.8**.

10.5.4 The court may consider a claim which is otherwise time-barred if, in all the circumstances of the case, the court considers that it is just and equitable to do so (Sch 3, para 6(3)).

Conciliation and advice in non-employment cases

10.5.5 Section 28(1) empowers the Secretary of State to make arrangements for the provision of advice and assistance to persons 'with a view to promoting the settlement of disputes ... otherwise than by recourse to the courts'.[1] This advice and assistance service will be available only in respect of disputes concerning the provision of goods, facilities or services, or in respect of the disposal or management of premises under Part III of the Act. It does not apply to cases of disability-related employment discrimination under Part II (including discrimination against contract workers or by trade organisations) nor to issues arising from the provisions in Parts IV and V concerning access to education and public transport. From 2 December 1996, help for advisers in respect of Part III will be provided by the Disability Access Rights Advice Service (DARAS) under this provision.

---

1   In Northern Ireland, the s 28 power is in the hands of the Department of Health and Social Services (Sch 8, para 14).

10.5.6 The service to be provided under s 28 is something of a hybrid creature. The Minister has indicated that:

'The main elements we envisage are the provision of a second tier advice and assistance service which will be available to local agencies providing advice to disabled people and small businesses ... and in certain circumstances directly to larger businesses, perhaps when their customer complaints departments have been unable to resolve a particularly tricky problem.'[1]

The intention is to build upon existing structures rather than to compete with them. Nevertheless, the Minister stated that 'the service would seek a resolution which ensured that the disabled person's rights were met' and would operate 'to serve the spirit in which the legislation was conceived', namely to increase the accessibility of the environment for disabled people.[2]

---

1   HL Deb, vol 566, col 988 (Lord Mackay of Ardbrecknish).
2   HL Deb, vol 566, col 1029 (Lord Mackay of Ardbrecknish).

10.5.7   However, the explicit reference in s 28(1) to the objective of dispute settlement would indicate that the Government does not view its advice and assistance service as being a substitute for a disability rights commission. This service does not appear to be an enforcement agency in the mould of the Equal Opportunities Commission or the Commission for Racial Equality. Instead, it would appear to have more in common with an agency like the Advisory, Conciliation and Arbitration Service[1] and will offer a conciliation or mediation facility to attempt to encourage the parties to resolve complaints and disputes without litigation. Disabled people will have to rely upon existing sources and advice agencies (such as citizens' advice bureaux) for direct advice and advocacy provision.

---

1   See the remarks of Lord Mackay of Ardbrecknish at HL Deb, vol 566, col 1030.

10.5.8   The Act makes provision for appointment of persons under the s 28 arrangements for the provision of advice and assistance. Such persons shall have such duties as the Secretary of State may direct (s 28(2)) and, subject to Treasury approval under s 28(5),[1] may be paid appropriate allowances and compensation for loss of earnings (s 28(3)). At his or her discretion, but with the necessary Treasury approval, the Secretary of State may make appropriate payments by way of grant to the advice and assistance service established under s 28 in order to meet its expenditure requirements (s 28(4)).

---

1   In Northern Ireland, the Treasury's powers under s 28 are to be exercised by the Department of Finance and Personnel (Sch 8, para 14(3)).

10.5.9   Normally, civil proceedings under s 25 for an alleged breach of the provisions of Part III of the Act must be commenced within six months of the act of discrimination (Sch 3, para 6(1)).[1] However, if a person has been appointed in connection with the advice and assistance arrangements to be made under s 28 and has been approached before the end of the six-month limitation period, then the limitation period within which civil proceedings must be commenced is extended by a further two months (Sch 3, para 6(2)).

---

1   See **10.5.2–10.5.4**.

Settlements

10.5.10   With effect from 2 December 1996, s 26(1) voids any term in a contract for the provision of goods, facilities or services so far as it purports to require any person to do anything which would contravene any provision of (or made under) Part III of the Act. This invalidating principle also applies to any term in any other agreement (which would presumably include a tenancy agreement or lease) that purports to have that effect. In like manner, a term in a contract or agreement which purports to exclude or limit the operation of any provision of Part III, or which seeks to prevent any person from making a claim under this part of the statute, is void.

10.5.11   The effect of such terms being avoided is to make them unenforceable, but this does not apparently render the contract or agreement itself null and void. Instead, a person interested in an agreement containing such a void term may apply to a county court or a sheriff court for an order modifying the agreement to take account of the effect of the term being void (s 26(3)). The court may make such an order as it thinks just and this may include provision as respects any period before the order was made (s 26(6)). The court may not make any such order unless the affected parties have been given notice of the application (subject to any rules of court to the contrary) and have been afforded an opportunity to make representations to the court (s 26(4)–(5)).

10.5.12   It is not intended that this provision concerning the validity of contract terms should prevent parties to a dispute under Part III of the 1995 Act settling legal proceedings by an agreement on terms. A claim by a person in civil proceedings brought under s 25 may be settled by an agreement that has the effect of excluding or limiting the operation of any provision of Part III or prevents a person from pursuing or continuing a claim under the Act (s 26(2)). It cannot, of course, require any person to do anything that would contravene the statute.

Remedies in non-employment cases

10.5.13   In any proceedings brought under s 25 in respect of discrimination in non-employment cases under Part III of the Act, any damages awarded by the court in respect of discrimination found to be unlawful may include compensation for injury to feelings (s 25(2)). Such a head of damages may be awarded alone or in tandem with compensation for other heads of loss. However, the amount of any damages awarded for injury to feelings shall not exceed a figure to be prescribed by regulations (Sch 3, para 7). That figure has not yet been determined. This is not a general ceiling on compensation that may be awarded in non-employment cases. It is a limit only upon that element of any award that reflects injury to feelings.[1] It is apparently the Government's intention that this limitation will help ensure that the majority of litigation brought under Part III of the Act will be pursued through the county court small claims procedure for claims under 3,000.[2]

---

1   HL Deb, vol 566, col 1065 (Lord Mackay of Ardbrecknish).
2   HL Deb, vol 565, cols 734–735 (Lord Mackay of Ardbrecknish).

10.5.14   Otherwise, the remedies available in civil proceedings under s 25 are those which are available in the High Court or, in Scotland, the Court of Session (s 25(5)). In appropriate cases, therefore, a successful plaintiff may be enabled to seek a declaration of his or her rights or an injunction to prevent further or continuing acts of discrimination. Note also the possibility of a plaintiff having rights to compensation against a commercial landlord where a service provider has been unable to comply with a s 21 duty to make adjustments to premises (s 27 and Sch 4).[1]

---

1   This has been discussed in Chapter 6.

Appendix I

DISABILITY DISCRIMINATION ACT 1995
(1995 c. 50)

(AS AMENDED)

ARRANGEMENT OF SECTIONS

PART I

DISABILITY

PART II

EMPLOYMENT

Discrimination by employers

Enforcement etc.

Discrimination by other persons

Premises occupied under leases

PART III

DISCRIMINATION IN OTHER AREAS

Goods, facilities and services

Premises

Enforcement, etc.

PART IV

EDUCATION

PART V

PUBLIC TRANSPORT

Taxis

PART VI

THE NATIONAL DISABILITY COUNCIL

PART VII

SUPPLEMENTAL

PART VIII

MISCELLANEOUS

An Act to make it unlawful to discriminate against disabled persons in connection with employment, the provision of goods, facilities and services or the disposal or management of premises; to make provision about the employment of disabled persons; and to establish a National Disability Council. [8 November 1995]

PART I

DISABILITY

1 Meaning of 'disability' and 'disabled person'

(1) Subject to the provisions of Schedule 1, a person has a disability for the purposes of this Act if he has a physical or mental impairment which has a substantial and long-term adverse effect on his ability to carry out normal day-to-day activities.

(2) In this Act 'disabled person' means a person who has a disability.

2 Past disabilities

(1) The provisions of this Part and Parts II and III apply in relation to a person who has had a disability as they apply in relation to a person who has that disability.

(2) Those provisions are subject to the modifications made by Schedule 2.

(3) Any regulations or order made under this Act may include provision with respect to persons who have had a disability.

(4) In any proceedings under Part II or Part III of this Act, the question whether a person had a disability at a particular time ('the relevant time') shall be determined, for the purposes of this section, as if the provisions of, or made under, this Act in force when the act complained of was done had been in force at the relevant time.

(5) The relevant time may be a time before the passing of this Act.

3 Guidance

(1) The Secretary of State may issue guidance about the matters to be taken into account in determining—

(a) whether an impairment has a substantial adverse effect on a person's ability to carry out normal day-to-day activities; or
(b) whether such an impairment has a long-term effect.

(2) The guidance may, among other things, give examples of—

(a) effects which it would be reasonable, in relation to particular activities, to regard for purposes of this Act as substantial adverse effects;
(b) effects which it would not be reasonable, in relation to particular activities, to regard for such purposes as substantial adverse effects;
(c) substantial adverse effects which it would be reasonable to regard, for such purposes, as long-term;
(d) substantial adverse effects which it would not be reasonable to regard, for such purposes, as long-term.

(3) A tribunal or court determining, for any purpose of this Act, whether an impairment has a substantial and long-term adverse effect on a person's ability to carry out normal

day-to-day activities, shall take into account any guidance which appears to it to be relevant.

(4) In preparing a draft of any guidance, the Secretary of State shall consult such persons as he considers appropriate.

(5) Where the Secretary of State proposes to issue any guidance, he shall publish a draft of it, consider any representations that are made to him about the draft and, if he thinks it appropriate, modify his proposals in the light of any of those representations.

(6) If the Secretary of State decides to proceed with any proposed guidance, he shall lay a draft of it before each House of Parliament.

(7) If, within the 40-day period, either House resolves not to approve the draft, the Secretary of State shall take no further steps in relation to the proposed guidance.

(8) If no such resolution is made within the 40-day period, the Secretary of State shall issue the guidance in the form of his draft.

(9) The guidance shall come into force on such date as the Secretary of State may appoint by order.

(10) Subsection (7) does not prevent a new draft of the proposed guidance from being laid before Parliament.

(11) The Secretary of State may—

  (a)   from time to time revise the whole or part of any guidance and re-issue it;
  (b)   by order revoke any guidance.

(12) In this section—

  '40-day period', in relation to the draft of any proposed guidance, means—
      (a)   if the draft is laid before one House on a day later than the day on which it is laid before the other House, the period of 40 days beginning with the later of the two days, and
      (b)   in any other case, the period of 40 days beginning with the day on which the draft is laid before each House,
  no account being taken of any period during which Parliament is dissolved or prorogued or during which both Houses are adjourned for more than 4 days; and
  'guidance' means guidance issued by the Secretary of State under this section and includes guidance which has been revised and re-issued.

PART II

EMPLOYMENT

Discrimination by employers

4   Discrimination against applicants and employees

(1) It is unlawful for an employer to discriminate against a disabled person—

  (a)   in the arrangements which he makes for the purpose of determining to whom he should offer employment;

(b)   in the terms on which he offers that person employment; or

(c)   by refusing to offer, or deliberately not offering, him employment.

(2) It is unlawful for an employer to discriminate against a disabled person whom he employs—

(a)   in the terms of employment which he affords him;

(b)   in the opportunities which he affords him for promotion, a transfer, training or receiving any other benefit;

(c)   by refusing to afford him, or deliberately not affording him, any such opportunity; or

(d)   by dismissing him, or subjecting him to any other detriment.

(3) Subsection (2) does not apply to benefits of any description if the employer is concerned with the provision (whether or not for payment) of benefits of that description to the public, or to a section of the public which includes the employee in question, unless—

(a)   that provision differs in a material respect from the provision of the benefits by the employer to his employees; or

(b)   the provision of the benefits to the employee in question is regulated by his contract of employment; or

(c)   the benefits relate to training.

(4) In this Part 'benefits' includes facilities and services.

(5) In the case of an act which constitutes discrimination by virtue of section 55, this section also applies to discrimination against a person who is not disabled.

(6) This section applies only in relation to employment at an establishment in Great Britain.

5   Meaning of 'discrimination'

(1) For the purposes of this Part, an employer discriminates against a disabled person if—

(a)   for a reason which relates to the disabled person's disability, he treats him less favourably than he treats or would treat others to whom that reason does not or would not apply; and

(b)   he cannot show that the treatment in question is justified.

(2) For the purposes of this Part, an employer also discriminates against a disabled person if—

(a)   he fails to comply with a section 6 duty imposed on him in relation to the disabled person; and

(b)   he cannot show that his failure to comply with that duty is justified.

(3) Subject to subsection (5), for the purposes of subsection (1) treatment is justified if, but only if, the reason for it is both material to the circumstances of the particular case and substantial.

(4) For the purposes of subsection (2), failure to comply with a section 6 duty is justified if, but only if, the reason for the failure is both material to the circumstances of the particular case and substantial.

(5) If, in a case falling within subsection (1), the employer is under a section 6 duty in relation to the disabled person but fails without justification to comply with that duty, his treatment of that person cannot be justified under subsection (3) unless it would have been justified even if he had complied with the section 6 duty.

(6) Regulations may make provision, for purposes of this section, as to circumstances in which—

    (a)   treatment is to be taken to be justified;

    (b)   failure to comply with a section 6 duty is to be taken to be justified;

    (c)   treatment is to be taken not to be justified;

    (d)   failure to comply with a section 6 duty is to be taken not to be justified.

(7) Regulations under subsection (6) may, in particular—

    (a)   make provision by reference to the cost of affording any benefit; and

    (b)   in relation to benefits under occupational pension schemes, make provision with a view to enabling uniform rates of contributions to be maintained.

6 Duty of employer to make adjustments

(1) Where—

    (a)   any arrangements made by or on behalf of an employer, or

    (b)   any physical feature of premises occupied by the employer,

place the disabled person concerned at a substantial disadvantage in comparison with persons who are not disabled, it is the duty of the employer to take such steps as it is reasonable, in all the circumstances of the case, for him to have to take in order to prevent the arrangements or feature having that effect.

(2) Subsection (1)(a) applies only in relation to—

    (a)   arrangements for determining to whom employment should be offered;

    (b)   any term, condition or arrangements on which employment, promotion, a transfer, training or any other benefit is offered or afforded.

(3) The following are examples of steps which an employer may have to take in relation to a disabled person in order to comply with subsection (1)—

    (a)   making adjustments to premises;

    (b)   allocating some of the disabled person's duties to another person;

    (c)   transferring him to fill an existing vacancy;

    (d)   altering his working hours;

    (e)   assigning him to a different place of work;

    (f)   allowing him to be absent during working hours for rehabilitation, assessment or treatment;

    (g)   giving him, or arranging for him to be given, training;

    (h)   acquiring or modifying equipment;

    (i)   modifying instructions or reference manuals;

    (j)   modifying procedures for testing or assessment;

    (k)   providing a reader or interpreter;

    (l)   providing supervision.

(4) In determining whether it is reasonable for an employer to have to take a particular step in order to comply with subsection (1), regard shall be had, in particular, to—

(a)   the extent to which taking the step would prevent the effect in question;

(b)   the extent to which it is practicable for the employer to take the step;

(c)   the financial and other costs which would be incurred by the employer in taking the step and the extent to which taking it would disrupt any of his activities;

(d)   the extent of the employer's financial and other resources;

(e)   the availability to the employer of financial or other assistance with respect to taking the step.

This subsection is subject to any provision of regulations made under subsection (8).

(5) In this section, 'the disabled person concerned' means—

(a)   in the case of arrangements for determining to whom employment should be offered, any disabled person who is, or has notified the employer that he may be, an applicant for that employment;

(b)   in any other case, a disabled person who is—

      (i) an applicant for the employment concerned; or

      (ii) an employee of the employer concerned.

(6) Nothing in this section imposes any duty on an employer in relation to a disabled person if the employer does not know, and could not reasonably be expected to know—

(a)   in the case of an applicant or potential applicant, that the disabled person concerned is, or may be, an applicant for the employment; or

(b)   in any case, that that person has a disability and is likely to be affected in the way mentioned in subsection (1).

(7) Subject to the provisions of this section, nothing in this Part is to be taken to require an employer to treat a disabled person more favourably than he treats or would treat others.

(8) Regulations may make provision, for the purposes of subsection (1)—

(a)   as to circumstances in which arrangements are, or a physical feature is, to be taken to have the effect mentioned in that subsection;

(b)   as to circumstances in which arrangements are not, or a physical feature is not, to be taken to have that effect;

(c)   as to circumstances in which it is reasonable for an employer to have to take steps of a prescribed description;

(d)   as to steps which it is always reasonable for an employer to have to take;

(e)   as to circumstances in which it is not reasonable for an employer to have to take steps of a prescribed description;

(f)   as to steps which it is never reasonable for an employer to have to take;

(g)   as to things which are to be treated as physical features;

(h)   as to things which are not to be treated as such features.

(9) Regulations made under subsection (8)(c), (d), (e) or (f) may, in particular, make provision by reference to the cost of taking the steps concerned.

(10) Regulations may make provision adding to the duty imposed on employers by this section, including provision of a kind which may be made under subsection (8).

(11) This section does not apply in relation to any benefits under an occupational pension scheme or any other benefit payable in money or money's worth under a scheme or arrangement for the benefit of employees in respect of—

    (a)   termination of service;
    (b)   retirement, old age or death;
    (c)   accident, injury, sickness or invalidity; or
    (d)   any other prescribed matter.

(12) This section imposes duties only for the purpose of determining whether an employer has discriminated against a disabled person; and accordingly a breach of any such duty is not actionable as such.

7   Exemption for small businesses

(1) Nothing in this Part applies in relation to an employer who has fewer than 20 employees.

(2) The Secretary of State may by order amend subsection (1) by substituting a different number (not greater than 20) for the number for the time being specified there.

(3) In this section—

'anniversary' means the anniversary of the coming into force of this section; and 'review' means a review of the effect of this section.

(4) Before making any order under subsection (2), the Secretary of State shall conduct a review.

(5) Unless he has already begun or completed a review under subsection (4), the Secretary of State shall begin to conduct a review immediately after the fourth anniversary.

(6) Any review shall be completed within nine months.

(7) In conducting any review, the Secretary of State shall consult—

    (a)   such organisations representing the interests of employers as he considers appropriate; and
    (b)   such organisations representing the interests of disabled persons in employment or seeking employment as he considers appropriate.

(8) If, on completing a review, the Secretary of State decides to make an order under subsection (2), he shall make such order to come into force not later than one year after the commencement of the review.

(9) If, on completing a review, the Secretary of State decides not to make such an order, he shall not later than one year after the commencement of the review lay before Parliament a report—

    (a)   summarising the results of the review; and
    (b)   giving the reasons for his decision.

(10) Any report made by the Secretary of State under subsection (9) shall include a summary of the views expressed to him in his consultations.

Enforcement etc.

8 Enforcement, remedies and procedure

(1) A complaint by any person that another person—

(a) has discriminated against him in a way which is unlawful under this Part, or

(b) is, by virtue of section 57 or 58, to be treated as having discriminated against him in such a way,

may be presented to an industrial tribunal.

(2) Where an industrial tribunal finds that a complaint presented to it under this section is well-founded, it shall take such of the following steps as it considers just and equitable—

(a) making a declaration as to the rights of the complainant and the respondent in relation to the matters to which the complaint relates;

(b) ordering the respondent to pay compensation to the complainant;

(c) recommending that the respondent take, within a specified period, action appearing to the tribunal to be reasonable, in all the circumstances of the case, for the purpose of obviating or reducing the adverse effect on the complainant of any matter to which the complaint relates.

(3) Where a tribunal orders compensation under subsection (2)(b), the amount of the compensation shall be calculated by applying the principles applicable to the calculation of damages in claims in tort or (in Scotland) in reparation for breach of statutory duty.

(4) For the avoidance of doubt it is hereby declared that compensation in respect of discrimination in a way which is unlawful under this Part may include compensation for injury to feelings whether or not it includes compensation under any other head.

(5) If the respondent to a complaint fails, without reasonable justification, to comply with a recommendation made by an industrial tribunal under subsection (2)(c) the tribunal may, if it thinks if just and equitable to do so—

(a) increase the amount of compensation required to be paid to the complainant in respect of the complaint, where an order was made under subsection (2)(b); or

(b) make an order under subsection (2)(b).

(6) Regulations may make provision—

(a) for enabling a tribunal, where an amount of compensation falls to be awarded under subsection (2)(b), to include in the award interest on that amount; and

(b) specifying, for cases where a tribunal decides that an award is to include an amount in respect of interest, the manner in which and the periods and rate by reference to which the interest is to be determined.

(7) Regulations may modify the operation of any order made under [section 14 of the Industrial Tribunals Act 1996] (power to make provision as to interest on sums payable in pursuance of industrial tribunal decisions) to the extent that it relates to an award of compensation under subsection (2)(b).

(8) Part I of Schedule 3 makes further provision about the enforcement of this Part and about procedure.

9   Validity of certain agreements

(1) Any term in a contract of employment or other agreement is void so far as it purports to—

- (a)   require a person to do anything which would contravene any provision of, or made under, this Part;
- (b)   exclude or limit the operation of any provision of this Part; or
- (c)   prevent any person from presenting a complaint to an industrial tribunal under this Part.

(2) Paragraphs (b) and (c) of subsection (1) do not apply to an agreement not to institute proceedings under section 8(1), or to an agreement not to continue such proceedings, if—

- (a)   a conciliation officer has acted under [section 18 of the Industrial Tribunals Act 1996] in relation to the matter; or
- (b)   the conditions set out in subsection (3) are satisfied.

(3) The conditions are that—

- (a)   the complainant must have received independent legal advice from a qualified lawyer as to the terms and effect of the proposed agreement (and in particular its effect on his ability to pursue his complaint before an industrial tribunal);
- (b)   when the adviser gave the advice there must have been in force a policy of insurance covering the risk of a claim by the complainant in respect of loss arising in consequence of the advice; and
- (c)   the agreement must be in writing, relate to the particular complaint, identify the adviser and state that the conditions are satisfied.

(4) In this section—

'independent', in relation to legal advice to the complainant, means that it is given by a lawyer who is not acting for the other party or for a person who is connected with that other party; and
'qualified lawyer' means—
- (a)   as respects proceedings in England and Wales, a barrister (whether in practice as such or employed to give legal advice) or a solicitor of the Supreme Court who holds a practising certificate; and
- (b)   as respects proceedings in Scotland, an advocate (whether in practice as such or employed to give legal advice) or a solicitor who holds a practising certificate.

(5) For the purposes of subsection (4), any two persons are to be treated as connected if—

- (a)   one is a company of which the other (directly or indirectly) has control, or
- (b)   both are companies of which a third person (directly or indirectly) has control.

10   Charities and support for particular groups of persons

(1) Nothing in this Part—

- (a)   affects any charitable instrument which provides for conferring benefits on one or more categories of person determined by reference to any physical or mental capacity; or (b)　makes unlawful any act done by a charity or recognised body in pursuance of any of its charitable purposes, so far as those purposes are connected with persons so determined.

(2) Nothing in this Part prevents—

(a)　a person who provides supported employment from treating members of a particular group of disabled persons more favourably than other persons in providing such employment; or

(b)　the Secretary of State from agreeing to arrangements for the provision of supported employment which will, or may, have that effect.

(3) In this section—

'charitable instrument' means an enactment or other instrument (whenever taking effect) so far as it relates to charitable purposes;

'charity' has the same meaning as in the Charities Act 1993;

'recognised body' means a body which is a recognised body for the purposes of Part I of the Law Reform (Miscellaneous Provisions) (Scotland) Act 1990; and

'supported employment' means facilities provided, or in respect of which payments are made, under section 15 of the Disabled Persons (Employment) Act 1944.

(4) In the application of this section to England and Wales, 'charitable purposes' means purposes which are exclusively charitable according to the law of England and Wales.

(5) In the application of this section to Scotland, 'charitable purposes' shall be construed in the same way as if it were contained in the Income Tax Acts.

11　Advertisements suggesting that employers will discriminate against disabled persons

(1) This section applies where—

(a)　a disabled person has applied for employment with an employer;

(b)　the employer has refused to offer, or has deliberately not offered, him the employment;

(c)　the disabled person has presented a complaint under section 8 against the employer;

(d)　the employer has advertised the employment (whether before or after the disabled person applied for it); and

(e)　the advertisement indicated, or might reasonably be understood to have indicated, that any application for the advertised employment would, or might, be determined to any extent by reference to—

(i) the successful applicant not having any disability or any category of disability which includes the disabled person's disability; or

(ii) the employer's reluctance to take any action of a kind mentioned in section 6.

(2) The tribunal hearing the complaint shall assume, unless the contrary is shown, that the employer's reason for refusing to offer, or deliberately not offering, the employment to the complainant was related to the complainant's disability.

(3) In this section 'advertisement' includes every form of advertisement or notice, whether to the public or not.

Discrimination by other persons

12   Discrimination against contract workers

(1) It is unlawful for a principal, in relation to contract work, to discriminate against a disabled person—

(a)   in the terms on which he allows him to do that work;
(b)   by not allowing him to do it or continue to do it;
(c)   in the way he affords him access to any benefits or by refusing or deliberately omitting to afford him access to them; or
(d)   by subjecting him to any other detriment.

(2) Subsection (1) does not apply to benefits of any description if the principal is concerned with the provision (whether or not for payment) of benefits of that description to the public, or to a section of the public which includes the contract worker in question, unless that provision differs in a material respect from the provision of the benefits by the principal to contract workers.

(3) The provisions of this Part (other than subsections (1) to (3) of section 4) apply to any principal, in relation to contract work, as if he were, or would be, the employer of the contract worker and as if any contract worker supplied to do work for him were an employee of his.

(4) In the case of an act which constitutes discrimination by virtue of section 55, this section also applies to discrimination against a person who is not disabled.

(5) This section applies only in relation to contract work done at an establishment in Great Britain (the provisions of section 68 about the meaning of 'employment at an establishment in Great Britain' applying for the purposes of this subsection with the appropriate modifications).

(6) In this section—

'principal' means a person ('A') who makes work available for doing by individuals who are employed by another person who supplies them under a contract made with A;
'contract work' means work so made available; and
'contract worker' means any individual who is supplied to the principal under such a contract.

13   Discrimination by trade organisations

(1) It is unlawful for a trade organisation to discriminate against a disabled person—

(a)   in the terms on which it is prepared to admit him to membership of the organisation; or
(b)   by refusing to accept, or deliberately not accepting, his application for membership.

(2) It is unlawful for a trade organisation, in the case of a disabled person who is a member of the organisation, to discriminate against him—

(a)   in the way it affords him access to any benefits or by refusing or deliberately omitting to afford him access to them;

(b)   by depriving him of membership, or varying the terms on which he is a member; or

(c)   by subjecting him to any other detriment.

(3) In the case of an act which constitutes discrimination by virtue of section 55, this section also applies to discrimination against a person who is not disabled.

(4) In this section 'trade organisation' means an organisation of workers, an organisation of employers or any other organisation whose members carry on a particular profession or trade for the purposes of which the organisation exists.

14   Meaning of 'discrimination' in relation to trade organisations

(1) For the purposes of this Part, a trade organisation discriminates against a disabled person if—

(a)   for a reason which relates to the disabled person's disability, it treats him less favourably than it treats or would treat others to whom that reason does not or would not apply; and

(b)   it cannot show that the treatment in question is justified.

(2) For the purposes of this Part, a trade organisation also discriminates against a disabled person if—

(a)   it fails to comply with a section 15 duty imposed on it in relation to the disabled person; and

(b)   it cannot show that its failure to comply with that duty is justified.

(3) Subject to subsection (5), for the purposes of subsection (1) treatment is justified if, but only if, the reason for it is both material to the circumstances of the particular case and substantial.

(4) For the purposes of subsection (2), failure to comply with a section 15 duty is justified if, but only if, the reason for the failure is both material to the circumstances of the particular case and substantial.

(5) If, in a case falling within subsection (1), the trade organisation is under a section 15 duty in relation to the disabled person concerned but fails wtihout justification to comply with that duty, its treatment of that person cannot be justified under subsection (3) unless the treatment would have been justified even if the organisation had complied with the section 15 duty.

(6) Regulations may make provision, for purposes of this section, as to circumstances in which—

(a)   treatment is to be taken to be justified;

(b)   failure to comply with a section 15 duty is to be taken to be justified;

(c)   treatment is to be taken not to be justified;

(d)   failure to comply with a section 15 duty is to be taken not to be justified.

15   Duty of trade organisation to make adjustments

(1) Where—

(a)   any arrangements made by or on behalf of a trade organisation, or

    (b)   any physical feature of premises occupied by the organisation,

place the disabled person concerned at a substantial disadvantage in comparison with persons who are not disabled, it is the duty of the organisation to take such steps as it is reasonable, in all the circumstances of the case, for it to have to take in order to prevent the arrangements or feature having that effect.

(2) Subsection (1)(a) applies only in relation to—

    (a)   arrangements for determining who should become or remain a member of the organisation;

    (b)   any term, condition or arrangements on which membership or any benefit is offered or afforded.

(3) In determining whether it is reasonable for a trade organisation to have to take a particular step in order to comply with subsection (1), regard shall be had, in particular, to—

    (a)   the extent to which taking the step would prevent the effect in question;

    (b)   the extent to which it is practicable for the organisation to take the step;

    (c)   the financial and other costs which would be incurred by the organisation in taking the step and the extent to which taking it would disrupt any of its activities;

    (d)   the extent of the organisation's financial and other resources;

    (e)   the availability to the organisation of financial or other assistance with respect to taking the step.

This subsection is subject to any provision of regulations made under subsection (7).

(4) In this section 'the disabled person concerned' means—

    (a)   in the case of arrangements for determining to whom membership should be offered, any disabled person who is, or has notified the organisation that he may be, an applicant for membership;

    (b)   in any other case, a disabled person who is—

        (i) an applicant for membership; or

        (ii) a member of the organisation.

(5) Nothing in this section imposes any duty on an organisation in relation to a disabled person if the organisation does not know, and could not reasonably be expected to know that the disabled person concerned—

    (a)   is, or may be, an applicant for membership; or

    (b)   has a disability and is likely to be affected in the way mentioned in subsection (1).

(6) Subject to the provisions of this section, nothing in this Part is to be taken to require a trade organisation to treat a disabled person more favourably than it treats or would treat others.

(7) Regulations may make provision for the purposes of subsection (1) as to any of the matters mentioned in paragraphs (a) to (h) of section 6(8) (the references in those paragraphs to an employer being read for these purposes as references to a trade organisation).

(8) Subsection (9) of section 6 applies in relation to such regulations as it applies in relation to regulations made under section 6(8).

(9) Regulations may make provision adding to the duty imposed on trade organisations by this section, including provision of a kind which may be made under subsection (7).

(10) This section imposes duties only for the purpose of determining whether a trade organisation has discriminated against a disabled person; and accordingly a breach of any such duty is not actionable as such.

Premises occupied under leases

16 Alterations to premises occupied under leases

(1) This section applies where—

- (a) an employer or trade organisation ('the occupier') occupies premises under a lease;
- (b) but for this section, the occupier would not be entitled to make a particular alteration to the premises; and
- (c) the alteration is one which the occupier proposes to make in order to comply with a section 6 duty or section 15 duty.

(2) Except to the extent to which it expressly so provides, the lease shall have effect by virtue of this subsection as if it provided—

- (a) for the occupier to be entitled to make the alteration with the written consent of the lessor;
- (b) for the occupier to have to make a written application to the lessor for consent if he wishes to make the alteration;
- (c) if such an application is made, for the lessor not to withhold his consent unreasonably; and
- (d) for the lessor to be entitled to make his consent subject to reasonable conditions.

(3) In this section—

'lease' includes a tenancy, sub-lease or sub-tenancy and an agreement for a lease, tenancy, sub-lease or sub-tenancy; and
'sub-lease' and 'sub-tenancy' have such meaning as may be prescribed.

(4) If the terms and conditions of a lease—

- (a) impose conditions which are to apply if the occupier alters the premises, or
- (b) entitle the lessor to impose conditions when consenting to the occupier's altering the premises,

the occupier is to be treated for the purposes of subsection (1) as not being entitled to make the alteration.

(5) Part I of Schedule 4 supplements the provisions of this section.

Occupational pension schemes and insurance services

17 Occupational pension schemes

(1) Every occupational pension scheme shall be taken to include a provision ('a non-discrimination rule')—

(a)   relating to the terms on which—
    (i)   persons become members of the scheme; and
    (ii) members of the scheme are treated; and

(b)   requiring the trustees or managers of the scheme to refrain from any act or omission which, if done in relation to a person by an employer, would amount to unlawful discrimination against that person for the purposes of this Part.

(2) The other provisions of the scheme are to have effect subject to the non-discrimination rule.

(3) Without prejudice to section 67, regulations under this Part may—

(a)   with respect to trustees or managers of occupational pension schemes make different provision from that made with respect to employers; or

(b)   make provision modifying the application to such trustees or managers of any regulations made under this Part, or of any provisions of this Part so far as they apply to employers.

(4) In determining, for the purposes of this section, whether an act or omission would amount to unlawful discrimination if done by an employer, any provision made under subsection (3) shall be applied as if it applied in relation to the notional employer.

18   Insurance services

(1) This section applies where a provider of insurance services ('the insurer') enters into arrangements with an employer under which the employer's employees, or a class of his employees—

(a)   receive insurance services provided by the insurer; or
(b)   are given an opportunity to receive such services.

(2) The insurer is to be taken, for the purposes of this Part, to discriminate unlawfully against a disabled person who is a relevant employee if he acts in relation to that employee in a way which would be unlawful discrimination for the purposes of Part III if—

(a)   he were providing the service in question to members of the public; and
(b)   the employee was provided with, or was trying to secure the provision of, that service as a member of the public.

(3) In this section—

  'insurance services' means services of a prescribed description for the provision of benefits in respect of—
    (a)   termination of service;
    (b)   retirement, old age or death;
    (c)   accident, injury, sickness or invalidity; or
    (d)   any other prescribed matter; and
  'relevant employee' means—
    (a)   in the case of an arrangement which applies to employees of the employer in question, an employee of his;
    (b)   in the case of an arrangement which applies to a class of employees of the employer, an employee who is in that class.

(4) For the purposes of the definition of 'relevant employee' in subsection (3), 'employee', in relation to an employer, includes a person who has applied for, or is

contemplating applying for, employment by that employer or (as the case may be) employment by him in the class in question.

PART III

DISCRIMINATION IN OTHER AREAS

Goods, facilities and services

19 Discrimination in relation to goods, facilities and services

(1) It is unlawful for a provider of services to discriminate against a disabled person—

(a) in refusing to provide, or deliberately not providing, to the disabled person any service which he provides, or is prepared to provide, to members of the public;

(b) in failing to comply with any duty imposed on him by section 21 in circumstances in which the effect of that failure is to make it impossible or unreasonably difficult for the disabled person to make use of any such service;

(c) in the standard of service which he provides to the disabled person or the manner in which he provides it to him; or

(d) in the terms on which he provides a service to the disabled person.

(2) For the purposes of this section and sections 20 and 21—

(a) the provision of services includes the provision of any goods or facilities;

(b) a person is 'a provider of services' if he is concerned with the provision, in the United Kingdom, of services to the public or to a section of the public; and

(c) it is irrelevant whether a service is provided on payment or without payment.

(3) The following are examples of services to which this section and sections 20 and 21 apply—

(a) access to and use of any place which members of the public are permitted to enter;

(b) access to and use of means of communication;

(c) access to and use of information services;

(d) accommodation in a hotel, boarding house or other similar establishment;

(e) facilities by way of banking or insurance or for grants, loans, credit or finance;

(f) facilities for entertainment, recreation or refreshment;

(g) facilities provided by employment agencies or under section 2 of the Employment and Training Act 1973;

(h) the services of any profession or trade, or any local or other public authority.

(4) In the case of an act which constitutes discrimination by virtue of section 55, this section also applies to discrimination against a person who is not disabled.

(5) Except in such circumstances as may be prescribed, this section and sections 20 and 21 do not apply to—

(a)   education which is funded, or secured, by a relevant body or provided at—
   (i) an establishment which is funded by such a body or by a Minister of the Crown; or
   (ii) any other establishment which is a school as defined in section 14(5) of the Further and Higher Education Act 1992 or section 135(1) of the Education (Scotland) Act 1980;
(b)   any service so far as it consists of the use of any means of transport; or
(c)   such other services as may be prescribed.

(6) In subsection (5) 'relevant body' means—

(a)   a local education authority in England and Wales;
(b)   an education authority in Scotland;
(c)   the Funding Agency for Schools;
(d)   the Schools Funding Council for Wales;
(e)   the Further Education Funding Council for England;
(f)   the Further Education Funding Council for Wales;
(g)   the Higher Education Funding Council for England;
(h)   the Scottish Higher Education Funding Council;
(i)   the Higher Education Funding Council for Wales;
(j)   the Teacher Training Agency;
(k)   a voluntary organisation; or
(l)   a body of a prescribed kind.

20   Meaning of 'discrimination'

(1) For the purposes of section 19, a provider of services discriminates against a disabled person if—

(a)   for a reason which relates to the disabled person's disability, he treats him less favourably than he treats or would treat others to whom that reason does not or would not apply; and
(b)   he cannot show that the treatment in question is justified.

(2) For the purposes of section 19, a provider of services also discriminates against a disabled person if—

(a)   he fails to comply with a section 21 duty imposed on him in relation to the disabled person; and
(b)   he cannot show that his failure to comply with that duty is justified.

(3) For the purposes of this section, treatment is justified only if—

(a)   in the opinion of the provider of services, one or more of the conditions mentioned in subsection (4) are satisfied; and
(b)   it is reasonable, in all the circumstances of the case, for him to hold that opinion.

(4) The conditions are that—

(a)   in any case, the treatment is necessary in order not to endanger the health or safety of any person (which may include that of the disabled person);
(b)   in any case, the disabled person is incapable of entering into an enforceable agreement, or of giving an informed consent, and for that reason the treatment is reasonable in that case;

(c)   in a case falling with section 19(1)(a), the treatment is necessary because the provider of services would otherwise be unable to provide the service to members of the public;

(d)   in a case falling within section 19(1)(c) or (d), the treatment is necessary in order for the provider of services to be able to provide the service to the disabled person or to other members of the public;

(e)   in a case falling within section 19(1)(d), the difference in the terms on which the service is provided to the disabled person and those on which it is provided to other members of the public reflects the greater cost to the provider of services in providing the service to the disabled person.

(5) Any increase in the cost of providing a service to a disabled person which results from compliance by a provider of services with a section 21 duty shall be disregarded for the purposes of subsection (4)(e).

(6) Regulations may make provision, for purposes of this section, as to circumstances in which—

(a)   it is reasonable for a provider of services to hold the opinion mentioned in subsection (3)(a);

(b)   it is not reasonable for a provider of services to hold that opinion.

(7) Regulations may make provision for subsection (4)(b) not to apply in prescribed circumstances where—

(a)   a person is acting for a disabled person under a power of attorney;

(b)   functions conferred by or under Part VII of the Mental Health Act 1983 are exercisable in relation to a disabled person's property or affairs; or

(c)   powers are exercisable in Scotland in relation to a disabled person's property or affairs in consequence of the appointment of a curator bonis, tutor or judicial factor.

(8) Regulations may make provision, for purposes of this section, as to circumstances (other than those mentioned in subsection (4)) in which treatment is to be taken to be justified.

(9) In subsections (3), (4) and (8) 'treatment' includes failure to comply with a section 21 duty.

21   Duty of providers of services to make adjustments

(1) Where a provider of services has a practice, policy or procedure which makes it impossible or unreasonably difficult for disabled persons to make use of a service which he provides, or is prepared to provide, to other members of the public, it is his duty to take such steps as it is reasonable, in all the circumstances of the case, for him to have to take in order to change that practice, policy or procedure so that it no longer has that effect.

(2) Where a physical feature (for example, one arising from the design or construction of a building or the approach or access to premises) makes it impossible or unreasonably difficult for disabled persons to make use of such a service, it is the duty of the provider of that service to take such steps as it is reasonable, in all the circumstances of the case, for him to have to take in order to—

(a)   remove the feature;

(b)   alter it so that it no longer has that effect;

(c)   provide a reasonable means of avoiding the feature; or

(d)   provide a reasonable alternative method of making the service in question available to disabled persons.

(3) Regulations may prescribe—

(a)   matters which are to be taken into account in determining whether any provision of a kind mentioned in subsection (2)(c) or (d) is reasonable; and

(b)   categories of providers of services to whom subsection (2) does not apply.

(4) Where an auxiliary aid or service (for example, the provision of information on audio tape or of a sign language interpreter) would—

(a)   enable disabled persons to make use of a service which a provider of services provides, or is prepared to provide, to members of the public, or

(b)   facilitate the use by disabled persons of such a service,

it is the duty of the provider of that service to take such steps as it is reasonable, in all the circumstances of the case, for him to have to take in order to provide that auxiliary aid or service.

(5) Regulations may make provision, for the purposes of this section—

(a)   as to circumstances in which it is reasonable for a provider of services to have to take steps of a prescribed description;

(b)   as to circumstances in which it is not reasonable for a provider of services to have to take steps of a prescribed description;

(c)   as to what is to be included within the meaning of 'practice, policy or procedure';

(d)   as to what is not to be included within the meaning of that expression;

(e)   as to things which are to be treated as physical features;

(f)   as to things which are not to be treated as such features;

(g)   as to things which are to be treated as auxiliary aids or services;

(h)   as to things which are not to be treated as auxiliary aids or services.

(6) Nothing in this section requires a provider of services to take any steps which would fundamentally alter the nature of the service in question or the nature of his trade, profession or business.

(7) Nothing in this section requires a provider of services to take any steps which would cause him to incur expenditure exceeding the prescribed maximum.

(8) Regulations under subsection (7) may provide for the prescribed maximum to be calculated by reference to—

(a)   aggregate amounts of expenditure incurred in relation to different cases;

(b)   prescribed periods;

(c)   services of a prescribed description;

(d)   premises of a prescribed description; or

(e)   such other criteria as may be prescribed.

(9) Regulations may provide, for the purposes of subsection (7), for expenditure incurred by one provider of services to be treated as incurred by another.

(10) This section imposes duties only for the purpose of determining whether a provider of services has discriminated against a disabled person; and accordingly a breach of any such duty is not actionable as such.

Premises

22 Discrimination in relation to premises

(1) It is unlawful for a person with power to dispose of any premises to discriminate against a disabled person—

   (a)   in the terms on which he offers to dispose of those premises to the disabled person;

   (b)   by refusing to dispose of those premises to the disabled person; or

   (c)   in his treatment of the disabled person in relation to any list of persons in need of premises of that description.

(2) Subsection (1) does not apply to a person who owns an estate or interest in the premises and wholly occupies them unless, for the purpose of disposing of the premises, he—

   (a)   use the services of an estate agent, or

   (b)   publishes an advertisement or causes an advertisement to be published.

(3) It is unlawful for a person managing any premises to discriminate against a disabled person occupying those premises—

   (a)   in the way he permits the disabled person to make use of any benefits or facilities;

   (b)   by refusing or deliberately omitting to permit the disabled person to make use of any benefits or facilities; or

   (c)   by evicting the disabled person, or subjecting him to any other detriment.

(4) It is unlawful for any person whose licence or consent is required for the disposal of any premises comprised in, or (in Scotland) the subject of, a tenancy to discriminate against a disabled person by withholding his licence or consent for the disposal of the premises to the disabled person.

(5) Subsection (4) applies to tenancies created before as well as after the passing of this Act.

(6) In this section—

   'advertisement' includes every form of advertisement or notice, whether to the public or not;

   'dispose', in relation to premises, includes granting a right to occupy the premises, and, in relation to premises comprised in, or (in Scotland) the subject of, a tenancy, includes—

      (a)   assigning the tenancy, and

      (b)   sub-letting or parting with possession of the premises or any part of the premises;

   and 'disposal' shall be construed accordingly;

   'estate agent' means a person who, by way of profession or trade, provides services for the purpose of finding premises for persons seeking to acquire them or assisting in the disposal of premises; and 'tenancy' means a tenancy created—

(a)   by a lease or sub-lease,

(b)   by an agreement for a lease or sub-lease,

(c)   by a tenancy agreement, or

(d)   in pursuance of any enactment.

(7) In the case of an act which constitutes discrimination by virtue of section 55, this section also applies to discrimination against a person who is not disabled.

(8) This section applies only in relation to premises in the United Kingdom.

23 Exemption for small dwellings

(1) Where the conditions mentioned in subsection (2) are satisfied, subsection (1), (3) or (as the case may be) (4) of section 22 does not apply.

(2) The conditions are that—

(a)   the relevant occupier resides, and intends to continue to reside, on the premises;

(b)   the relevant occupier shares accommodation on the premises with persons who reside on the premises and are not members of his household;

(c)   the shared accommodation is not storage accommodation or a means of access; and

(d)   the premises are small premises.

(3) For the purposes of this section, premises are 'small premises' if they fall within subsection (4) or (5).

(4) Premises fall within this subsection if—

(a)   only the relevant occupier and members of his household reside in the accommodation occupied by him;

(b)   the premises comprise, in addition to the accommodation occupied by the relevant occupier, residential accommodation for at least one other household;

(c)   the residential accommodation for each other household is let, or available for letting, on a separate tenancy or similar agreement; and

(d)   there are not normally more than two such other households.

(5) Premises fall within this subsection if there is not normally residential accommodation on the premises for more than six persons in addition to the relevant occupier and any members of his household.

(6) For the purposes of this section 'the relevant occupier' means—

(a)   in a case falling within section 22(1), the person with power to dispose of the premises, or a near relative of his;

(b)   in a case falling within section 22(4), the person whose licence or consent is required for the disposal of the premises, or a near relative of his.

(7) For the purposes of this section—

'near relative' means a person's spouse, partner, parent, child, grandparent, grandchild, or brother or sister (whether of full or half blood or by affinity); and

'partner' means the other member of a couple consisting of a man and a woman who are not married to each other but are living together as husband and wife.

24 Meaning of 'discrimination'

(1) For the purposes of section 22, a person ('A') discriminates against a disabled person if—

- (a) for a reason which relates to the disabled person's disability, he treats him less favourably than he treats or would treat others to whom that reason does not or would not apply; and
- (b) he cannot show that the treatment in question is justified.

(2) For the purposes of this section, treatment is justified only if—

- (a) in A's opinion, one or more of the conditions mentioned in subsection (3) are satisfied; and
- (b) it is reasonable, in all the circumstances of the case, for him to hold that opinion.

(3) The conditions are that—

- (a) in any case, the treatment is necessary in order not to endanger the health or safety of any person (which may include that of the disabled person);
- (b) in any case, the disabled person is incapable of entering into an enforceable agreement, or of giving an informed consent, and for that reason the treatment is reasonable in that case;
- (c) in a case falling within section 22(3)(a), the treatment is necessary in order for the disabled person or the occupiers of other premises forming part of the building to make use of the benefit or facility;
- (d) in a case falling within section 22(3)(b), the treatment is necessary in order for the occupiers of other premises forming part of the building to make use of the benefit or facility.

(4) Regulations may make provision, for purposes of this section, as to circumstances in which—

- (a) it is reasonable for a person to hold the opinion mentioned in subsection 2(a);
- (b) it is not reasonable for a person to hold that opinion.

(5) Regulations may make provision, for purposes of this section, as to circumstances (other than those mentioned in subsection (3)) in which treatment is to be taken to be justified.

Enforcement, etc.

25 Enforcement, remedies and procedure

(1) A claim by any person that another person—

- (a) has discriminated against him in a way which is unlawful under this Part; or
- (b) is by virtue of section 57 or 58 to be treated as having discriminated against him in such a way,

may be made the subject of civil proceedings in the same way as any other claim in tort or (in Scotland) in reparation for breach of statutory duty.

(2) For the avoidance of doubt it is hereby declared that damages in respect of discrimination in a way which is unlawful under this Part may include compensation for injury to feelings whether or not they include compensation under any other head.

(3) Proceedings in England and Wales shall be brought only in a county court.

(4) Proceedings in Scotland shall be brought only in a sheriff court.

(5) The remedies available in such proceedings are those which are available in the High Court or (as the case may be) the Court of Session.

(6) Part II of Schedule 3 makes further provision about the enforcement of this Part and about procedure.

26 Validity and revision of certain agreements

(1) Any term in a contract for the provision of goods, facilities or services or in any other agreement is void so far as it purports to—

    (a)   require a person to do anything which would contravene any provision of, or made under, this Part,

    (b)   exclude or limit the operation of any provision of this Part, or

    (c)   prevent any person from making a claim under this Part.

(2) Paragraphs (b) and (c) of subsection (1) do not apply to an agreement settling a claim to which section 25 applies.

(3) On the application of any person interested in an agreement to which subsection (1) applies, a county court or a sheriff court may make such order as it thinks just for modifying the agreement to take account of the effect of subsection (1).

(4) No such order shall be made unless all persons affected have been—

    (a)   given notice of the application; and

    (b)   afforded an opportunity to make representations to the court.

(5) Subsection (4) applies subject to any rules of court providing for that notice to be dispensed with.

(6) An order under subsection (3) may include provision as respects any period before the making of the order.

27 Alterations to premises occupied under leases

(1) This section applies where—

    (a)   a provider of services ('the occupier') occupies premises under a lease;

    (b)   but for this section, he would not be entitled to make a particular alteration to the premises; and

    (c)   the alteration is one which the occupier proposes to make in order to comply with a section 21 duty.

(2) Except to the extent to which it expressly so provides, the lease shall have effect by virtue of this subsection as if it provided—

    (a)   for the occupier to be entitled to make the alteration with the written consent of the lessor;

    (b)   for the occupier to have to make a written application to the lessor for consent if he wishes to make the alteration;

    (c)   if such an application is made, for the lessor not to withhold his consent unreasonably; and

(d)   for the lessor to be entitled to make his consent subject to reasonable conditions.

(3) In this section—

'lease' includes a tenancy, sub-lease or sub-tenancy and an agreement for a lease, tenancy, sub-lease or sub-tenancy; and

'sub-lease' and 'sub-tenancy' have such meaning as may be prescribed.

(4) If the terms and conditions of a lease—

(a)   impose conditions which are to apply if the occupier alters the premises, or

(b)   entitle the lessor to impose conditions when consenting to the occupier's altering the premises,

the occupier is to be treated for the purposes of subsection (1) as not being entitled to make the alteration.

(5) Part II of Schedule 4 supplements the provisions of this section.

28   Advice and assistance

(1) The Secretary of State may make arrangements for the provision of advice and assistance to persons with a view to promoting the settlement of disputes arising under this Part otherwise than by recourse to the courts.

(2) Any person appointed by the Secretary of State in connection with arrangements made under subsection (1) shall have such duties as the Secretary of State may direct.

(3) The Secretary of State may pay to any person so appointed such allowances and compensation for loss of earnings as he considers appropriate.

(4) The Secretary of State may make such payments, by way of grants, in respect of expenditure incurred, or to be incurred, by any person exercising functions in accordance with arrangements made by the Secretary of State under this section as he considers appropriate.

(5) The approval of the Treasury is required for any payment under subsection (3) or (4).

PART IV

EDUCATION

29   Education of disabled persons

(1) In section 161(5) of the Education Act 1993 (information relating to pupils with special educational needs to be included in annual report), omit the words from 'and in this subsection' to the end.

(2) After section 161(5) of that Act insert—

'(6) The annual report for each county, voluntary or grant-maintained school shall include a report containing information as to—

(a)   the arrangements for the admission of disabled pupils;

(b)   the steps taken to prevent disabled pupils from being treated less favourably than other pupils; and

     (c)   the facilities provided to assist access to the school by disabled pupils.

(7) In this section—
    "annual report" means the report prepared under the articles of government
        for the school in accordance with section 30 of the Education (No. 2) Act
        1986 or, as the case may be, paragraph 8 of Schedule 6 to this Act; and
    "disabled pupils" means pupils who are disabled persons for the purposes of
        the Disability Discrimination Act 1995.'

(3) In section 1 of the Education Act 1994 (establishment of the Teacher Training
Agency) add, at the end—

    '(4) In exercising their functions, the Teacher Training Agency shall have regard to
the requirements of persons who are disabled persons for the purposes of the
Disability Discrimination Act 1995.'

30   Further and higher education of disabled persons

(1) The Further and Higher Education Act 1992 is amended as set out in subsections (2)
to (6).

(2) In section 5 (administration of funds by further education funding councils), in
subsection (6)(b), after 'may' insert ', subject to subsection (7A) below,'.

(3) After section 5(7) insert—

    '(7A) Without prejudice to the power to impose conditions given by subsection
(6)(b) above, the conditions subject to which a council gives financial support
under this section to the governing body of an institution within the further
education sector—
    (a)   shall require the governing body to publish disability statements at such
         intervals as may be prescribed; and
    (b)   may include conditions relating to the provision made, or to be made, by
         the institution with respect to disabled persons.

    (7B) For the purposes of subsection (7A) above—
        "disability statement" means a statement containing information of a pre-
           scribed description about the provision of facilities for education made by
           the institution in respect of disabled persons;
        "disabled persons" means persons who are disabled persons for the purposes
           of the Disability Discrimination Act 1995; and
        "prescribed" means prescribed by regulations.'

(4) In section 8 (supplementary functions) add, at the end—

    '(6) As soon as is reasonably practicable after the end of its financial year, each
council shall make a written report to the Secretary of State on—
    (a)   the progress made during the year to which the report relates in the
         provision of further education for disabled students in their area; and
    (b)   their plans for the future provision of further education for disabled
         students in their area.

    (7) In subsection (6) above—
        "disabled students" means students who are disabled persons for the purposes
           of the Disability Discrimination Act 1995; and

"financial year" means the period of twelve months ending with 31st March 1997 and each successive period of twelve months.'

(5) In section 62 (establishment of higher education funding councils), after subsection (7) insert—

'(7A) In exercising their functions, each council shall have regard to the requirements of disabled persons.

(7B) In subsection (7A) "disabled persons" means persons who are disabled persons for the purposes of the Disability Discrimination Act 1995.'

(6) In section 65 (administration of funds by higher education funding councils), after subsection (4) insert—

'(4A) Without prejudice to the power to impose conditions given by subsection (3) above, the conditions subject to which a council makes grants, loans or other payments under this section to the governing body of a higher education institution shall require the governing body to publish disability statements at such intervals as may be specified.

(4B) For the purposes of subsection (4A) above—
   "disability statement" means a statement containing information of a specified description about the provision of facilities for education and research made by the institution in respect of persons who are disabled persons for the purposes of the Disability Discrimination Act 1995; and
   "specified" means specified in the conditions subject to which grants, loans or other payments are made by a council under this section.'

(7) The Education Act 1944 is amended as set out in subsection (8) and (9).

(8) In section 41 (functions of local education authorities in respect of further education), after subsection (2) insert—

'(2A) It shall be the duty of every local education authority to publish disability statements at such intervals as may be prescribed.

(2B) For the purposes of subsection (2A) above—
   "disability statement" means a statement containing information of a prescribed description about the provision of facilities for further education made by the local education authority in respect of persons who are disabled persons for the purposes of the Disability Discrimination Act 1995; and
   "prescribed" means prescribed by regulations made by the Secretary of State.'

(9) In section 41(7), (8) and (11), for 'this section' substitute 'subsections (1) and (6) above'.

31   Further and higher education of disabled persons: Scotland

(1) The Further and Higher Education (Scotland) Act 1992 is amended as follows.

(2) In section 37 (establishment of Scottish Higher Education Funding Council) after subsection (4) insert—

'(4A) In exercising their functions, the Council shall have regard to the requirements of disabled persons.

(4B) In subsection (4A) above, "disabled persons" means persons who are disabled persons for the purpose of the Disability Discrimination Act 1995.'

(3) In section 40 (administration of funds by the Council), after subsection (4) insert—

'(5) Without prejudice to the power to impose conditions given by subsection (3) above, the conditions subject to which the Council make grants, loans or other payments under this section to the governing body of an institution within the higher education sector shall require the governing body to publish disability statements at such intervals as may be specified.

(6) For the purposes of subsection (5) above—
    "disability statement" means a statement containing information of a specified description about the provision of facilities for education and research made by the institution in respect of persons who are disabled persons for the purpose of the Disability Discrimination Act 1995; and
    "specified" means specified in the conditions subject to which grants, loans or other payments are made by the Council under this section.'

PART V

PUBLIC TRANSPORT

Taxis

32   Taxi accessibility regulations

(1) The Secretary of State may make regulations ('taxi accessibility regulations') for the purpose of securing that it is possible—

(a)   for disabled persons—
    (i) to get into and out of taxis in safety;
    (ii) to be carried in taxis in safety and in reasonable comfort; and
(b)   for disabled persons in wheelchairs—
    (i) to be conveyed in safety into and out of taxis while remaining in their wheelchairs; and
    (ii) to be carried in taxis in safety and in reasonable comfort while remaining in their wheelchairs.

(2) Taxi accessibility regulations may, in particular—

(a)   require any regulated taxi to conform with provisions of the regulations as to—
    (i) the size of any door opening which is for the use of passengers;
    (ii) the floor area of the passenger compartment;
    (iii) the amount of headroom in the passenger compartment;
    (iv) the fitting of restraining devices designed to ensure the stability of a wheelchair while the taxi is moving;
(b)   require the driver of any regulated taxi which is plying for hire, or which has been hired, to comply with provisions of the regulations as to the carrying of ramps or other devices designed to facilitate the loading and unloading of wheelchairs;

(c)   require the driver of any regulated taxi in which a disabled person who is in a wheelchair is being carried (while remaining in his wheelchair) to comply with provisions of the regulations as to the position in which the wheelchair is to be secured.

(3) The driver of a regulated taxi which is plying for hire, or which has been hired, is guilty of an offence it—

(a)   he fails to comply with any requirement imposed on him by the regulations; or
(b)   the taxi fails to conform with any provision of the regulations with which it is required to conform.

(4) A person who is guilty of such an offence is liable, on summary conviction, to a fine not exceeding level 3 on the standard scale.

(5) In this section—

'passenger compartment' has such meaning as may be prescribed;
'regulated taxi' means any taxi to which the regulations are expressed to apply;
'taxi' means a vehicle licensed under—
(a)   section 37 of the Town Police Clauses Act 1847, or
(b)   section 6 of the Metropolitan Public Carriage Act 1869,
but does not include a taxi which is drawn by a horse or other animal.

33   Designated transport facilities

(1) In this section 'a franchise agreement' means a contract entered into by the operator of a designated transport facility for the provision by the other party to the contract of hire car services—

(a)   for members of the public using any part of the transport facility; and
(b)   which involve vehicles entering any part of that facility.

(2) The Secretary of State may by regulations provide for the application of any taxi provision in relation to—

(a)   vehicles used for the provision of services under a franchise agreement; or
(b)   the drivers of such vehicles.

(3) Any regulations under subsection (2) may apply any taxi provision with such modifications as the Secretary of State considers appropriate.

(4) In this section—

'designated' means designated for the purposes of this section by an order made by the Secretary of State;
'hire car' has such meaning as may be prescribed;
'operator', in relation to a transport facility, means any person who is concerned with the management or operation of the facility;
'taxi provision' means any provision of—
(a)   this Act, or
(b)   regulations made in pursuance of section 20(2A) of the Civic Government (Scotland) Act 1982,
which applies in relation to taxis or the drivers of taxis; and
'transport facility' means any premises which form part of any port, airport, railway station or bus station.

34 New licences conditional on compliance with taxi accessibility regulations

(1) No licensing authority shall grant a licence for a taxi to ply for hire unless the vehicle conforms with those provisions of the taxi accessibility regulations with which it will be required to conform if licensed.

(2) Subsection (1) does not apply if such a licence was in force with respect to the vehicle at any time during the period of 28 days immediately before the day on which the licence is granted.

(3) The Secretary of State may by order provide for subsection (2) to cease to have effect on such date as may be specified in the order.

(4) Separate orders may be made under subsection (3) with respect to different areas or localities.

35 Exemption from taxi accessibility regulations

(1) The Secretary of State may make regulations ('exemption regulations') for the purpose of enabling any relevant licensing authority to apply to him for an order (an 'exemption order') exempting the authority from the requirements of section 34.

(2) Exemption regulations may, in particular, make provision requiring a licensing authority proposing to apply for an exemption order—

- (a)   to carry out such consultations as may be prescribed;
- (b)   to publish the proposal in the prescribed manner;
- (c)   to consider any representations made to it about the proposal, before applying for the order;
- (d)   to make its application in the prescribed form.

(3) A licensing authority may apply for an exemption order only if it is satisfied—

- (a)   that, having regard to the circumstances prevailing in its area, it would be inappropriate for the requirements of section 34 to apply; and
- (b)   that the application of section 34 would result in an unacceptable reduction in the number of taxis in its area.

(4) After considering any application for an exemption order and consulting the Disabled Persons Transport Advisory Committee and such other persons as he considers appropriate, the Secretary of State may—

- (a)   make an exemption order in the terms of the application;
- (b)   make an exemption order in such other terms as he considers appropriate; or
- (c)   refuse to make an exemption order.

(5) The Secretary of State may by regulations ('swivel seat regulations') make provision requiring any exempt taxi plying for hire in an area in respect of which an exemption order is in force to conform with provisions of the regulations as to the fitting and use of swivel seats.

(6) The Secretary of State may by regulations make provision with respect to swivel seat regulations similar to that made by section 34 with respect to taxi accessibility regulations.

(7) In this section—

'exempt taxi' means a taxi in relation to which section 34(1) would apply if the exemption order were not in force;

'relevant licensing authority' means a licensing authority responsible for licensing taxis in any area of England and Wales other than the area to which the Metropolitan Public Carriage Act 1869 applies; and

'swivel seats' has such meaning as may be prescribed.

36   Carrying of passengers in wheelchairs

(1) This section imposes duties on the driver of a regulated taxi which has been hired—

(a)   by or for a disabled person who is in a wheelchair; or
(b)   by a person who wishes such a disabled person to accompany him in the taxi.

(2) In this section—

'carry' means carry in the taxi concerned; and
'the passenger' means the disabled person concerned.

(3) The duties are—

(a)   to carry the passenger while he remains in his wheelchair;
(b)   not to make any additional charge for doing so;
(c)   if the passenger chooses to sit in a passenger seat, to carry the wheelchair;
(d)   to take such steps as are necessary to ensure that the passenger is carried in safety and in reasonable comfort;
(e)   to give such assistance as may be reasonably required—
    (i) to enable the passenger to get into or out of the taxi;
    (ii) if the passenger wishes to remain in his wheelchair, to enable him to be conveyed into and out of the taxi while in his wheelchair;
    (iii) to load the passenger's luggage into or out of the taxi;
    (iv) if the passenger does not wish to remain in his wheelchair, to load the wheelchair into or out of the taxi.

(4) Nothing in this section is to be taken to require the driver of any taxi—

(a)   except in the case of a taxi of a prescribed description, to carry more than one person in a wheelchair, or more than one wheelchair, on any one journey; or
(b)   to carry any person in circumstances in which it would otherwise be lawful for him to refuse to carry that person.

(5) A driver of a regulated taxi who fails to comply with any duty imposed on him by this section is guilty of an offence and liable, on summary conviction, to a fine not exceeding level 3 on the standard scale.

(6) In any proceedings for an offence under this section, it is a defence for the accused to show that, even though at the time of the alleged offence the taxi conformed with those provisions of the taxi accessibility regulations with which it was required to conform, it would not have been possible for the wheelchair in question to be carried in safety in the taxi.

(7) If the licensing authority is satisfied that it is appropriate to exempt a person from the duties imposed by this section—

(a)   on medical grounds, or

(b)   on the ground that his physical condition makes it impossible or unreasonably difficult for him to comply with the duties imposed on drivers by this section,

it shall issue him with a certificate of exemption.

(8) A certificate of exemption shall be issued for such period as may be specified in the certificate.

(9) The driver of a regulated taxi is exempt from the duties imposed by this section if—

(a)   a certificate of exemption issued to him under this section is in force; and

(b)   the prescribed notice of his exemption is exhibited on the taxi in the prescribed manner.

37 Carrying of guide dogs and hearing dogs

(1) This section imposes duties on the driver of a taxi which has been hired—

(a)   by or for a disabled person who is accompanied by his guide dog or hearing dog, or

(b)   by a person who wishes such a disabled person to accompany him in the taxi.

(2) The disabled person is referred to in this section as 'the passenger'.

(3) The duties are—

(a)   to carry the passenger's dog and allow it to remain with the passenger; and

(b)   not to make any additional charge for doing so.

(4) A driver of a taxi who fails to comply with any duty imposed on him by this section is guilty of an offence and liable, on summary conviction, to a fine not exceeding level 3 on the standard scale.

(5) If the licensing authority is satisfied that it is appropriate on medical grounds to exempt a person from the duties imposed by this section, it shall issue him with a certificate of exemption.

(6) In determining whether to issue a certificate of exemption, the licensing authority shall, in particular, have regard to the physical characteristics of the taxi which the applicant drives or those of any kind of taxi in relation to which he requires the certificate.

(7) A certificate of exemption shall be issued—

(a)   with respect to a specified taxi or a specified kind of taxi; and

(b)   for such period as may be specified in the certificate.

(8) The driver of a taxi is exempt from the duties imposed by this section if—

(a)   a certificate of exemption issued to him under this section is in force with respect to the taxi; and

(b)   the prescribed notice of his exemption is exhibited on the taxi in the prescribed manner.

(9) The Secretary of State may, for the purposes of this section, prescribe any other category of dog trained to assist a disabled person who has a disability of a prescribed kind.

(10) This section applies in relation to any such prescribed category of dog as it applies in relation to guide dogs.

(11) In this section—

'guide dog' means a dog which has been trained to guide a blind person; and
'hearing dog' means a dog which has been trained to assist a deaf person.

38 Appeal against refusal of exemption certificate

(1) Any person who is aggrieved by the refusal of a licensing authority to issue an exemption certificate under section 36 or 37 may appeal to the appropriate court before the end of the period of 28 days beginning with the date of the refusal.

(2) On an appeal to it under this section, the court may direct the licensing authority concerned to issue the appropriate certificate of exemption to have effect for such period as may be specified in the direction.

(3) 'Appropriate court' means the magistrates' court for the petty sessions area in which the licensing authority has its principal office.

39 Requirements as to disabled passengers in Scotland

(1) Part II of the Civic Government (Scotland) Act 1982 (licensing and regulation) is amended as follows.

(2) In subsection (4) of section 10 (suitability of vehicle for use as taxi)—

(a)   after 'authority' insert '—(a)'; and
(b)   at the end add '; and
          (b) as not being so suitable if it does not so comply.'

(3) In section 20 (regulations relating to taxis etc.) after subsection (2) insert—

'(2A) Without prejudice to the generality of subsections (1) and (2) above, regulations under those subsections may make such provision as appears to the Secretary of State to be necessary or expedient in relation to the carrying in taxis of disabled persons (within the meaning of section 1(2) of the Disability Discrimination Act 1995) and such provision may in particular prescribe—
    (a)   requirements as to the carriage of wheelchairs, guide dogs, hearing dogs and other categories of dog;
    (b)   a date from which any such provision is to apply and the extent to which it is to apply; and
    (c)   the circumstances in which an exemption from such provision may be granted in respect of any taxi or taxi driver,
and in this subsection—
        "guide dog" means a dog which has been trained to guide a blind person;
        "hearing dog" means a dog which has been trained to assist a deaf person; and
        "other categories of dog" means such other categories of dog as the Secretary of State may prescribe, trained to assist disabled persons who have disabilities of such kinds as he may prescribe.'

Public service vehicles

40 PSV accessibility regulations

(1) The Secretary of State may make regulations ('PSV accessibility regulations') for the purpose of securing that it is possible for disabled persons—

(a)   to get on to and off regulated public service vehicles in safety and without unreasonable difficulty (and, in the case of disabled persons in wheelchairs, to do so while remaining in their wheelchairs); and

(b)   to be carried in such vehicles in safety and in reasonable comfort.

(2) PSV accessibility regulations may, in particular, make provision as to the construction, use and maintenance of regulated public service vehicles including provision as to—

(a)   the fitting of equipment to vehicles;

(b)   equipment to be carried by vehicles;

(c)   the design of equipment to be fitted to, or carried by, vehicles;

(d)   the fitting and use of restraining devices designed to ensure the stability of wheelchairs while vehicles are moving;

(e)   the position in which wheelchairs are to be secured while vehicles are moving.

(3) Any person who—

(a)   contravenes or fails to comply with any provision of the PSV accessibility regulations,

(b)   uses on a road a regulated public service vehicle which does not conform with any provision of the regulations with which it is required to conform, or

(c)   causes or permits to be used on a road such a regulated public service vehicle,

is guilty of an offence.

(4) A person who is guilty of such an offence is liable, on summary conviction, to a fine not exceeding level 4 on the standard scale.

(5) In this section—

'public service vehicle' means a vehicle which is—
  (a)   adapted to carry more than eight passengers; and
  (b)   a public service vehicle for the purposes of the Public Passenger Vehicles Act 1981;
'regulated public service vehicle' means any public service vehicle to which the PSV accessibility regulations are expressed to apply.

(6) Different provision may be made in regulations under this section—

(a)   as respects different classes or descriptions of vehicle;

(b)   as respects the same class or description of vehicle in different circumstances.

(7) Before making any regulations under this section or section 41 or 42 the Secretary of State shall consult the Disabled Persons Transport Advisory Committee and such other representative organisations as he thinks fit.

41 Accessibility certificates

(1) A regulated public service vehicle shall not be used on a road unless—

   (a) a vehicle examiner has issued a certificate (an 'accessibility certificate') that such provisions of the PSV accessibility regulations as may be prescribed are satisfied in respect of the vehicle; or
   (b) an approval certificate has been issued under section 42 in respect of the vehicle.

(2) The Secretary of State may make regulations—

   (a) with respect to applications for, and the issue of, accessibility certificates;
   (b) providing for the examination of vehicles in respect of which applications have been made;
   (c) with respect to the issue of copies of accessibility certificates in place of certificates which have been lost or destroyed.

(3) If a regulated public service vehicle is used in contravention of this section, the operator of the vehicle is guilty of an offence and liable on summary conviction to a fine not exceeding level 4 on the standard scale.

(4) In this section 'operator' has the same meaning as in the Public Passenger Vehicles Act 1981.

42 Approval certificates

(1) Where the Secretary of State is satisfied that such provisions of the PSV accessibility regulations as may be prescribed for the purposes of section 41 are satisfied in respect of a particular vehicle he may approve the vehicle for the purposes of this section.

(2) A vehicle which has been so approved is referred to in this section as a 'type vehicle'.

(3) Subsection (4) applies where a declaration in the prescribed form has been made by an authorised person that a particular vehicle conforms in design, construction and equipment with a type vehicle.

(4) A vehicle examiner may, after examining (if he thinks fit) the vehicle to which the declaration applies, issue a certificate in the prescribed form ('an approval certificate') that it conforms to the type vehicle.

(5) The Secretary of State may make regulations—

   (a) with respect to applications for, and grants of, approval under subsection (1);
   (b) with respect to applications for, and the issue of, approval certificates;
   (c) providing for the examination of vehicles in respect of which applications have been made;
   (d) with respect to the issue of copies of approval certificates in place of certificates which have been lost or destroyed.

(6) The Secretary of State may at any time withdraw his approval of a type vehicle.

(7) Where an approval is withdrawn—

   (a) no further approval certificates shall be issued by reference to the type vehicle; but
   (b) any approval certificate issued by reference to the type vehicle before the withdrawal shall continue to have effect for the purposes of section 41.

(8) In subsection (3) 'authorised person' means a person authorised by the Secretary of State for the purposes of that subsection.

43   Special authorisations

(1) The Secretary of State may by order authorise the use on roads of—

    (a)   any regulated public service vehicle of a class or description specified by the order, or

    (b)   any regulated public service vehicle which is so specified,

and nothing in section 40, 41, or 42 prevents the use of any vehicle in accordance with the order.

(2) Any such authorisation may be given subject to such restrictions and conditions as may be specified by or under the order.

(3) The Secretary of State may by order make provision for the purpose of securing that, subject to such restrictions and conditions as may be specified by or under the order, provisions of the PSV accessibility regulations apply to regulated public service vehicles of a description specified by the order subject to such modifications or exceptions as may be specified by the order.

44   Reviews and appeals

(1) Subsection (2) applies where—

    (a)   the Secretary of State refuses an application for the approval of a vehicle under section 42(1); and

    (b)   before the end of the prescribed period, the applicant asks the Secretary of State to review the decision and pays any fee fixed under section 45;

(2) The Secretary of State shall—

    (a)   review the decision; and

    (b)   in doing so, consider any representations made to him in writing, before the end of the prescribed period, by the applicant.

(3) A person applying for an accessibility certificate or an approval certificate may appeal to the Secretary of State against the refusal of a vehicle examiner to issue such a certificate.

(4) An appeal must be made within the prescribed time and in the prescribed manner.

(5) Regulations may make provision as to the procedure to be followed in connection with appeals.

(6) On the determination of an appeal, the Secretary of State may—

    (a)   confirm, vary or reverse the decision appealed against;

    (b)   give such directions as he thinks fit to the vehicle examiner for giving effect to his decision.

45   Fees

(1) Such fees, payable at such times, as may be prescribed may be charged by the Secretary of State in respect of—

(a)   applications for, and grants of, approval under section 42(1);
(b)   applications for, and the issue of, accessibility certificates and approval certificates;
(c)   copies of such certificates;
(d)   reviews and appeals under section 44.

(2) Any such fees received by the Secretary of State shall be paid by him into the Consolidated Fund.

(3) Regulations under subsection (1) may make provision for the repayment of fees, in whole or in part, in such circumstances as may be prescribed.

(4) Before making any regulations under subsection (1) the Secretary of State shall consult such representative organisations as he thinks fit.

Rail vehicles

46   Rail vehicle accessibility regulations

(1) The Secretary of State may make regulations ('rail vehicle accessibility regulations') for the purpose of securing that it is possible—

(a)   for disabled persons—
    (i)   to get on to and off regulated rail vehicles in safety and without unreasonable difficulty;
    (ii)   to be carried in such vehicles in safety and in reasonable comfort; and
(b)   for disabled persons in wheelchairs—
    (i)   to get on to and off such vehicles in safety and without unreasonable difficulty while remaining in their wheelchairs, and
    (ii)   to be carried in such vehicles in safety and in reasonable comfort while remaining in their wheelchairs.

(2) Rail vehicle accessibility regulations may, in particular, make provision as to the construction, use and maintenance of regulated rail vehicles including provision as to—

(a)   the fitting of equipment to vehicles;
(b)   equipment to be carried by vehicles;
(c)   the design of equipment to be fitted to, or carried by, vehicles;
(d)   the use of equipment fitted to, or carried by, vehicles;
(e)   the toilet facilities to be provided in vehicles;
(f)   the location and floor area of the wheelchair accommodation to be provided in vehicles;
(g)   assistance to be given to disabled persons.

(3) If a regulated rail vehicle which does not conform with any provision of the rail vehicle accessibility regulations with which it is required to conform is used for carriage, the operator of the vehicle is guilty of an offence.

(4) A person who is guilty of such an offence is liable, on summary conviction, to a fine not exceeding level 4 on the standard scale.

(5) Different provision may be made in rail vehicle accessibility regulations—

(a)   as respects different classes or descriptions of rail vehicle;

(b)   as respects the same class or description of rail vehicle in different circumstances;

(c)   as respects different networks.

(6) In this section—

'network' means any permanent way or other means of guiding or supporting rail vehicles or any section of it;

'operator', in relation to any rail vehicle, means the person having the management of that vehicle;

'rail vehicle' means a vehicle—

(a)   constructed or adapted to carry passengers on any railway, tramway or prescribed system; and

(b)   first brought into use, or belonging to a class of vehicle first brought into use, after 31st December 1998;

'regulated rail vehicle' means any rail vehicle to which the rail vehicle accessibility regulations are expressed to apply; and

'wheelchair accommodation' has such meaning as may be prescribed.

(7) In subsection (6)—

'prescribed system' means a system using a prescribed mode of guided transport ('guided transport' having the same meaning as in the Transport and Works Act 1992); and

'railway' and 'tramway' have the same meaning as in that Act.

(8) The Secretary of State may by regulations make provision as to the time when a rail vehicle, or a class of rail vehicle, is to be treated, for the purposes of this section, as first brought into use.

(9) Regulations under subsection (8) may include provision for disregarding periods of testing and other prescribed periods of use.

(10) For the purposes of this section and section 47, a person uses a vehicle for carriage if he uses it for the carriage of members of the public for hire or reward at separate fares.

(11) Before making any regulations under subsection (1) or section 47 the Secretary of State shall consult the Disabled Persons Transport Advisory Committee and such other representative organisations as he thinks fit.

47   Exemption from rail vehicle accessibility regulations

(1) The Secretary of State may by order (an 'exemption order') authorise the use for carriage of any regulated rail vehicle of a specified description, or in specified circumstances, even though that vehicle does not conform with the provisions of the rail vehicle accessibility regulations with which it is required to conform.

(2) Regulations may make provision with respect to exemption orders including, in particular, provision as to—

(a)   the persons by whom applications for exemption orders may be made;

(b)   the form in which such applications are to be made;

(c)   information to be supplied in connection with such applications;

(d)   the period for which exemption orders are to continue in force;

(e)   the revocation of exemption orders.

(3) After considering any application for an exemption order and consulting the Disabled Persons Transport Advisory Committee and such other persons as he considers appropriate, the Secretary of State may—

(a)   make an exemption order in the terms of the application;

(b)   make an exemption order in such other terms as he considers appropriate;

(c)   refuse to make an exemption order.

(4) An exemption order may be made subject to such restrictions and conditions as may be specified.

(5) In this section 'specified' means specified in an exemption order.

Supplemental

48   Offences by bodies corporate etc.

(1) Where an offence under section 40 or 46 committed by a body corporate is committed with the consent or connivance of, or is attributable to any neglect on the part of, a director, manager, secretary or other similar officer of the body, or a person purporting to act in such a capacity, he as well as the body corporate is guilty of the offence.

(2) In subsection (1) 'director' , in relation to a body corporate whose affairs are managed by its members, means a member of the body corporate.

(3) Where, in Scotland, an offence under section 40 or 46 committed by a partnership or by an unincorporated association other than a partnership is committed with the consent or connivance of, or is attributable to any neglect on the part of, a partner in the partnership of (as the case may be) a person concerned in the management or control of the association, he, as well as the partnership or association, is guilty of the offence.

49   Forgery and false statements

(1) In this section 'relevant document' means—

(a)   a certificate of exemption issued under section 36 or 37;

(b)   a notice of a kind mentioned in section 36(9)(b) or 37(8)(b);

(c)   an accessibility certificate; or

(d)   an approval certificate.

(2) A person is guilty of an offence if, with intent to deceive, he—

(a)   forges, alters or uses a relevant document;

(b)   lends a relevant document to any other person;

(c)   allows a relevant document to be used by any other person; or

(d)   makes or has in his possession any document which closely resembles a relevant document.

(3) A person who is guilty of an offence under subsection (2) is liable—

(a)   on summary conviction, to a fine not exceeding the statutory maximum;

(b) on conviction on indictment, to imprisonment for a term not exceeding two years or to a fine or to both.

(4) A person who knowingly makes a false statement for the purpose of obtaining an accessibility certificate or an approval certificate is guilty of an offence and liable on summary conviction to a fine not exceeding level 4 on the standard scale.

PART VI

THE NATIONAL DISABILITY COUNCIL

50 The National Disability Council

(1) There shall be a body to be known as the National Disability Council (but in this Act referred to as 'the Council').

(2) It shall be the duty of the Council to advise the Secretary of State, either on its own initiative or when asked to do so by the Secretary of State—

(a) on matters relevant to the elimination of discrimination against disabled persons and persons who have had a disability;
(b) on measures which are likely to reduce or eliminate such discrimination; and
(c) on matters related to the operation of this Act or of provisions made under this Act.

(3) The Secretary of State may by order confer additional functions on the Council.

(4) The power conferred by subsection (3) does not include power to confer on the Council any functions with respect to the investigation of any complaint which may be the subject of proceedings under this Act.

(5) In discharging its duties under this section, the Council shall in particular have regard to—

(a) the extent and nature of the benefits which would be likely to result from the implementation of any recommendation which it makes; and
(b) the likely cost of implementing any such recommendation.

(6) Where the Council makes any recommendation in the discharge of any of its functions under this section it shall, if it is reasonably practicable to do so, make an assessment of—

(a) the likely cost of implementing the recommendation; and
(b) the likely financial benefits which would result from implementing it.

(7) Where the Council proposes to give the Secretary of State advice on a matter, it shall before doing so—

(a) consult any body—
    (i) established by any enactment or by a Minister of the Crown for the purpose of giving advice in relation to disability, or any aspect of disability; and
    (ii) having functions in relation to the matter to which the advice relates;
(b) consult such other persons as it considers appropriate; and
(c) have regard to any representations made to it as a result of any such consultations.

(8) Schedule 5 makes further provision with respect to the Council, including provision about its membership.

(9) The power conferred on the Council by subsection (2) to give advice on its own initiative does not include power to give advice—

    (a)   by virtue of paragraph (a) or (b), in respect of any matter which relates to the operation of any provision of or arrangements made under—
        (i)   the Disabled Persons (Employment) Acts 1944 and 1958;
        (ii)   the Employment and Training Act 1973;
        (iii) the [Employment Rights Act 1996]; or
        (iv) section 2(3) of the Enterprise and New Towns (Scotland) Act 1990; or
    (b)   by virtue of paragraph (c), in respect of any matter arising under Part II or section 53, 54, 56 or 61.

(10) Subsection (9) shall not have effect at any time when there is neither a national advisory council established under section 17(1)(a) of the Disabled Persons (Employment) Act 1944 nor any person appointed to act generally under section 60(1) of this Act.

51   Codes of practice prepared by the Council

(1) It shall be the duty of the Council, when asked to do so by the Secretary of State—

    (a)   to prepare proposals for a code of practice dealing with the matters to which the Secretary of State's request relates; or
    (b)   to review a code and, if it considers it appropriate, propose alterations.

(2) The Secretary of State may, in accordance with the procedural provisions of section 52, issue codes of practice in response to proposals made by the Council under this section.

(3) A failure on the part of any person to observe any provision of a code does not of itself make that person liable to any proceedings.

(4) A code is admissible in evidence in any proceedings under this Act before an industrial tribunal, a county court or a sheriff court.

(5) If any provision of a code appears to a tribunal or court to be relevant to any question arising in any proceedings under this Act, it shall be taken into account in determining that question.

(6) In this section and section 52 'code' means a code issued by the Secretary of State under this section and includes a code which has been altered and re-issued.

52   Further provision about codes issued under section 51

(1) In this section 'proposal' means a proposal made by the Council to the Secretary of State under section 51.

(2) In preparing any proposal, the Council shall consult—

(a) such persons (if any) as the Secretary of State has specified in making his request to the Council; and

(b) such other persons (if any) as the Council considers appropriate.

(3) Before making any proposal, the Council shall publish a draft, consider any representations made to it about the draft and, if it thinks it appropriate, modify its proposal in the light of any of those representations.

(4) Where the Council makes any proposal, the Secretary of State may—

(a) approve it;

(b) approve it subject to such modifications as he considers appropriate; or

(c) refuse to approve it.

(5) Where the Secretary of State approves any proposal (with or without modifications), he shall prepare a draft of the proposed code and lay it before each House of Parliament.

(6) If, within the 40-day period, either House resolves not to approve the draft, the Secretary of State shall take no further steps in relation to the proposed code.

(7) If no such resolution is made within the 40-day period, the Secretary of State shall issue the code in the form of his draft.

(8) The code shall come into force on such date as the Secretary of State may appoint by order.

(9) Subsection (6) does not prevent a new draft of the proposed code from being laid before Parliament.

(10) If the Secretary of State refuses to approve a proposal, he shall give the Council a written statement of his reasons for not approving it.

(11) The Secretary of State may by order revoke a code.

(12) In this section '40-day period', in relation to the draft of a proposed code, means—

(a) if the draft is laid before one House on a day later than the day on which it is laid before the other House, the period of 40 days beginning with the later of the two days, and

(b) in any other case, the period of 40 days beginning with the day on which the draft is laid before each House,

no account being taken of any period during which Parliament is dissolved or prorogued or during which both Houses are adjourned for more than four days.

PART VII

SUPPLEMENTAL

53 Codes of practice prepared by the Secretary of State

(1) The Secretary of State may issue codes of practice containing such practical guidance as he considers appropriate with a view to—

(a) eliminating discrimination in the field of employment against disabled persons and persons who have had a disability; or

(b)   encouraging good practice in relation to the employment of disabled persons and persons who have had a disability.

(2) The Secretary of State may from time to time revise the whole or any part of a code and re-issue it.

(3) Without prejudice to subsection (1), a code may include practical guidance as to—

(a)   the circumstances in which it would be reasonable, having regard in particular to the costs involved, for a person to be expected to make adjustments in favour of a disabled person or a person who has had a disability; or

(b)   what steps it is reasonably practicable for employers to take for the purpose of preventing their employees from doing, in the course of their employment, anything which is made unlawful by this Act.

(4) A failure on the part of any person to observe any provision of a code does not of itself make that person liable to any proceedings.

(5) A code is admissible in evidence in any proceedings under this Act before an industrial tribunal, a county court or a sheriff court.

(6) If any provision of a code appears to a tribunal or court to be relevant to any question arising in any proceedings under this Act, it shall be taken into account in determining that question.

(7) In this section and section 54 'code' means a code issued by the Secretary of State under this section and includes a code which has been revised and re-issued.

(8) In subsection (1)(a), 'discrimination in the field of employment' includes discrimination of a kind mentioned in section 12 or 13.

(9) In subsections (1)(b) and (3), 'employment' includes contract work (as defined by section 12(6)).

54   Further provision about codes issued under section 53

(1) In preparing a draft of any code under section 53, the Secretary of State shall consult such organisations representing the interests of employers or of disabled persons in, or seeking, employment as he considers appropriate.

(2) Where the Secretary of State proposes to issue a code, he shall publish a draft of it, consider any representations that are made to him about the draft and, if he thinks it appropriate, modify his proposals in the light of any of those representations.

(3) If the Secretary of State decides to proceed with a proposed code, he shall lay a draft of it before each House of Parliament.

(4) If, within the 40-day period, either House resolves not to approve the draft, the Secretary of State shall take no further steps in relation to the proposed code.

(5) If no such resolution is made within the 40-day period, the Secretary of State shall issue the code in the form of his draft.

(6) The code shall come into force on such date as the Secretary of State may appoint by order.

(7) Subsection (4) does not prevent a new draft of the proposed code from being laid before Parliament.

(8) The Secretary of State may by order revoke a code.

(9) In this section '40-day period', in relation to the draft of a proposed code, means—

    (a)   if the draft is laid before one House on a day later than the day on which it is laid before the other House, the period of 40 days beginning with the later of the two days, and

    (b)   in any other case, the period of 40 days beginning with the day on which the draft is laid before each House,

no account being taken of any period during which Parliament is dissolved or prorogued or during which both Houses are adjourned for more than four days.

55 Victimisation

(1) For the purposes of Part II or Part III, a person ('A') discriminates against another person ('B') if—

    (a)   he treats B less favourably than he treats or would treat other persons whose circumstances are the same as B's; and

    (b)   he does so for a reason mentioned in subsection (2).

(2) The reasons are that—

    (a)   B has—

        (i) brought proceedings against A or any other person under this Act; or

        (ii) given evidence or information in connection with such proceedings brought by any person; or

        (iii) otherwise done anything under this Act in relation to A or any other person; or

        (iv) alleged that A or any other person has (whether or not the allegation so states) contravened this Act; or

    (b)   A believes or suspects that B has done or intends to do any of those things.

(3) Where B is a disabled person, or a person who has had a disability, the disability in question shall be disregarded in comparing his circumstances with those of any other person for the purposes of subsection (1)(a).

(4) Subsection (1) does not apply to treatment of a person because of an allegation made by him if the allegation was false and not made in good faith.

56 Help for persons suffering discrimination

(1) For the purposes of this section—

    (a)   a person who considers that he may have been discriminated against, in contravention of any provision of Part II, is referred to as 'the complainant'; and

    (b)   a person against whom the complainant may decide to make, or has made, a complaint under Part II is referred to as 'the respondent'.

(2) The Secretary of State shall, with a view to helping the complainant to decide whether to make a complaint against the respondent and, if he does so, to formulate and present his case in the most effective manner, by order prescribe—

(a) forms by which the complainant may question the respondent on his reasons for doing any relevant act, or on any other matter which is or may be relevant; and

(b) forms by which the respondent may if he so wishes reply to any questions.

(3) Where the complainant questions the respondent in accordance with forms prescribed by an order under subsection (2)—

(a) the question, and any reply by the respondent (whether in accordance with such an order or not), shall be admissible as evidence in any proceedings under Part II;

(b) if it appears to the tribunal in any such proceedings—
    (i) that the respondent deliberately, and without reasonable excuse, omitted to reply within a reasonable period, or
    (ii) that the respondent's reply is evasive or equivocal,
it may draw any inference which it considers it just and equitable to draw, including an inference that the respondent has contravened a provision of Part II.

(4) The Secretary of State may by order prescribe—

(a) the period within which questions must be duly served in order to be admissible under subsection (3)(a); and

(b) the manner in which a question, and any reply by the respondent, may be duly served.

(5) This section is without prejudice to any other enactment or rule of law regulating interlocutory and preliminary matters in proceedings before an industrial tribunal, and has effect subject to any enactment or rule of law regulating the admissibility of evidence in such proceedings.

57 Aiding unlawful acts

(1) A person who knowingly aids another person to do an act made unlawful by this Act is to be treated for the purposes of this Act as himself doing the same kind of unlawful act.

(2) For the purposes of subsection (1), an employee or agent for whose act the employer of principal is liable under section 58 (or would be so liable but for section 58(5)) shall be taken to have aided the employer or principal to do the act.

(3) For the purposes of this section, a person does not knowingly aid another to do an unlawful act if—

(a) he acts in reliance on a statement made to him by that other person that, because of any provision of this Act, the act would not be unlawful; and

(b) it is reasonable for him to rely on the statement.

(4) A person who knowingly or recklessly makes such a statement which is false or misleading in a material respect is guilty of an offence.

(5) Any person guilty of an offence under subsection (4) shall be liable on summary conviction to a fine not exceeding level 5 on the standard scale.

58   Liability of employers and principals

(1) Anything done by a person in the course of his employment shall be treated for the purposes of this Act as also done by his employer, whether or not it was done with the employer's knowledge or approval.

(2) Anything done by a person as agent for another person with the authority of that other person shall be treated for the purposes of this Act as also done by that other person.

(3) Subsection (2) applies whether the authority was—

   (a)   express or implied; or
   (b)   given before or after the act in question was done.

(4) Subsections (1) and (2) do not apply in relation to an offence under section 57(4).

(5) In proceedings under this Act against any person in respect of an act alleged to have been done by an employee of his, it shall be a defence for that person to prove that he took such steps as were reasonably practicable to prevent the employee from—

   (a)   doing that act; or
   (b)   doing, in the course of his employment, acts of that description.

59   Statutory authority and national security etc.

(1) Nothing in this Act makes unlawful any act done—

   (a)   in pursuance of any enactment; or
   (b)   in pursuance of any instrument made by a Minister of the Crown under any enactment; or
   (c)   to comply with any condition or requirement imposed by a Minister of the Crown (whether before or after the passing of this Act) by virtue of any enactment.

(2) In subsection (1) 'enactment' includes one passed or made after the date on which this Act is passed and 'instrument' includes one made after that date.

(3) Nothing in this Act makes unlawful any act done for the purpose of safeguarding national security.

PART VIII

MISCELLANEOUS

60   Appointment by Secretary of State of advisers

(1) The Secretary of State may appoint such persons as he thinks fit to advise or assist him in connection with matters relating to the employment of disabled persons and persons who have had a disability.

(2) Persons may be appointed by the Secretary of State to act generally or in relation to a particular area or locality.

(3) The Secretary of State may pay to any person appointed under this section such allowances and compensation for loss of earnings as he considers appropriate.

(4) The approval of the Treasury is required for any payment under this section.

(5) In subsection (1) 'employment' includes self-employment.

(6) The Secretary of State may by order—

    (a)   provide for section 17 of, and Schedule 2 to, the Disabled Persons (Employment) Act 1944 (national advisory council and district advisory committees) to cease to have effect—
        (i)   so far as concerns the national advisory council; or
        (ii) so far as concerns district advisory committees; or
    (b)   repeal that section and Schedule.

(7) At any time before the coming into force of an order under paragraph (b) of subsection (6), section 17 of the Act of 1944 shall have effect as if in subsection (1), after 'disabled persons' in each case there were inserted ', and persons who have had a disability,' and as if at the end of the section there were added—

    '(3) For the purposes of this section—
        (a)   a person is a disabled person if he is a disabled person for the purposes of the Disability Discrimination Act 1995; and
        (b)   "disability" has the same meaning as in that Act.'

(8) At any time before the coming into force of an order under paragraph (a)(i) or (b) of subsection (6), section 16 of the Chronically Sick and Disabled Persons Act 1970 (which extends the functions of the national advisory council) shall have effect as if after 'disabled persons' in each case there were inserted ', and persons who have had a disability,' and as if at the end of the section there were added—

    '(2) For the purposes of this section—
        (a)   a person is a disabled person if he is a disabled person for the purposes of the Disability Discrimination Act 1995; and
        (b)   "disability" has the same meaning as in that Act.'

61   Amendment of Disabled Persons (Employment) Act 1944

(1) Section 15 of the Disabled Persons (Employment) Act 1944 (which gives the Secretary of State power to make arrangements for the provision of supported employment) is amended as set out in subsections (2) to (5).

(2) In subsection (1)—

    (a)   for 'persons registered as handicapped by disablement' substitute 'disabled persons';
    (b)   for 'their disablement' substitute 'their disability'; and
    (c)   for 'are not subject to disablement' substitute 'do not have a disability'.

(3) In subsection (2), for the words from 'any of one or more companies' to 'so required and prohibited' substitute 'any company, association or body'.

(4) After subsection (2) insert—

    '(2A) The only kind of company which the Minister himself may form in exercising his powers under this section is a company which is—
        (a)   required by its constitution to apply its profits, if any, or other income in promoting its objects; and
        (b)   prohibited by its constitution from paying any dividend to its members.'

(5) After subsection (5) insert—

'(5A) For the purposes this section—
- (a)   a person is a disabled person if he is a disabled person for the purposes of the Disability Discrimination Act 1995; and
- (b)   "disability" has the same meaning as in that Act.'

(6) The provisions of section 16 (preference to be given under section 15 of that Act to ex-service men and women) shall become subsection (1) of that section and at the end insert—

'and whose disability is due to that service.

(2) For the purposes of subsection (1) of this section, a disabled person's disability shall be treated as due to service of a particular kind only in such circumstances as may be prescribed.'

(7) The following provisions of the Act of 1944 shall cease to have effect—
- (a)   section 1 (definition of 'disabled person');
- (b)   sections 6 to 8 (the register of disabled persons);
- (c)   sections 9 to 11 (obligations on employers with substantial staffs to employ a quota of registered persons);
- (d)   section 12 (the designated employment scheme for persons registered as handicapped by disablement);
- (e)   section 13 (interpretation of provisions repealed by this Act);
- (f)   section 14 (records to be kept by employers);
- (g)   section 19 (proceedings in relation to offences); and
- (h)   section 21 (application as respects place of employment, and nationality).

(8) Any provision of subordinate legislation in which 'disabled person' is defined by reference to the Act of 1944 shall be construed as if that expression had the same meaning as in this Act.

(9) Subsection (8) does not prevent the further amendment of any such provision by subordinate legislation.

62   Restriction of publicity: industrial tribunals

(1) This section applies to proceedings on a complaint under section 8 in which evidence of a personal nature is likely to be heard by the industrial tribunal hearing the complaint.

(2) The power of the Secretary of State to make regulations with respect to the procedure of industrial tribunals includes power to make provision in relation to proceedings to which this section applies for—
- (a)   enabling an industrial tribunal, on the application of the complainant or of its own motion, to make a restricted reporting order having effect (if not revoked earlier) until the promulgation of the tribunal's decision; and
- (b)   where a restricted reporting order is made in relation to a complaint which is being dealt with by the tribunal together with any other proceedings, enabling the tribunal to direct that the order is to apply also in relation to those other proceedings or such part of them as the tribunal may direct.

(3) If any identifying matter is published or included in a relevant programme in contravention of a restricted reporting order—

(a) in the case of publication in a newspaper or periodical, any proprietor, any editor and any publisher of the newspaper or periodical,

(b) in the case of publication in any other form, the person publishing the matter, and

(c) in the case of matter included in a relevant programme—

    (i) any body corporate engaged in providing the service in which the programme is included, and

    (ii) any person having functions in relation to the programme corresponding to those of an editor of a newspaper,

shall be guilty of an offence and liable on summary conviction to a fine not exceeding level 5 on the standard scale.

(4) Where a person is charged with an offence under subsection (3), it is a defence to prove that at the time of the alleged offence—

(a) he was not aware, and

(b) he neither suspected nor had reason to suspect,

that the publication or programme in question was of, or included, the matter in question.

(5) Where an offence under subsection (3) committed by a body corporate is proved to have been committed with the consent or connivance of, or to be attributable to any neglect on the part of—

(a) a director, manager, secretary or other similar officer of the body corporate, or

(b) a person purporting to act in any such capacity,

he as well as the body corporate is guilty of the offence and liable to be proceeded against and punished accordingly.

(6) In relation to a body corporate whose affairs are managed by its members 'director', in subsection (5), means a member of the body corporate.

(7) In this section—

'evidence of a personal nature' means any evidence of a medical, or other intimate, nature which might reasonably be assumed to be likely to cause significant embarrassment to the complainant if reported;

'identifying matter' means any matter likely to lead members of the public to identify the complainant or such other persons (if any) as may be named in the order;

'promulgation' has such meaning as may be prescribed by the regulations;

'relevant programme' means a programme included in a programme service, within the meaning of the Broadcasting Act 1990;

'restricted reporting order' means an order—

(a) made in exercise of the power conferred by regulations made by virtue of this section; and

(b) prohibiting the publication in Great Britain of identifying matter in a written publication available to the public or its inclusion in a relevant programme for reception in Great Britain; and

'written publication' includes a film, a soundtrack and any other record in permanent form but does not include an indictment or other document prepared for use in particular legal proceedings.

63   Restriction of publicity: Employment Appeal Tribunal

(1) This section applies to proceedings—

(a)   on an appeal against a decision of an industrial tribunal to make, or not to make, a restricted reporting order, or

(b)   on an appeal against any interlocutory decision of an industrial tribunal in proceedings in which the industrial tribunal has made a restricted reporting order which it has not revoked.

(2) The power of the Lord Chancellor to make rules with respect to the procedure of the Employment Appeal Tribunal includes power to make provision in relation to proceedings to which this section applies for—

(a)   enabling the Tribunal, on the application of the complainant or of its own motion, to make a restricted reporting order having effect (if not revoked earlier) until the promulgation of the Tribunal's decision; and

(b)   where a restricted reporting order is made in relation to an appeal which is being dealt with by the Tribunal together with any other proceedings, enabling the Tribunal to direct that the order is to apply also in relation to those other proceedings or such part of them as the Tribunal may direct.

(3) Subsections (3) to (6) of section 62 apply in relation to a restricted reporting order made by the Tribunal as they apply in relation to one made by an industrial tribunal.

(4) In subsection (1), 'restricted reporting order' means an order which is a restricted reporting order for the purposes of section 62.

(5) In subsection (2), 'restricted reporting order' means an order—

(a)   made in exercise of the power conferred by rules made by virtue of this section; and

(b)   prohibiting the publication in Great Britain of identifying matter in a written publication available to the public or its inclusion in a relevant programme for reception in Great Britain.

(6) In this section—

'complainant' means the person who made the complaint to which the proceedings before the Tribunal relate;

'identifying matter', 'written publication' and 'relevant programme' have the same meaning as in section 62; and

'promulgation' has such meaning as may be prescribed by the rules.

64   Application to Crown etc.

(1) This Act applies—

(a)   to an act done by or for purposes of a Minister of the Crown or government department, or

(b)   to an act done on behalf of the Crown by a statutory body, or a person holding a statutory office,

as it applies to an act done by a private person.

(2) Subject to subsection (5), Part II applies to service—

(a) for purposes of a Minister of the Crown or government department, other than service of a person holding a statutory office, or

(b) on behalf of the Crown for purposes of a person holding a statutory office or purposes of a statutory body,

as it applies to employment by a private person.

(3) The provisions of Parts II to IV of the 1947 Act apply to proceedings against the Crown under this Act as they apply to Crown proceedings in England and Wales; but section 20 of that Act (removal of proceedings from county court to High Court) does not apply.

(4) The provisions of Part V of the 1947 Act apply to proceedings against the Crown under this Act as they apply to proceedings in Scotland which by virtue of that Part are treated as civil proceedings by or against the Crown; but the proviso to section 44 of that Act (removal of proceedings from the sheriff court to the Court of Session) does not apply.

(5) Part II does not apply to service—

(a) as a member of the Ministry of Defence Police, the British Transport Police, the Royal Parks Constabulary or the United Kingdom Atomic Energy Authority Constabulary;

(b) as a prison officer; or

(c) for purposes of a Minister of the Crown or government department having functions with respect to defence as a person who is or may be required by his terms of service to engage in fire fighting.

(6) Part II does not apply to service as a member of a fire brigade who is or may be required by his terms of service to engage in fire fighting.

(7) It is hereby declared (for the avoidance of doubt) that Part II does not apply to service in any of the naval, military or air forces of the Crown.

(8) In this section—

'the 1947 Act' means the Crown Proceedings Act 1947;

'British Transport Police' means the constables appointed, or deemed to have been appointed, under section 53 of the British Transport Commission Act 1949;

'Crown proceedings' means proceedings which, by virtue of section 23 of the 1947 Act, are treated for the purposes of Part II of that Act as civil proceedings by or against the Crown;

'fire brigade' means a fire brigade maintained in pursuance of the Fire Services Act 1947;

'Ministry of Defence Police' means the force established under section 1 of the Ministry of Defence Police Act 1987;

'prison officer' means a person who is a prison officer within the meaning of section 127 of the Criminal Justice and Public Order Act 1994, apart from those who are custody officers within the meaning of Part I of that Act;

'Royal Parks Constabulary' means the park constables appointed under the Parks Regulation Act 1872;

'service for purposes of a Minister of the Crown or government department' does not
  include service in any office for the time being mentioned in Schedule 2
  (Ministerial offices) to the House of Commons Disqualification Act 1975;
'statutory body' means a body set up by or under an enactment;
'statutory office' means an office so set up; and
'United Kingdom Atomic Energy Authority Constabulary' means the special constables appointed under section 3 of the Special Constables Act 1923 on the
  nomination of the United Kingdom Atomic Energy Authority.

65　Application to Parliament

(1) This Act applies to an act done by or for purposes of the House of Lords or the House
of Commons as it applies to an act done by a private person.

(2) For the purposes of the application of Part II in relation to the House of Commons,
the Corporate Officer of that House shall be treated as the employer of a person who is
(or would be) a relevant member of the House of Commons staff for the purposes of
section [195 of the Employment Rights Act 1996].

(3) Except as provided in subsection (4), for the purposes of the application of sections
19 to 21, the provider of services is—

(a)　as respects the House of Lords, the Corporate Officer of that House; and
(b)　as respects the House of Commons, the Corporate Officer of that House.

(4) Where the service is question is access to and use of any place in the Palace of
Westminster which members of the public are permitted to enter, the Corporate
Officers of both Houses jointly are the provider of that service.

(5) Nothing in any rule of law or the law or practice of Parliament prevents proceedings
being instituted before an industrial tribunal under Part II or before any court under
Part III.

66　Government appointments outside Part II

(1) Subject to regulations under subsection (3), this section applies to any appointment
made by a Minister of the Crown or government department to an office or post where
Part II does not apply in relation to the appointment.

(2) In making the appointment, and in making arrangements for determining to whom
the office or post should be offered, the Minister of the Crown or government
department shall not act in a way which would contravene Part II if he or the department
were the employer for the purposes of this Act.

(3) Regulations may provide for this section not to apply to such appointments as may be
prescribed.

67　Regulations and orders

(1) Any power under this Act to make regulations or orders shall be exercisable by
statutory instrument.

(2) Any such power may be exercised to make different provision for different cases,
including different provision for different areas or localities.

(3) Any such power includes power—

(a) to make such incidental, supplemental, consequential or transitional provision as appears to the Secretary of State to be expedient; and
(b) to provide for a person to exercise a discretion in dealing with any matter.

(4) No order shall be made under section 50(3) unless a draft of the statutory instrument containing the order has been laid before Parliament and approved by a resolution of each House.

(5) Any other statutory instrument made under this Act, other than one made under section 3(9), 52(8), 54(6) or 70(3), shall be subject to annulment in pursuance of a resolution of either House of Parliament.

(6) Subsection (1) does not require an order under section 43 which applies only to a specified vehicle, or to vehicles of a specified person, to be made by statutory instrument but such an order shall be as capable of being amended or revoked as an order which is made by statutory instrument.

(7) Nothing in section 34(4), 40(6) or 46(5) affects the powers conferred by subsections (2) and (3).

68 Interpretation

(1) In this Act—

'accessibility certificate' means a certificate issued under section 41(1)(a);
'act' includes a deliberate omission;
'approval certificate' means a certificate issued under section 42(4);
'benefits', in Part II, has the meaning given in section 4(4);
'conciliation officer' means a person designated under section 211 of the Trade Union and Labour Relations (Consolidation) Act 1992;
'employment' means, subject to any prescribed provision, employment under a contract of service or of apprenticeship or a contract personally to do any work, and related expressions are to be construed accordingly;
'employment at an establishment in Great Britain' is to be construed in accordance with subsections (2) to (5);
'enactment' includes subordinate legislation and any Order in Council;
'licensing authority' means—
  (a) in relation to the area to which the Metropolitan Public Carriage Act 1869 applies, the Secretary of State or the holder of any office for the time being designated by the Secretary of State; or
  (b) in relation to any other area in England and Wales, the authority responsible for licensing taxis in that area;
'mental impairment' does not have the same meaning as in the Mental Health Act 1983 or the Mental Health (Scotland) Act 1984 but the fact that an impairment would be a mental impairment for the purposes of either of those Acts does not prevent it from being a mental impairment for the purposes of this Act;
'Minister of the Crown' includes the Treasury;
'occupational pension scheme' has the same meaning as in the Pension Schemes Act 1993;
'premises' includes land of any description;
'prescribed' means prescribed by regulations;
'profession' includes any vocation or occupation;
'provider of services' has the meaning given in section 19(2)(b);

'public service vehicle' and 'regulated public service vehicle' have the meaning given
 in section 40;

'PSV accessibility regulations' means regulations made under section 40(1);

'rail vehicle' and 'regulated rail vehicle' have the meaning given in section 46;

'rail vehicle accessibility regulations' means regulations made under section 46(1);

'regulations' means regulations made by the Secretary of State;

'section 6 duty' means any duty imposed by or under section 6;

'section 15 duty' means any duty imposed by or under section 15;

'section 21 duty' means any duty imposed by or under section 21;

'subordinate legislation' has the same meaning as in section 21 of the Interpretation
 Act 1978;

'taxi' and 'regulated taxi' have the meaning given in section 32;

'taxi accessibility regulations' means regulations made under section 32(1);

'trade' includes any business;

'trade organisation' has the meaning given in section 13;

'vehicle examiner' means an examiner appointed under section 66A of the Road
 Traffic Act 1988.

(2) Where an employee does his work wholly or mainly outside Great Britain, his
employment is not to be treated as being work at an establishment in Great Britain even
if he does some of his work at such an establishment.

(3) Except in prescribed cases, employment on board a ship, aircraft or hovercraft is to
be regarded as not being employment at an establishment in Great Britain.

(4) Employment of a prescribed kind, or in prescribed circumstances, is to be regarded
as not being employment at an establishment in Great Britain.

(5) Where work is not done at an establishment it shall be treated as done—

 (a) at the establishment from which it is done; or
 (b) where it is not done from any establishment, at the establishment with which it
   has the closest connection.

69 Financial provisions

(1) There shall be paid out of money provided by Parliament—

 (a) any expenditure incurred by a Minister of the Crown under this Act;
 (b) any increase attributable to this Act in the sums payable out of money so
   provided under or by virtue of any other enactment.

70 Short title, commencement, extent etc.

(1) This Act may be cited as the Disability Discrimination Act 1995.

(2) This section (apart from subsections (4), (5) and (7)) comes into force on the
passing of this Act.

(3) The other provisions of this Act come into force on such day as the Secretary of State
may by order appoint and different days may be appointed for different purposes.

(4) Schedule 6 makes consequential amendments.

(5) The repeals set out in Schedule 7 shall have effect.

(6) This Act extends to Northern Ireland, but in their application to Northern Ireland the provisions of this Act mentioned in Schedule 8 shall have effect subject to the modifications set out in that Schedule.

(7) In Part II of Schedule 1 to the House of Commons Disqualification Act 1975 and in Part II of Schedule 1 to the Northern Ireland Assembly Disqualification Act 1975 (bodies whose members are disqualified) in each case insert at the appropriate places—

'The National Disability Council.'
'The Northern Ireland Disability Council.'

(8) Consultations which are required by any provision of this Act to be held by the Secretary of State may be held by him before the coming into force of that provision.

SCHEDULES

SCHEDULE 1

PROVISIONS SUPPLEMENTING SECTION 1

Section 1(1)

Impairment

1   (1) 'Mental impairment' includes an impairment resulting from or consisting of a mental illness only if the illness is a clinically well-recognised illness.

(2) Regulations may make provision, for the purposes of this Act—

- (a)   for conditions of a prescribed description to be treated as amounting to impairments;
- (b)   for conditions of a prescribed description to be treated as not amounting to impairments.

(3) Regulations made under sub-paragraph (2) may make provision as to the meaning of 'condition' for the purposes of those regulations.

Long-term effects

2   (1) The effect of an impairment is a long-term effect if—

- (a)   it has lasted at least 12 months;
- (b)   the period for which it lasts is likely to be at least 12 months; or
- (c)   it is likely to last for the rest of the life of the person affected.

(2) Where an impairment ceases to have a substantial adverse effect on a person's ability to carry out normal day-to-day activities, it is to be treated as continuing to have that effect if that effect is likely to recur.

(3) For the purposes of sub-paragraph (2), the likelihood of an effect recurring shall be disregarded in prescribed circumstances.

(4) Regulations may prescribe circumstances in which, for the purposes of this Act—

- (a)   an effect which would not otherwise be a long-term effect is to be treated as such an effect; or
- (b)   an effect which would otherwise be a long-term effect is to be treated as not being such an effect.

Severe disfigurement

3   (1) An impairment which consists of a severe disfigurement is to be treated as having a substantial adverse effect on the ability of the person concerned to carry out normal day-to-day activities.

(2) Regulations may provide that in prescribed circumstances a severe disfigurement is not to be treated as having that effect.

(3) Regulations under sub-paragraph (2) may, in particular, make provision with respect to deliberately acquired disfigurements.

Normal day-to-day activities

4 (1) An impairment is to be taken to affect the ability of the person concerned to carry out normal day-to-day activities only if it affects one of the following—

    (a)   mobility;
    (b)   manual dexterity;
    (c)   physical co-ordination;
    (d)   continence;
    (e)   ability to lift, carry or otherwise move everyday objects;
    (f)   speech, hearing or eyesight;
    (g)   memory or ability to concentrate, learn or understand; or
    (h)   perception of the risk of physical danger.

(2) Regulations may prescribe—

    (a)   circumstances in which an impairment which does not have an effect falling within sub-paragraph (1) is to be taken to affect the ability of the person concerned to carry out normal day-to-day activities;
    (b)   circumstances in which an impairment which has an effect falling within sub-paragraph (1) is to be taken not to affect the ability of the person concerned to carry out normal day-to-day activities.

Substantial adverse effects

5 Regulations may make provision for the purposes of this Act—

    (a)   for an effect of a prescribed kind on the ability of a person to carry out normal day-to-day activities to be treated as a substantial adverse effect;
    (b)   for an effect of a prescribed kind on the ability of a person to carry out normal day-to-day activities to be treated as not being a substantial adverse effect.

Effect of medical treatment

6 (1) An impairment which would be likely to have a substantial adverse effect on the ability of the person concerned to carry out normal day-to-day activities, but for the fact that measures are being taken to treat or correct it, is to be treated as having that effect.

(2) In sub-paragraph (1) 'measures' includes, in particular, medical treatment and the use of a prosthesis or other aid.

(3) Sub-paragraph (1) does not apply—

    (a)   in relation to the impairment of a person's sight, to the extent that the impairment is, in his case, correctable by spectacles or contact lenses or in such other ways as may be prescribed; or

(b)   in relation to such other impairments as may be prescribed, in such
       circumstances as may be prescribed.

Persons deemed to be disabled

7 (1) Sub-paragraph (2) applies to any person whose name is, both on 12th January
1995 and on the date when this paragraph comes into force, in the register of disabled
persons maintained under section 6 of the Disabled Persons (Employment) Act 1944.

(2) That person is to be deemed—

(a)   during the initial period, to have a disability, and hence to be a disabled person;
       and
(b)   afterwards, to have had a disability and hence to have been a disabled person
       during that period.

(3) A certificate of registration shall be conclusive evidence, in relation to the person
with respect to whom it was issued, of the matters certified.

(4) Unless the contrary is shown, any document purporting to be a certificate of
registration shall be taken to be such a certificate and to have been validly issued.

(5) Regulations may provide for prescribed descriptions of person to be deemed to have
disabilities, and hence to be disabled persons, for the purposes of this Act.

(6) Regulations may prescribe circumstances in which a person who has been deemed
to be a disabled person by the provisions of sub-paragraph (1) or regulations made
under sub-paragraph (5) is to be treated as no longer being deemed to be such a person.

(7) In this paragraph—

   'certificate of registration' means a certificate issued under regulations made under
       section 6 of the Act of 1944; and
   'initial period' means the period of three years beginning with the date on which this
       paragraph comes into force.

Progressive conditions

8 (1) Where—

(a)   a person has a progressive condition (such as cancer, multiple sclerosis or
       muscular dystrophy or infection by the human immunodeficiency virus),
(b)   as a result of that condition, he has an impairment which has (or had) an effect
       on his ability to carry out normal day-to-day activities, but
(c)   that effect is not (or was not) a substantial adverse effect,

he shall be taken to have an impairment which has such a substantial adverse effect if the
condition is likely to result in his having such an impairment.

(2) Regulations may make provision, for the purposes of this paragraph—

(a) for conditions of a prescribed description to be treated as being progressive;

(b) for conditions of a prescribed description to be treated as not being progressive.

SCHEDULE 2

PAST DISABILITIES

Section 2(2)

1 The modifications referred to in section 2 are as follows.

2 References in Parts II and III to a disabled person are to be read as references to a person who has had a disability.

3 In section 6(1), after 'not disabled' insert 'and who have not had a disability'.

4 In section 6(6), for 'has' substitute 'has had'.

5 For paragraph 2(1) to (3) of Schedule 1, substitute—

'(1) The effect of an impairment is a long-term effect if it has lasted for at least 12 months.

(2) Where an impairment ceases to have a substantial adverse effect on a person's ability to carry out normal day-to-day activities, it is to be treated as continuing to have that effect if that effect recurs.

(3) For the purposes of sub-paragraph (2), the recurrence of an effect shall be disregarded in prescribed circumstances.'

SCHEDULE 3

ENFORCEMENT AND PROCEDURE

Sections 8(8) and 25(6)

PART I

EMPLOYMENT

Conciliation

[Schedule 3, para 1 repealed by the Industrial Tribunals Act 1996, Sch 3, Part I.]

Restriction on proceedings for breach of Part II

2 (1) Except as provided by section 8, no civil or criminal proceedings may be brought against any person in respect of an act merely because the act is unlawful under Part II.

(2) Sub-paragraph (1) does not prevent the making of an application for judicial review.

Period within which proceedings must be brought

3 (1) An industrial tribunal shall not consider a complaint under section 8 unless it is presented before the end of the period of three months beginning when the act complained of was done.

(2) A tribunal may consider any such complaint which is out of time if, in all the circumstances of the case, it considers that it is just and equitable to do so.

(3) For the purposes of sub-paragraph (1)—

(a) where an unlawful act of discrimination is attributable to a term in a contract, that act is to be treated as extending throughout the duration of the contract;
(b) any act extending over a period shall be treated as done at the end of that period; and
(c) a deliberate omission shall be treated as done when the person in question decided upon it.

(4) In the absence of evidence establishing the contrary, a person shall be taken for the purposes of this paragraph to decide upon an omission—

(a) when he does an act inconsistent with doing the omitted act; or
(b) if he has done no such inconsistent act, when the period expires within which he might reasonably have been expected to do the omitted act if it was to be done.

Evidence

4 (1) In any proceedings under section 8, a certificate signed by or on behalf of a Minister of the Crown and certifying—

(a) that any conditions or requirements specified in the certificate were imposed by a Minister of the Crown and were in operation at a time or throughout a time so specified, or
(b) that an act specified in the certificate was done for the purpose of safeguarding national security,

shall be conclusive evidence of the matters certified.

(2) A document purporting to be such a certificate shall be received in evidence and, unless the contrary is proved, be deemed to be such a certificate.

PART II

DISCRIMINATION IN OTHER AREAS

Restriction on proceedings for breach of Part III

5 (1) Except as provided by section 25 no civil or criminal proceedings may be brought against any person in respect of an act merely because the act is unlawful under Part III.

(2) Sub-paragraph (1) does not prevent the making of an application for judicial review.

Period within which proceedings must be brought

6 (1) A county court or a sheriff court shall not consider a claim under section 25 unless proceedings in respect of the claim are instituted before the end of the period of six months beginning when the act complained of was done.

(2) Where, in relation to proceedings or prospective proceedings under section 25, a person appointed in connection with arrangements under section 28 is approached before the end of the period of six months mentioned in sub-paragraph (1), the period allowed by that sub-paragraph shall be extended by two months.

(3) A court may consider any claim under section 25 which is out of time if, in all the circumstances of the case, it considers that it is just and equitable to do so.

(4) For the purposes of sub-paragraph (1)—

    (a)   where an unlawful act of discrimination is attributable to a term in a contract, that act is to be treated as extending throughout the duration of the contract;

    (b)   any act extending over a period shall be treated as done at the end of that period; and

    (c)   a deliberate omission shall be treated as done when the person in question decided upon it.

(5) In the absence of evidence establishing the contrary, a person shall be taken for the purposes of this paragraph to decide upon an omission—

    (a)   when he does an act inconsistent with doing the omitted act; or

    (b)   if he has done no such inconsistent act, when the period expires within which he might reasonably have been expected to do the omitted act if it was to be done.

Compensation for injury to feelings

7 In any proceedings under section 25, the amount of any damages awarded as compensation for injury to feelings shall not exceed the prescribed amount.

Evidence

8 (1) In any proceedings under section 25, a certificate signed by or on behalf of a Minister of the Crown and certifying—

    (a)   that any conditions or requirements specified in the certificate were imposed by a Minister of the Crown and were in operation at a time or throughout a time so specified, or

    (b)   that an act specified in the certificate was done for the purpose of safeguarding national security,

shall be conclusive evidence of the matters certified.

(2) A document purporting to be such a certificate shall be received in evidence and, unless the contrary is proved, be deemed to be such a certificate.

SCHEDULE 4

PREMISES OCCUPIED UNDER LEASES

Sections 16(5) and 27(5)

PART I

OCCUPATION BY EMPLOYER OR TRADE ORGANISATION

Failure to obtain consent to alteration

1   If any question arises as to whether the occupier has failed to comply with the section 6 or section 15 duty, by failing to make a particular alteration to the premises, any constraint attributable to the fact that he occupies the premises under a lease is to be ignored unless he has applied to the lessor in writing for consent to the making of the alteration.

Joining lessors in proceedings under section 8

2   (1) In any proceedings under section 8, in a case to which section 16 applies, the complainant or the occupier may ask the tribunal hearing the complaint to direct that the lessor be joined or sisted as a party to the proceedings.

(2) The request shall be granted if it is made before the hearing of the complaint begins.

(3) The tribunal may refuse the request if it is made after the hearing of the complaint begins.

(4) The request may not be granted if it is made after the tribunal has determined the complaint.

(5) Where a lessor has been so joined or sisted as a party to the proceedings, the tribunal may determine—

    (a)   whether the lessor has—
         (i) refused consent to the alteration, or
         (ii) consented subject to one or more conditions, and
    (b)   if so, whether the refusal or any of the conditions was unreasonable,

(6) If, under sub-paragraph (5), the tribunal determines that the refusal or any of the conditions was unreasonable it may take one or more of the following steps—

    (a)   make such declaration as it considers appropriate;
    (b)   make an order authorising the occupier to make the alteration specified in the order;
    (c)   order the lessor to pay compensation to the complainant.

(7) An order under sub-paragraph (6)(b) may require the occupier to comply with conditions specified in the order.

(8) Any step taken by the tribunal under sub-paragraph (6) may be in substitution for, or in addition to, any step taken by the tribunal under section 8(2).

(9) If the tribunal orders the lessor to pay compensation it may not make an order under section 8(2) ordering the occupier to do so.

Regulations

3 Regulations may make provision as to circumstances in which—

(a) a lessor is to be taken, for the purposes of section 16 of this Part of this Schedule to have—
   (i) withheld his consent;
   (ii) withheld his consent unreasonably;
   (iii) acted reasonably in withholding his consent;
(b) a condition subject to which a lessor has given his consent is to be taken to be reasonable;
(c) a condition subject to which a lessor has given his consent is to be taken to be unreasonable.

Sub-leases etc.

4 The Secretary of State may by regulations make provision supplementing, or modifying, the provision made by section 16 or any provision made by or under this Part of this Schedule in relation to cases where the occupier occupies premises under a sub-lease or sub-tenancy.

PART II

OCCUPATION BY PROVIDER OF SERVICES

Failure to obtain consent to alteration

5 If any question arises as to whether the occupier has failed to comply with the section 21 duty, by failing to make a particular alteration to premises, any constraint attributable to the fact that he occupies the premises under a lease is to be ignored unless he has applied to the lessor in writing for consent to the making of the alteration.

Reference to court

6 (1) If the occupier has applied in writing to the lessor for consent to the alteration and—

(a) that consent has been refused, or
(b) the lessor has made his consent subject to one or more conditions,

the occupier or a disabled person who has an interest in the proposed alteration to the premises being made, may refer the matter to a county court or, in Scotland, to the sheriff.

(2) In the following provisions of this Schedule 'court' includes 'sheriff'.

(3) On such a reference the court shall determine whether the lessor's refusal was unreasonable or (as the case may be) whether the condition is, or any of the conditions are, unreasonable.

(4) If the court determines—

(a)   that the lessor's refusal was unreasonable, or
(b)   that the condition is, or any of the conditions are, unreasonable,

it may make such declaration as it considers appropriate or an order authorising the occupier to make the alteration specified in the order.

(5) An order under sub-paragraph (4) may require the occupier to comply with conditions specified in the order.

Joining lessors in proceedings under section 25

7   (1) In any proceedings on a claim under section 25, in a case to which this Part of this Schedule applies, the plaintiff, the pursuer or the occupier concerned may ask the court to direct that the lessor be joined or sisted as a party to the proceedings.

(2) The request shall be granted if it is made before the hearing of the claim begins.

(3) The court may refuse the request if it is made after the hearing of the claim begins.

(4) The request may not be granted if it is made after the court has determined the claim.

(5) Where a lessor has been so joined or sisted as a party to the proceedings, the court may determine—

(a)   whether the lessor has—
           (i) refused consent to the alteration, or
           (ii) consented subject to one or more conditions, and
(b)   if so, whether the refusal or any of the conditions was unreasonable.

(6) If, under sub-paragraph (5), the court determines that the refusal or any of the conditions was unreasonable it may take one or more of the following steps—

(a)   make such declaration as it considers appropriate;
(b)   make an order authorising the occupier to make the alteration specified in the order;
(c)   order the lessor to pay compensation to the complainant.

(7) An order under sub-paragraph (6)(b) may require the occupier to comply with conditions specified in the order.

(8) If the court orders the lessor to pay compensation it may not order the occupier to do so.

Regulations

8   Regulations may make provision as to circumstances in which—

(a)   a lessor is to be taken, for the purposes of section 27 and this Part of this Schedule to have—

     (i) withheld his consent;

     (ii) withheld his consent unreasonably;

     (iii) acted unreasonably in withholding his consent;

(b)   a condition subject to which a lessor has given his consent is to be taken to be reasonable;

(c)   a condition subject to which a lessor has given his consent is to be taken to be unreasonable.

Sub-leases etc.

9   The Secretary of State may by regulations make provision supplementing, or modifying, the provision made by section 27 or any provision made by or under this Part of this Schedule in relation to cases where the occupier occupies premises under a sub-lease or sub-tenancy.

SCHEDULE 5

THE NATIONAL DISABILITY COUNCIL

Section 50(8)

Status

1   (1) The Council shall be a body corporate.

(2) The Council is not the servant or agent of the Crown and does not enjoy any status, immunity or privilege of the Crown.

Procedure

2   The Council has power to regulate its own procedure (including power to determine its quorum).

Membership

3   (1) The Council shall consist of at least 10, but not more than 20, members.

(2) In this Schedule 'member', except in sub-paragraph (5)(b), means a member of the Council.

(3) Each member shall be appointed by the Secretary of State.

(4) The Secretary of State shall appoint one member to be chairman of the Council and another member to be its deputy chairman.

(5) The members shall be appointed from among persons who, in the opinion of the Secretary of State—

(a)   have knowledge or experience of the needs of disabled persons or the needs of a particular group, or particular groups, of disabled persons;

(b)   have knowledge or experience of the needs of persons who have had a disability or the needs of a particular group, or particular groups, of such persons; or

(c)   are members of, or otherwise represent, professional bodies or bodies which represent industry or other business interests.

(6) Before appointing any member, the Secretary of State shall consult such persons as he considers appropriate.

(7) In exercising his powers of appointment, the Secretary of State shall try to secure that at all times at least half the membership of the Council consists of disabled persons, persons who have had a disability or the parents or guardians of disabled persons.

Term of office of members

4   (1) Each member shall be appointed for a term which does not exceed five years but shall otherwise hold and vacate his office in accordance with the terms of his appointment.

(2) A person shall not be prevented from being appointed as a member merely because he has previously been a member.

(3) Any member may at any time resign his office by written notice given to the Secretary of State.

(4) Regulations may make provision for the Secretary of State to remove a member from his office in such circumstances as may be prescribed.

Remuneration

5   (1) The Secretary of State may pay such remuneration or expenses to any member as he considers appropriate.

(2) The approval of the Treasury is required for any payment made under this paragraph.

Staff

6   The Secretary of State shall provide the Council with such staff as he considers appropriate.

Supplementary regulation-making power

7   The Secretary of State may by regulations make provision—

   (a)   as to the provision of information to the Council by the Secretary of State;
   (b)   as to the commissioning by the Secretary of State of research to be undertaken on behalf of the Council;
   (c)   as to the circumstances in which and conditions subject to which the Council may appoint any person as an adviser;
   (d)   as to the payment by the Secretary of State, with the approval of the Treasury, of expenses incurred by the Council.

Annual report

8   (1) As soon as is practicable after the end of each financial year, the Council shall report to the Secretary of State on its activities during the financial year to which the report relates.

(2) The Secretary of State shall lay a copy of every annual report of the Council before each House of Parliament and shall arrange for such further publication of the report as he considers appropriate.

SCHEDULE 6

CONSEQUENTIAL AMENDMENTS

Section 70(4)

Employment and Training Act 1973 (c. 50)

1 In section 12(1) of the Employment and Training Act 1973 (duty of Secretary of State to give preference to ex-service men and women in exercising certain powers in respect of disabled persons)—

    (a)   for 'persons registered as handicapped by disablement' substitute 'disabled persons'; and

    (b)   for the words after 'disabled person' substitute 'has the same meaning as in the Disability Discrimination Act 1995.'

Employment Protection (Consolidation) Act 1978 (c. 44)

[Schedule 6, para 2 repealed by the Industrial Tribunals Act 1996, Sch 3, Part I.]

[Schedule 6, para 3 repealed by the Employment Rights Act 1996, Sch 3, Part I.]

Companies Act 1985 (c. 6)

4 In paragraph 9 of Schedule 7 to the Companies Act 1985 (disclosure in directors' report of company policy in relation to disabled persons), in the definition of 'disabled person' in sub-paragraph (4)(b), for 'Disabled Persons (Employment) Act 1944' substitute 'Disability Discrimination Act 1995'.

Local Government and Housing Act 1989 (c. 42)

5 In section 7 of the Local Government and Housing Act 1989 (all staff of a local authority etc. to be appointed on merit), in subsection (2)—

    (a)   paragraph (a) shall be omitted;

    (b)   the word 'and' at the end of paragraph (d) shall be omitted; and

    (c)   after paragraph (e) insert—

    '; and

        (f)   sections 5 and 6 of the Disability Discrimination Act 1995 (meaning of discrimination and duty to make adjustments).'

Enterprise and New Towns (Scotland) Act 1990 (c. 35)

6 In section 16 of the Enterprise and New Towns (Scotland) Act 1990 (duty of certain Scottish bodies to give preference to ex-service men and women in exercising powers to select disabled persons for training), in subsection (2), for 'said Act of 1944' substitute 'Disability Discrimination Act 1995'.

SCHEDULE 7

REPEALS

Section 70(5)

Chapter	Short title	Extent of repeal
7 & 8 Geo. 6 c. 10.	The Disabled Persons (Employment) Act 1944.	Section 1. Sections 6 to 14. Section 19. Section 21. Section 22(4).
6 & 7 Eliz. 2 c. 33.	The Disabled Persons (Employment) Act 1958.	Section 2.
1970 c. 44.	The Chronically Sick and Disabled Persons Act 1970.	Section 16.
1978 c. 44.	The Employment Protection (Consolidation) Act 1978.	In Schedule 13, in paragraph 20(3), the word "or" in the definitions of "relevant complaint of dismissal" and "relevant conciliation powers".
1989 c. 42.	The Local Government and Housing Act 1989.	In section 7(2), paragraph (a) and the word "and" at the end of paragraph (d).
1993 c. 62.	The Education Act 1993.	In section 161(5), the words from "and in this subsection" to the end.

SCHEDULE 8

MODIFICATIONS OF THIS ACT IN ITS APPLICATION TO NORTHERN IRELAND

Section 70(6)

1 In its application to Northern Ireland this Act shall have effect subject to the following modifications.

2 (1) In section 3(1) for 'Secretary of State' substitute 'Department'.

(2) In section 3 for subsections (4) to (12) substitute—

'(4) In preparing a draft of any guidance, the Department shall consult such persons as it considers appropriate.

(5) Where the Department proposes to issue any guidance, the Department shall publish a draft of it, consider any representations that are made to the Department about the draft and, if the Department thinks it appropriate, modify its proposals in the light of any of those representations.

(6) If the Department decides to proceed with any proposed guidance, the Department shall lay a draft of it before the Assembly.

(7) If, within the statutory period, the Assembly resolves not to approve the draft, the Department shall take no further steps in relation to the proposed guidance.

(8) If no such resolution is made within the statutory period, the Department shall issue the guidance in the form of its draft.

(9) The guidance shall come into force on such date as the Department may by order appoint.

(10) Subsection (7) does not prevent a new draft of the proposed guidance being laid before the Assembly.

(11) The Department may—
    (a)   from time to time revise the whole or any part of any guidance and re-issue it;
    (b)   by order revoke any guidance.

(12) In this section—
    "the Department" means the Department of Economic Development;
    "guidance" means guidance issued by the Department under this section and includes guidance which has been revised and re-issued;
    "statutory period" has the meaning assigned to it by section 41(2) of the Interpretation Act (Northern Ireland) 1954.'

3   In section 4(6) for 'Great Britain' substitute 'Northern Ireland'.

4   (1) In section 7(2) for 'Secretary of State' substitute 'Department of Economic Development'.

(2) In section 7(4) to (10) for 'Secretary of State' wherever it occurs substitute 'Department of Economic Development', for 'he' and 'him' wherever they occur substitute 'it' and for 'his' wherever it occurs substitute 'its'.

(3) In section 7(9) for 'Parliament' substitute 'the Assembly'.

5   (1) In section 8(3) omit 'or (in Scotland) in reparation'.

(2) In section 8(7) for 'paragraph 6A of Schedule 9 to the Employment Protection (Consolidation) Act 1978' substitute 'Article 61(3) of the Industrial Relations (Northern Ireland) Order 1976'.

6   (1) In section 9(2)(a) for 'a conciliation officer' substitute 'the Agency'.

(2) In section 9(4) in the definition of 'qualified lawyer' for the words from 'means' to the end substitute 'means a barrister (whether in practice as such or employed to give legal advice) or a solicitor of the Supreme Court who holds a practising certificate.'.

7   (1) In section 10(1)(b) omit 'or recognised body'.

(2) In section 10(2)(b) for 'Secretary of State' substitute 'Department of Economic Development'.

(3) In section 10(3) in the definition of 'charity' for '1993' substitute '(Northern Ireland) 1964', omit the definition of 'recognised body' and in the definition of 'supported employment' for 'Act 1944' substitute 'Act (Northern Ireland) 1945'.

(4) In section 10(4) for 'England and Wales' where it twice occurs substitute 'Northern Ireland'.

(5) Omit section 10(5).

8 In section 12(5) for 'Great Britain' where it twice occurs substitute 'Northern Ireland'.

9 (1) In section 19(3)(g) for 'section 2 of the Employment and Training Act 1973' substitute 'sections 1 and 2 of the Employment and Training Act (Northern Ireland) 1950'.

(2) In section 19(5) for paragraph (a) substitute—

'(a)   education which is funded, or secured, by a relevant body or provided at—
    (i)   an establishment which is funded by such a body or by the Department of Education for Northern Ireland; or
    (ii) any other establishment which is a school within the meaning of the Education and Libraries (Northern Ireland) Order 1986;'.

(3) For section 19(6) substitute—

'(6) In subsection (5) "relevant body" means—
    (a)   an education and library board;
    (b)   a voluntary organisation; or
    (c)   a body of a prescribed kind.'.

10   In section 20(7) for paragraphs (b) and (c) substitute '; or

   (b)   functions conferred by or under Part VIII of the Mental Health (Northern Ireland) Order 1986 are exercisable in relation to a disabled person's property or affairs.'.

11   In section 22(4) and (6) omit 'or (in Scotland) the subject of'.

12   (1) In section 25(1) omit 'or (in Scotland) in reparation'.

(2) In section 25(3) for 'England and Wales' substitute 'Northern Ireland'.

(3) Omit section 25(4).

(4) In section 25(5) omit the words from 'or' to the end.

13   In section 26(3) omit 'or a sheriff court'.

14   (1) In section 28 for 'Secretary of State' wherever it occurs substitute 'Department of Health and Social Services'.

(2) In section 28(3) and (4) for 'he' substitute 'it'.

(3) In section 28(5) for 'Treasury' substitute 'Department of Finance and Personnel in Northern Ireland'.

15   Omit sections 29, 30 and 31.

16   (1) In section 32(1) for 'Secretary of State' substitute 'Department of the Environment'.

(2) In section 32(5) for the definition of 'taxi' substitute—

' "taxi" means a vehicle which—
  (a)   is licensed under Article 61 of the Road Traffic (Northern Ireland) Order 1981 to stand or ply for hire; and
  (b)   seats not more than 8 passengers in addition to the driver'.

17   In section 33, for 'Secretary of State', wherever it occurs, substitute 'Department of the Environment'.

18   For section 34 substitute—

'34   New licences conditional on compliance with accessibility taxi regulations

(1) The Department of the Environment shall not grant a public service vehicle licence under Article 61 of the Road Traffic (Northern Ireland) Order 1981 for a taxi unless the vehicle conforms with those provisions of the taxi accessibility regulations with which it will be required to confirm if licensed.

(2) Subsection (1) does not apply if such a licence was in force with respect to the vehicle at any time during the period of 28 days immediately before the day on which the licence is granted.

(3) The Department of the Environment may by order provide for subsection (2) to cease to have effect on such date as may be specified in the order.'.

19   Omit section 35.

20   In section 36(7) for 'licensing authority' substitute 'Department of the Environment'.

21   (1) In section 37(5) and (6) for 'licensing authority' substitute 'Department of the Environment'.

(2) In section 37(9) for 'Secretary of State' substitute 'Department of the Environment'.

22   (1) In section 38(1) for 'a licensing authority' substitute 'the Department of the Environment'.

(2) In section 38(2) for 'licensing authority concerned' substitute 'Department of the Environment'.

(3) In section 38(3) for the words from 'the magistrates' court' to the end substitute 'a court of summary jurisdiction acting for the petty sessions district in which the aggrieved person resides'.

23   Omit section 39.

24   (1) In section 40 for 'Secretary of State' wherever it occurs substitute 'Department of the Environment'.

(2) In section 40(5) for the definition of 'public service vehicle' substitute—

' "public service vehicle" means a vehicle which—
  (a)   seats more than 8 passengers in addition to the driver; and
  (b)   is a public service vehicle for the purposes of the Road Traffic (Northern Ireland) Order 1981;'.

(3) In section 40(7) for the words for 'the Disabled' to the end substitute 'such representative organisations as it thinks fit'.

25 (1) In section 41(2) for 'Secretary of State' substitute 'Department of the Environment'.

(2) In section 41 for subsections (3) and (4) substitute—

'(3) Any person who uses a regulated public service vehicle in contravention of this section is guilty of an offence and liable on summary conviction to a fine not exceeding level 4 on the standard scale.'.

26 (1) In section 42 for 'Secretary of State' wherever it occurs substitute 'Department of the Environment'.

(2) In section 42(1) for 'he' substitute 'it'.

(3) In section 42(6) for 'his' substitute 'its'.

27 In section 43 for 'Secretary of State' wherever it occurs substitute 'Department of the Environment'.

28 (1) In section 44 for 'Secretary of State' wherever it occurs substitute 'Department of the Environment'.

(2) In section 44(2) for 'him' substitute 'it'.

(3) In section 44(6) for 'he' substitute 'it' and for 'his' substitute 'its'.

29 (1) In section 45 for 'Secretary of State' wherever it occurs substitute 'Department of the Environment'.

(2) In section 45(2) for 'him' substitute 'it' and at the end add 'of Northern Ireland'.

(3) In section 45(4) for 'he' substitute 'it'.

30 (1) In section 46 for 'Secretary of State' wherever it occurs substitute 'Department of the Environment'.

(2) In section 46(6) in the definition of 'rail vehicle' for the words 'on any railway, tramway or prescribed system' substitute 'by rail'.

(3) Omit section 46(7).

(4) In section 46(11) for the words from 'the Disabled' to the end substitute 'such representative organisations as it thinks fit'.

31 (1) In section 47 for 'Secretary of State' wherever it occurs substitute 'Department of the Environment'.

(2) In section 47(3) for the words 'the Disabled Persons Transport Advisory Committee and such other persons as he' substitute 'such persons as it' and for 'he' substitute 'it'.

32 Omit section 48(3).

33 (1) In the heading to Part VI of this Act and in section 50(1) for 'National Disability Council' substitute 'Northern Ireland Disability Council'.

(2) In section 50(2) for 'Secretary of State' in the first place where it occurs substitute 'a Northern Ireland department' and in the other place where it occurs substitute 'that department'.

(3) In section 50(3) for 'Secretary of State' substitute 'Department of Health and Social Services'.

(4) In section 50(7) for 'Secretary of State' substitute 'a Northern Ireland department' and after 'Crown' insert 'or a Northern Ireland department'.

(5) In section 50(9)(a) for sub-paragraphs (i) to (iv) substitute—

'(i)   the Disabled Persons (Employment) Act (Northern Ireland) 1945;
(ii)   the Contracts of Employment and Redundancy Payments Act (Northern Ireland) 1965;
(iii) the Employment and Training Act (Northern Ireland) 1950;
(iv)   the Industrial Relations (Northern Ireland) Orders 1976; or'.

(6) In section 50(10) for the words from 'time when' to the end substitute 'time when—

(a)   there are no committees in existence under section 17 of the Disabled Persons (Employment) Act (Northern Ireland) 1945; and
(b)   there is no person appointed to act generally under section 60(1) of this Act.'.

34 (1) In section 51(1) for 'the Secretary of State' substitute 'any Northern Ireland department' and for 'the Secretary of State's' substitute 'that department's'.

(2) In section 51(2) for 'The Secretary of State' substitute 'A Northern Ireland department'.

(3) In section 51(4) for 'a county court or a sheriff court' substitute 'or a county court'.

(4) In section 51(6) for 'the Secretary of State' substitute 'a Northern Ireland department'.

35 For section 52 substitute—

'52   Further provisions about codes issued under section 51

(1) In this section—
"proposal" means a proposal made by the Council to a Northern Ireland department under section 51;
"responsible department"—
(a)   in relation to a proposal, means the Northern Ireland department to which the proposal is made,
(b)   in relation to a code, means the Northern Ireland department by which the code is issued; and
"statutory period" has the meaning assigned to it by section 41(2) of the Interpretation Act (Northern Ireland) 1954.

(2) In preparing any proposal, the Council shall consult—
(a)   such persons (if any) as the responsible department has specified in making its request to the Council; and
(b)   such other persons (if any) as the Council considers appropriate.

(3) Before making any proposal the Council shall publish a draft, consider any representations made to it about the draft and, if it thinks it appropriate, modify its proposal in the light of any of those representations.

(4) Where the Council makes any proposal, the responsible department may—

  (a)   approve it;
  (b)   approve it subject to such modifications as that department thinks appropriate; or
  (c)   refuse to approve it.

(5) Where the responsible department approves any proposal (with or without modifications) that department shall prepare a draft of the proposed code and lay it before the Assembly.

(6) If, within the statutory period, the Assembly resolves not to approve the draft, the responsible department shall take no further steps in relation to the proposed code.

(7) If no such resolution is made within the statutory period, the responsible department shall issue the code in the form of its draft.

(8) The code shall come into force on such date as the responsible department may appoint by order.

(9) Subsection (6) does not prevent a new draft of the proposed code from being laid before the Assembly.

(10) If the responsible department refuses to approve a proposal, that department shall give the Council a written statement of the department's reasons for not approving it.

(11) The responsible department may by order revoke a code.'.

36   (1) In section 53 for 'Secretary of State' wherever it occurs substitute 'Department of Economic Development'.

(2) In section 53(1) for 'he' substitute 'it'.

(3) In section 53(3) for 'a county court or a sheriff court' substitute 'or a county court'.

37   For section 54 substitute—

'54   Further provisions about codes issued under section 53

(1) In preparing a draft of any code under section 53, the Department shall consult such organisations representing the interests of employers or of disabled persons in, or seeking, employment as the Department considers appropriate.

(2) Where the Department proposes to issue a code, the Department shall publish a draft of the code, consider any representations that are made to the Department about the draft and, if the Department thinks it appropriate, modify its proposals in the light of any of those representations.

(3) If the Department decides to proceed with the code, the Department shall lay a draft of it before the Assembly.

(4) If, within the statutory period, the Assembly resolves not to approve the draft, the Department shall take no further steps in relation to the proposed code.

(5) If no such resolution is made within the statutory period, the Department shall issue the code in the form of its draft.

(6) The code shall come into force on such date as the Department may appoint by order.

(7) Subsection (4) does not prevent a new draft of the proposed code from being laid before the Assembly.

(8) The Department may by order revoke a code.

(9) In this section—
"the Department" means the Department of Economic Development; and
"statutory period" has the meaning assigned to it by section 41(2) of the Interpretation Act (Northern Ireland) 1954.'.

38 In section 56(2) and (4) for 'Secretary of State' substitute 'Department of Economic Development'.

39 In section 59(1) after 'Crown' where it twice occurs insert 'or a Northern Ireland department'.

40 (1) In section 60(1) to (3) for 'Secretary of State' wherever it occurs substitute 'Department of Economic Development' and for 'he' and 'him' wherever they occur substitute 'it'.

(2) In section 60(4) for 'Treasury' substitute 'Department of Finance and Personnel in Northern Ireland'.

(3) For section 60(6) substitute—

'(6) The Department of Economic Development may by order repeal section 17 of, and Schedule 2 to, the Disabled Persons (Employment) Act (Northern Ireland) 1945 (district advisory committees).'.

(4) In section 60(7) omit 'paragraph (b) of', for '1944' substitute '1945' and omit 'in each case'.

(5) In section 60, omit subsection (8).

41 For section 61 substitute—

'61 Amendments of Disabled Persons (Employment) Act (Northern Ireland) 1945

(1) Section 15 of the Disabled Persons (Employment) Act (Northern Ireland) 1945 (which gives the Department of Economic Development power to make arrangements for the provision of supported employment) is amended as set out in subsection (2) to (5).

(2) In subsection (1)—
(a) for "persons registered as handicapped by disablement" substitute "disabled persons";
(b) for "their disablement" substitute "their disability"; and
(c) for "are not subject to disablement" substitute "do not have a disability".

(3) In subsection (2) for the words from "any of one or more companies" to "so required and prohibited" substitute "any company, association or body".

(4) After subsection (2) insert—

"(2A) The only kind of company which the Department itself may form in exercising its powers under this section is a company which is—
- (a)　required by its constitution to apply its profits, if any, or other income in promoting its objects; and
- (b)　prohibited by its constitution from paying any dividend to its members.".

(5) After subsection (5) insert—

"(5A) For the purposes of this section—
- (a)　a person is a disabled person if he is a disabled person for the purposes of the Disability Discrimination Act 1995; and
- (b)　'disability' has the same meaning as in that Act.".

(6) The provisions of section 16 of the Act of 1945 (preference to be given under section 15 of that Act to ex-service men and women) shall become subsection (1) of that section and at the end insert—

"and whose disability is due to that service.

(2) For the purposes of subsection (1) of this section, a disabled person's disability shall be treated as due to service of a particular kind only in such circumstances as may be prescribed."

(7) The following provisions of the Act of 1945 shall cease to have effect—
- (a)　section 1 (definition of "disabled person");
- (b)　sections 2 to 4 (training for disabled persons);
- (c)　sections 6 to 8 (the register of disabled persons);
- (d)　sections 9 to 11 (obligations on employers with substantial staffs to employ quota of registered persons);
- (e)　section 12 (the designated employment scheme for persons registered as handicapped by disablement);
- (f)　section 13 (interpretation of provisions repealed by this Act);
- (g)　section 14 (records to be kept by employer);
- (h)　section 19 (proceedings in relation to offences);
- (j)　sections 21 and 22 (supplementary).

(8) Any statutory provision in which "disabled person" is defined by reference to the Act of 1945 shall be construed as if that expression had the same meaning as in this Act.'.

42　(1) In section 62(2) for 'Secretary of State' substitute 'Department of Economic Development'.

(2) In section 62(7) for 'Great Britain' where it twice occurs substitute 'Northern Ireland'.

43　Omit section 63.

44　(1) In section 64(3) for 'England and Wales' substitute 'Northern Ireland'.

(2) Omit section 64(4).

(3) In section 64(5)(a) omit the words from ', the British' to the end.

(4) In section 64(8)—

(a)   omit the definitions of 'British Transport Police', 'Royal Parks Constabulary' and 'United Kingdom Atomic Energy Authority Constabulary';

(b)   in the definition of 'the 1947 Act' at the end add 'as it applies both in relation to the Crown in right of Her Majesty's Government in Northern Ireland and in relation to the Crown in right of Her Majesty's Government in the United Kingdom';

(c)   in the definition of 'fire brigade' for the words from 'means' to the end substitute 'has the same meaning as in the Fire Services (Northern Ireland) Order 1984';

(d)   in the definition of 'prison officer' for the words from 'means' to the end substitute 'means any individual who holds any post, otherwise than as a medical officer, to which he has been appointed under section 2(2) of the Prison Act (Northern Ireland) 1953 or who is a prison custody officer within the meaning of Chapter III of Part VIII of the Criminal Justice and Public Order Act 1994';

(e)   in the definition of 'service for purposes of a Minister of the Crown or government department' at the end add 'or service as the head of a Northern Ireland department'.

45   Omit section 65.

46   For section 67 substitute—

'67   Regulations and orders etc.

(1) Any power under this Act to make regulations or orders shall be exercisable by statutory rule for the purposes of the Statutory Rules (Northern Ireland) Order 1979.

(2) Any such power may be exercised to make different provision for different cases, including different provision for different areas or localities.

(3) Any such power, includes power—
(a)   to make such incidental, supplementary, consequential or transitional provision as appears to the Northern Ireland department exercising the power to be expedient; and
(b)   to provide for a person to exercise a discretion in dealing with any matter.

(4) No order shall be made under section 50(3) unless a draft of the order has been laid before and approved by a resolution of the Assembly.

(5) Any other order made under this Act, other than an order under section 3(9), 52(8), 54(6) or 70(3), and any regulations made under this Act shall be subject to negative resolution within the meaning of section 41(6) of the Interpretation Act (Northern Ireland) 1954 as if they were statutory instruments within the meaning of that Act.

(6) Section 41(3) of the Interpretation Act (Northern Ireland) 1954 shall apply in relation to any instrument or document which by virtue of this Act is required to be laid before the Assembly as if it were a statutory instrument or statutory document within the meaning of that Act.

(7) Subsection (1) does not require an order under section 43 which applies only to a specified vehicle, or to vehicles of a specified person, to be made by statutory rule.

(8) Nothing in section 40(6) or 46(5) affects the powers conferred by subsections (2) and (3).'

47 (1) For section 68(1) substitute—

'(1) In this Act—

"accessibility certificate" means a certificate issued under section 41(1)(a);

"act" includes a deliberate omission;

"the Agency" means the Labour Relations Agency;

"approval certificate" means a certificate issued under section 42(4);

"the Assembly" means the Northern Ireland Assembly;

"benefits", in Part II, has the meaning given in section 4(4);

"the Department of Economic Development" means the Department of Economic Development in Northern Ireland;

"the Department of the Environment" means the Department of the Environment for Northern Ireland;

"the Department of Health and Social Services" means the Department of Health and Social Services for Northern Ireland;

"employment" means, subject to any prescribed provision, employment under a contract of service or of apprenticeship or a contract personally to do work and related expressions are to be construed accordingly;

"employment at an establishment in Northern Ireland" is to be construed in accordance with subsections (2) to (5);

"enactment" means any statutory provision within the meaning of section 1(f) of the Interpretation Act (Northern Ireland) 1954;

"government department" means a Northern Ireland department or a department of the Government of the United Kingdom;

"Minister of the Crown" includes the Treasury;

"Northern Ireland department" includes (except in sections 51 and 52) the head of a Northern Ireland department;

"occupational pension scheme" has the same meaning as in the Pension Schemes (Northern Ireland) Act 1993;

"premises", includes land of any description;

"prescribed" means prescribed by regulations;

"profession" includes any vocation or occupation;

"provider of services" has the meaning given in section 19(2)(b);

"public service vehicle" and "regulated public service vehicle" have the meaning given in section 40;

"PSV accessibility regulations" means regulations made under section 40(1);

"rail vehicle" and "regulated rail vehicle" have the meaning given in section 46;

"rail vehicle accessibility regulations" means regulations made under section 46(1);

"regulations" means—

    (a)   in Parts I and II of this Act, section 66, the definition of "employment" above and subsections (3) and (4) below, regulations made by the Department of Economic Development;

    (b)   in Part V of this Act, regulations made by the Department of the Environment;

    (c)   in any other provision of this Act, regulations made by the Department of Health and Social Services.

"section 6 duty" means any duty imposed by or under section 6;

"section 15 duty" means any duty imposed by or under section 15;

"section 21 duty" means any duty imposed by or under section 21;

"taxi" and "regulated taxi" have the meaning given in section 32;

"taxi accessibility regulations" means regulations made under section 32(1);

"trade" includes any business;

"trade organisation" has the meaning given in section 13;

"vehicle examiner" means an officer of the Department of the Environment authorised by that Department for the purposes of sections 41 and 42.'.

(2) In section 68(2) to (4) for 'Great Britain' wherever it occurs substitute 'Northern Ireland'.

48   (1) In section 70(3) for 'Secretary of State' substitute 'Department of Health and Social Services'.

(2) In section 70(8) for 'the Secretary of State' substitute 'a Northern Ireland department' and for 'him' substitute 'it'.

49   (1) In Schedule 1 in paragraph 7(1) for 'Act 1944' substitute 'Act (Northern Ireland) 1945'.

(2) In Schedule 1 in paragraph 7(7) for '1944' substitute '1945'.

50   (1) In Schedule 3 in paragraph 1—

  (a)   for 'a conciliation officer' wherever it occurs substitute 'the Agency';
  (b)   in sub-paragraphs (1) and (4) for 'he' substitute 'it';
  (c)   in sub-paragraph (3) for 'the conciliation officer' substitute 'the Agency'.

(2) In Schedule 3 for paragraph 4(1) substitute—

  '(1) In any proceedings under section 8—
  (a)   a certificate signed by or on behalf of a Minister of the Crown or a Northern Ireland department and certifying that any conditions or requirements specified in the certificate were imposed by that Minister or that department (as the case may be) and were in operation at a time or throughout a time so specified; or
  (b)   a certificate signed by or on behalf of the Secretary of State and certifying that an act specified in the certificate was done for the purpose of safeguarding national security,
  shall be conclusive evidence of the matters certified.'.

(3) In Schedule 3 in paragraph 6(1) omit 'or a sheriff court'.

(4) In Schedule 3 for paragraph 8(1) substitute—

  '(1) In any proceedings under section 25—
  (a)   a certificate signed by or on behalf of a Minister of the Crown or a Northern Ireland department and certifying that any conditions or requirements specified in the certificate were imposed by that Minister or that department (as the case may be) and were in operation at a time or throughout a time so specified; or
  (b)   a certificate signed by or on behalf of the Secretary of State and certifying that an act specified in the certificate was done for the purpose of safeguarding national security,
  shall be conclusive evidence of the matters certified.'.

51   (1) In Schedule 4 in paragraphs 2(1) and (5) and 7(1) and (5) omit 'or sisted'.

(2) In Schedule 4 in paragraph 4 for 'Secretary of State' substitute 'Department of Economic Development'.

(3) In Schedule 4 in paragraph 6(1) omit 'or, in Scotland, to the sheriff'.

(4) In Schedule 4 omit paragraph 6(2).

(5) In Schedule 4 in paragraph 9 for 'Secretary of State' substitute 'Department of Health and Social Services'.

52   (1) In Schedule 5 in the heading for 'National' substitute 'Northern Ireland'.

(2) In Schedule 5 for 'Secretary of State' wherever it occurs substitute 'Department of Health and Social Services'.

(3) In Schedule 5 in paragraphs 3(6), 5(1), 6 and 8(2) for 'he' substitute 'it' and in paragraph 3(7) for 'his' substitute 'its'.

(4) In Schedule 5 in paragraphs 5(2) and 7(d) for 'Treasury' substitute 'Department of Finance and Personnel in Northern Ireland'.

(5) In Schedule 5 in paragraph 8(2) for 'each House of Parliament' substitute 'the Assembly'.

53   For Schedules 6 and 7 substitute—

'SCHEDULE 6

CONSEQUENTIAL AMENDMENTS

The Industrial Relations (Northern Ireland) Order 1976 (NI 16)

1   In Article 68(6) of the Industrial Relations (Northern Ireland) Order 1976 (reinstatement or re-engagement of dismissed employees)—

(a)   in the definition of 'relevant complaint of dismissal', omit 'or' and at the end insert 'or a complaint under section 8 of the Disability Discrimination Act 1995 arising out of a dismissal';

(b)   in the definition of 'relevant conciliation powers' omit 'or' and at the end insert 'or paragraph 1 of Schedule 3 to the Disability Discrimination Act 1995';

(c)   in the definition of 'relevant compromise contract' for 'or Article' substitute 'Article' and at the end insert 'or section 9(2) of the Disability Discrimination Act 1995'.

The Companies (Northern Ireland) Order 1986 (NI 6)

3   In paragraph 9 of Schedule 7 to the Companies (Northern Ireland) Order 1986 (disclosure in directors' report of company policy in relation to disabled persons) in the definition of 'disabled person' in sub-paragraph (4) (b) for 'Disabled Persons (Employment) Act (Northern Ireland) 1945' substitute 'Disability Discrimination Act 1995'.

SCHEDULE 7

REPEALS

Chapter	Short Title	Extent of repeal
1945 c. 6 (N.I.)	The Disabled Persons (Employment) Act (Northern Ireland) 1945.	Sections 1 to 4. Sections 6 to 14. In section 16 the words "vocational training and industrial rehabilitation courses and", the words "courses and" and the words from "and in selecting" to "engagement". Section 19. Section 21. Section 22.
1960 c. 4 (N.I.)	The Disabled Persons (Employment) Act (Northern Ireland) 1960.	The whole Act.
1976 NI16	The Industrial Relations (Northern Ireland) Order 1976.	In Article 68(6) the word "or" in the definitions of "relevant complaint of dismissal" and "relevant conciliation powers".'.

Appendix II

Statutory Instruments

The Disability Discrimination (Meaning of Disability) Regulations 1996

SI 1996/1455

1 Citation and commencement

These Regulations may be cited as the Disability Discrimination (Meaning of Disability) Regulations 1996 and shall come into force on 30th July 1996.

2 Interpretation

In these Regulations—

'the Act' means the Disability Discrimination Act 1995; and
'addiction' includes a dependency.

3 Addictions

(1) Subject to paragraph (2) below, addiction to alcohol, nicotine or any other substance is to be treated as not amounting to an impairment for the purposes of the Act.

(2) Paragraph (1) above does not apply to addiction which was originally the result of administration of medically prescribed drugs or other medical treatment.

4 Other conditions not to be treated as impairments

(1) For the purposes of the Act the following conditions are to be treated as not amounting to impairments—

(a)   a tendency to set fires,
(b)   a tendency to steal,
(c)   a tendency to physical or sexual abuse of other persons,
(d)   exhibitionism, and
(e)   voyeurism.

(2) Subject to paragraph (3) below for the purposes of the Act the condition known as seasonal allergic rhinitis shall be treated as not amounting to an impairment.

(3) Paragraph (2) above shall not prevent that condition from being taken into account for the purposes of the Act where it aggravates the effect of another condition.

5 Tattoos and piercings

For the purposes of paragraph 3 of Schedule 1 to the Act a severe disfigurement is not to be treated as having a substantial adverse effect on the ability of the person concerned to carry out normal day-to-day activities if it consists of—

(a)   a tattoo (which has not been removed), or

(b)   a piercing of the body for decorative or other non-medical purposes, including any object attached through the piercing for such purposes.

6 Babies and young children

For the purposes of the Act where a child under six years of age has an impairment which does not have an effect falling within paragraph 4(1) of Schedule 1 to the Act that impairment is to be taken to have a substantial and long-term adverse effect on the ability of that child to carry out normal day-to-day activities where it would normally have a substantial and long-term adverse effect on the ability of a person aged 6 years or over to carry out normal day-to-day activities.

The Disability Discrimination (Employment) Regulations 1996

SI 1996/1456

1 Citation and commencement

These Regulations may be cited as the Disability Discrimination (Employment) Regulations 1996 and shall come into force on 2nd December 1996.

2 Interpretation

In these Regulations—

'the Act' means the Disability Discrimination Act 1995;
'binding obligation' means a legally binding obligation (not contained in a lease) in relation to the premises whether arising from an agreement or otherwise;
'building' means an erection or structure of any kind;
'building regulations' has the meaning given by section 122 of the Building Act 1984;
'lease' has the meaning assigned by section 16(3) of the Act;
'pay' means remuneration of any kind including any benefit;
'performance' includes performance as assessed by reference to any measure, whether relative or absolute, of output, efficiency or effectiveness in an employment;
'section 6 duty' means any duty imposed by or under section 6 of the Act;
'Technical Standards' means the technical standards for compliance with the Building Standards (Scotland) Regulations 1990 issued by the Scottish Office in 1990 and as amended by the substitute pages issued by the Scottish Office in and dated July 1993 and July 1994.

3 Pay

(1) For the purposes of section 5 of the Act, treatment is to be taken to be justified if it results from applying to the disabled person a term or practice—

(a) under which the amount of a person's pay is wholly or partly dependent on that person's performance; and
(b) which is applied to all of the employer's employees or to all of a class of his employees which includes the disabled person but which is not defined by reference to any disability.

(2) Arrangements consisting of the application to a disabled person of a term or practice of the kind referred to in paragraph (1) above are not to be taken to place that disabled person at a substantial disadvantage of the kind mentioned in section 6(1) of the Act.

(3) Nothing in this regulation affects the operation of section 6 of the Act in relation to any arrangements or physical features of premises which, by placing a disabled person at a substantial disadvantage, cause reduced performance by him.

4 Occupational pension schemes

(1) For the purposes of section 5(1) of the Act less favourable treatment of a disabled person is to be taken to be justified in the circumstances described in paragraph (2) below if it results from applying the eligibility conditions set for receiving any benefit referred to in paragraph (3) below or from determining the amount of any such benefit.

(2) The circumstances are that by reason of the disabled person's disability (including any clinical prognosis flowing from the disability) the cost of providing any benefit referred to in paragraph (3) below is likely to be substantially greater than it would be for a comparable person without that disability.

(3) The benefits are those provided under an occupational pension scheme in respect of any of the following—

(a)   termination of service;
(b)   retirement, old age or death; or
(c)   accident, injury, sickness or invalidity.

5 Uniform rates of contributions

For the purposes of section 5 of the Act, treatment is always to be taken to be justified if an employer requires from a disabled person the same rate of contribution to an occupational pension scheme as he requires from his other employees (or from any class of his employees which includes the disabled person but which is not defined by reference to any disability), notwithstanding that the disabled person is not eligible under that scheme, for a reason related to his disability, to receive a benefit or to receive a benefit at the same rate as a comparable person to whom that reason does not apply.

6 Agricultural wages

For the purposes of section 5 of the Act—

(a)   treatment of a disabled person is to be taken to be justified to the extent that the treatment relates to a matter within the terms and conditions of a permit granted to that person under section 5 of the Agricultural Wages Act 1948 or section 5 of the Agricultural Wages (Scotland) Act 1949 (permits to incapacitated persons) and accords with those terms and conditions, and
(b)   failure to take a step otherwise required to comply with a section 6 duty is to be taken to be justified if that step would relate to a matter within the terms and conditions of the permit referred to in (a) above but would exceed the requirements of those terms and conditions.

7 Contract work

(1) Paragraph (2) below applies for the purposes of section 6 of the Act (and that section as applied by section 12(3) of the Act) where a contract worker is likely to be placed at a similar substantial disadvantage by arrangements made by or on behalf of, or premises occupied by, all or most of the principals to whom he is or might be supplied.

(2) It is reasonable for the employer to have to take such steps as are within his power as it would be reasonable for him to have to take if the arrangements were made by him or on his behalf or, as the case may be, the premises were occupied by him.

(3) For the purposes of section 6 of the Act (and that section as applied by section 12(3) of the Act) it is not reasonable for any principal to whom a contract worker is supplied to

have to take any step which it is reasonable for the employer to have to take pursuant to paragraph (2) above or otherwise.

8 Building regulations

(1) This regulation applies only to a physical characteristic included within building works which—

    (a)   was adopted with a view to meeting the requirements for the time being of—
        (i) (in England and Wales) Part M of the building regulations, and
        (ii) (in Scotland) Part T of the Technical Standards,
        with regard to access and facilities for disabled people, and
    (b)   met those requirements at the time the building works were carried out and continues substantially to meet those requirements which applied at the time the building works were carried out.

(2) For the purposes of section 6(1) of the Act it is never reasonable for an employer to have to take steps in relation to a disabled person to the extent that this would involve altering any physical characteristic to which this regulation applies.

9 Physical features

For the purposes of section 6(1) of the Act the following are to be treated as physical features (whether permanent or temporary)—

    (a)   any feature arising from the design or construction of a building on the premises;
    (b)   any feature on the premises of any approach to, exit from or access to such a building;
    (c)   any fixtures, fittings, furnishings, furniture, equipment or materials in or on the premises;
    (d)   any other physical element or quality of any land comprised in the premises.

10 Consent to an adjustment

(1) For the purposes of section 6(1) of the Act where under any binding obligation the employer is required to obtain the consent of any person to any alteration of the premises occupied by him it is always reasonable for the employer to have to take steps to obtain that consent and it is never reasonable for the employer to have to make that alteration before that consent is obtained.

(2) The steps referred to in paragraph (1) above shall not be taken to include an application to a court or tribunal.

11 Lessor withholding consent

(1) For the purposes of section 16 of and Part I of Schedule 4 to the Act a lessor is to be taken to have withheld his consent to an alteration where he has received a written application by or on behalf of the occupier for consent to make the alteration and has failed to meet the requirements specified in paragraph (2) below.

(2) The requirements are that the lessor within a period of 21 days (beginning with the day on which he receives the application referred to in paragraph (1) above) or such longer period as is reasonable—

(a)   replies consenting to or refusing the application, or

(b)   (i) replies consenting to the application subject to obtaining the consent of another person required under a superior lease or pursuant to a binding obligation, and

        (ii) seeks that consent.

(3) A lessor who fails to meet the requirements in paragraph (2) above but who subsequently meets those requirements (except as to time)—

(a)   shall be taken to have withheld his consent from the date of such failure, and

(b)   shall be taken not to have withheld his consent from the time he met those requirements (except as to time).

(4) For the purposes of this regulation, a lessor is to be treated as not having sought another person's consent unless he has applied in writing to that person, indicating—

(i)   that the lessor's consent to the alteration has been applied for in order to comply with a section 6 duty, and

(ii)   that he has given his consent conditionally upon obtaining the other person's consent.

12 Lessor withholding consent unreasonably

For the purposes of section 16 of and Part I of Schedule 4 to the Act, a lessor is to be taken to have withheld his consent unreasonably where—

(a)   the lease provides that consent shall or will be given to an alteration of the kind in question; or

(b)   the lease provides that consent shall or will be given to an alteration of the kind in question if the consent is sought in a particular way and the consent has been sought in that way; or

(c)   the lessor is to be taken to have withheld his consent by virtue of regulation 11 above.

13 Lessor withholding consent reasonably

(1) For the purposes of section 16 of and Part I of Schedule 4 to the Act a lessor is to be taken to have acted reasonably in withholding his consent where—

(a)   there is a binding obligation requiring the consent of any person to the alteration;

(b)   he has taken steps to seek that consent; and

(c)   that consent has not been given or has been given subject to a condition making it reasonable for him to withhold his consent.

(2) For the purposes of section 16 of and Part I of Schedule 4 to the Act a lessor is to be taken to have acted reasonably in withholding his consent where—

(a)   he is bound by an agreement which allows him to consent to the alteration in question subject to a condition that he makes a payment, and

(b)   that condition does not permit the lessor to make his own consent subject to a condition that the occupier reimburse him the payment.

14 Lessor's consent subject to conditions

(1) For the purposes of section 16 of and Part I of Schedule 4 to the Act a condition subject to which a lessor has given his consent is to be taken to be reasonable in all circumstances if it is any of the following (or a condition to similar effect)—

(a)   that the occupier must obtain any necessary planning permission and any other consent or permission required by or under any enactment;

(b)   that the occupier must submit any plans or specifications for the alteration to the lessor for approval (provided that the condition binds the lessor not to withhold approval unreasonably) and that the work is carried out in accordance with such plans or specifications;

(c)   that the lessor must be permitted a reasonable opportunity to inspect the work when completed; and

(d)   that the occupier must repay to the lessor the costs reasonably incurred in connection with the giving of his consent.

(2) For the purposes of section 16 of and Part I of Schedule 4 to the Act in a case where it would be reasonable for the lessor to withhold consent, a condition that upon expiry of the lease the occupier (or any assignee or successor) must reinstate any relevant part of the premises which is to be altered to its state before the alteration was made is to be taken as reasonable.

15 Steps contrary to the terms of the lease

For the purposes of section 6 of the Act it is not reasonable for an employer to have to take a step in relation to premises occupied by him which would otherwise be required in order to comply with a section 6 duty and which is contrary to the terms of any lease under which he occupies those premises if—

(a)   he has applied to the lessor in writing to take the step,

(b)   he has indicated in writing that he proposes to take the step, subject to that consent, in order to comply with a section 6 duty,

(c)   the lessor has withheld that consent, and

(d)   the occupier has informed the disabled person that he has applied for the consent of the lessor and that the lessor has withheld it.

The Disability Discrimination (Services and Premises) Regulations 1996

SI 1996/1836

1 Citation, commencement and interpretation

(1) These Regulations may be cited as the Disability Discrimination (Services and Premises) Regulations 1996 and shall come into force on 2nd December 1996.

(2) In these Regulations—

'the Act' means the Disability Discrimination Act 1995;
'incepted' refers to the time when the liability to risk of an insurer under a policy of insurance commenced;
'insurance business' has the same meaning as in the Insurance Companies Act 1982;
'insurer' means an insurance company as defined in section 96 of the Insurance Companies Act 1982.

(3) In these Regulations, unless the context otherwise requires, a reference—

(a) to a numbered regulation is to the regulation in these Regulations bearing that number;
(b) in a regulation to a numbered paragraph is to the paragraph in that regulation bearing that number;
(c) in a paragraph to a lettered or numbered sub-paragraph is to the sub-paragraph in that paragraph bearing that letter or number.

2 Circumstances in which less favourable treatment is justified: insurance

(1) Where, for a reason which relates to the disabled person's disability, a provider of services treats a disabled person less favourably than he treats or would treat others to whom that reason does not or would not apply, that treatment shall be taken to be justified for the purposes of section 20 of the Act in the circumstances specified in paragraph (2).

(2) The circumstances referred to in paragraph (1) are that the less favourable treatment is—

(a) in connection with insurance business carried on by the provider of services;
(b) based upon information (for example, actuarial or statistical data or a medical report) which is relevant to the assessment of the risk to be insured and is from a source on which it is reasonable to rely; and
(c) reasonable having regard to the information relied upon and any other relevant factors.

3 Existing policies of insurance: transitional provisions

(1) Subject to paragraph (2), and except where regulation 4 applies, where, for a reason which relates to the disabled person's disability, a provider of services treats a

disabled person less favourably than he treats or would treat others to whom that reason does not or would not apply, that treatment shall be taken to be justified for the purposes of section 20 of the Act if the treatment is in connection with insurance business carried on by the provider of services and relates to an existing policy.

(2) Subject to paragraph (3), where an existing policy is due to be renewed, or the terms of such a policy are due to be reviewed, on or after 2nd December 1996, any less favourable treatment which occurs on or after the date that the review or renewal is due shall not be taken to be justified under paragraph (1).

(3) A review of an existing policy which is part of, or incidental to, a general reassessment by the provider of services of the pricing structure for a group of policies shall not be treated as a review for the purposes of paragraph (2).

(4) In this regulation 'an existing policy' means a policy of insurance which incepted before 2nd December 1996.

4 Cover documents and master policies: transitional provisions

(1) Subject to paragraphs (2) and (3), where, for a reason which relates to the disabled person's disability, a provider of services treats a disabled person less favourably than he treats or would treat others to whom that reason does not or would not apply, that treatment shall be taken to be justified for the purposes of section 20 of the Act if the treatment is in connection with insurance business carried on by the provider of services and—

(a)   results in a refusal to issue a cover document to or in respect of the disabled person, and the refusal occurs before 2nd December 1997; or
(b)   relates to a cover document which incepted before 2nd December 1997.

(2) Paragraph (1) does not apply in a case where—

(a)   the relevant master policy was entered into or renewed on or after 2nd December 1996; or
(b)   the terms of the relevant master policy were reviewed on or after 2nd December 1996,
and for this purpose 'the relevant master policy' means the master policy under which the cover document was issued, or under which a cover document would have been issued but for the refusal to issue it.

(3) Where a cover document is due to be renewed, or the terms of a cover document are due to be reviewed, on or after 2nd December 1997, any less favourable treatment which occurs on or after the date that the review or renewal is due shall not be taken to be justified under paragraph (1).

(4) In this regulation—

'cover document' means a certificate or policy issued under a master policy;
'master policy' means a contract between an insurer and another person under which that person is entitled to issue certificates or policies to individuals, and which details the terms on which that person may do so.

5 Circumstances in which less favourable treatment is justified: guarantees

(1) Where, for a reason which relates to the disabled person's disability, a provider of services ('the provider') treats a disabled person less favourably than he treats or would treat others to whom that reason does not or would not apply, that treatment shall be taken to be justified for the purposes of section 20 of the Act in the circumstances specified in paragraph (2).

(2) The circumstances referred to in paragraph (1) are that—

(a) the provider provides a guarantee (whether or not legally enforceable) that—
   (i) the purchase price of services that he has provided will be refunded if the services are not of satisfactory quality; or
   (ii) services in the form of goods that he has provided will be replaced or repaired if those goods are not of satisfactory quality; and
(b) the provider refuses to provide a replacement, repair or refund under the guarantee because damage has occurred for a reason which relates to the disabled person's disability, and the damage is above the level at which the provider would normally provide a replacement, repair or refund under the guarantee; and
(c) it is reasonable in all the circumstances of the case for the provider to refuse to provide a replacement, repair or refund under the guarantee.

(3) In this regulation 'guarantee' includes any document having the effect referred to in paragraph (2)(a) whether or not that document is described as a guarantee by the provider.

6 Circumstances in which less favourable treatment is justified: deposits in respect of goods and facilities

(1) Where, for a reason which relates to the disabled person's disability, a provider of services ('the provider') treats a disabled person less favourably than he treats or would treat others to whom that reason does not or would not apply, that treatment shall be taken to be justified for the purposes of section 20 of the Act in the circumstances specified in paragraph (2).

(2) The circumstances referred to in paragraph (1) are that—

(a) when goods or facilities are provided, the disabled person is required to provide a deposit which is refundable if the goods or facilities are undamaged; and
(b) the provider refuses to refund some or all of the deposit because damage has occurred to the goods or facilities for a reason which relates to the disabled person's disability, and the damage is above the level at which the provider would normally refund the deposit in full; and
(c) it is reasonable in all the circumstances of the case for the provider to refuse to refund the deposit in full.

7 Circumstances in which less favourable treatment is justified: deposits in respect of premises

(1) Where, for a reason which relates to the disabled person's disability, a person with power to dispose of any premises ('the provider') treats a disabled person less favourably than he treats or would treat others to whom that reason does not or would not apply,

that treatment shall be taken to be justified for the purposes of section 24 of the Act in the circumstances specified in paragraph (2).

(2) The circumstances referred to in paragraph (1) are that—

(a)   the provider grants a disabled person a right to occupy premises (whether by means of a formal tenancy agreement or otherwise);

(b)   in respect of that occupation the disabled person is required to provide a deposit which is refundable at the end of the occupation provided that the premises and contents are not damaged;

(c)   the provider refuses to refund some or all of the deposit because the premises or contents have been damaged for a reason which relates to the disabled person's disability, and the damage is above the level at which the provider would normally refund the deposit in full; and

(d)   it is reasonable in all the circumstances of the case for the provider to refuse to refund the deposit in full.

8 Mental incapacity

Section 20(4)(b) of the Act (treatment justified where disabled person is incapable of entering into an enforceable agreement or giving informed consent) shall not apply where a disabled person is acting through another person by virtue of—

(a)   a power of attorney; or

(b)   functions conferred by or under Part VII of the Mental Health Act 1983; or

(c)   powers exercisable in Scotland in relation to the disabled person's property or affairs in consequence of the appointment of a curator bonis, tutor or judicial factor.

9 Exemption from sections 19 to 21 of the Act for certain educational services

(1) Sections 19 to 21 of the Act shall not apply to the following services (insofar as they do not fall within section 19(5)(a) of the Act)—

(a)   services provided by a local education authority in carrying out their functions under section 41 or 53 of the Education Act 1944 or by an education authority in carrying out their functions under section 1(3) of the Education (Scotland) Act 1980;

(b)   the provision by a voluntary organisation of social, cultural and recreational activities and facilities for physical education and training, where such activities are designed to promote the personal or educational development of persons taking part in them;

(c)   the provision of facilities for research (including the supervision of or guidance of research) at any relevant establishment;

(d)   the assessment at a relevant establishment—

    (i)   of pupils or students in connection with education provided to them by the establishment or by another relevant establishment; or

    (ii)   of pupils or students to whom education has not been provided by the establishment where the assessment is undertaken as part of an assessment referred to in head (i) above.

(2) In this regulation 'relevant establishment' means—

    (a)   an establishment which is funded by a body mentioned in paragraphs (a) to (k) of section 19(6) of the Act or by a Minister of the Crown; or

    (b)   an establishment referred to in section 19(5)(a)(ii) of the Act.

Appendix III

Department for Education and Employment Guidance and Codes of Practice

DOCUMENT 1

Guidance on matters to be taken into account in determining questions relating to the definition of disability

CONTENTS

Status and purpose of the guidance

This guidance is issued by the Secretary of State under section 3 of the Disability Discrimination Act 1995. It concerns the definition of disability in the Act. Section 3 of the Act enables the Secretary of State to issue guidance about matters to be taken into account in determining whether an impairment has a **substantial adverse effect** on a person's ability to carry out normal day-to-day activities and/or whether an impairment has a **long-term effect**. The guidance may give examples.

This guidance does not impose any legal obligations in itself, nor is it an authoritative statement of the law. However, section 3(3) of the Act requires that an industrial tribunal or a court, which is determining for any purpose of the Act whether a person's impairment has a substantial and long-term adverse effect on his or her ability to carry out normal day-to-day activities, must take into account any of this guidance which appears to it to be relevant.

Part I Introduction

Using the guidance

1.   Although this guidance is primarily designed for courts and tribunals, it is likely to be of value to a range of people and organisations. **In the vast majority of cases there is unlikely to be any doubt whether or not a person has or has had a disability, but this guidance should prove helpful in cases where it is not clear.**

2.   The definition of disability has a number of elements. The guidance covers each of these elements in turn. Each section contains an explanation of the relevant provisions of the Act which supplement the basic definition; guidance and examples are provided where relevant. Those using this guidance for the first time may wish to read it all, as each part of the guidance builds upon the part(s) preceding it.

3.   Part II of this guidance relates to matters to be taken into account when considering whether an effect is substantial and/or long term. Most of the examples are to be found here, and particularly in **Section C**. Because the purpose of this guidance is to help in the cases where there is doubt, examples of cases where there will not be any doubt are not included.

4.   Throughout the guidance descriptions of the provisions in the legislation are immediately preceded by bold italic text. They are immediately followed by a reference to the relevant provision of the Act or Regulations. References to sections of the Act are marked *"S"*; references to schedules are marked *"Sch"*; and references to paragraphs in schedules are marked *"Para"*. References in footnotes to "Definition Regulations" mean The Disability Discrimination (Meaning of Disability) Regulations 1996.

Main elements of the definition of disability

5.   *The Act defines* "disabled person" as a person with "**a physical or mental impairment which has a substantial and long-term adverse effect on his ability to carry out normal day-to-day activities**" *(S1)*.

6.   This means that:

■   the person must have an *impairment,* that is either physical or mental (see paragraphs 10–15 below);

■   the impairment must have adverse effects which are *substantial* (see **Section A**);

- the substantial effects must be *long-term* (see **Section B**); and

- the long-term substantial effects must be *adverse* effects on *normal day-to-day activities* (see **Section C**).

This definition is subject to the provisions in Schedule 1 *(Sch1)*.

Inclusion of people who have had a disability in the past

7.   ***The Act says*** that Part I of the Act (definition), Part II (employment) and Part III (goods, facilities, services and premises) also apply in relation to a person who has had a disability as defined in paragraphs 5 and 6 above. For this purpose, those Parts of the Act are subject to the provisions in Schedule 2 to the Act *(S2, Sch2)*.

Exclusions from the definition

8.   Certain conditions are not to be regarded as impairments for the purposes of the Act. These are:

- addiction to or dependency on alcohol, nicotine, or any other substance (other than in consequence of the substance being medically prescribed);

- the condition known as seasonal allergic rhinitis (e.g. hayfever), except where it aggravates the effect of another condition;

- tendency to set fires;

- tendency to steal;

- tendency to physical or sexual abuse of other persons;

- exhibitionism;

- voyeurism.

Also, disfigurements which consist of a tattoo (which has not been removed), non-medical body piercing, or something attached though such piercing, are to be treated as not having a substantial adverse effect on the person's ability to carry-out normal day-to-day activities.[1]

Registered disabled people

9.   The introduction of the employment provisions in the Act coincides with the abolition of the Quota scheme which operated under the Disabled Persons (Employment) Act 1944. ***The Disability Discrimination Act says*** that anyone who was registered as a disabled person under the Disabled Persons (Employment) Act 1944 and whose name appeared on

1   Definition Regulations

the register both on 12 January 1995 and on 2 December 1996 (the date the employment provisions come into force) is to be treated as having a disability for the purposes of the Disability Discrimination Act during the period of three years starting on 2 December 1996. This applies regardless of whether the person otherwise meets the definition of "disabled person" during that period. Those who are treated by this provision as being disabled for the three-year period are also to be treated after this period has ended as having had a disability in the past *(Sch1, Para 7)*.

Impairment

10.   The definition requires that the effects which a person may experience arise from a physical or mental impairment. In many cases there will be no dispute whether a person has an impairment. Any disagreement is more likely to be about whether the effects of the impairment are sufficient to fall within the definition. Even so, it may sometimes be necessary to decide whether a person has an impairment so as to be able to deal with the issues about its effects.

11.   It is not necessary to consider how an impairment was caused, even if the cause is a consequence of a condition which is excluded. For example, liver disease as a result of alcohol dependency would count as an impairment.

12.   *Physical or mental impairment* includes sensory impairments, such as those affecting sight or hearing.

13.   *Mental impairment* includes a wide range of impairments relating to mental functioning, including what are often known as learning disabilities (formerly known as "mental handicap"). However, **the Act states** that it does not include any impairment resulting from or consisting of a mental illness unless that illness is a clinically well-recognised illness *(Sch1, Para 1)*.

14.   *A clinically well-recognised illness* is a mental illness which is recognised by a respected body of medical opinion. It is very likely that this would include those specifically mentioned in publications such as the World Health Organisation's International Classification of Diseases.

15.   **The Act states** that mental impairment does not have the special meaning used in the Mental Health Act 1983 or the Mental Health (Scotland) Act 1984, although this does not preclude a mental impairment within the meaning of that legislation from coming within the definition in the Disability Discrimination Act *(S68)*.

Part II Guidance on matters to be taken into account in determining questions relating to the definition of disability

A   Substantial

Meaning of "substantial" adverse effect

A1. The requirement that an adverse effect be substantial reflects the general understanding of "disability" as a limitation going beyond the normal differences in ability which may exist among people. A "substantial" effect is more than would be produced by the sort of physical or mental conditions experienced by many people which have only minor effects. A "substantial" effect is one which is more than "minor" or "trivial".

The time taken to carry out an activity

A2. The time taken by a person with an impairment to carry out a normal day-to-day activity should be considered when assessing whether the effect of that impairment is substantial. It should be compared with the time that might be expected if the person did not have the impairment.

The way in which an activity is carried out

A3. Another factor to be considered when assessing whether the effect of an impairment is substantial is the way in which a person with that impairment carries out a normal day-to-day activity. The comparison should be with the way the person might be expected to carry out the activity if he or she did not have the impairment.

Cumulative effects of an impairment

A4. **The Act provides** that an impairment is to be taken to affect the ability of a person to carry out normal day-to-day activities only if it affects that person in one (or more) of the respects listed in paragraph C4 **(Sch1, Para 4)**. An impairment might not have a substantial adverse effect on a person in any one of these respects, but its effects in more than one of these respects taken together could result in a substantial adverse effect on the person's ability to carry out normal day-to-day activities.

A5. For example, although the great majority of people with cerebral palsy will experience a number of substantial effects, someone with mild cerebral palsy may experience minor effects in a number of the respects listed in paragraph C4 which together could create substantial adverse effects on a range of normal day-to-day activities: fatigue may hinder walking, visual perception may be poor, co-ordination and balance may cause some difficulties. Similarly, a person whose impairment causes breathing difficulties may experience minor effects in a number of respects but which overall have a substantial adverse effect on their ability to carry out normal day-to-day activities. For some people, mental illness may have a clear effect in one of the respects in C4. However, for others, depending on the extent of the condition, there may be effects in a number of different respects which, taken together, substantially adversely affect their ability to carry out normal day-to-day activities.

A6.   A person may have more than one impairment, any one of which alone would not have a substantial effect. In such a case, account should be taken of whether the impairments together have a substantial effect overall on the person's ability to carry out normal day-to-day activities. For example a minor impairment which affects physical co-ordination and an irreversible but minor injury to a leg which affects mobility, taken together, might have a substantial effect on the person's ability to carry out certain normal day-to-day activities.

Effects of behaviour

A7.   Account should be taken of how far a person can reasonably be expected to modify behaviour to prevent or reduce the effects of an impairment on normal day-to-day activities. If a person can behave in such a way that the impairment ceases to have a substantial adverse effect on his or her ability to carry out normal day-to-day activities the person would no longer meet the definition of disability.

A8.   In some cases people have such "coping" strategies which cease to work in certain circumstances (for example, where someone who stutters or has dyslexia is placed under stress). If it is possible that a person's ability to manage the effects of an impairment will break down so that effects will sometimes still occur, this possibility must be taken into account when assessing the effects of the impairment.

A9.   If a disabled person is advised by a medical practitioner to behave in a certain way in order to reduce the impact of the disability, that might count as treatment to be disregarded (see paragraph A11 below).

Effects of environment

A10. Whether adverse effects are substantial may depend on environmental conditions which may vary; for example, the temperature, humidity, the time of day or night, how tired the person is or how much stress he or she is under may have an impact on the effects. When assessing whether adverse effects are substantial, the extent to which such environmental factors are likely to have an impact should also therefore be considered.

Effects of treatment

A11. **The Act provides** that where an impairment is being *treated or corrected* the impairment is to be treated as having the effect it would have without the measures in question **(Sch1, Para 6(1))**. **The Act states** that the treatment or correction measures to be disregarded for these purposes include medical treatment and the use of a prosthesis or other aid **(Sch1, Para 6(2))**.

A12. This applies even if the measures result in the effects being completely under control or not at all apparent.

A13. For example, if a person with a hearing impairment wears a hearing aid the question whether his or her impairment has a substantial adverse effect is to be decided by reference to what the hearing level would be without the hearing aid. And in the case of someone with diabetes, whether or not the effect is substantial should be decided by reference to what the condition would be if he or she was not taking medication.

A14. However, **the Act states** that this provision does not apply to sight impairments to the extent that they are capable of correction by spectacles or contact lenses. In other words the only effects on ability to carry out normal day-to-day activities to be considered are those which remain when spectacles or contact lenses are used (or would remain if they were used). This does not include the use of devices to correct sight which are not spectacles or contact lenses **(Sch1, Para 6(3))**.

Progressive conditions

A15. A progressive condition is one which is likely to change and develop over time. **The Act gives** the following examples of progressive conditions: cancer, multiple sclerosis, muscular dystrophy, HIV infection. **The Act provides** for a person with such a condition to be regarded as having an impairment which has a substantial adverse effect on his or her ability to carry out normal day-to-day activities before it actually does so. Where a person has a progressive condition, he or she will be treated as having an impairment which has a *substantial* adverse effect from the moment any impairment resulting from that condition first has *some* effect on ability to carry out normal day-to-day activities. The effect need not be continuous and need not be substantial. For this rule to operate medical diagnosis of the condition is not by itself enough **(Sch1, Para 8)**.

Severe disfigurements

A16. **The Act provides** that where an impairment consists of a severe disfigurement, it is to be treated as having a substantial adverse effect on the person's ability to carry out normal day-to-day activities. There is no need to demonstrate such an effect **(Sch1, Para 3)**. **Regulations** *provide* that a disfigurement which consists of a tattoo (which has not been removed) is not to be considered as a severe disfigurement. Also excluded is a piercing of the body for decorative purposes including anything attached through the piercing.[2]

A17. Examples of disfigurements include scars, birthmarks, limb or postural deformation or diseases of the skin. Assessing severity will be mainly a matter of the degree of the disfigurement. However, it may be necessary to take account of where the feature in question is (e.g. on the back as opposed to the face).

B   Long term

Meaning of long-term effects
B1. *The Act states* that, for the purpose of deciding whether a person is disabled, a long-term effect of an impairment is one:

■ which has lasted at least twelve months; or

■ where the total period for which it lasts, from the time of the first onset, is likely to be at least twelve months; or

■ which is likely to last for the rest of the life of the person affected *(Sch1, Para 2)*.

For the purpose of deciding whether a person has had a disability in the past, a long-term effect of an impairment is one which lasted at least 12 months *(Sch2, Para 5)*.

B2.   It is not necessary for the effect to be the same throughout the relevant period. It may change, as where activities which are initially very difficult become possible to a much greater extent. The main adverse effect might even disappear – or it might disappear temporarily – while one or other effects on ability to carry out normal day-to-day activities continue or develop. Provided the impairment continues to have, or is likely to have, such an effect throughout the period, there is a long-term effect.

Recurring effects
B3. *The Act states* that if an impairment has had a substantial adverse effect on a person's ability to carry out normal day-to-day activities but that effect ceases, the substantial effect is treated as continuing if it is likely to recur; that is, it is more likely than not that the effect will recur. (In deciding whether a person has had a disability in the past, the question is whether a substantial adverse effect has in fact recurred.) Conditions which recur only sporadically or for short periods (e.g. epilepsy) can still

2   Definition Regulations

qualify. *(Sch1, Para 2(2), Sch2, Para 5)*. **Regulations specifically exclude** seasonal allergic rhinitis (e.g. hayfever) from this category, except where it aggravates the effects of an existing condition.[3]

B4.   For example, a person with rheumatoid arthritis may experience effects from the first occurrence for a few weeks and then have a period of remission. But, if the effects are likely to recur, they are to be treated as if they were continuing. If the effects are likely to recur beyond twelve months after the first occurrence, they are to be treated as long-term.

B5.   Likelihood of recurrence should be considered taking all the circumstances of the case into account. This should include what the person could reasonably be expected to do to prevent the recurrence; for example, the person might reasonably be expected to take action which prevents the impairment from having such effects (e.g. avoiding substances to which he or she is allergic). This may be unreasonably difficult with some substances. In addition, it is possible that the way in which a person can control or cope with the effects of a condition may not always be successful because, for example, a routine is not followed or the person is in an unfamiliar environment. If there is an increased likelihood that the control will break down, it will be more likely that there will be a recurrence. That possibility should be taken into account when assessing the likelihood of a recurrence.

Effects of treatment

B6.   If medical or other treatment is likely to cure an impairment, so that recurrence of its effects would then be unlikely even if there were no further treatment, this should be taken into consideration when looking at the likelihood of recurrence of those effects. However, as **Section A** describes, if the treatment simply delays or prevents a recurrence, and a recurrence would be likely if the treatment stopped, then the treatment is to be ignored and the effect is to be regarded as likely to recur.

Meaning of "likely"

B7.   It is *likely* that an event will happen if it is more probable than not that it will happen.

B8.   In assessing the likelihood of an effect lasting for any period, account should be taken of the total period for which the effect exists. This includes any time before the point when the discriminatory behaviour occurred as well as time afterwards. Account should also be taken of both the typical length of such an effect on an individual, and any relevant factors specific to this individual (for example, general state of health, age).

3   Definition Regulations

Assessing whether a past disability was long-term

B9. ***The Act provides that*** a person who has had a disability within the definition is protected from discrimination even if he or she has since recovered or the effects have become less than substantial. In deciding whether a past condition was a disability, its effects count as long-term if they lasted twelve months or more after the first occurrence, or if a recurrence happened or continued until more than twelve months after the first occurrence ***(S2, Sch2, Para 5)***.

C   Normal day-to-day activities

Meaning of "normal day-to-day activities"

C1. ***The Act states*** that an impairment must have a long-term substantial adverse effect on normal day-to-day activities ***(S1)***.

C2.   The term "normal day-to-day activities" is not intended to include activities which are normal only for a particular person or group of people. Therefore in deciding whether an activity is a "normal day-to-day activity" account should be taken of how far it is normal for most people and carried out by most people on a daily or frequent and fairly regular basis.

C3.   The term "normal day-to-day activities" does not, for example, include work of any particular form, because no particular form of work is "normal" for most people. In any individual case, the activities carried out might be highly specialised. The same is true of playing a particular game, taking part in a particular hobby, playing a musical instrument, playing sport, or performing a highly skilled task. Impairments which affect only such an activity and have no effect on "normal day-to-day activities" are not covered. The examples included in this section give an indication of what are to be taken as normal day-to-day activities.

C4. ***The Act states*** that an impairment is only to be treated as affecting the person's ability to carry out *normal day-to-day activities* if it affects one of the following:

- mobility;
- manual dexterity;
- physical co-ordination;
- continence;
- ability to lift, carry or otherwise move everyday objects;
- speech, hearing or eyesight;
- memory or ability to concentrate, learn or understand; or
- perception of the risk of physical danger ***(Sch1, Para 4)***.

C5.　In many cases an impairment will adversely affect the person's ability to carry out a range of normal day-to-day activities and it will be obvious that the overall adverse effect is substantial or the effect on at least one normal day-to-day activity is substantial. In such a case it is unnecessary to consider precisely how the person is affected in each of the respects listed in paragraph C4. For example, a person with a clinically well-recognised mental illness may experience an adverse effect on concentration which prevents the person from remembering why he or she is going somewhere; the person would not also have to demonstrate that there was an effect on, say, speech. A person with an impairment which has an adverse effect on sight might be unable to go shopping unassisted; he or she would not also have to demonstrate that there was an effect on, say, mobility.

C6.　Many impairments will, by their nature, adversely affect a person directly in one of the respects listed in C4. An impairment may also indirectly affect a person in one or more of these respects, and this should be taken into account when assessing whether the impairment falls within the definition. For example:

- ■ medical advice: where a person has been professionally advised to change, limit or refrain from a normal day-to-day activity on account of an impairment or only do it in a certain way or under certain conditions;

- ■ pain or fatigue: where an impairment causes pain or fatigue in performing normal day-to-day activities, so the person may have the capacity to do something but suffer pain in doing so; or the impairment might make the activity more than usually fatiguing so that the person might not be able to repeat the task over a sustained period of time.

C7.　Where a person has a mental illness such as depression account should be taken of whether, although that person has the physical ability to perform a task, he or she is, in practice, unable to sustain an activity over a reasonable period.

C8.　Effects of impairments may not be apparent in babies and young children because they are too young to have developed the ability to act in the respects listed in C4. *Regulations provide* that where an impairment to a child under six years old does not have an effect in any of the respects in C4, it is to be treated as having a substantial and long-term adverse effect on the ability of that child to carry out normal day-to-day activities where it would normally have a substantial and long-term adverse effect on the ability of a person aged six years or over to carry out normal day-to-day activities.[4]

4　Definition Regulations

C9. In deciding whether an effect on the ability to carry out a normal day-to-day activity is a substantial adverse effect, account should be taken of factors such as those mentioned under each heading below. The headings are exhaustive – the person must be affected in one of these respects. The lists of examples are not exhaustive; they are only meant to be illustrative. The assumption is made in each example that there is an adverse effect on the person's ability to carry out normal day-to-day activities. A person only counts as disabled if the substantial effect is adverse.

C10. The examples below of what it would, and what it would not, be reasonable to regard as substantial adverse effects are indicators and not tests. They do not mean that if a person can do an activity listed then he or she does not experience any substantial adverse effects; the person may be inhibited in other activities, and this instead may indicate a substantial effect.

C11. In reading examples of effects which it would not be reasonable to regard as substantial, the effect described should be thought of as if it were the only effect of the impairment. That is, if the effect listed in the example were the only effect it would not be reasonable to regard it as substantial in itself.

C12. Examples of effects which are obviously within the definition are not included below. So for example, inability to dress oneself, inability to stand up, severe dyslexia or a severe speech impairment would clearly be covered by the definition and are not included among the examples below. The purpose of these lists is to provide help in cases where there may be doubt as to whether the effects on normal day-to-day activities are substantial.

C13. The examples below describe the effect which would occur when the various factors described in Parts A and B above have been allowed for. This includes, for example the effects of a person making such modifications of behaviour as might reasonably be expected, or of disregarding the impact of medical or other treatment.

Mobility
C14. This covers moving or changing position in a wide sense. Account should be taken of the extent to which, because of either a physical or a mental condition, a person is inhibited in getting around unaided or using a normal means of transport, in leaving home with or without assistance, in walking a short distance, climbing stairs, travelling in a car or completing a journey on public transport, sitting, standing, bending, or reaching, or getting around in an unfamiliar place.

Examples
___

It **would be reasonable** to regard as having a substantial adverse effect:

- ■ inability to travel a short journey as a passenger in a vehicle;

- ■ inability to walk other than at a slow pace or with unsteady or jerky movements;

- ■ difficulty in going up or down steps, stairs or gradients;

- ■ inability to use one or more forms of public transport;

- ■ inability to go out of doors unaccompanied.

It **would not be reasonable** to regard as having a substantial adverse effect:

- ■ difficulty walking unaided a distance of about 1.5 kilometres or a mile without discomfort or having to stop – the distance in question would obviously vary according to the age of the person concerned and the type of terrain;

- ■ inability to travel in a car for a journey lasting more than two hours without discomfort.

Manual dexterity

C15. This covers the ability to use hands and fingers with precision. Account should be taken of the extent to which a person can manipulate the fingers on each hand or co-ordinate the use of both hands together to do a task. This includes the ability to do things like pick up or manipulate small objects, operate a range of equipment manually, or communicate through writing or typing on standard machinery. Loss of function in the dominant hand would be expected to have a greater effect than equivalent loss in the non-dominant hand.

Examples
___

It **would be reasonable** to regard as having a substantial adverse effect:

- ■ loss of function in one or both hands such that the person cannot use the hand or hands;

- ■ inability to handle a knife and fork at the same time;

- ■ ability to press the buttons on keyboards or keypads but only much more slowly than is normal for most people.

It **would not be reasonable** to regard as having a substantial adverse effect:

- inability to undertake activities requiring delicate hand movements, such as threading a small needle;
- inability to reach typing speeds standardised for secretarial work;
- inability to pick up a single small item, such as a pin.

Physical co-ordination

C16. This covers balanced and effective interaction of body movement, including hand and eye co-ordination. In the case of a child, it is necessary to take account of the level of achievement which would be normal for a person of the particular age. In any case, account should be taken of the ability to carry out "composite" activities such as walking and using hands at the same time.

Examples

It **would be reasonable** to regard as having a substantial adverse effect:

- ability to pour liquid into another vessel only with unusual slowness or concentration;
- inability to place food into one's own mouth with fork/spoon without unusual concentration or assistance.

It **would not be reasonable** to regard as having a substantial adverse effect:

- mere clumsiness;
- inability to catch a tennis ball.

Continence

C17. This covers the ability to control urination and/or defecation. Account should be taken of the frequency and extent of the loss of control and the age of the individual.

Examples

It **would be reasonable** to regard as having a substantial adverse effect:

- even infrequent loss of control of the bowels;

- loss of control of the bladder while asleep at least once a month;

- frequent minor faecal incontinence or frequent minor leakage from the bladder.

It **would not be reasonable** to regard as having a substantial adverse effect:

- infrequent loss of control of the bladder while asleep;

- infrequent minor leakage from the bladder.

Ability to lift, carry or otherwise move everyday objects

C18. Account should be taken of a person's ability to repeat such functions or, for example, to bear weights over a reasonable period of time. Everyday objects might include such items as books, a kettle of water, bags of shopping, a briefcase, an overnight bag, a chair or other piece of light furniture.

Examples

It **would be reasonable** to regard as having a substantial adverse effect:

- inability to pick up objects of moderate weight with one hand

- inability to carry a moderately loaded tray steadily.

It **would not be reasonable** to regard as having a substantial adverse effect:

- inability to carry heavy luggage without assistance;

- inability to move heavy objects without a mechanical aid.

Speech, hearing or eyesight

C19. This covers the ability to speak, hear or see and includes face-to-face, telephone and written communication.

(i) Speech

Account should be taken of how far a person is able to speak clearly at a normal pace and rhythm and to understand someone else speaking normally in the person's native language. It is necessary to consider any effects on speech patterns or which impede the acquisition or processing of one's native language, for example by someone who has had a stroke.

Examples

It **would be reasonable** to regard as having a substantial adverse effect:

- inability to give clear basic instructions orally to colleagues or providers of a service;

- inability to ask specific questions to clarify instructions;

- taking significantly longer than average to say things.

It **would not be reasonable** to regard as having a substantial adverse effect:

- inability to articulate fluently due to a minor stutter, lisp or speech impediment;

- inability to speak in front of an audience;

- having a strong regional or foreign accent;

- inability to converse in a language which is not the speaker's native language.

(ii) Hearing

If a person uses a hearing aid or similar device, what needs to be considered is the effect that would be experienced if the person were not using the hearing aid or device. Account should be taken of effects where the level of background noise is within such a range and of such a type that most people would be able to hear adequately.

Examples

It would be reasonable to regard as having a substantial adverse effect:

- inability to hold a conversation with someone talking in a normal voice in a moderately noisy environment;
- inability to hear and understand another person speaking clearly over the voice telephone.

It would not be reasonable to regard as having a substantial adverse effect:

- inability to hold a conversation in a very noisy place, such as a factory floor;
- inability to sing in tune.

(iii) Eyesight

If a person's sight is corrected by spectacles or contact lenses, or could be corrected by them, what needs to be considered is the effect remaining while they are wearing such spectacles or lenses, in light of a level and type normally acceptable to most people for normal day-to-day activities.

Examples

It would be reasonable to regard as having a substantial adverse effect:

- inability to see to pass the eyesight test for a standard driving test;
- inability to recognise by sight a known person across a moderately-sized room;
- total inability to distinguish colours;
- inability to read ordinary newsprint;
- inability to walk safely without bumping into things.

It would not be reasonable to regard as having a substantial adverse effect:

- inability to read very small or indistinct print without the aid of a magnifying glass;
- inability to distinguish a known person across a substantial distance (e.g. playing field);
- inability to distinguish between red and green.

Memory or ability to concentrate, learn or understand

C20. Account should be taken of the person's ability to remember, organise his or her thoughts, plan a course of action and carry it out, take in new knowledge, or understand spoken or written instructions. This includes considering whether the person learns to do things significantly more slowly than is normal. Account should be taken of whether the person has persistent and significant difficulty in reading text in standard English or straightforward numbers.

Examples

It **would be reasonable** to regard as having a substantial adverse effect:

- intermittent loss of consciousness and associated confused behaviour;

- persistent inability to remember the names of familiar people such as family or friends;

- inability to adapt after a reasonable period to minor change in work routine;

- inability to write a cheque without assistance;

- considerable difficulty in following a short sequence such as a simple recipe or a brief list of domestic tasks.

It **would not be reasonable** to regard as having a substantial adverse effect:

- occasionally forgetting the name of a familiar person, such as a colleague;

- inability to concentrate on a task requiring application over several hours;

- inability to fill in a long, detailed, technical document without assistance;

- inability to read at faster than normal speed;

- minor problems with writing or spelling.

Perception of the risk of physical danger

C21. This includes both the underestimation and overestimation of physical danger, including danger to well-being. Account should be taken, for example, of whether the person is inclined to neglect basic functions such as eating, drinking, sleeping, keeping warm or personal hygiene; reckless behaviour which puts the person or others at risk; or excessive avoidance behaviour without a good cause.

Examples

It **would be reasonable** to regard as having a substantial adverse effect:

- inability to operate safely properly-maintained equipment;

- persistent inability to cross a road safely;

- inability to nourish oneself (assuming nourishment is available);

- inability to tell by touch that an object is very hot or cold.

It **would not be reasonable** to regard as having a substantial adverse effect:

- fear of significant heights;

- underestimating the risk associated with dangerous hobbies, such as mountain climbing;

- underestimating risks – other than obvious ones – in unfamiliar workplaces.

DOCUMENT 2

Code of Practice for the elimination of discrimination in the field of employment against disabled persons or persons who have had a disability

CONTENTS

Introduction

Purpose and status of the Code

1.1   Pages 3 to 58 are a Code of Practice issued by the Secretary of State for Education and Employment under section 53 (1) (a) of the Disability Discrimination Act 1995 ("the Act"). The Code comes into effect on 2 December 1996.

1.2   The employment provisions of the Act and the Disability Discrimination (Employment) Regulations 1996 protect disabled people, and people who have been disabled, from discrimination in the field of employment. Although the Code is written in terms of "disabled" people, it also applies to people who no longer have a disability but have had one in the past. The date from which the employment provisions take effect is 2 December 1996 (but see paragraph 7.12). The Code of Practice gives practical guidance to help employers and others – including trade organisations and people who hire staff from employment businesses – in eliminating discrimination and should assist in avoiding complaints to industrial tribunals.

1.3   The Code applies in England, Scotland and Wales. It does not itself impose legal obligations and is not an authoritative statement of the law. Authoritative interpretation of the Act and regulations is for the tribunals and courts. However, the Code is admissible in evidence in any proceedings under the Act before an industrial tribunal or court. If any provision in the Code appears to the tribunal or court to be relevant to a question arising in the proceedings, it must be taken into account in determining that question.

Using the Code

1.4   The Code describes – and gives general guidance on – the main employment provisions of the Act in paragraphs 4.1 to 4. 66. More specific guidance on how these provisions operate in different situations is in later paragraphs but it may be necessary to refer back to the general guidance occasionally. For example, someone thinking of recruiting new staff will need to read paragraphs 5.1 to 5.29 and also, unless already familiar with it, the general guidance on the provisions in paragraphs 4.1 to 4.66. Someone dealing with a new or existing employee should read paragraphs 6.1 to 6.23, again with reference to the general guidance as necessary. Examples of how the Act is likely to work in practice are given in boxes (see also paragraph 3.1). Annexes 1–3 are not part of the Code but include information on related subjects. There is a detailed index at the end of the Code.

1.5   References to the legal provisions relevant to the guidance in the Code are generally just on the first, or only, main mention of a provision. For example, "S5(1)" means Section 5, subsection (1) of the Act. "Sch 1 Para 1 (1)" means Schedule 1, paragraph 1 subparagraph (1) of the Act.

1.6   References in footnotes to "Employment Regulations" mean The Disability Discrimination (Employment) Regulations 1996 and to "Definition Regulations" mean The Disability Discrimination (Meaning of Disability) Regulations 1996.

1.7   In the examples, references to male and female individual disabled people are given for realism. All other references are masculine for simplicity but could, of course, apply to either sex.

2 Who is, and who is not, covered by the employment provisions

What is the main purpose of the employment provisions of the Act?

2.1   The Act protects disabled people from discrimination in the field of employment. As part of this protection employers may have to make "reasonable adjustments" if their employment arrangements or premises place disabled people at a substantial disadvantage compared with non-disabled people. These provisions replace the quota scheme, the designated employment scheme and registration as a disabled person *(S61(7))*.

2.2   The Act does not prohibit an employer from appointing the best person for the job. Nor does it prevent employers from treating disabled people more favourably than those without a disability.

Who has rights or obligations under the Act?

2.3   Disabled people have rights under the Act, as do people who have had disabilities but have fully or largely recovered. The Act defines a disabled person as someone with a physical or mental impairment which has a substantial and long-term adverse effect on his ability to carry out normal day-to-day activities *(S1 and Sch1)*. (See Annex 1)

2.4   The following people and organisations may have obligations under the Act:

■   employers;

■   the Crown (including Government Departments and Agencies) *(S64)*;

■   employees and agents of an employer;

■   landlords of premises occupied by employers;

■   people who hire contract workers;

■   trustees or managers of occupational pension schemes;

■   people who provide group insurance schemes for an employer's employees;

■   trade organisations.

2.5   This Act does not confer rights on people who do not have – and have not had – a disability, with the exception of the provisions covering victimisation (see paragraphs 4.53 and 4.54).

Who does not have obligations or rights under the Act?

2.6   The employment provisions do not apply to employers with fewer than 20 employees *(S7)*. The Act applies when an employer has 20 or more employees in total, regardless of the size of individual workplaces or branches. However, if the number of employees falls below 20 the employer will be exempted for as long as there are fewer than 20 employees. Independent franchise holders are exempt if they employ fewer than 20 people even if the franchise network has 20 or more employees. The Government must carry out a review of the threshold for the exclusion of small firms within 5 years of the employment provisions coming into force.

2.7   The employment provisions do not apply to:

- members of the Armed Forces *(S64(7))*;

- prison officers *(S64(5)(b))*;

- firefighters *(S64(5)(c) and (6))*;

- employees who work wholly or mainly outside Great Britain *(S68(2))*;

- employees who work on board ships, aircraft or hovercraft *(S68(3))*;

- members of the Ministry of Defence Police, the British Transport Police, the Royal Parks Constabulary and the United Kingdom Atomic Energy Authority Constabulary *(S68(5)(a));* and

- other police officers who are in any event not employees as defined in *S68(1)*.

Who counts as an employee under the Act?

2.8   "Employment" means employment under a contract of service or of apprenticeship, or a contract personally to do any work *(S68)*. The last category covers persons who are self-employed and agree to perform the work personally. "Employee" means anyone whose contract is within that definition of employment, whether or not, for example, he works full-time.

3 General guidance to help avoid discrimination

Be flexible

3.1   There may be several ways to avoid discrimination in any one situation. Examples in this Code are *illustrative only*, to indicate what should or should not be done in those and other broadly similar types of situations. They cannot cover every possibility, so it is important to consider carefully how the guidance applies in any specific circumstances. **Many ways of avoiding discrimination will cost little or nothing**. The Code should not be read narrowly; for instance, its guidance on recruitment might help avoid discrimination when promoting employees.

Do not make assumptions

3.2   It will probably be helpful to talk to each disabled person about what the real effects of the disability might be or what might help. There is less chance of a dispute where the person is involved from the start. Such discussions should not, of course, be conducted in a way which would itself give the disabled person any reason to believe that he was being discriminated against.

Consider whether expert advice is needed

3.3   It is possible to avoid discrimination using personal, or in-house, knowledge and expertise, particularly if the views of the disabled person are sought. The Act does not oblige anyone to get expert advice but it could help in some circumstances to seek independent advice on the extent of a disabled person's capabilities. This might be particularly appropriate where a person is newly disabled or the effects of someone's disability become more marked. It may also help to get advice on what might be done to change premises or working arrangements, especially if discussions with the disabled person do not lead to a satisfactory solution. Annex 2 gives information about getting advice or help.

Plan ahead

3.4   Although the Act does not require an employer to make changes in anticipation of ever having a disabled applicant or employee, nevertheless when planning for change it could be cost-effective to consider the needs of a range of possible future disabled employees and applicants. There may be helpful improvements that could be built into plans. For example, a new telecommunications system might be made accessible to deaf people even if there are currently no deaf employees.

Promote equal opportunities

3.5   If an employer has an equal opportunities policy or is thinking of introducing one, it would probably help to avoid a breach of the Act if that policy covered disability issues. Employers who have, and follow, a good policy – including monitoring its effectiveness – are likely to have that counted in their favour by a tribunal if a complaint is made. But employers should remember that treating people equally will not always avoid a breach of the Act. An employer may be under a duty to make a reasonable adjustment. This could apply at any time in the recruitment process or in the course of a disabled person's employment.

4. The main employment provisions of the Act

Discrimination

What does the Act say about discrimination?

4.1   *The Act makes it unlawful* for an employer to discriminate against a disabled person in the field of employment *(S4). The Act says* "discrimination" occurs in two ways.

4.2   One way in which discrimination occurs is when:

- ■ for a reason which relates to a disabled person's disability, the employer treats that disabled person less favourably than the employer treats or would treat others to whom the reason does not or would not apply; *and*

- ■ the employer cannot show that this treatment is justified *(S5(1))*.

A woman with a disability which requires use of a wheelchair applies for a job. She can do the job but the employer thinks the wheelchair will get in the way in the office. He gives the job to a person who is no more suitable for the job but who does not use a wheelchair. The employer has therefore treated the woman *less favourably* than the other person because he did not give her the job. The treatment was *for a reason related to the disability* – the fact that she used a wheelchair. And the reason for treating her less favourably *did not apply to the other person* because that person did not use a wheelchair.

If the employer could not justify his treatment of the disabled woman then he would have unlawfully discriminated against her.

An employer decides to close down a factory and makes all the employees redundant, including a disabled person who works there. This is not discrimination as the disabled employee is not being dismissed for a reason which relates to the disability.

4.3   A disabled person may not be able to point to other people who were actually treated more favourably. However, it is still "less favourable treatment" if the employer would give better treatment to someone else to whom the reason for the treatment of the disabled person did not apply. This comparison can also be made with other disabled people, not just non-disabled people. For example, an employer might be discriminating by treating a person with a mental illness less favourably than he treats or would treat a physically disabled person.

4.4   The other way *the Act says* that discrimination occurs is when:

- an employer fails to comply with a duty of reasonable adjustment imposed on him by section 6 in relation to the disabled person; *and*

- he cannot show that this failure is justified *(S5(2))*.

4.5   The relationship between the duty of reasonable adjustment and the need to justify less favourable treatment is described in paragraphs 4.7–4.9. The duty itself is described from paragraph 4.12 onwards and the need to justify a failure to comply with it is described in paragraph 4.34.

What will, and what will not, be justified treatment?

4.6   *The Act says* that less favourable treatment of a disabled person will be justified only if the reason for it is both material to the circumstances of the particular case *and* substantial *(S5(3))*. This means that the reason has to relate to the individual circumstances in question and not just be trivial or minor.

> Someone who is blind is not shortlisted for a job involving computers because the employer thinks blind people cannot use them. The employer makes no effort to look at the individual circumstances. A general assumption that blind people cannot use computers would not in itself be a material reason – it is not related to the particular circumstances.

> A factory worker with a mental illness is sometimes away from work due to his disability. Because of that he is dismissed. However, the amount of time off is very little more than the employer accepts as sick leave for other employees and so is very unlikely to be a substantial reason.

> A clerical worker with a learning disability cannot sort papers quite as quickly as some of his colleagues. There is very little difference in productivity but he is dismissed. That is very unlikely to be a substantial reason.

> An employer seeking a clerical worker turns down an applicant with a severe facial disfigurement solely on the ground that other employees would be uncomfortable working alongside him. This will be unlawful because such a reaction by other employees will not in itself justify less favourable treatment of this sort – it is not substantial. The same would apply if it were thought that a customer would feel uncomfortable.

An employer moves someone with a mental illness to a different workplace solely because he mutters to himself while he works. If the employer accepts similar levels of noise from other people, the treatment of the disabled person would probably be unjustified – that level of noise is unlikely to be a substantial reason.

Someone who has psoriasis (a skin condition) is rejected for a job involving modelling cosmetics on a part of the body which in his case is severely disfigured by the condition. That would be lawful if his appearance would be incompatible with the purpose of the work. This is a substantial reason which is clearly related – material – to the individual circumstance.

4.7 **The Act says** that less favourable treatment cannot be justified where the employer is under a duty to make a reasonable adjustment but fails (without justification) to do so, *unless* the treatment would have been justified even after that adjustment *(S5(5))*.

An employee who uses a wheelchair is not promoted, solely because the work station for the higher post is inaccessible to wheelchairs – though it could readily be made so by rearrangement of the furniture. If the furniture had been re-arranged, the reason for refusing promotion would not have applied. The refusal of promotion would therefore not be justified.

An applicant for a typing job is not the best person on the face of it, but only because her typing speed is too slow due to arthritis in her hands. If a reasonable adjustment – perhaps an adapted keyboard – would overcome this, her typing speed would not in itself be a substantial reason for not employing her. Therefore the employer would be unlawfully discriminating if on account of her typing speed he did not employ her and provide the adjustment.

An employer refuses a training course for an employee with an illness which is very likely to be terminal within a year because, even with a reasonable adjustment to help in the job after the course, the benefits of the course could not be adequately realised. This is very likely to be a substantial reason. It is clearly material to the circumstances. The refusal of training would therefore very likely be justified.

Someone who is blind applies for a job which requires a significant amount of driving. If it is not reasonable for the employer to adjust the job so that the driving duties are given to someone else, the employer's need for a driver might well be a substantial reason for not employing the blind person. It is clearly material to the particular circumstances. The non-appointment could therefore be justified.

How does an employer avoid unlawful discrimination?

4.8   An employer should not treat a disabled employee or disabled job applicant less favourably, for a reason relating to the disability, than others to whom that reason does not apply, unless that reason is material to the particular circumstances and substantial. If the reason is material and substantial, the employer may have to make a reasonable adjustment to remove it or make it less than substantial *(S5(3) and (5))*.

4.9   Less favourable treatment is therefore justified if the disabled person cannot do the job concerned, and no adjustment which would enable the person to do the job (or another vacant job) is practicable *(S5(3) and (5))*. (See paragraph 4.20 for examples of adjustments which employers may have to make.)

4.10 *The Act says* that some charities (and Government-funded supported employment) are allowed to treat some groups of disabled people more favourably than others. But they can do this only if the group being treated more favourably is one with whom the charitable purposes of the charity are connected and the more favourable treatment is in pursuance of those purposes (or, in the case of supported employment, those treated more favourably are severely disabled people whom the programme aims to help) *(S10)*.

What does the Act say about helping others to discriminate?

4.11 *The Act says* that a person who knowingly helps another to do something made unlawful by the Act will also be treated as having done the same kind of unlawful act *(S 57(1))*.

A recruitment consultant engaged by an engineering company refuses to consider a disabled applicant for a vacancy, because the employer has told the consultant that he does not want the post filled by someone who is "handicapped". Under the Act the consultant could be liable for aiding the company.

Reasonable adjustment

What does the Act say about the duty of "reasonable adjustment"?

4.12 *The Act says* that the duty applies where any physical feature of premises occupied by the employer, or any arrangements made by or on behalf of the employer, cause a substantial disadvantage to a disabled person compared with non-disabled people. An employer has to take such steps as it is reasonable for him to have to take in all the circumstances to prevent that disadvantage – in other words the employer has to make a "reasonable adjustment" *(S6(1))*.

> A man who is disabled by dyslexia applies for a job which involves writing letters within fairly long deadlines. The employer gives all applicants a test of their letter-writing ability. The man can generally write letters very well but finds it difficult to do so in stressful situations. The *employer's arrangements* would mean he had to begin his test immediately on arrival and to do it in a short time. He would be *substantially disadvantaged compared to non-disabled people* who would not find such arrangements stressful or, if they did, would not be so affected by them. The employer therefore gives him a little time to settle in and longer to write the letter. These new arrangements do not inconvenience the employer very much and only briefly delay the decision on an appointment. These are *steps that it is reasonable for the employer to have to take in the circumstances to prevent the disadvantage* – a "reasonable adjustment".

4.13 If a disabled person cannot point to an existing non-disabled person compared with whom he is at a substantial disadvantage, then the comparison should be made with how the employer would have treated a non-disabled person.

4.14 How to comply with this duty in recruitment and during employment is explained in paragraphs 5.1–5.29 and 6.1–6.21. The following paragraphs explain how to satisfy this duty more generally.

What "physical features" and "arrangements" are covered by the duty?

4.15 *Regulations define* the term "physical features" to include anything on the premises arising from a building's design or construction or from an approach to, exit from or access to such a building; fixtures, fittings, furnishings, furniture, equipment or materials; and any other physical element or quality of land in the premises. All of these are covered whether temporary or permanent.[1]

4.16 **The Act says** that the duty applies to "arrangements" for determining to whom employment should be offered and any term, condition or arrangement on which employment, promotion, transfer, training or any other benefit is offered or afforded **(S6(2))**. The duty applies in recruitment and during employment; for example, selection and interview procedures and the arrangements for using premises for such procedures as well as job offers, contractual arrangements, and working conditions.

> The design of a particular workplace makes it difficult for someone with a hearing impairment to hear. That is a disadvantage caused by the *physical features*. There may be nothing that can reasonably be done in the circumstances to change these features. However, requiring someone to work in such a workplace is an *arrangement made by the employer* and it might be reasonable to overcome the disadvantage by a transfer to another workplace or by ensuring that the supervisor gives instructions in an office rather than in the working area.

What "disadvantages" give rise to the duty?

4.17 **The Act says** that only substantial disadvantages give rise to the duty **(S6(1))**. Substantial disadvantages are those which are not minor or trivial.

> An employer is unlikely to be required to widen a particular doorway to enable passage by an employee using a wheelchair if there is an easy alternative route to the same destination.

4.18 An employer cannot be required to prevent a disadvantage caused by premises or by non-pay arrangements by increasing the disabled person's pay. (See paragraph 5.29).

4.19 The duty of reasonable adjustment does not apply in relation to benefits under occupational pension schemes or certain benefits under other employment-related benefit schemes although there is a duty not to discriminate in relation to such benefits (see paragraphs 6.9–6.16).

1   Employment Regulations (see paragraph 1.6)

What adjustments might an employer have to make?

4.20 **The Act gives** a number of examples of "steps" which employers may have to take, if it is reasonable for them to have to do so in all the circumstances of the case **(S6(3))**. Steps other than those listed here, or a combination of steps, will sometimes have to be taken. The steps in the Act are:

- *making adjustments to premises*

  An employer might have to make structural or other physical changes such as: widening a doorway, providing a ramp or moving furniture for a wheelchair user; relocating light switches, door handles or shelves for someone who has difficulty in reaching; providing appropriate contrast in decor to help the safe mobility of a visually impaired person.

- *allocating some of the disabled person's duties to another person*

  Minor or subsidiary duties might be reallocated to another employee if the disabled person has difficulty in doing them because of the disability. For example, if a job occasionally involves going onto the open roof of a building an employer might have to transfer this work away from an employee whose disability involves severe vertigo.

- *transferring the person to fill an existing vacancy*

  If an employee becomes disabled, or has a disability which worsens so she cannot work in the same place or under the same arrangements and there is no reasonable adjustment which would enable the employee to continue doing the current job, then she might have to be considered for any suitable alternative posts which are available. (Such a case might also involve reasonable retraining.)

- *altering the person's working hours*

  This could include allowing the disabled person to work flexible hours to enable additional breaks to overcome fatigue arising from the disability, or changing the disabled person's hours to fit with the availability of a carer.

■ *assigning the person to a different place of work*

This could mean transferring a wheelchair user's work station from an inaccessible third floor office to an accessible one on the ground floor. It could mean moving the person to other premises of the same employer if the first building is inaccessible.

■ *allowing the person to be absent during working hours for rehabilitation, assessment or treatment*

For example, if a person were to become disabled, the employer might have to allow the person more time off during work, than would be allowed to non-disabled employees, to receive physiotherapy or psychoanalysis or undertake employment rehabilitation. A similar adjustment might be appropriate if a disability worsens or if a disabled person needs occasional treatment anyway.

■ *giving the person, or arranging for him to be given, training*

This could be training in the use of particular pieces of equipment unique to the disabled person, or training appropriate for all employees but which needs altering for the disabled person because of the disability. For example, all employees might need to be trained in the use of a particular machine but an employer might have to provide slightly different or longer training for an employee with restricted hand or arm movements,or training in additional software for a visually impaired person so that he can use a computer with speech output.

■ *acquiring or modifying equipment*

An employer might have to provide special equipment (such as an adapted keyboard for a visually impaired person or someone with arthritis), or an adapted telephone for someone with a hearing impairment or modified equipment (such as longer handles on a machine). There is no requirement to provide or modify equipment for personal purposes unconnected with work, such as providing a wheelchair if a person needs one in any event but does not have one: the disadvantage in such a case does not flow from the employer's arrangements or premises.

■ *modifying instructions or reference manuals*

The way instruction is normally given to employees might need to be revised when telling a disabled person how to do a task. The format of instructions or manuals may need to be modified (e.g. produced in braille or on audio tape) and instructions for people with learning disabilities may need to be conveyed orally with individual demonstration.

■ *modifying procedures for testing or assessment*

This could involve ensuring that particular tests do not adversely affect people with particular types of disability. For example, a person with restricted manual dexterity might be disadvantaged by a written test, so an employer might have to give that person an oral test.

■ *providing a reader or interpreter*

This could involve a colleague reading mail to a person with a visual impairment at particular times during the working day or, in appropriate circumstances, the hiring of a reader or sign language interpreter.

■ *providing supervision*

This could involve the provision of a support worker, or help from a colleague, in appropriate circumstances, for someone whose disability leads to uncertainty or lack of confidence.

When is it "reasonable" for an employer to have to make an adjustment?

4.21 Effective and practicable adjustments for disabled people often involve little or no cost or disruption and are therefore very likely to be reasonable for an employer to have to make. *The Act lists* a number of factors which may, in particular, have a bearing on whether it will be reasonable for the employer to have to make a particular adjustment *(S6(4))*. These factors make a useful checklist, particularly when considering more substantial adjustments. The effectiveness and practicability of a particular adjustment might be considered first. If it is practicable and effective, the financial aspects might be looked at as a whole – cost of the adjustment and resources available to fund it. Other factors might also have a bearing. The factors in the Act are listed below.

The effectiveness of the step in preventing the disadvantage

4.22 It is unlikely to be reasonable for an employer to have to make an adjustment involving little benefit to the disabled employee.

> A disabled person is significantly less productive than his colleagues and so is paid less. A particular adjustment would improve his output and thus his pay. It is more likely to be reasonable for the employer to have to make that adjustment if it would significantly improve his pay, than if the adjustment would make only a relatively small improvement.

The practicability of the step

4.23 It is more likely to be reasonable for an employer to have to take a step which is easy to take than one which is difficult.

> It might be impracticable for an employer who needs to appoint an employee urgently to have to wait for an adjustment to be made to an entrance. How long it might be reasonable for the employer to have to wait would depend on the circumstances. However, it might be possible to make a temporary adjustment in the meantime, such as using another, less convenient entrance.

The financial and other costs of the adjustment and the extent of any disruption caused

4.24 If an adjustment costs little or nothing and is not disruptive, it would be reasonable unless some other factor (such as practicability or effectiveness) made it unreasonable. The costs to be taken into account include staff and other resource costs. The significance of the cost of a step may depend in part on what the employer might otherwise spend in the circumstances.

> It would be reasonable for an employer to have to spend at least as much on an adjustment to enable the retention of a disabled person – including any retraining – as might be spent on recruiting and training a replacement.

4.25 The significance of the cost of a step may also depend in part on the value of the employee's experience and expertise to the employer.

Examples of the factors that might be considered as relating to the value of an employee would include:

- the amount of resources (such as training) invested in the individual by the employer;

- the employee's length of service;

- the employee's level of skill and knowledge;

- the employee's quality of relationships with clients;

- the level of the employee's pay.

4.26 It is more likely to be reasonable for an employer to have to make an adjustment with significant costs for an employee who is likely be in the job for some time than for a temporary employee.

4.27 An employer is more likely to have to make an adjustment which might cause only minor inconvenience to other employees or the employer than one which might unavoidably prevent other employees from doing their job, or cause other significant disruption.

The extent of the employer's financial or other resources

4.28 It is more likely to be reasonable for an employer with substantial financial resources to have to make an adjustment with a significant cost, than for an employer with fewer resources. The resources in practice available to the employer as a whole should be taken into account as well as other calls on those resources. The reasonableness of an adjustment will depend, however, not only on the resources in practice available for the adjustment but also on all other relevant factors (such as effectiveness and practicability).

4.29 Where the resources of the employer are spread across more than one "business unit" or "profit centre" the calls on them should also be taken into account in assessing reasonableness.

> A large retailer probably could not show that the limited resources for which an individual shop manager is responsible meant it was not reasonable for the retailer to have to make an adjustment at that shop. Such an employer may, however, have a number – perhaps a large number – of other disabled employees in other shops. The employer's expenditure on other adjustments, or his potential expenditure on similar adjustments for other existing disabled employees, might then be taken into account in assessing the reasonableness of having to make a new adjustment for the disabled employee in question.

4.30 It is more likely to be reasonable for an employer with a substantial number of staff to have to make certain adjustments, than for a smaller employer.

> It would generally be reasonable for an employer with many staff to have to make significant efforts to reallocate duties, identify a suitable alternative post or provide supervision from existing staff. It could also be reasonable for a small company covered by the Act to have to make any of these adjustments but not if it involved disproportionate effort.

The availability to the employer of financial or other assistance to help make an adjustment.

4.31 The availability of outside help may well be a relevant factor.

> An employer, in recruiting a disabled person, finds that the only feasible adjustment is too costly for him alone. However, if assistance is available e.g. from a Government programme or voluntary body, it may well be reasonable for him to have to make the adjustment after all.

A disabled person is not required to contribute to the cost of a reasonable adjustment. However, if a disabled person has a particular piece of special or adapted equipment which he is prepared to use for work, this might make it reasonable for the employer to have to take some other step (as well as allowing use of the equipment).

> An employer requires his employees to use company cars for all business travel. One employee's disability means she would have to use an adapted car or an alternative form of transport. If she has an adapted car of her own which she is willing to use on business, it might well be reasonable for the employer to have to allow this and pay her an allowance to cover the cost of doing so, even if it would not have been reasonable for him to have to provide an adapted company car, or to pay an allowance to cover alternative travel arrangements in the absence of an adapted car.

Other factors

4.32 Although the Act does not mention any further factors, others might be relevant depending on the circumstances. For example:

■ effect on other employees

Employees' adverse reaction to an adjustment being made
for the disabled employee which involves something they too
would like (such as a special working arrangement) is unlikely
to be significant.

■ adjustments made for other disabled employees

An employer may choose to give a particular disabled employee,
or group of disabled employees, an adjustment which goes
beyond the duty – that is, which is more than it is reasonable
for him to have to do. This would not mean he necessarily had
to provide a similar adjustment for other employees with a
similar disability.

■ the extent to which the disabled person is willing to cooperate

An employee with a mobility impairment works in a team
located on an upper floor, to which there is no access by lift.
Getting there is very tiring for the employee, and the employer
could easily make a more accessible location available for him
(though the whole team could not be relocated). If that was the
only adjustment which it would be reasonable for the employer
to have to make but the employee refused to work there then
the employer would not have to make any adjustment at all.

Could an employer have to make more than one adjustment?

4.33 Yes, if it is reasonable for the employer to have to make more
than one.

A woman who is deafblind is given a new job with her employer
in an unfamiliar part of the building. The employer (i) arranges
facilities for her guide dog in the new area, (ii) arranges for her
new instructions to be in Braille and (iii) suggests to visitors
ways in which they can communicate with her.

Does an employer have to justify not making an adjustment?

4.34 **The Act says** that it is discrimination if an employer fails to take a
step which it is reasonable for him to have to take, and he cannot justify
that failure **(S5(2))**. However, if it is unreasonable (under **S6**) for an
employer to have to make any, or a particular, adjustment, he would not

then also have to justify (under **S5**) not doing so. Failure to comply with the duty of reasonable adjustment can only be justified if the reason for the failure is material to the circumstances of the particular case and substantial **(S5(4))**.

> An employer might not make an adjustment which it was reasonable for him to have to make because of ignorance or wrong information about appropriate adjustments or about the availability of help with making an adjustment. He would then need to justify failing in his duty. It is unlikely that he could do so unless he had made a reasonable effort to obtain good information from a reputable source such as contacting the local Placing Assessment and Counselling Team or an appropriate disability organisation.

> If either of two possible adjustments would remove a disadvantage, but the employer has cost or operational reasons for preferring one rather than the other, it is unlikely to be reasonable for him to have to make the one that is not preferred. If, however, the employee refuses to cooperate with the proposed adjustment the employer is likely to be justified in not providing it.

> A disabled employee refuses to follow specific occupational medical advice provided on behalf of an employer about methods of working or managing his condition at work. If he has no good reason for this and his condition deteriorates as a result, the refusal may justify the employer's subsequent failure to make an adjustment for the worsened condition.

Building regulations, listed buildings, leases

How do building regulations affect reasonable adjustments?

4.35 A building or extension to a building may have been constructed in accordance with Part M of the building regulations (or the Scottish parallel, Part T of the Technical Standards) which is concerned with access and facilities for disabled people. **Regulations provide** in these circumstances that the employer does not have to alter any physical characteristic of the building or extension which still complies with the building regulations in force at the time the building works were carried out.[2]

2 Employment Regulations (see paragraph 1.6)

Where the building regulations in force at the time of a building's construction required that a door should be a particular width, the employer would not have to alter the width of the door later. However, he might have to alter other aspects of the door (eg the type of handle).

4.36 Employers can only rely upon this defence if the feature still satisfies the requirement of the building regulations that applied when the building or extension was constructed.

What about the need to obtain statutory consent for some building changes?

4.37 Employers might have to obtain statutory consent before making adjustments involving changes to premises. Such consents include planning permission, listed building consent, scheduled monument consent and fire regulations approval. The Act does not override the need to obtain such consents *(S59)*. Therefore an employer does not have to make an adjustment if it requires a statutory consent which has not been given.

4.38 The time it would take to obtain consent may make a particular adjustment impracticable and therefore one which it is not reasonable for the employer to have to make. However, the employer would then also need to consider whether it was reasonable to have to make a temporary adjustment – one that does not require consent – in the meantime.

4.39 Employers should explore ways of making reasonable adjustments which either do not require statutory consent or are likely to receive it. They may well find it useful to consult their local planning authority (in England and Wales) or planning authority (in Scotland).

An employer needs statutory consent to widen an internal doorway in a listed building for a woman disabled in an accident who returned to work in a wheelchair. The employer considers using a different office but this is not practicable. In the circumstances the widening would be a reasonable adjustment. The employer knows from the local planning authority that consent is likely to be given in a few weeks. In the meantime the employer arranges for the woman to share an accessible office which is inconvenient for both employees, but does not prevent them doing their jobs and is tolerable for that limited period.

What happens where a lease says that certain changes to premises cannot be made?

4.40 Special provisions apply where a lease would otherwise prevent a reasonable adjustment involving an alteration to premises. *The Act modifies* the effect of the lease so far as necessary to enable the employer to make the alteration if the landlord consents, and to provide that the landlord must not withhold consent unreasonably but may attach reasonable conditions to the consent *(S16)*.

How will arrangements for getting the landlord's consent work?

4.41 *The Act says* that the employer must write to the landlord (called the "lessor" in the Act) asking for consent to make the alteration. If an employer fails to apply to the landlord for consent, anything in the lease which would prevent that alteration must be ignored in deciding whether it was reasonable for the employer to have to make that alteration *(Sch4 Para 1)*. If the landlord consents, the employer can then carry out the alteration. If the landlord refuses consent the employer must notify the disabled person, but then has no further obligation.[3] Where the landlord fails to reply within 21 days or a reasonable period after that he is deemed to have withheld his consent. In those circumstances the withholding of the consent will be unreasonable (see paragraph 4.44).[4]

4.42 If the landlord attaches a condition to the consent and it is reasonable for the employer to have to carry out the alteration on that basis, the employer must then carry out the alteration. If it would not be reasonable for the employer to have to carry out the alteration on that basis, the employer must notify the disabled person, but then has no further obligation.

When is it unreasonable for a landlord to withhold consent?

4.43 This will depend on the circumstances but a trivial or arbitrary reason would almost certainly be unreasonable. Many reasonable adjustments to premises will not harm a landlord's interests and so it would generally be unreasonable to withhold consent for them.

> A particular adjustment helps make a public building more accessible generally and is therefore likely to benefit the landlord. It would very probably be unreasonable for consent to be withheld in these circumstances.

3 Employment Regulations (see paragraph 1.6)
4 Employment Regulations (see paragraph 1.6)

4.44 *Regulations provide* that withholding consent will be unreasonable where:

- a landlord has failed to act within the time limits referred to in paragraph 4.41 above (ie 21 days of receipt of the employer's application or a reasonable period after that); or

- the lease says that consent will be given to alterations of that type or says that such consent will be given if it is sought in a particular way and it has been sought in that way.[5]

When is it reasonable for a landlord to withhold consent?

4.45 This will depend on the particular circumstances.

A particular adjustment is likely to result in a substantial permanent reduction in the value of the landlord's interest in the premises. The landlord would almost certainly be acting reasonably in withholding consent.

A particular adjustment would cause significant disruption or inconvenience to other tenants (for example, where the premises consist of multiple adjoining units). The landlord would be likely to be acting reasonably in withholding consent.

What conditions would it be reasonable for a landlord to make when giving consent?

4.46 This will depend on the particular circumstances. However, *Regulations provide* that it would be reasonable for the landlord to require the employer to meet any of the following conditions:

- obtain planning permission and other statutory consents;

- submit any plans to the landlord for approval (provided that the landlord then confirms that approval will not be withheld unreasonably);

- allow the landlord a reasonable opportunity to inspect the work when completed;

- reimburse the landlord's reasonable costs incurred in connection with the giving of his consent;

- reinstate the altered part of the premises to its former state when the lease expires but only if it would have been reasonable for the landlord to have refused consent in the first place.[6]

---

5   Employment Regulations (see paragraph 1.6)
6   Employment Regulations (see paragraph 1.6)

What happens if the landlord has a "superior" landlord?

4.47 The employer's landlord may also hold a lease which prevents him from consenting to the alteration without the consent of the "superior" landlord. The statutory provisions have been modified by regulations to cover this. The employer's landlord will be acting reasonably by notifying the employer that consent will be given if the superior landlord agrees. The employer's landlord must then apply to the superior landlord to ask for agreement. The provisions in paragraphs 4.41–4.46, including the requirements not to withhold consent unreasonably and not to attach unreasonable conditions, then apply to the superior landlord.[7]

What if some agreement other than a lease prevents the premises being altered?

4.48 An employer or landlord may be bound by the terms of an agreement or other legally binding obligation (for example, a mortgage or charge or restrictive covenant or, in Scotland, a feu disposition) under which the employer or landlord cannot alter the premises without someone else's consent. In these circumstances *Regulations provide* that it is always reasonable for the employer or landlord to have to take steps to obtain the necessary consent so that a reasonable adjustment can be made. Unless or until that consent is obtained the employer or landlord is not required to make the alteration in question. The step of seeking consent which it is always reasonable to have to take does not extend to having to apply to a court or tribunal.[8] Whether it is reasonable for the employer or landlord to have to apply to a court or tribunal would depend on the circumstances of the case.

Agreements which breach the Act's provisions

Can a disabled person waive rights, or an employer's duties, under the Act?

4.49 *The Act says* that any term in a contract of employment or other agreement is "void" (i.e. not valid) to the extent that it would require a person to do anything that would breach any of the Act's employment provisions, or exclude or limit the operation of those provisions *(S9)*.

4.50 An employer should not include in an agreement any provision intended to avoid obligations under the Act, or to prevent someone from fulfilling obligations. An agreement should not, therefore, be used to try to justify less favourable treatment or deem an adjustment unreasonable. Moreover, even parts of agreements which have such an effect (even

---

7 The Disability Discrimination (Sub-leases and Sub-tenancies) Regulations 1996
8 Employment Regulations (see paragraph 1.6)

though unintended) are made void if they would restrict the working of the employment provisions in the Act. However, special arrangements cover leases and other agreements which might prevent a change to premises which could be an adjustment under the Act but where the possible restrictions to the Act's working were unintentional. These are described in paragraphs 4.40–4.48.

4.51 The Act also says that a contract term is void if it would prevent anyone from making a claim under the employment provisions in an industrial tribunal *(S9)*. Further information is given in Annex 3 about such agreements.

What about permits issued in accordance with the Agricultural Wages Acts?

4.52 Under the Agricultural Wages Act 1948 and the Agricultural Wages (Scotland) Act 1949 minimum wages, and terms and conditions, can be set for agricultural workers. Permits can be issued to individuals who are "incapacitated" for the purposes of those Acts and they can then be paid such lower minimum rates or be subject to such revised terms and conditions of employment that the permit specifies. *Regulations provide* that the treatment of a disabled person in accordance with such a permit would be taken to be justified.[9] This would not prevent the employer from having to comply with the duty not to discriminate, including the duty of reasonable adjustment, for matters other than those covered by the permit.

Victimisation

What does the Act say about victimisation?

4.53 Victimisation is a special form of discrimination covered by the Act. *The Act makes* it unlawful for one person to treat another (the victim) less favourably than he would treat other people in the same circumstances because the "victim" has:

- brought, or given evidence or information in connection with, proceedings under the Act (whether or not proceedings are later withdrawn);

- done anything else under the Act; or

- alleged someone has contravened the Act (whether or not the allegation is later dropped);

9 Employment Regulations (see paragraph 1.6)

or because the person believes or suspects that the victim has done or intends to do any of these things *(S55)*.

It is unlawful for an employer to victimise either disabled or non-disabled people.

> A disabled employee complains of discrimination. It would be unlawful for the employer to subject non-disabled colleagues to any detriment (e.g. suspension) for telling the truth about the alleged discrimination at an industrial tribunal hearing or in any internal grievance procedures.

4.54 It is not victimisation to treat a person less favourably because that person has made an allegation which was false and not made in good faith *(S55(b))*.

(Harassment is covered in paragraphs 6.22–6.23.)

Setting up management systems to help avoid discrimination

What management systems might be set up to help avoid discrimination?

4.55 *The Act says* that employers are responsible for the actions done by their employees in the course of their employment. In legal proceedings against an employer based on actions of an employee, it is a defence that the employer took such steps as were reasonably practicable to prevent such actions. It is not a defence for the employer simply to show the action took place without his knowledge or approval. Employers who act through agents will also be liable for the actions of their agents done with the employer's express or implied authority *(S58)*.

> An employer makes it clear to a recruitment agency that the company will not take kindly to recruits with learning disabilities being put forward by the agency. The agency complies by not putting such candidates forward. Both the employer and the agency will be liable if such treatment cannot be justified in an individual case.

4.56 Employers should communicate to their employees and agents any policy they may have on disability matters, and any other policies which have elements relevant to disabled employees (such as health, absenteeism or equal opportunities). All staff should be made aware that it is unlawful to discriminate against disabled people, and be familiar with the policies and practices adopted by their employer to ensure compliance with the law. Employers should provide guidance on non-discriminatory practices for all employees, so they will be aware what they should do and how to deal with disabled colleagues and disabled applicants for vacancies in the organisation, and should ensure so far as possible that these policies and practices are implemented. Employers should also make it clear to their agents what is required of them with regard to their duties under the Act, and the extent of their authority.

4.57 **The Act says** that an employer is not under an obligation to make an adjustment if he does not know, and could not reasonably be expected to know, that a person has a disability which is likely to place the person at a substantial disadvantage **(S6(6))**. An employer must therefore do all he could reasonably be expected to do to find out whether this is the case.

> An employee has a disability which sometimes causes him to cry at work although the cause of this behaviour is not known to the employer. The employer's general approach on such matters is to tell staff to leave their personal problems at home and to make no allowance for such problems in the work arrangements. The employer disciplines the employee without giving him any opportunity to explain that the problem in fact arises from a disability. The employer would be unlikely to succeed in a claim that he could not reasonably be expected to have known of the disability or that it led to the behaviour for which the employee was disciplined.

> An employer has an annual appraisal system which specifically provides an opportunity to notify the employer in confidence if any employees are disabled and are put at a substantial disadvantage by the work arrangements or premises. This practice enables the employer to show that he could not reasonably be expected to know that an employee was put at such a disadvantage as a result of disability, if this was not obvious and was not brought to the employer's attention through the appraisal system.

4.58 In some cases a reasonable adjustment will not work without the co-operation of other employees. Employees may therefore have an important role in helping to ensure that a reasonable adjustment is carried out in practice.

It is a reasonable adjustment for an employer to communicate
in a particular way to an employee with autism (a disability
which can make it difficult for someone to understand normal
social interaction among people). As part of the reasonable
adjustment it is the responsibility of that employer to seek the
co-operation of other employees in communicating in that way.

4.59 It may be necessary to tell one or more of a disabled person's
colleagues (in confidence) about a disability which is not obvious and/or
whether any special assistance is required. This may be limited to the
person's supervisor, or it may be necessary to involve other colleagues,
depending on the nature of the disability and the reason they need to
know about it.

In order for a person with epilepsy to work safely in a
particular factory, it may be necessary to advise fellow workers
about the effects of the condition, and the methods for assisting
with them.

An office worker with cancer says that he does not want
colleagues to know of his condition. As an adjustment he needs
extra time away from work to receive treatment and to rest.
Neither his colleagues nor the line manager needs to be told
the precise reasons for the extra leave but the latter will need
to know that the adjustment is required in order to carry it
out effectively.

4.60 The extent to which an employer is entitled to let other staff know
about an employee's disability will depend at least in part on the terms of
employment. An employer could be held to be discriminating in revealing
such information about a disabled employee if the employer would not
reveal similar information about another person for an equally legitimate
management purpose; or if the employer revealed such information without
consulting the individual, whereas the employer's usual practice would be
to talk to an employee before revealing personal information about him.

4.61 The Act does not prevent a disabled person keeping a disability
confidential from an employer. But this is likely to mean that unless the
employer could reasonably be expected to know about the person's
disability anyway, the employer will not be under a duty to make a
reasonable adjustment. If a disabled person expects an employer to
make a reasonable adjustment, he will need to provide the employer
– or, as the case may be, someone acting on the employer's behalf –
with sufficient information to carry out that adjustment.

An employee has symptomatic HIV. He prefers not to tell his employer of the condition. However, as the condition progresses, he finds it increasingly difficult to work the required number of hours in a week. Until he tells his employer of his condition – or the employer becomes or could reasonably be expected to be aware of it – he cannot require the employer to change his working hours to overcome the difficulty. However, once the employer is informed he may then have to make a reasonable adjustment.

4.62 If an employer's agent or employee (for example, an occupational health officer, a personnel officer or line manager) knows in that capacity of an employee's disability, then the employer cannot claim that he does not know of that person's disability, and that he is therefore excluded from the obligation to make a reasonable adjustment. This will be the case even if the disabled person specifically asked for such information to be kept confidential. Employers will therefore need to ensure that where information about disabled people may come through different channels, there is a means – suitably confidential – for bringing the information together, so the employer's duties under the Act are fulfilled.

In a large company an occupational health officer is engaged by the employer to provide him with information about his employees' health. The officer becomes aware of an employee's disability, which the employee's line manager does not know about. The employer's working arrangements put the employee at a substantial disadvantage because of the effects of her disability and she claims that a reasonable adjustment should have been made. It will not be a defence for the employer to claim that he did not know of her disability. This is because the information gained by the officer on the employer's behalf is imputed to the employer. Even if the person did not want the line manager to know that she had a disability, the occupational health officer's knowledge means that the employer's duty under the Act applies. It might even be necessary for the line manager to implement reasonable adjustments without knowing precisely why he has to do so.

4.63 Information will not be imputed to the employer if it is gained by a person providing services to employees independently of the employer. This is the case even if the employer has arranged for those services to be provided.

An employer contracts with an agency to provide an independent counselling service to employees. The contract says that the counsellors are not acting on the employer's behalf while in the counselling role. Any information about a person's disability obtained by a counsellor during such counselling would not be imputed to the employer and so could not itself place a duty of reasonable adjustment on the employer.

What if someone says they have a disability and the employer is not convinced?

4.64 If a candidate asks for an adjustment to be made because of an impairment whose effects are not obvious, nothing in the Act or Regulations would prohibit the employer from asking for evidence that the impairment is one which gives rise to a disability as defined in the Act.

An applicant says she has a mental illness whose effects require her to take time off work on a frequent, but irregular, basis. If not satisfied that this is true, the employer would be entitled to ask for evidence that the woman has a mental illness which was likely to have the effects claimed and that it is clinically well recognised (as required by the Act).

Effects of other legislation

What about the effects of other legislation?

4.65 An employer is not required to make an adjustment – or do anything under the Act – that would result in a breach of statutory obligations *(S59)*.

If a particular adjustment would breach health and safety or fire legislation then an employer would not have to make it. However, the employer would still have to consider whether he was required to make any other adjustment which would not breach any legislation. For instance, if someone in a wheelchair could not use emergency evacuation arrangements such as a fire escape on a particular floor, it might be reasonable for the employer to have to relocate that person's job to an office where that problem did not arise.

An employer shortlisting applicants to fill a junior office post is considering whether to include a blind applicant who the employer believes might present a safety risk moving around the crowded office. A reasonable adjustment might be to provide mobility training to familiarise the applicant with the work area, so removing any risk there might otherwise be.

What about legislation which places restrictions on what employers can do to recruit disabled people?

4.66 The Disability Discrimination Act does not prevent posts being advertised as open only to disabled candidates. However, the requirement, for example, under Section 7 of the Local Government and Housing Act 1989 that every appointment to local authorities must be made on merit means that a post cannot be so advertised. Applications from disabled people can nevertheless be encouraged. However, this requirement to appoint "on merit" does not exclude the duty under the 1995 Act to make adjustments so a disabled person's "merit" must be assessed taking into account any such adjustments which would have to be made.

5 Recruitment

Discrimination against applicants

How does the Act affect recruitment?

5.1 *The Act says* that it is unlawful for an employer to discriminate against a disabled person:

- in the arrangements made for determining who should be offered employment;

- in the terms on which the disabled person is offered employment; or

- by refusing to offer, or deliberately not offering, the disabled person employment *S4(1)*.

5.2 The word "arrangements" has a wide meaning. Employers should avoid discrimination in, for example, specifying the job, advertising the job, and the processes of selection, including the location and timing of interviews, assessment techniques, interviewing, and selection criteria.

Specifying the job

Does the Act affect how an employer should draw up a job specification?

5.3 Yes. The inclusion of unnecessary or marginal requirements in a job specification can lead to discrimination.

An employer stipulates that employees must be "energetic", when in fact the job in question is largely sedentary in nature. This requirement could unjustifiably exclude some people whose disabilities result in them getting tired more easily than others.

An employer specifies that a driving licence is required for a job which involves limited travelling. An applicant for the job has no driving licence because of the particular effects in his case of cerebral palsy. He is otherwise the best candidate for that job, he could easily and cheaply do the travelling involved other than by driving and it would be a reasonable adjustment for the employer to let him do so. It would be discriminatory to insist on the specification and reject his application solely because he had no driving licence.

5.4 Blanket exclusions (i.e. exclusions which do not take account of individual circumstances) may lead to discrimination.

> An employer excludes people with epilepsy from all driving jobs. One of the jobs, in practice, only requires a standard licence and normal insurance cover. If, as a result, someone with epilepsy, who has such a licence and can obtain such cover, is turned down for the job then the employer will probably have discriminated unlawfully in excluding her from consideration.

> An employer stipulates that candidates for a job must not have a history of mental illness, believing that such candidates will have poor attendance. The employer rejects an applicant solely because he has had a mental illness without checking the individual's probable attendance. Even if good attendance is genuinely essential for the job, this is not likely to be justified and is therefore very likely to be unlawful discrimination.

Can an employer stipulate essential health requirements?

5.5 Yes, but the employer may need to justify doing so, and to show that it would not be reasonable for him to have to waive them, in any individual case.

Can employers simply prefer a certain type of person?

5.6 Stating that a certain personal, medical or health-related characteristic is desirable may also lead to discrimination if the characteristic is not necessary for the performance of the job. Like a requirement, a preference may be decisive against an otherwise well-qualified disabled candidate and may have to be justified in an individual case.

> An employer prefers all employees to have a certain level of educational qualification. A woman with a learning disability, which has prevented her from obtaining the preferred qualification, is turned down for a job because she does not have that qualification. If the qualification is not necessary in order to do the job and she is otherwise the best candidate, then the employer will have discriminated unlawfully against her.

Publicising the vacancy

What does the Act say about how an employer can advertise vacancies?

5.7   Where a job is advertised, and a disabled person who applies is refused or deliberately not offered it and complains to an industrial tribunal about disability discrimination, the Act requires the tribunal to assume (unless the employer can prove otherwise) that the reason the person did not get the job was related to his disability if the advertisement could reasonably be taken to indicate:

- that the success of a person's application for the job might depend to any extent on the absence of a disability such as the applicant's; or

- that the employer is unwilling to make an adjustment for a disabled person *(S11)*.

An employer puts in an advertisement for an office worker, "Sorry, but gaining access to our building can be difficult for some people". A man, who as a result of an accident some years previously can only walk with the aid of crutches but can do office work, applies for the job and is turned down. He complains to an industrial tribunal. Because of the wording of the advertisement, the tribunal would have to assume that he did not get the job for a reason relating to his disability unless the employer could prove otherwise.

What is an "advertisement" for the purposes of the Act?

5.8   *According to the Act* "advertisement" includes every form of advertisement or notice, whether to the public or not *(S11(3))*. This would include advertisements internal to a company or office.

Does an employer have to provide information about jobs in alternative formats?

5.9   In particular cases, this may be a reasonable adjustment.

A person whom the employer knows to be disabled asks to be given information about a job in a medium that is accessible to her (in large print, in braille, on tape or on computer disc). It is often likely to be a reasonable adjustment for the employer to comply, particularly if the employer's information systems, and the time available before the new employee is needed, mean it can easily be done.

Can an employer say that he would welcome applications from disabled people?

5.10 Yes. *The Act does not prevent* this and it would be a positive and public statement of the employer's policy.

Can an employer include a question on an application form asking whether someone is disabled?

5.11 Yes. *The Act does not prevent* employers including such a question on application forms. Employers can also ask whether the individual might need an adjustment and what it might be.

Selection

Does the duty of reasonable adjustment apply to applicants?

5.12 *The Act says* that the duty to make a reasonable adjustment does not apply where the employer does not know, and could not reasonably be expected to know, that the disabled person in question is or may be an applicant for the post, or, that a particular applicant has a disability which is likely to place him at a disadvantage *(S6(a))*.

Does an employer have to take special care when considering applications?

5.13 Yes. Employers and their staff or agents must not discriminate against disabled people in the way in which they deal with applications. They may also have to make reasonable adjustments.

> Because of his disability, a candidate asks to submit an application in a particular medium, different from that specified for candidates in general (e.g. typewritten, by telephone, or on tape). It would normally be a reasonable adjustment for the employer to allow this.

Whom can an employer shortlist for interview?

5.14 If an employer knows that an applicant has a disability and is likely to be at a substantial disadvantage because of the employer's arrangements or premises, the employer should consider whether there is any reasonable adjustment which would bring the disabled person within the field of applicants to be considered even though he would not otherwise be within that field because of that disadvantage. If the employer could only make this judgement with more information it would be discriminatory for him not to put the disabled person on the shortlist for interview if that is how he would normally seek additional information about candidates.

What should an employer do when arranging interviews?

5.15 Employers should think ahead for interviews. Giving applicants the opportunity to indicate any relevant effects of a disability and to suggest adjustments to help overcome any disadvantage the disability may cause, could help the employer avoid discrimination in the interview and in considering the applicant, by clarifying whether any reasonable adjustments may be required.

5.16 Nevertheless, if a person, whom the employer previously did not know, and could not have known, to be disabled, arrives for interview and is placed at a substantial disadvantage because of the arrangements, the employer may still be under a duty to make a reasonable adjustment from the time that he first learns of the disability and the disadvantage. However, what the employer has to do in such circumstances might be less extensive than if advance notice had been given.

What changes might an employer have to make to arrangements for interviews?

5.17 There are many possible reasonable adjustments, depending on the circumstances.

> A person has difficulty attending at a particular time because of a disability. It will very likely be reasonable for the employer to have to rearrange the time.

> A hearing impaired candidate has substantial difficulties with the interview arrangements. The interviewer may simply need to ensure he faces the applicant and speaks clearly or is prepared to repeat questions. The interviewer should make sure that his face is well lit when talking to someone with a hearing or visual impairment. It will almost always be reasonable for an employer to have to provide such help with communication support if the interviewee would otherwise be at a substantial disadvantage.

An employer who pays expenses to candidates who come for interview could well have to pay additional expenses to meet any special requirements of a disabled person arising from any substantial disadvantage to which she would otherwise be put by the interview arrangements. This might include paying travelling expenses for a support worker or reasonable cost of travel by taxi, rather than by bus or train, if this is necessary because of the disability.

A job applicant does not tell an employer (who has no knowledge of her disability) in advance that she uses a wheelchair. On arriving for the interview she discovers that the room is not accessible. The employer did not know of the disability and so could not have been expected to make changes in advance. However, it would still be a reasonable adjustment for the employer to hold the interview in an alternative accessible room, if a suitable one was easily available at the time with no, or only an acceptable level of, disruption or additional cost.

Should an employer consider making changes to the way the interview is carried out?

5.18 Yes, although whether any change is needed – and, if so, what change – will depend on the circumstances.

It would almost always be reasonable to allow an applicant with a learning disability to bring a supportive person such as a friend or relative to assist when answering questions that are not part of tests.

It would normally be reasonable to allow a longer time for an interview to someone with a hearing impairment using a sign language interpreter to communicate.

Does an employer have to make changes to anticipate *any* disabled person applying for a job?

5.19 No. An employer is not required to make changes in anticipation of applications from disabled people in general. It is only if the employer knows or could be reasonably expected to know that a particular disabled person is, or may be, applying and is likely to be substantially disadvantaged by the employer's premises or arrangements, that the employer may have to make changes.

Should an employer ask about a disability?

5.20 The Act does not prohibit an employer from seeking information about a disability but an employer must not use it to discriminate against a disabled person. An employer should ask only about a disability if it is, or may be, relevant to the person's ability to do the job – after a reasonable adjustment, if necessary. Asking about the effects of a disability might be important in deciding what adjustments ought to be made. The employer should avoid discriminatory questions.

> An applicant whose disability has left him using a wheelchair but healthy, is asked by an employer whether any extra leave might be required because of the condition. This is unlikely to be discriminatory because a need for extra time off work may be a substantial factor relevant to the person's ability to do the job. Therefore such a question would normally be justified. Similarly, a reasonable question about whether any changes may need to be made to the workplace to accommodate the use of the wheelchair would probably not be discriminatory.

Does the Act prevent employers carrying out aptitude or other tests in the recruitment process?

5.21 No, but routine testing of all candidates may still discriminate against particular individuals or substantially disadvantage them. If so, the employer would need to revise the tests – or the way the results of such tests are assessed – to take account of specific disabled candidates, except where the nature and form of the test were necessary to assess a matter relevant to the job. It may, for instance, be a reasonable adjustment to accept a lower "pass rate" for a person whose disability inhibits performance in such a test. The extent to which this is required would depend on how closely the test is related to the job in question and what adjustments the employer might have to make if the applicant were given the job.

> An employer sets a numeracy test for prospective employees. A person with a learning disability takes the test and does not achieve the level the employer normally stipulates. If the job in fact entails very little numerical work and the candidate is otherwise well suited for the job it is likely to be a reasonable adjustment for the employer to waive the requirement.

An employer sets candidates a short oral test. An applicant is disabled by a bad stammer, but only under stress. It may be a reasonable adjustment to allow her more time to complete the test, or to give the test in written form instead, though not if oral communication is relevant to the job and assessing this was the purpose of the test.

Can an employer specify qualifications?

5.22 An employer is entitled to specify that applicants for a job must have certain qualifications. However, if a disabled person is rejected for the job because he lacks a qualification, the employer will have to justify that rejection if the reason why the person is rejected (i.e. the lack of a qualification) is connected with his disability. Justification will involve showing that the qualification is relevant and significant in terms of the particular job and the particular applicant, and that there is no reasonable adjustment which would change this. In some circumstances it might be feasible to reassign those duties to which the qualification relates, or to waive the requirement for the qualification if this particular applicant has alternative evidence of the necessary level of competence.

An employer seeking someone to work in an administrative post specifies that candidates must have the relevant NVQ Level 4 qualification. If Level 4 fairly reflects the complex and varied nature and substantial personal responsibility of the work, and these aspects of the job cannot reasonably be altered, the employer will be able to justify rejecting a disabled applicant who has only been able to reach Level 3 because of his disability and who cannot show the relevant level of competence by other means.

An employer specifies that two GCSEs are required for a certain post. This is to show that a candidate has the general level of ability required. No particular subjects are specified. An applicant whose dyslexia prevented her from passing written examinations cannot meet this requirement, but the employer would be unable to justify rejecting her on this account alone if she could show she nevertheless had the skill and intelligence called for in the post.

Can an employer insist on a disabled person having a medical examination?

5.23 Yes. However, if an employer insists on a medical check for a disabled person and not others, without justification, he will probably be discriminating unlawfully. The fact that a person has a disability is unlikely in itself to justify singling out that person to have a health check, although such action might be justified in relation to some jobs

> An employer requires all candidates for employment to have a medical examination. That employer would normally be entitled to include a disabled person.

> An applicant for a job has a disabling heart condition. The employer routinely issues a health questionnaire to job applicants, and requires all applicants who state they have a disability to undergo a medical examination. Under the Act, the employer would not be justified in requiring a medical examination whenever an applicant states he has a disability – for example, this would not normally be justified if the disability is clearly relevant neither to the job nor to the environment in which the job is done. However, the employer would probably be justified in asking the applicant with the disabling heart condition to have a medical examination restricted to assessing its implications for the particular job in its context. If, for example, the job required lifting and carrying but these abilities were limited by the condition, the employer would also have to consider whether it would be reasonable for him to have to make a change such as providing a mechanical means of lifting and/or carrying, or arranging for the few items above the person's limit to be dealt with by another person, whilst ensuring that any health and safety provisions were not breached.

How can an employer take account of medical evidence?

5.24 In most cases, having a disability does not adversely affect a person's general health. Medical evidence about a disability can justify an adverse employment decision (such as dismissing or not promoting). It will not generally do so if there is no effect on the person's ability to do the work (or any effect is less than substantial), however great the effects of the disability are in other ways. The condition or effects must be relevant to the employer's decision.

An applicant for a post on a short-term contract has a progressive condition which has some effects, but is likely to have substantial adverse effects only in the long term. The likelihood of these long-term effects would not itself be a justifiable reason for the employer to reject him.

An employer requires all candidates for a certain job to be able to work for at least two years to complete a particular work project. Medical evidence shows that a particular candidate is unlikely to be able to continue working for that long. It would be lawful to reject that candidate if the two-year requirement was justified in terms of the work, and if it would not be reasonable for the employer to have to waive it in the particular circumstances.

Advice from an occupational health expert simply that an employee was "unfit for work" would not mean that the employer's duty to make a reasonable adjustment was waived.

What will help an employer decide to select a particular disabled person?

5.25 The employer must take into account any adjustments that it is reasonable for him to have to make. Suggestions made by the candidate at any stage may assist in identifying these.

What if a disabled person just isn't the right person for the job?

5.26 An employer must not discriminate against a disabled candidate, but there is no requirement (aside from reasonable adjustment) to treat a disabled person more favourably than he treats or would treat others. An employer will have to assess an applicant's merits as they would be if any reasonable adjustments required under the Act had been made. If, after allowing for those adjustments, a disabled person would not be the best person for the job the employer would not have to recruit that person.

Terms and conditions of service

Are there restrictions on the terms and conditions an employer can offer a disabled person?

5.27 Terms and conditions of service should not discriminate against a disabled person. The employer should consider whether any reasonable adjustments need to be made to the terms and conditions which would otherwise apply.

> An employer's terms and conditions state the hours an employee has to be in work. It might be a reasonable adjustment to change these hours for someone whose disability means that she has difficulty using public transport during rush hours.

Does that mean that an employer can never offer a disabled person a less favourable contract?

5.28 No. Such a contract may be justified if there is a material and substantial reason and there is no reasonable adjustment which can be made to remove that reason.

> A person's disability means she has significantly lower output than other employees doing similar work, even after an adjustment. Her work is of neither lower nor higher quality than theirs. The employer would be justified in paying her less in proportion to the lower output if it affected the value of her work to the business.

Can employers still operate performance-related pay?

5.29 *Regulations provide* that this is justified so long as the scheme applies equally to all employees, or all of a particular class of employees. There would be no requirement to make a reasonable adjustment to an arrangement of this kind to ensure (for example) that a person's pay was topped up if a deteriorating condition happened to lead to lower performance.[10] However, there would still be a duty to make a reasonable adjustment to any aspect of the premises or work arrangements if that would prevent the disability reducing the employee's performance.

---

10 Employment Regulations (see paragraph 1.6)

6   Employment

Discrimination against employees

Does the Act cover all areas of employment?

6.1   Yes. *The Act* says that it is unlawful for an employer to discriminate against a disabled person whom he employs:

■   in the terms of employment which he affords him;

■   in the opportunities which he affords him for promotion, a transfer, training or receiving any other benefit;

■   by refusing to afford him, or deliberately not affording him, any such opportunity; or

■   by dismissing him, or subjecting him to any other detriment *(S4(2))*.

6.2 Therefore, an employer should not discriminate in relation to, for example: terms and conditions of service, arrangements made for induction, arrangements made for employees who become disabled (or who have a disability which worsens), opportunities for promotion, transfer, training or receiving any other benefit, or refusal of such opportunities, pensions, dismissal or any detriment.

Induction

What is the effect on induction procedures?

6.3   Employers must not discriminate in their induction procedures. The employer may have to make adjustments to ensure a disabled person is introduced into a new working environment in a clearly structured and supported way with, if necessary, an individually tailored induction programme *(S4(2) and S6(1))*.

> An employer runs a one day induction course for new recruits. A recruit with a learning disability is put at a substantial disadvantage by the way the course is normally run. The employer might have to make an alternative arrangement: for example running a separate, longer course for the person, or permitting someone to sit in on the normal course to provide support, assistance or encouragement.

Promotion and transfer

What are an employer's duties as far as promotion and transfer are concerned?

6.4   Employers must not discriminate in assessing a disabled person's suitability for promotion or transfer, in the practical arrangements necessary to enable the promotion or transfer to take place, in the operation of the appraisal, selection and promotion or transfer process, or in the new job itself – and may have to make a reasonable adjustment *(S4(2)(b) and (c) and S6(1))*.

> A garage owner does not consider for promotion to assistant manager a clerk who has lost the use of her right arm, because he wrongly and unreasonably believes that her disability might prevent her performing competently in a managerial post. The reason used by the employer to deny the clerk promotion has meant that she was discriminated against.

> An employer considering a number of people for a job on promotion is aware that one of the candidates for interview has a hearing impairment, but does not find out whether the person needs any special arrangements for the interview, for example a sign language interpreter. If the candidate requires such an adjustment, and it would be reasonable for the employer to have to make it, the employer would fail in his duty if he did not make that adjustment.

> A civil engineer whose disability involves kidney dialysis treatment, is based in London and regularly visits hospital for the treatment. She wishes to transfer to a vacant post in her company's Scottish office. She meets all the requirements for the post, but her transfer is turned down on the ground that her need for treatment would mean that, away from the facilities in London, she would be absent from work for longer. The employer had made no attempt to discuss this with her or get medical advice. If the employer had done so, it would have been clear that similar treatment would be equally available in the new locality. In these circumstances, the employer probably could not show that relying on this reason was justified.

Someone disabled by a back injury is seeking promotion to supervisor. A minor duty involves assisting with the unloading of the weekly delivery van, which the person's back injury would prevent. In assessing her suitability for promotion, the employer should consider whether reallocating this duty to another person would be a reasonable adjustment.

What should an employer do to check that promotion and transfer arrangements do not discriminate?

6.5   The employer should review the arrangements to check that qualifications required are justified for the job to be done. He should also check that other arrangements, for example systems which determine other criteria for a particular job, do not exclude disabled people who may have been unable to meet those criteria because of their disability but would be capable of performing well in the job.

Training and other benefits provided by the employer

Does the Act apply to the provision of training?

6.6   Yes. Employers must not discriminate in selection for training and must make any necessary reasonable adjustments *(S4(2)(b) and (c) and S6(1))*.

An employer wrongly assumes that a disabled person will be unwilling or unable to undertake demanding training or attend a residential training course, instead of taking an informed decision. He may well not be able to justify a decision based on that assumption.

An employer may need to alter the time or the location of the training for someone with a mobility problem, make training manuals, slides or other visual media accessible to a visually impaired employee, perhaps by providing braille versions or having them read out, or ensure that an induction loop is available for someone with a hearing impairment.

An employer refuses to allow a disabled employee to be coached for a theory examination relating to practical work which the disability prevented the employee from doing. The employer would almost always be justified in refusing to allow the coaching because it was designed to equip employees for an area of work for which, because of the disability, the person could not be suited even by a reasonable adjustment.

What about other benefits provided by employers?

6.7   An employer must not discriminate in providing disabled people with opportunities for receiving benefits (which include "facilities" and "services") which are available to other employees *(S4(2)(b) and (c))*. The employer must make any necessary reasonable adjustment to the way the benefits are provided *(S6(1))* although this does not apply to benefits under occupational pension schemes or certain other employment related benefit schemes (paragraph 6.16).

Benefits might include canteens, meal vouchers, social clubs and other recreational activities, dedicated car parking spaces, discounts on products, bonuses, share options, hairdressing, clothes allowances, financial services, healthcare, medical assistance/insurance, transport to work, company car, education assistance, workplace nurseries, and rights to special leave.

If physical features of a company's social club would inhibit a disabled person's access it might be a reasonable adjustment for the employer to make suitable modifications.

An employer provides dedicated car parking spaces near to the workplace. It is likely to be reasonable for the employer to have to allocate one of these spaces to a disabled employee who has significant difficulty getting from the public car parks further away that he would otherwise have to use.

6.8   If an employer provides benefits to the public, or to a section of the public which includes the disabled employee, provision of those benefits will normally fall outside the duty not to discriminate in employment. Instead, the duty in the Act not to discriminate in providing goods, facilities and services will apply. However, the employment duty will apply if the benefit to employees is materially different (eg. at a discount), is governed by the contract of employment, or relates to training *(S4(2) and (3))*.

A disabled employee of a supermarket chain who believes he has been discriminated against when buying goods as a customer at any branch of the supermarket would have no claim under the employment provisions. However, if that employee were using a discount card provided only to employees, then the employment provisions would apply if any less favourable treatment related to his use of the card.

Occupational pension schemes and insurance

What does the Act say about occupational pension schemes?

6.9 **The Act inserts** into every scheme a "non-discrimination" rule. The trustees or managers of the scheme are prohibited by that rule from doing – or omitting to do – anything to members or non-members of schemes that would be unlawful discrimination if done by an employer **(S17)**. References to employers in paragraphs 6.11–6.15 should therefore be read as if they also apply to trustees or managers when appropriate.

When is less favourable treatment justified?

6.10 Less favourable treatment for a reason relating to a disability can be justified only if the reason is material and substantial.

> Trustees of a pension scheme would not be justified in excluding a woman simply because she had a visual impairment. That fact, in itself, would be no reason why she should not receive the same pension benefits as any other employee.

6.11 There are circumstances when a disabled person's health or health prognosis is such that the cost of providing benefits under a pension scheme is substantially greater than it would be for a person without the disability. In these circumstances **Regulations provide** that an employer is regarded as justified in treating a disabled person less favourably in applying the eligibility conditions for receiving the benefit. Employers should satisfy themselves, if necessary with actuarial advice and/or medical evidence, of the likelihood of there being a substantially greater cost.[11]

When could the justification be used?

6.12 The justification would be available whenever the disabled person is considered for admission to the scheme. However, the justification cannot be applied to a disabled member, unless a term was imposed at the time of admission which allowed this.

11 Employment Regulations (see paragraph 1.6)

Which benefits does this justification apply to?

6.13 The justification can apply to the following types of benefits provided by an occupational pension scheme: termination of service, retirement, old age or death, accident, injury, sickness or invalidity.[12]

Would a minor degree of extra cost amount to a justification for less favourable treatment?

6.14 No. Only the likelihood of a substantial additional cost should be taken to be a justification. Substantial means something more than minor or trivial.[13]

> An employer receives medical advice that an individual with multiple sclerosis is likely to retire early on health grounds. The employer obtains actuarial advice that the cost of providing that early retirement benefit would be substantially greater than an employee without MS and so the individual is refused access to the scheme. This is justified.

What happens to an employee's rate of contributions if the employer is justified in refusing the employee access to some benefits but not others?

6.15 *Regulations provide* that if the employer sets a uniform rate of contribution the employer would be justified in applying it to a disabled person. A disabled person could therefore be required to pay the same rate of contributions as other employees, even if not eligible for some of the benefits.[14]

Does the duty to make a reasonable adjustment apply?

6.16 No. The duty of reasonable adjustment does not apply to the provision of benefits under an occupational pension scheme or any other benefit payable in money or money's worth under a scheme or arrangement for the benefit of employees in respect of:

- ■ termination of service;

- ■ retirement, old age or death; or

- ■ accident, injury, sickness or invalidity *(S6(11))*. (Although there is power to add other matters to this list by regulations, none have been added at the date of this Code).

12 Employment Regulations (see paragraph 1.6)
13 Employment Regulations (see paragraph 1.6)
14 Employment Regulations (see paragraph 1.6)

Therefore, neither the employer nor the scheme's trustees or managers need to make any adjustment for a disabled person who, without that adjustment, will be justifiably denied access either to such a scheme or to a benefit under the scheme. Nor will they have to make an adjustment for someone receiving less benefit because they justifiably receive a lower rate of pay.

Does the Act cover the provision of insurance schemes for individual employees?

6.17 The Act also applies to provision of group insurance, such as permanent health insurance or life insurance, by an insurance company for employees under an arrangement with their employer. A disabled person in, or who applies or is considering applying to join, a group of employees covered by such an arrangement is protected from discrimination in the provision of the insurance services in the same way as if he were a member of the public seeking the services of that insurance company under the part of the Act relating to the provision of goods, facilities and services. However, the right of redress in this case would be exercised through an industrial tribunal (and not the courts) *(S18).*

Does the Act cover the provision of insurance to an employer?

6.18 The employer may have to make reasonable adjustments to remove any disadvantage caused to a disabled person which arose from the arrangements made by the employer to provide himself with insurance cover. Such adjustments could include measures which would reduce any risk otherwise posed by the disabled person, so that the insurer would then provide cover, or seeking alternative cover. If cover could not be obtained at all at realistic cost it is most unlikely that the employer would have to bear the risk himself.

> It comes to an employer's attention that someone who works for his antiques business has epilepsy. The employer is obliged to notify his insurance company who refuse to cover the employer against damage caused by the disabled person. To avoid dismissing the employee, it might be reasonable for the employer to have to bar the person from contact with valuable items, if this would mean the insurance company then provided cover.

Retention of disabled employees

6.19 An employer must not discriminate against an employee who becomes disabled, or has a disability which worsens *(S4(2))*. The issue of retention might also arise when an employee has a stable impairment but the nature of his employment changes.

6.20 If as a result of the disability an employer's arrangements or a physical feature of the employer's premises place the employee at a substantial disadvantage in doing his existing job, the employer must first consider any reasonable adjustment that would resolve the difficulty. The employer may also need to consult the disabled person at appropriate stages about what his needs are and what effect the disability might have on future employment, for example, where the employee has a progressive condition. The nature of the reasonable adjustments which an employer may have to consider will depend on the circumstances of the case.

> It may be possible to modify a job to accommodate an employee's changed needs. This might be by rearranging working methods or giving another employee certain minor tasks the newly disabled person can no longer do, providing practical aids or adaptations to premises or equipment, or allowing the disabled person to work at different times or places from those with equivalent jobs (for instance, it may be that a change to part-time work might be appropriate for someone who needed to spend some time each week having medical treatment).

> A newly disabled employee is likely to need time to readjust. For example, an employer might allow: a trial period to assess whether the employee is able to cope with the current job, or a new one; the employee initially to work from home; a gradual build-up to full time hours; or additional training for a person with learning disabilities who moves to another workplace.

> It may be a reasonable adjustment for an employer to move a newly disabled person to a different post within the organisation if a suitable vacancy exists or is expected shortly.

> Additional job coaching may be necessary to enable a disabled person to take on a new job.

In many cases where no reasonable adjustment would overcome a particular disability so as to enable the disabled person to continue with similar terms or conditions, it might be reasonable for the employer to have to offer a disabled employee a lower-paying job, applying the rate of pay that would apply to such a position under his usual pay practices.

If new technology (for instance a telephone or information technology system) puts a disabled person at a substantial disadvantage compared with non-disabled people, then the employer would be under a duty to make a reasonable adjustment. For example, some telephone systems may interfere with hearing aids for people with hearing impairments and the quality of the inductive coupler may need to be improved.

Termination of employment

6.21 Dismissal – including compulsory early retirement – of a disabled person for a reason relating to the disability would need to be justified and the reason for it would have to be one which could not be removed by any reasonable adjustment.

It would be justifiable to terminate the employment of an employee whose disability makes it impossible for him any longer to perform the main functions of his job, if an adjustment such as a move to a vacant post elsewhere in the business is not practicable or otherwise not reasonable for the employer to have to make.

It would be justifiable to terminate the employment of an employee with a worsening progressive condition if the increasing degree of adjustment necessary to accommodate the effects of the condition (shorter hours of work or falling productivity, say) became unreasonable for the employer to have to make.

An employer who needs to reduce the workforce would have to ensure that any scheme which was introduced for choosing candidates for redundancy did not discriminate against disabled people. Therefore, if a criterion for redundancy would apply to a disabled person for a reason relating to the disability, that criterion would have to be "material" and "substantial" and the employer would have to consider whether a reasonable adjustment would prevent the criterion applying to the disabled person after all.

Harassment

What does the Act say about harassment?

6.22 The Act does not refer to harassment as a separate issue. However, harassing a disabled person on account of a disability will almost always amount to a "detriment" under the Act. (Victimisation is covered in paragraphs 4.53–4.54).

Are employers liable for harassment by their employees?

6.23 An employer is responsible for acts of harassment by employees in the course of their employment unless the employer took such steps as were reasonable practicable to prevent it. As a minimum first step harassment because of disability should be made a disciplinary matter and staff should be made aware that it will be taken seriously.

Particular provisions

Discrimination against contract workers

7.1   The Act deals specifically with work which is carried out by individuals ("contract workers") for a person (a "principal") who hires them under contract from their employer (generally an employment business) – referred to below as the "sending" employer.

What does the Act say about contract workers?

7.2   *The Act says* that it is unlawful for a principal to discriminate against a disabled person:

- in the terms on which the person is allowed to do the contract work;

- by not allowing the person to do, or continue to do, the contract work;

- in the way he affords the person access to, or by failing to afford him access to, benefits in relation to contract work; or

- by subjecting the person to any other detriment in relation to contract work *(S12(1))*.

7.3   *The Act and Regulations apply*, generally speaking, as if the principal were, or would be, the actual employer of the contract worker. Therefore, the same definition of "discrimination" – including the need to justify less favourable treatment – applies as for employers *(S12(3))*.

> The employer of a labourer, who some years ago was disabled by clinical depression but has since recovered, proposes to supply him to a contractor to work on a building site. Although his past disability is covered by the Act, the site manager refuses to accept him because of his medical history. Unless the contractor can show that the manager's action is justified, the contractor would be acting unlawfully.

What will be the effect of the duty to make adjustments for principals?

7.4   The duty to make a reasonable adjustment applies to a principal as to an employer *(S12(3))*.

7.5   In deciding whether any, and if so, what, adjustment would be reasonable for a principal to have to make, the period for which the contract worker will work for the principal is important. It might well be unreasonable for a principal to have to make certain adjustments if the worker will be with the principal for only a short time.

An employment business enters into a contract with a firm of accountants to provide an assistant for two weeks to cover an unexpected absence. The employment business wishes to put forward a person who, because of his disability, finds it difficult to travel during the rush hour and would like his working hours to be modified accordingly. It might not be reasonable for the firm to have to agree given the short time in which to negotiate and implement the new hours.

Will the principal and the "sending" employer both have duties to make reasonable adjustments?

7.6   Both the "sending" employer and the principal may separately be under a duty of reasonable adjustment in the case of a contract worker who is disabled. If the "sending" employer's own premises or arrangements place the contract worker at a substantial disadvantage, then the "sending" employer may have a duty to make a reasonable adjustment *(S6(1))*. The "sending" employer may also have a duty to make a reasonable adjustment where a similar substantial disadvantage is likely to affect a contract worker as a result of the arrangements or premises of all or most of the principals to whom he might be supplied. The employer would not have to take separate steps in relation to each principal, but would have to make any reasonable adjustment within his power which would overcome the disadvantage wherever it might arise. The principal would not have to make any adjustment which the employer should make.[15] However, subject to that the principal would be responsible only for any additional reasonable adjustment which is necessary solely because of the principal's own arrangements or premises *(S6(1)* applied by *S12(3))*. It would also usually be reasonable for a principal and a "sending" employer to have to cooperate with any steps taken by the other to assist a disabled contract worker.

A travel agency hires a clerical worker from an employment business to fulfil a three month contract to file travel invoices during the busy summer holiday period. The contract worker is a wheelchair user, and is quite capable of doing the job if a few minor, temporary changes are made to the arrangement of furniture in the office. It would be reasonable for the travel agency to make this adjustment.

---

15 Employment Regulations (see paragraph 1.6)

A bank hires a blind word processor operator as a contract worker from an employment business. The employment business provides her with a specially adapted portable computer because she would otherwise be at a similar substantial disadvantage in doing the work wherever she does it. (In such circumstances the bank would not have to provide a specially adapted computer if the employment business did not.) The bank would have to cooperate by letting the contract worker use her computer whilst working for the bank if it is compatible with the bank's systems. If not, it could be a reasonable adjustment for the bank to make the computer compatible and for the employment business to allow that change to be made.

What about contract workers in small firms?

7.7 The Act applies to any employment business which has 20 or more employees (including people currently employed by it but hired out to principals). It also applies to any principal who has 20 or more workers (counting both the principal's own employees and any contract workers currently working for the principal). It does not apply to employment businesses or principals with fewer than 20 employees. Note the extended definition of "employment" in the Act (see paragraph 2.8).

An employment business has 15 employees (including people currently hired out to others) and enters a contract to provide a worker in a shop. The shop employs 29 people. Neither the duty not to discriminate nor the duty to make a reasonable adjustment applies to the employment business, but both duties apply to the owner of the shop. However, the length of time the worker was contracted to work at the shop would be an important factor in assessing whether the shop-owner had to make any significant adjustment.

A deaf individual is employed by an employment business that has 100 employees (including people currently hired out to others). He is hired regularly to do contract work and, as a reasonable adjustment, the business provides a portable induction loop for assignments. If he works for a principal with, say, 17 workers, (counting both employees and contract workers) that principal would not be required to cooperate with use of the induction loop. However, if the principal has 20 or more such workers the principal would be obliged to cooperate.

What about the Supported Placement Scheme (SPS)?

7.8   These arrangements also apply to the Employment Service's Supported Placement Scheme (SPS) for severely disabled people. The "contractor" under the scheme (usually a local authority or voluntary body) is the equivalent of the "sending" employer, and the "host employer" is the equivalent of the principal. A local authority can even be both the contractor and the host employer at the same time (as can a voluntary body) in which case the duty not to discriminate and the duty of reasonable adjustment would apply to it as to an employer.

Provisions applying to trade organisations

What does the Act say about trade organisations?

7.9   A trade organisation is defined as an organisation of workers or of employers, or any other organisation whose members carry on a particular profession or trade for the purposes of which the organisation exists *(S13(4))*. Therefore trade unions, employers' associations, and similar bodies like the Law Society and chartered professional institutions, for example, must comply with the legislation.

7.10 *The Act says* that it is unlawful for a trade organisation to discriminate against a disabled person:

- in the terms on which it is prepared to admit the person to membership; or

- by refusing to accept, or deliberately not accepting, an application for membership.

It is also unlawful for a trade organisation to discriminate against a disabled member of the organisation:

- in the way it affords the person access to any benefits or by refusing or deliberately omitting to afford access to them;

- by depriving the person of membership, or varying the terms of membership; or

- by subjecting the person to any other detriment *(S13)*.

Trade organisations should therefore check that they do not discriminate as regards, for example, training facilities, welfare or insurance schemes, invitations to attend events, processing of grievances, assistance to members in their employers' disciplinary or dismissal procedures.

7.11 **The Act defines** discrimination by a trade organisation in similar terms to the definition relating to discrimination by an employer. Therefore, the need to justify less favourable treatment for a reason relating to disability applies as in the case of an employer **(S14(3))**.

> A trade organisation is arranging a trip to some of its members' workplaces but it decides to exclude a member in a wheelchair because too many of the sites are inaccessible to make participation worthwhile. This could well be justified. (Note, however, paragraph 7.12)

Do trade organisations have a duty to make adjustments?

7.12 **The Act includes** a requirement on trade organisations to make reasonable adjustments **(S15)**. However, this duty will not be brought into force until after the other employment provisions, at a date which will be subject to consultation.

What about the actions of employees or representatives of trade organisations?

7.13 Individual employees or agents of trade organisations who have dealings with members or applicants are treated in the same way as individual employees or agents of employers who deal with job applicants or employees: the trade organisation is responsible for their actions **(S58)**.

8   Resolving disagreements within the employing organisation

What does the Act say about resolving disagreements?

8.1   The Act does not require employers to resolve disputes within their organisations. However, it is in an employer's interests to resolve problems as they arise where possible. This should be in a non-discriminatory way to comply with the Act's general provisions.

8.2   One method might be the use of a grievance procedure. Grievance procedures provide an open and fair way for employees to make known their concerns and enable grievances to be resolved quickly before they become major difficulties. Use of the procedures can highlight areas where the employer's duty of reasonable adjustment may not have been observed, and can prevent misunderstandings in this area leading to tribunal complaints.

Do existing grievance and disciplinary procedures need changing?

8.3   Where grievance or disciplinary procedures are in place, the employer might wish to review, and where necessary adapt, them to ensure that they are flexible enough to be used by disabled employees. Where a formal grievance (or disciplinary) procedure operates, it must be open, or applied, to disabled employees on the same basis as to others. Employers will have to ensure that grievance (or disciplinary) procedures do not, in themselves, discriminate against disabled employees and may have to make reasonable adjustments to enable some disabled employees to use grievance procedures effectively or to ensure disciplinary procedures have the same impact on disabled employees as on others.

> An employee with a learning disability has to attend an interview under the employer's disciplinary procedures. The employee would like his guardian or a friend to be present. The employer agrees to this but refuses to rearrange the interview to a time which is more convenient to the guardian or friend. The employer may be in breach of the duty to make a reasonable adjustment.

(See Annex 3 for information about industrial tribunals.)

Annex 1   What is meant by disability

1   This Annex is included to aid understanding about who is covered by the Act and should provide sufficient information on the definition of disability to cover the large majority of cases. The definition of disability in the Act is designed to cover only people who would generally be considered to be disabled. A Government publication *Guidance on matters to be taken into account in determining questions relating to the definition of disability*, is also available.

When is a person disabled?

2   A person has a disability if he has a physical or mental impairment which has a substantial and long-term adverse effect on his ability to carry out normal day-to-day activities.

What about people who have recovered from a disability?

3   People who have had a disability within the definition are protected from discrimination even if they have since recovered.

What does "impairment" cover?

4   It covers physical or mental impairments; this includes sensory impairments, such as those affecting sight or hearing.

Are all mental impairments covered?

5   The term "mental impairment" is intended to cover a wide range of impairments relating to mental functioning, including what are often known as learning disabilities. However, the Act states that it does not include any impairment resulting from or consisting of a mental illness, unless that illness is a clinically well-recognised illness. A clinically well-recognised illness is one that is recognised by a respected body of medical opinion.

What is a "substantial" adverse effect?

6   A substantial adverse effect is something which is more than a minor or trivial effect. The requirement that an effect must be substantial reflects the general understanding of disability as a limitation going beyond the normal differences in ability which might exist among people.

What is a "long-term" effect?

7   A long-term effect of an impairment is one:

■ which has lasted at least 12 months; or

■ where the total period for which it lasts is likely to be at least 12 months; or

■ which is likely to last for the rest of the life of the person affected.

8   Effects which are not long-term would therefore include loss of mobility due to a broken limb which is likely to heal within 12 months and the effects of temporary infections, from which a person would be likely to recover within 12 months.

What if the effects come and go over a period of time?

9   If an impairment has had a substantial adverse effect on normal day-to-day activities but that effect ceases, the substantial effect is treated as continuing if it is likely to recur; that is if it is more probable than not that the effect will *recur*. To take the example of a person with rheumatoid arthritis whose impairment has a substantial adverse effect, which then ceases to be substantial (i.e. the person has a period of remission). The effects are to be treated as if they are continuing, and are likely to continue beyond 12 months, *if:*

■ the impairment remains; and

■ at least one recurrence of the substantial effect is likely to take place 12 months or more after the initial occurrence.

This would then be a long-term effect.

What are "normal day-to-day activities"?

10   They are activities which are carried out by most people on a fairly regular and frequent basis. The term is not intended to include activities which are normal only for a particular person or group of people, such as playing a musical instrument, or a sport, to a professional standard or performing a skilled or specialised task at work. However, someone who is affected in such a specialised way but is *also* affected in normal day-to-day activities, would be covered by this part of the definition. The test of whether an impairment affects normal day-to-day activities is whether it affects one of the broad categories of capacity listed in Schedule 1 to the Act. They are:

- mobility;

- manual dexterity;

- physical co-ordination;

- continence;

- ability to lift, carry or otherwise move everyday objects;

- speech, hearing or eyesight;

- memory or ability to concentrate, learn or understand; or

- perception of the risk of physical danger.

What about treatment?

11   Someone with an impairment may be receiving medical or other treatment which alleviates or removes the effects (though not the impairment). In such cases, the treatment is ignored and the impairment is taken to have the effect it would have had without such treatment. This does not apply if substantial adverse effects are not likely to recur even if the treatment stops (i.e. the impairment has been cured).

Does this include people who wear spectacles?

12   No. The sole exception to the rule about ignoring the effects of treatment is the wearing of spectacles or contact lenses. In this case, the effect while the person is wearing spectacles or contact lenses should be considered.

Are people who have disfigurements covered?

13   People with severe disfigurements are covered by the Act. They do not need to demonstrate that the impairment has a substantial adverse effect on their ability to carry out normal day-to-day activities.

What about people who know their condition is going to get worse over time?

14   Progressive conditions are conditions which are likely to change and develop over time. Examples given in the Act are cancer, multiple sclerosis, muscular dystrophy and HIV infection. Where a person has a progressive condition he will be covered by the Act from the moment the condition leads to an impairment which has *some* effect on ability to carry out normal day-to-day activities, even though not a *substantial* effect, if that impairment is likely eventually to have a substantial adverse effect on such ability.

What about people who are registered disabled?

15   Those registered as disabled under the Disabled Persons (Employment) Act 1944 both on 12 January 1995 and 2 December 1996 will be treated as being disabled under the Disability Discrimination Act 1995 for three years from the latter date. At all times from 2 December 1996 onwards they will be covered by the Act as people who have had a disability. This does not preclude them from being covered as having a current disability any time after the three year period has finished. Whether they are or not will depend on whether they – like anyone else – meet the definition of disability in the Act.

Are people with genetic conditions covered?

16   If a genetic condition has no effect on ability to carry out normal day-to-day activities, the person is not covered. Diagnosis does not in itself bring someone within the definition. If the condition is progressive, then the rule about progressive conditions applies.

Are any conditions specifically excluded from the coverage of the Act?

17   Yes. Certain conditions are to be regarded as not amounting to impairments for the purposes of the Act. These are:

- addiction to or dependency on alcohol, nicotine, or any other substance (other than as a result of the substance being medically prescribed);

- seasonal allergic rhinitis (e.g. hayfever), except where it aggravates the effect of another condition;

- tendency to set fires;

- tendency to steal;

- tendency to physical or sexual abuse of other persons;

- exhibitionism;

- voyeurism.

Also, disfigurements which consist of a tattoo (which has not been removed), non-medical body piercing, or something attached through such piercing, are to be treated as not having a substantial adverse effect on the person's ability to carry out normal day-to-day activities.[16]

16 Definition Regulations (see paragraph 1.6)

Annex 2 How to get further information, help and advice

1   A range of leaflets about various aspects of the Act is available. To obtain copies, call 0345 622 633 (local rate), or textphone 0345 622 644. Copies of the leaflets are also available in braille and audio cassette.

2   Statutory Guidance on the definition of disability is produced separately. This can be obtained from HMSO bookshops – see back cover of this Code. This Guidance should prove helpful where it is not clear whether or not a person has or has had a disability.

3   There is a wide range of practical help and advice available to assist employers in the recruitment and employment of people, including disabled people, for example from Jobcentres, Careers Service offices, Training and Enterprise Councils (in England and Wales) and Local Enterprise Companies (in Scotland). Addresses and telephone numbers are available in local telephone directories.

4   Where necessary, specialist help and advice for disabled people and for employers who might, or do, employ disabled people is available from the Employment Service through its local Placing, Assessment and Counselling Teams (PACTs). PACTs can help with issues related to employing disabled people, but cannot advise on an employer's specific legal obligations.

5   PACTs may be able to provide help with special aids, equipment and other measures to overcome the effects of disability in the working environment.

6   The addresses and telephone numbers of PACTs are listed in local telephone directories under "Employment Service", or can be obtained from the nearest Jobcentre.

7   Many specialist organisations for disabled people also offer a range of employment help and advice. The Employment Service publish a booklet called *Sources of Information and Advice (Ref: PGP6)* which lists many of the specialist organisations offering help to employers on employment and disability issues. The booklet can be obtained from PACTs.

8   The Advisory, Conciliation and Arbitration Service (ACAS) can help employers and individuals with factual information on the legislation and assistance related to its effects on industrial relations practices and procedures. The address and telephone numbers of ACAS offices are listed in local telephone directories under "ACAS".

9   Employers working in historic buildings, or other heritage properties, may also wish to obtain a copy of *Easy Access to Historic Properties* from English Heritage at 23 Savile Row, London W1X 1AB. Tel: 0171 973 3434.

10   Disability can take a very large number of forms and the action an employer may be required to take will depend to a very large extent on the particular circumstances of the case. Any advice and information employers receive should be considered in that light. In some circumstances employers may wish to consider whether they should seek legal advice.

Annex 3 Complaints under the employment provisions

What does the Act say about making complaints?

1   **The Act says** that a person who believes that an employer has unlawfully discriminated or failed to make a reasonable adjustment, or that a person has aided an employer to do such an act, may present a complaint to an industrial tribunal *(S8(1))*.

What does the Act say about conciliation?

2   When a formal complaint has been made to an industrial tribunal **the Act places a duty** on the Advisory, Conciliation and Arbitration Service's (ACAS) conciliation officers to try to promote settlement of the dispute without a tribunal hearing *(Sch 3, Para 1)*. ACAS can also assist in this way without a formal application to a tribunal being made.

What does the Act say about obtaining a remedy for unlawful discrimination?

3   **The Act says** that a disabled person who believes someone has unlawfully discriminated against him or failed to make a reasonable adjustment, in breach of the employment provisions of the Act or Regulations, may present a complaint to an industrial tribunal *(S8(1))*.

4   If the tribunal upholds the complaint it may:

■   declare the rights of the disabled person (the complainant), and the other person (the respondent) in relation to the complaint;

■   order the other person to pay the complainant compensation; and

■   recommend that, within a specified time, the other person take reasonable action to prevent or reduce the adverse effect in question *(S8(2))*.

5   **The Act allows** compensation for injury to feelings to be awarded whether or not other compensation is awarded *(S8(4))*.

6   **The Act says** that if a respondent fails, without reasonable justification, to comply with an industrial tribunal's recommendation, the tribunal may:

■   increase the amount of compensation to be paid; or

■   order the respondent to pay compensation if it did not make such an order earlier *(S8(5))*.

Who can be taken to an Industrial Tribunal?

7   The tribunal complaints procedure applies to anyone who, it is claimed, has discriminated in the employment field – employers (and their employees and agents for whose acts they are responsible), trade organisations, people who hire contract workers and people who aid any of these to discriminate.

Complaints involving landlords

8   If a reasonable adjustment requiring the consent of the employer's landlord (or a superior landlord) is not made, for whatever reason, the disabled person may bring a complaint against the employer in an industrial tribunal. Either the disabled person or the employer may ask the tribunal to make the landlord a party to the proceedings. If the industrial tribunal finds that the landlord acted unreasonably in withholding consent, or gave consent but attached an unreasonable condition, it can make any appropriate declaration, order that the alteration may be made, or award compensation against the landlord *(S27 and Sch 4 Para 2).*

Complaining about pension schemes

9   A disabled person who considers that the trustees or managers of a pension scheme have discriminated against him, may complain through the pensions dispute resolution mechanism. Information about the scheme should give details about this. If necessary, a complaint may be made to the Pensions Ombudsman.

10   From April 1997, all occupational pension schemes will be required to set up and operate procedures for resolving disputes between individual pension scheme members and the trustees or managers.

11   The Occupational Pensions Advisory Service (OPAS) can provide an advice and conciliation service for members of the public who have problems with their occupational pension. OPAS can be contacted at 11 Belgrave Road, London SW1U 1RB. Tel: 0171 233 8080.

12   A disabled person who considers that an employer has discriminated against him in providing access to a pension scheme can complain to an industrial tribunal following the same process for other complaints against employers.

What is the "Questionnaire Procedure"?

13. *The Act provides for* a procedure (the questionnaire procedure) to assist a person who believes that discrimination has occurred, to decide whether or not to start proceedings and, if the person does, to formulate and present a case in the most effective manner *(S56)*. Questionnaire forms will be obtainable from Jobcentres.

Can compromise agreements be an alternative to making tribunal complaints?

14 *The Act says* that, in general, the terms of an agreement (such as a contract of employment) cannot prevent a disabled person from complaining to an industrial tribunal, or force a complaint to be stopped *(S9)*. However, *the Act also says* that in some circumstances a disabled person can make an agreement not to make a complaint or to stop one *(S9)*.

15 These circumstances are if:

■ an ACAS conciliation officer has acted under the Act on the matter; *or* the following conditions apply:

■ the disabled person must have received independent legal advice from a qualified lawyer about the terms and effects of the agreement, particularly its effect on his ability to complain to a tribunal;

■ the adviser must have an insurance policy covering any loss arising from the advice; and

■ the agreement must be in writing, relate to the complaint, identify the adviser and say that these conditions are satisfied.

16 It may be in the interests of some disabled people to make such "compromise" agreements instead of pursuing complaints to industrial tribunal hearings, but care should be taken to ensure that the above conditions are met.

How is a complaint made to an Industrial Tribunal?

17   Complaints to an industrial tribunal can be made on an application form (IT1). Forms are obtainable from Jobcentres. Completed applications should be returned to the Industrial Tribunals Central Office. The address is on the form.

18   Applications to an industrial tribunal must be made within three months of the time when the incident being complained of occurred. The time limit will not normally be extended to allow for the time it might take to try to settle the dispute within the organisation eg. by way of internal grievance procedures (see paragraphs 8.1–8.3). A tribunal may, however, consider a complaint which is out of time, if it considers, in all the circumstances of the case, that it is just and equitable to do so *(Sch 3, Para 3)*.

What does the Act say about reporting restrictions?

19   *The Act empowers* a tribunal to make "restricted reporting orders" if it considers that evidence of a personal nature is likely to be heard by the tribunal. Such orders prohibit the publication, for example in a newspaper, of any matter likely to lead members of the public to identify the complainant or any other person mentioned in the order, until the tribunal's decision is promulgated.

Index

References are to paragraph numbers (including the associated examples) in this Code and its annexes. References to specific disabilities in the examples contained in the Code are not shown separately in the index. The examples are illustrative only (see paragraph 3.1) and it could be misleading to suggest that particular examples apply only to the type of disability specifically mentioned in them. The approach taken in this index is to refer to the kinds of situations which employers might face in relation to the employment of disabled people or to particular provisions in the Act. Cross references to other index items are given in brackets. References to "the Act" are to the Disability Discrimination Act 1995.

DOCUMENT 3

Code of Practice
Rights of Access
Goods, Facilities, Services and Premises

CONTENTS

1   INTRODUCTION

Purpose of Code

1.1   The Disability Discrimination Act 1995 (the Act) brings in new measures to prevent discrimination against disabled people. Part III of the Act is based on the principle that disabled people should not be treated less favourably, simply because of their disability, by those **providing goods, facilities or services to the public** or by those **selling, letting or managing premises.** If you are in either of these categories, you must comply with the duties set out in the Act, which are described and explained in this Code of Practice (the Code).

1.2   The Code gives practical advice on how to comply with the new duties. The Code will also help disabled people to understand the law. The Code is issued by the Secretary of State on the basis of proposals prepared by the National Disability Council. It applies to England, Scotland and Wales and comes into effect on 2 December 1996. A separate Code applies to Northern Ireland.

Status of Code

1.3   The Code does not impose legal obligations. Nor is it an authoritative statement of the law – that is a matter for the courts. However, the Code can be used in evidence in any legal proceedings under the Act. Courts must take into account any part of the Code that appears to them relevant to any question arising. If you follow the advice in the Code, you may avoid an adverse judgement by the court in any proceedings taken against you.

Using the Code

1.4   **Chapter two** describes who is and who is not affected by the Act, and explains the meaning of discrimination. You will need to read this chapter to have a proper understanding of the Code. Provision of goods, facilities and services is covered in **chapter three**. If you are selling or letting premises you will need to read **chapter four**. There are some exceptions to the duties set out in chapters three and four – these are covered in **chapter five**. **Chapter six** describes other actions which are unlawful under the access to goods, facilities, services and premises provisions of the Act. **Chapter seven** explains what happens if discrimination is alleged.

1.5   The Code should not be read narrowly. Each section should be viewed as part of an overall explanation of the Act.

1.6   Examples of how the Act is likely to work in practice are given in boxes. The examples are given **for illustrative purposes** only and should not be treated as a complete or authoritative statement of the law. References to the Act are shown in {} (for example {S1(1)} means Section 1(1) of the Act).

General Approach

1.7   Discrimination may stem from lack of awareness about disability. It may also be the result of making assumptions. For example, you might assume that a disabled person would not benefit from a service or that you could not cope with serving him or her. When in doubt, ask the disabled person.

1.8   You will need to think about your **attitude towards disabled people** and the way you and your staff deal with customers. For example, you should consider:

●   informing all staff dealing with customers that it is unlawful to discriminate against disabled people;

●   establishing a policy towards disabled customers which is communicated to all staff;

●   providing disability awareness training for all staff serving customers and monitoring its implementation; and

●   having an appropriate complaints mechanism.

Further Information

1.9　Copies of the Act, and any regulations made under it, are available from
HMSO. A separate code, covering the rights of disabled employees, is
also available from the same source. Further information on the Act
is available from Disability on the Agenda (telephone 0345 622 633,
textphone 0345 622 644). Organisations providing information or
advice to business, and advice agencies, may also be able to help.

2   WHO IS AFFECTED BY THE ACT?

What does the Act mean by "disabled people"?

2.1   An adult or child is disabled if he or she has a physical or mental impairment which has an effect which is:

- substantial (not just trivial or minor);

- adverse; and

- long term (lasting or expected to last for at least a year)

on his or her ability to carry out normal day-to-day activities {S1(1)}. Physical or mental impairment includes a sensory impairment.

2.2   People who have had a disability within the definition are protected from discrimination even if they have since recovered.

2.3   The appendix to the Code gives some more detail about who is covered.

Providing goods, facilities and services – who is affected?

2.4   In the Act the provision of services includes the provision of goods and facilities. Subject to the exclusions set out in paragraph 2.9, the Act affects anyone concerned with the provision of services to the public, whether in the public, private or voluntary sectors. It does not matter if the service in question is provided free (such as access to a public park) or in return for payment (for example, a meal in a restaurant).

2.5   Unlike the Act's employment provisions, there is no exemption for small employers.

2.6   Services not generally available to the public, such as those provided by private clubs, are not covered. Nor does the Act cover the manufacture or design of products. Where clubs or manufacturers do provide services to the public – for example, a company selling the goods it produces by mail order or a private golf club hiring out its facilities for a wedding reception – the Act applies to those services.

2.7 Among the services covered are those provided by local councils, hotels, banks, solicitors, advice agencies, pubs, theatres, hairdressers, any kind of shop, telesales businesses, places of worship, courts and doctors {S19(3)}. All those involved in providing the service are affected – from the most senior person to the most junior employee, whether full or part-time, permanent or temporary.

Premises – who is affected?

2.8 Subject to the exemptions set out in paragraphs 2.10 and 2.11, the Act also covers anyone involved in the sale, letting and management of all types of premises, for example, land, houses, flats and business premises. Local councils, housing associations, private landlords, estate agencies, accommodation agencies, property developers, managing agents and private owner-occupiers could be affected.

What is not affected?

2.9 The only services which are excluded are:

● **education,** and some services which are very closely related to it – such as the youth service (whether provided by a local education authority or the voluntary sector), some examination and assessment services and facilities for research students. Any other services which are provided on school, college or university premises (for example, where a Parent Teachers' Association organises a fund-raising event) are subject to the duties described in the Code. (Part IV of the Act requires schools, colleges and universities to provide information on access).

● **transport vehicles,** although the transport infrastructure, for example, bus stations and airports, is covered (Part V of the Act allows the Government to set access standards for buses, trains, trams and taxis).

2.10 You are exempt from the measures that apply to selling, letting and managing premises if you, or a near relative of yours:

- live on the premises; and

- share accommodation, other than storage accommodation or a means of access, with others who are not members of your household.

This applies only if the premises in question are small which means:

- only you and your household live in the accommodation you occupy, and there is accommodation, let on a separate tenancy or similar agreement, for normally no more than two other households; **or**

- you do not normally let accommodation in your own home to more than six people {S23}.

2.11 In addition, you are exempt from the measures that apply to selling and letting premises if you are an owner-occupier and you do not use an estate agent or advertise publicly {S22(2)}.

What is "discrimination"?

2.12 It is unlawful for you to discriminate against a disabled person in the circumstances described in chapter 3 and chapter 4 {S19(1) & S21(1)}. The Act says discrimination occurs when:

- for a reason which relates to a disabled person's disability,

- you treat him or her less favourably than you treat or would treat others to whom that reason does not or would not apply, and

- you cannot show this treatment was justified {S20(1) & S24(1)}.

A waiter asks a disabled customer to leave the restaurant because she has difficulty eating as a result of her disability. He serves other customers who have no difficulty eating. The waiter has therefore treated her **less favourably** than other customers. The treatment was for **a reason related to her disability** – her difficulty when eating. And the reason for her less favourable treatment did **not apply to the other customers.**

If the waiter could not justify the less favourable treatment, he would have discriminated unlawfully.

2.13 The disabled person does not have to point to others who **were** treated more favourably than he or she was. It is still "less favourable" treatment if others **would have been** treated better.

2.14 Less favourable treatment is not necessarily the same as bad treatment. Treatment must be less favourable by comparison with others (including other disabled people). If, for example, all customers were given the same poor standard of service and a disabled customer was treated no worse than others, no less favourable treatment would have occurred.

2.15 Treating a disabled person less favourably cannot be justified on the basis that anyone who behaves in a like manner is treated in the same way. In the above example, the waiter could not justify refusing to serve the disabled customer on the grounds that he would also have refused to serve anyone who was eating messily, for example, a child. Less favourable treatment of a disabled person is unlawful if it is for a reason which relates to his or her disability **and** it cannot be justified in one of the specified circumstances explained in more detail in chapter 5.

2.16 The Act cannot be used as an excuse for disruptive or anti-social behaviour. For example, if a publican refuses to serve a disabled person because he or she is abusive or drunk, the treatment would not be for a reason which related to the disabled person's disability. It would therefore be lawful to treat him or her in the same way as any other customer who was drunk. For such treatment to be caught by the Act, there must be a direct connection between the disabled person's disability and his or her less favourable treatment.

3 DUTIES UNDER THE ACT – Goods, Facilities & Services

What does the Act say?

3.1 **The Act says** it is unlawful for you to discriminate against a disabled person:

- in refusing to provide or deliberately not providing any service which you provide, or are prepared to provide, to members of the public (paragraphs 3.3 to 3.5) {S19(1)(a)};

- in the standard of service you provide or the manner in which you provide it (paragraphs 3.6 to 3.7) {S19(1)(c)}; or

- in the terms on which you provide a service (paragraph 3.8) {S19(1)(d)}.

3.2 Discrimination is unlawful if it is for a reason relating to a person's disability (discussed in more detail in paragraphs 2.12 to 2.16) and you cannot justify your actions. There are only limited circumstances in which you may be able to justify treating a disabled person less favourably (see chapter 5). The rest of this chapter should be read in this light.

What is the duty not to refuse service?

3.3 It is unlawful for you to refuse to serve, or deliberately not provide a service to, a disabled person for any reason related to his or her disability {S19(1)(a)}.

A group of deaf people is refused entry to a night club because the doorman thinks that communication using sign language might be seen as threatening. **This is against the law.**

3.4 Discrimination is unlawful whatever the intention. Even where you think you are helping the disabled person, but are nonetheless refusing to serve them, you may still be breaking the law. For example, you cannot refuse to serve disabled customers on the grounds that another service provider caters better for their needs.

A sweet shop refuses to serve a deaf child because the owner of a nearby sweet shop can communicate using British Sign Language and is therefore able to offer a better service. **This is against the law.**

3.5 Spurious reasons cannot be used to justify refusing to serve a disabled person.

A hotel pretends that all rooms are taken in order to refuse a booking from a mentally ill customer. **This is against the law.**

What is the duty not to provide a worse standard or manner of service?

3.6 It is against the law for you to offer a disabled person a lower level of service than the service you offer to other people {S19(1)(c)}. It is also against the law to adopt a worse manner in serving disabled people. Abusive behaviour towards disabled customers, especially the use of insulting language about their disability, is very likely to be used as evidence that they have been provided with a worse standard of service.

A restaurant tells a severely disfigured person he must sit at a table out of sight of other customers, despite other tables being free. **This is against the law.**

3.7 This duty does not mean that you have to change the service you provide to overcome the effects of the disability. Nor do you have to stock special products for disabled people. In due course, however, the later duties in the Act might require you to make adjustments to the way you provide your services to disabled customers (see inside front cover).

A shop selling telephones does not stock telephones with keyboards and screens for deaf customers. **This is within the law.**

What is the duty not to provide a service on worse terms?

3.8   It is unlawful for you to provide a service to a disabled person on terms
       which are worse than the terms offered to other people {S19(1)(d)}. This
       includes charging more for a service or imposing extra restrictions.

       A travel agent asks a person who is deaf and blind for a larger deposit
       than she requires from others because she assumes without good
       reason that the customer will be more likely to cancel his holiday.
       This is against the law.

Can you treat disabled people more favourably?

3.9   The Act does not prohibit positive action in favour of disabled people.
       You can therefore provide services on more favourable terms to a
       disabled person.

       A theatre manager offers a better seat to a blind person to allow room
       for her guide dog. **This is within the law.**

4   DUTIES UNDER THE ACT – Premises

What does the Act say?

4.1   It is unlawful for you to discriminate against a disabled person:

- in the terms on which you offer to dispose of premises to him or her (paragraph 4.10) {S22(1)(a)};

- by refusing to dispose of premises to him or her (paragraph 4.11) {S22(1)(b)}; or

- in the way you treat him or her in relation to a list of people needing premises (paragraph 4.12) {S22(1)(c)}.

4.2   The Act also says that if you manage premises it is unlawful for you to discriminate against a disabled person:

- in the way that you allow him or her to make use of any benefits or facilities (paragraph 4.13) {S22(3)(a)};

- by refusing or deliberately omitting to allow him or her to make use of any benefits or facilities (paragraph 4.13) {S22(3)(b)}; or

- by evicting him or her or subjecting him or her to any other detriment (paragraph 4.14) {S22(3)(c)}.

4.3   If your consent is required to dispose of premises to a tenant, you must not discriminate against a disabled person by withholding it. This applies to tenancies that were created both before and after the passing of the Act {S22(4)}.

4.4   However, you do not have to make adjustments to the premises to make them more suitable for a disabled person.

4.5   Some landlords and owner-occupiers are exempt from these duties (see paragraphs 2.10 – 2.11).

4.6 Discrimination is unlawful if it is for a reason relating to a person's disability (discussed in more detail in paragraphs 2.12 to 2.16) and you cannot justify your actions. There are only limited circumstances in which you may be able to justify treating a disabled person less favourably (see chapter 5). The rest of this chapter should be read in this light.

What is "disposing of premises"?

4.7 Disposing of premises includes selling and letting premises. Premises includes land and buildings, for example, houses, flats and business premises. Disposing of premises does not cover the hire of premises or rooms booked in hotels and guest houses. These are covered by the provisions relating to services (see chapter 3).

What is "managing premises"?

4.8 The term "managing premises" could include actions by accommodation agencies, housekeepers and estate agents who, for example, may collect the rent or provide access to particular benefits or facilities.

What are "benefits and facilities"?

4.9 Examples of benefits and facilities include laundry facilities, access to a garden and parking facilities.

What is the duty not to sell or let premises on worse terms?

4.10 It is unlawful for you to discriminate against a disabled person in the terms on which premises are sold or let {S22(1)(a)}.

A landlord asks a mentally ill person for a deposit when others have to pay none. **This is against the law.**

What is the duty not to refuse to sell or let premises?

4.11 It is against the law for you to refuse to sell or let premises to a disabled person {S22(1)(b)}.

Without any supporting evidence, a landlord refuses to let a flat to a person who has fully recovered from cancer because he believes her former disability might recur and would prevent her from keeping up the rent payments. **This is against the law**.

Are housing lists affected?

4.12 It is unlawful for you to treat a disabled person less favourably when maintaining housing lists {S22(1)(c)}.

A housing association keeps all disabled people at the bottom of its waiting list. **This is against the law**.

Using benefits and facilities

4.13 It is against the law for you to discriminate in the way in which a disabled tenant is allowed to make use of the benefits or facilities of premises, such as shared recreational areas {S22(3)(a)}. It is also against the law for you to prevent him or her from using them {S22(3)(b)}.

A landlord prevents a person with a severe facial disfigurement from using the swimming pool in a block of flats. **This is against the law**.

Eviction and other detriments

4.14 It is against the law for you to evict a disabled person simply because of his or her disability or otherwise place him or her at a disadvantage, such as harassment {S22(3)(c)}.

A landlord charges a person with a learning disability more than he charges other tenants for repairs to his flat. **This is against the law**.

Can you treat disabled people more favourably?

4.15 The Act does not prohibit positive action in favour of disabled people. You can therefore offer premises on better terms.

A local authority gives priority to disabled people ahead of other people on their waiting list for housing. **This is within the law**.

5   WHEN LESS FAVOURABLE TREATMENT CAN BE JUSTIFIED UNDER THE ACT

Introduction

5.1   This chapter sets out the limited circumstances in which you may be able to justify less favourable treatment of a disabled person for a reason which relates to his or her disability. No other form of justification is available. You should read this chapter in conjunction with the explanation of the meaning of discrimination (paragraphs 2.12 to 2.16).

5.2   You may be able to justify treating a disabled person less favourably **only if you believed that one or more of the conditions below applied and it was reasonable in all the circumstances of the case for you to have held that opinion.** You do not have to be an expert on disability but you are expected to take account of all the circumstances, including the information available to you, at the time.

A swimming pool attendant refuses to allow a child who uses a wheelchair to use the swimming pool because he believes the child is unable to swim. In the absence of further information, **this may be within the law.**

Despite being told subsequently by the child's mother that the child is a competent swimmer, the attendant persists in refusing him admission. **This is likely to be against the law.**

5.3   If a disabled person can show that he or she has been treated less favourably, you will have to prove that your actions were justified.

5.4   **Some of the conditions specified below (for example, those relating to health or safety) apply both to service providers and to those involved in disposing of premises. Others apply to one group alone. The heading for each section makes clear to whom it applies.**

Health or safety – services and premises

5.5 The Act does not require you to do anything which would endanger the health or safety of any person, including that of the disabled person {S20(4)(a) & S24(3)(a)}.

A driving instructor refuses to give lessons to a person with such severely impaired vision that he fails the eyesight test, even with glasses. **This is within the law.**

A landlord refuses to let a third floor flat to a disabled person living alone who is clearly unable to negotiate the stairs in safety or use the fire escape or other escape routes in an emergency. **This is within the law.**

5.6 Spurious health and safety reasons will provide no defence. For example, fire regulations should not be used as an excuse to place **unnecessary** restrictions on disabled people. It is for the management of the establishment concerned, in conjunction with the licensing authority, to make any special provision needed.

Although there are adequate means of escape, a cinema manager turns away a wheelchair user because he assumes, without checking, that she could be in danger in the event of a fire. **This is against the law.**

Despite knowing that there is no health risk, a landlord refuses to let a flat to someone with AIDS on the grounds that other tenants might be put at risk. **This is against the law.**

5.7 Every opportunity should be taken, as far as practicable, to enable disabled people to use cinemas, theatres, leisure centres and other entertainment venues. Equally, disabled people should not be prevented from living where they choose through unfounded concerns for safety.

Incapacity to contract – services and premises

5.8   The Act does not require you to contract with a disabled person who is incapable of entering into a legally enforceable agreement or of giving an informed consent {S20(4)(b) & S24(3)(b)}. If a disabled person is unable to understand a particular transaction due to mental incapacity, you may refuse to enter into a contract.

A landlord refuses to let a flat to a person with a severe learning disability who does not understand that rent would have to be paid. **This is within the law.**

5.9   Your refusal must be reasonable. A person may be able to understand less complicated transactions, but have difficulty with more complex ones. Unless there is clear evidence to the contrary, you should assume that a disabled person is able to enter into any contract.

Staff in a bakery refuse to sell a loaf of bread to a person with a severe learning disability because they claim she does not understand the nature of the agreement even though her order is clear and she is able to pay. **This is against the law.**

5.10 Regulations will prevent a service provider from justifying less favourable treatment of a disabled person on the grounds of incapacity to contract in a situation where another person is legally acting on his or her behalf (for example, under a power of attorney).

A salesman refuses to rent a television to someone simply because she is legally acting on behalf of someone who is mentally ill. **This is against the law.**

Providing the service – services

5.11 You may be able to justify refusing to serve a disabled person if this is necessary to serve other customers {S20(4)(c)}.

A tour guide refuses to allow an unaccompanied wheelchair user on a tour of old city walls because he has well-founded reasons to believe that the extra help he has to give her would prevent the party from completing the tour. **This is within the law.**

5.12 Similarly, you may be able to justify providing a lower standard of service or on worse terms if this is necessary to serve the disabled person or other customers {S20(4)(d)}.

A hotel restricts a wheelchair user to rooms on the ground floor because rooms on other floors are not accessible. This restriction of his choice of rooms is necessary in order to provide the service to him. **This is within the law.**

5.13 These conditions will justify less favourable treatment only where not treating the disabled person less favourably would effectively prevent other customers or the disabled person from using the service. They cannot be used to justify refusal simply because other people would be inconvenienced or delayed. The distinction is between people who have paid for a service and cannot receive it at all and those who are merely being delayed. It is most unlikely, for example, that you could justify asking a disabled person to go to the back of the queue so as not to delay other customers waiting to be served.

A clerk in a post office refuses to serve a deaf person because the extra time taken means that other customers have to queue for longer. **This is against the law**.

Greater expense – services

5.14 In general, it is unlawful for you to charge a disabled person more for a service than you charge anyone else, **except** where **additional costs** are incurred in providing a special service to the disabled person's particular requirements {S20(4)(e)}. Charging more can be justified only where the service is individually tailored to the needs of the customer and the disabled person's particular requirements increase costs due to greater materials or work.

A furniture shop charges more for an orthopaedic bed, made to the disabled person's specification, but does not charge more for a standard bed. **This is within the law.**

Necessary to provide the benefits or facilities – premises

5.15 You may be able to justify restricting access to benefits or facilities associated with premises if this is necessary to allow access to others or to the disabled person {S24(3)(c)}.

A landlord refuses to allow a mentally ill tenant to use the shared laundry facilities because he frequently breaks the washing machine. **This is within the law.**

5.16 Similarly, you may be able to justify denying access to benefits or facilities if this is necessary to allow access to others {S24(3)(d)}.

A landlord requires a disabled tenant to park her car at the side of the building as otherwise it would block the main entrance for other tenants. **This is within the law**.

5.17 These conditions will justify less favourable treatment only where not treating the disabled tenant less favourably would effectively prevent other tenants, or the disabled person, from using the benefit or facility. They cannot be used to justify less favourable treatment simply because other tenants would be inconvenienced or delayed.

A landlord refuses to allow a mentally ill tenant to use the shared kitchen because he sometimes takes a little longer and so delays other tenants. **This is against the law.**

What about the effects of other legislation?

5.18 The Act does not:

- make unlawful anything done to comply with other legislation (if you are required to do something under another law this takes precedence over anything required by the Act);

- make unlawful any act done to safeguard national security {S59}.

Special rules for insurance

5.19 Regulations will make special rules for insurance which recognise the need for insurers to be able to distinguish between individuals on the basis of the risks against which they seek to insure. Insurers will be able to justify less favourable treatment only if that treatment is based on actuarial or other statistical data or other information on which it is reasonable to rely. If a disabled person establishes in a court that less favourable treatment has occurred, it will be up to the insurer to prove that there is an additional risk associated with the disabled person which arises from his or her disability.

An insurance company charges a higher premium to a deaf person for car insurance although it has no evidence of an increased risk. **This is against the law.**

Special rules for guarantees and warranties

5.20 Many retailers go beyond their statutory duties by replacing goods if they wear out or break within a specified period of time. Generally speaking, they do this if the goods have been subjected to only an average amount of wear and tear. However, there are situations in which a person's disability might result in higher than average wear and tear. Regulations will exempt service providers from replacing goods in the latter circumstances.

A person with mobility problems buys a pair of shoes but wears out the left shoe after a few months because his left foot has to bear most of his weight. The retailer refuses to provide a new pair of shoes because the old pair has undergone abnormal wear and tear. **This is within the law.**

6   OTHER UNLAWFUL ACTIONS

Victimisation

6.1   It is unlawful for you to victimise (to pick on or treat less favourably) any person, **whether disabled or not**, who has:

- brought legal proceedings under the Act;

- given evidence or information in connection with such proceedings;

- done anything else under the Act; or

- alleged that the Act has been broken;

or because you believe that he or she has done or intends to do any of the above {S55}.

6.2   It is not victimisation to treat a person less favourably because that person has made an allegation which was false and not made in good faith.

Aiding unlawful actions

6.3   It is unlawful for you to aid anyone to discriminate against a disabled person, unless you are relying on a statement that the action is allowed under the Act and it is reasonable for you to rely on that statement. However, anyone who knowingly or recklessly makes a false statement of this kind is committing an offence {S57}.

A receptionist in a small hairdresser's, following his employer's instructions, refuses to book an appointment for a person with cerebral palsy. His employer has told him that small firms are exempt from Part III of the Act, despite knowing that this exemption applies only to the employment provisions in Part II. **The employee is within the law but the employer is not**.

Liability of employers for their employees' actions

6.4   Each of your employees is individually responsible for complying with the law. However, if one of your employees breaks the law in the course of his or her employment, action could also be taken against you even if you were unaware or did not approve of what he or she had done {S58(1)}. However, in a case where one of your employees breaks the law, you may have a defence if you can prove that you took such steps as were reasonably practicable to prevent him or her from discriminating {S58(5)}. Examples of the type of steps which might be reasonably practicable are set out in paragraph 1.8.

A sales assistant refuses to serve a disabled person, despite the employer having provided relevant and recent training, instructing staff to serve disabled people and checking regularly that they are complying. **The employer is likely to be within the law but the employee is not.**

6.5   If someone you authorise to act on your behalf – for example an agent – breaks the law, action could also be taken against you {S58(2)}. This applies whether the authority was express or implied and whether it was given before or after the unlawful act. You may, however, have a defence if you can show that your agent was not acting with your authority.

Terms of agreements

6.6   Any term in an agreement, such as a lease, is void if its effect is to:

- require someone to do something which would be unlawful under Part III of the Act (the part relating to services and premises);

- exclude or limit the operation of Part III; or

- prevent someone making a claim under Part III {S26}.

A landlord's lease includes a term forbidding the tenant from subletting to people with learning disabilities. **This term is not legally binding.**

7   DISPUTES AND PENALTIES

What happens if there is a dispute?

7.1 If you unlawfully discriminate against a disabled person he or she may seek to discuss the problem with you in order to resolve it. He or she may also seek assistance from an organisation representing his or her interests. Similarly, you might wish to seek advice from a business or service providers' organisation.

7.2 The Government will establish a service to provide advice and assistance to the many general or specialist advisers who are already operating. This will ensure that those providing advice on the Act will have access to specialist knowledge of its provisions and a pool of experience in dealing with cases of particular difficulty.

What happens if a dispute cannot be resolved?

7.3 If you cannot resolve a dispute in this way, a disabled person would be able to take you to court and, if successful, could receive compensation for any financial loss or injury to his or her feelings. A disabled person may also be able to seek an injunction or, in Scotland, interdict, against you to prevent the repeat of any discriminatory act {S25}.

Making false statements

7.4 If you are found guilty of making a false statement of the kind described in paragraph 6.3 you will be liable to a fine up to level 5 on the standard scale (£5,000 as of May 1996) {S57(5)}.

APPENDIX – WHAT IS MEANT BY DISABILITY

This Appendix does not form part of the Code. It is included to aid understanding about who is covered by the Act and should provide sufficient information on the definition of disability to cover the large majority of cases. The definition of disability in the Act is designed to cover only people who would generally be considered to be disabled. A Government publication "Guidance on matters to be taken into account in determining questions relating to the definition of disability", is also available.

When is a person disabled?

A person has a disability if he has a physical or mental impairment which has a substantial and long-term adverse effect on his ability to carry out normal day-to-day activities.

What about people who have recovered from a disability?

People who have had a disability within the definition are protected from discrimination even if they have since recovered.

What does "impairment" cover?

It covers physical or mental impairments; this includes sensory impairments, such as those affecting sight or hearing.

Are all mental impairments covered?

The term "mental impairment" is intended to cover a wide range of impairments relating to mental functioning, including what are often known as learning disabilities. However, the Act states that it does not include any impairment resulting from or consisting of a mental illness, unless that illness is a clinically well-recognised illness. A clinically well-recognised illness is one that is recognised by a respected body of medical opinion.

What is a "substantial" adverse effect?

A substantial adverse effect is something which is more than a minor or trivial effect. The requirement that an effect must be substantial reflects the general understanding of disability as a limitation going beyond the normal differences in ability which might exist among people.

What is a "long-term" effect?

A long-term effect of an impairment is one:

- which has lasted at least 12 months; or

- where the total period for which it lasts is likely to be at least 12 months; or

- which is likely to last for the rest of the life of the person affected.

Effects which are not long-term would therefore include loss of mobility due to a broken limb which is likely to heal within 12 months and the effects of temporary infections, from which a person would be likely to recover within 12 months.

What if the effects come and go over a period of time?

If an impairment has had a substantial adverse effect on normal day-to-day activities but that effect ceases, the substantial effect is treated as continuing if it is likely to **recur**; that is, if it is more probable than not that the effect will recur. Take the example of a person with rheumatoid arthritis whose impairment has a substantial adverse effect, which then ceases to be substantial (i.e. the person has a period of remission). The effects are to be treated as if they are continuing, and are likely to continue beyond 12 months, **if**:

- the impairment remains; and

- at least one recurrence of the substantial effect is likely to take place 12 months or more after the initial occurrence.

This would then be a long-term effect.

What are "normal day-to-day activities"?

They are activities which are carried out by most people on a fairly regular and frequent basis. The term is not intended to include activities which are normal only for a particular person or group of people, such as playing a musical instrument, or a sport, to a professional standard or performing a skilled or specialised task at work. However, someone who is affected in such a specialised way but is **also** affected in normal day-to-day activities would be covered by this part of the definition. The test of whether an impairment affects normal day-to-day activities is whether it affects one of the broad categories of capacity listed in Schedule 1 to the Act. They are:

- mobility;

- manual dexterity;

- physical co-ordination;

- continence;

- ability to lift, carry or otherwise move everyday objects;

- speech, hearing or eyesight;

- memory or ability to concentrate, learn or understand; or

- perception of the risk of physical danger.

What about treatment?

Someone with an impairment may be receiving medical or other treatment which alleviates or removes the effects (though not the impairment). In such cases, the treatment is ignored and the impairment is taken to have the effect it would have had without such treatment. This does not apply if substantial adverse effects are not likely to recur even if the treatment stops (i.e. the impairment has been cured).

Does this include people who wear spectacles?

No. The sole exception to the rule about ignoring the effects of treatment is the wearing of spectacles or contact lenses. In this case, the effect while the person is wearing spectacles or contact lenses should be considered.

Are people who have disfigurements covered?

People with severe disfigurements are covered by the Act. They do not need to demonstrate that the impairment has a substantial adverse effect on their ability to carry out normal day-to-day activities.

What about people who know their condition is going to get worse over time?

Progressive conditions are conditions which are likely to change and develop over time. Examples given in the Act are cancer, multiple sclerosis, muscular dystrophy and HIV infection. Where a person has a progressive condition he will be covered by the Act from the moment the condition leads to an impairment which has **some** effect on ability to carry out normal day-to-day activities, even though not a **substantial** effect, if that impairment is likely eventually to have a substantial adverse effect on such ability.

What about people who are registered disabled?

Those registered as disabled under the Disabled Persons (Employment) Act 1944 both on 12 January 1995 and 2 December 1996 will be treated as being disabled under the Disability Discrimination Act 1995 for three years from the latter date. At all times from 2 December 1996 onwards they will be covered by the Act as people who have had a disability. This does not preclude them from being covered as having a current disability any time after the three year period has finished. Whether they are or not will depend on whether they – like anyone else – meet the definition of disability in the Act.

Are people with genetic conditions covered?

If a genetic condition has no effect on ability to carry out normal day-to-day activities, the person is not covered. Diagnosis does not in itself bring someone within the definition. If the condition is progressive, then the rule about progressive conditions applies.

Are any conditions specifically excluded from the coverage of the Act?

Yes. Certain conditions are to be regarded as not amounting to impairments for the purposes of the Act. These are:

- addiction to or dependency on alcohol, nicotine, or any other substance (other than as a result of the substance being medically prescribed);

- seasonal allergic rhinitis (e.g. hayfever), except where it aggravates the effect of another condition;

- tendency to set fires;

- tendency to steal;

- tendency to physical or sexual abuse of other persons;

- exhibitionism;

- voyeurism.

Also, disfigurements which consist of a tattoo (which has not been removed), non-medical body piercing, or something attached through such piercing, are to be treated as not having a substantial adverse effect on the person's ability to carry out normal day-to-day activities.

THE DISABILITY DISCRIMINATION ACT 1995

The Disability Discrimination Act introduces new laws and measures aimed at ending the discrimination which many disabled people face. Over time, the Act will give disabled people new rights in the areas of:

- employment

- access to goods, facilities and services

- buying or renting land or property.

In addition the Act:

- requires schools, colleges and universities to provide information for disabled people

- allows the Government to set minimum standards so that disabled people can use public transport easily

- sets up the National Disability Council (in Northern Ireland, the Northern Ireland Disability Council) to advise the Government on discrimination against disabled people.

There is a separate Code of Practice containing guidance on the elimination of discrimination against disabled people in the field of employment. This can be obtained from HMSO bookshops.

NORTHERN IRELAND

The Act (as modified by Schedule 8) also applies in Northern Ireland. A Code of Practice reflecting those modifications is published in Northern Ireland.

INDEX

References in the right-hand column are to paragraph numbers.